New Perspectives on

Microsoft®
Excel 97

INTRODUCTORY

The New Perspectives Series

The New Perspectives Series consists of texts and technology that teach computer concepts and microcomputer applications (listed below). You can order these New Perspectives texts in many different lengths, software releases, custom-bound combinations, CourseKits™ and Custom Editions®. Contact your Course Technology sales representative or customer service representative for the most up-to-date details.

The New Perspectives Series

Computer Concepts

Borland® dBASE®

Borland® Paradox®

Corel® Presentations™

Corel® Quattro Pro®

Corel® WordPerfect®

DOS

HTML

Lotus® 1-2-3®

Microsoft® Access

Microsoft® Excel

Microsoft® Internet Explorer

Microsoft® Office Professional

Microsoft® PowerPoint®

Microsoft® Windows® 3.1

Microsoft® Windows® 95

Microsoft® Windows NT® Server 4.0

Microsoft® Windows NT® Workstation 4.0

Microsoft® Word

Microsoft® Works

Netscape Navigator™

Netscape Navigator™ Gold

Microsoft® Visual Basic® 4 and 5

New Perspectives on
Microsoft®
Excel 97

June Jamrich Parsons
University of the Virgin Islands

Dan Oja
GuildWare, Inc.

Roy Ageloff
University of Rhode Island

COURSE
TECHNOLOGY

ONE MAIN STREET, CAMBRIDGE, MA 02142

an International Thomson Publishing company I(T)P®

Cambridge • Albany • Bonn • Boston • Cincinnati • London • Madrid • Melbourne • Mexico City
New York • Paris • San Francisco • Singapore • Tokyo • Toronto • Washington

New Perspectives on Microsoft® Excel 97— Introductory is published by Course Technology.

Associate Publisher	Mac Mendelsohn
Series Consulting Editor	Susan Solomon
Product Manager	Donna Gridley
Developmental Editor	Kim T. M. Crowley
Production Editor	Nancy Ray
Text and Cover Designer	Ella Hanna
Cover Illustrator	Douglas Goodman

© 1997 by Course Technology—I(T)P®

For more information contact:

Course Technology
One Main Street
Cambridge, MA 02142

ITP Europe
Berkshire House 168-173
High Holborn
London WCIV 7AA
England

Nelson ITP, Australia
102 Dodds Street
South Melbourne, 3205
Victoria, Australia

ITP Nelson Canada
1120 Birchmount Road
Scarborough, Ontario
Canada M1K 5G4

International Thomson Editores
Seneca, 53
Colonia Polanco
11560 Mexico D.F. Mexico

ITP GmbH
Königswinterer Strasse 418
53227 Bonn
Germany

ITP Asia
60 Albert Street, #15-01
Albert Complex
Singapore 189969

ITP Japan
Hirakawacho Kyowa Building, 3F
2-2-1 Hirakawacho
Chiyoda-ku, Tokyo 102
Japan

Trademarks
Course Technology and the Open Book logo are registered trademarks and CourseKits is a trademark of Course Technology. Custom Editions and the ITP logo are registered trademarks of International Thomson Publishing Inc.

Microsoft and the Office logo are either registered trademarks or trademarks of Microsoft Corporation in the United States and/or other countries. Course Technology is an independent entity from Microsoft Corporation, and not affiliated with Microsoft Corporation in any manner. This text may be used in assisting students to prepare for a Certified Microsoft Office User Exam. Neither Microsoft Corporation, its designated review company, nor Course Technology warrants that use of this text will ensure passing the relevant CMOU Exam.

Some of the product names and company names used in this book have been used for identification purposes only and may be trademarks or registered trademarks of their respective manufacturers and sellers.

Disclaimer
Course Technology reserves the right to revise this publication and make changes from time to time in its content without notice.

ISBN 0-7600-5260-3

Printed in the United States of America

7 8 9 BM 01 00 99

From the New Perspectives Series Team

At **Course Technology** we have one foot in education and the other in technology. We believe that technology is transforming the way people teach and learn, and we are excited about providing instructors and students with materials that use technology to teach about technology.

Our development process is unparalleled in the higher education publishing industry. Every product we create goes through an exacting process of design, development, review, and testing.

Reviewers give us direction and insight that shape our manuscripts and bring them up to the latest standards. Every manuscript is quality tested. Students whose backgrounds match the intended audience work through every keystroke, carefully checking for clarity and pointing out errors in logic and sequence. Together with our own technical reviewers, these testers help us ensure that everything that carries our name is error-free and easy to use.

We show both how and why technology is critical to solving problems in college and in whatever field you choose to teach or pursue. Our time-tested, step-by-step instructions provide unparalleled clarity. Examples and applications are chosen and crafted to motivate students.

As the New Perspectives Series team at Course Technology, our goal is to produce the most timely, accurate, creative, and technologically sound product in the entire college publishing industry. We strive for consistent high quality. This takes a lot of communication, coordination, and hard work. But we love what we do. We are determined to be the best. Write to us and let us know what you think. You can also e-mail us at *NewPerspectives@course.com*.

The New Perspectives Series Team

Joseph J. Adamski	Jessica Evans	Dan Oja
Judy Adamski	Marilyn Freedman	David Paradice
Roy Ageloff	Kathy Finnegan	June Parsons
David Auer	Robin Geller	Harry Phillips
Dirk Baldwin	Donna Gridley	Sandra Poindexter
Daphne Barbas	Roger Hayen	Mark Reimold
Rachel Bunin	Charles Hommel	Ann Shaffer
Joan Carey	Janice Jutras	Susan Solomon
Patrick Carey	Chris Kelly	Susanne Walker
Sharon Caswell	Mary Kemper	John Zeanchock
Barbara Clemens	Terry Ann Kremer	Beverly Zimmerman
Rachel Crapser	John Leschke	Scott Zimmerman
Kim Crowley	Mac Mendelsohn	
Michael Ekedahl	William Newman	

What is the New Perspectives Series?

Course Technology's **New Perspectives Series** is an integrated system of instruction that combines text and technology products to teach computer concepts and microcomputer applications. Users consistently praise this series for innovative pedagogy, creativity, supportive and engaging style, accuracy, and use of interactive technology. The first New Perspectives text was published in January of 1993. Since then, the series has grown to more than 100 titles and has become the best-selling series on computer concepts and microcomputer applications. Others have imitated the New Perspectives features, design, and technologies, but none have replicated its quality and its ability to consistently anticipate and meet the needs of instructors and students.

What is the Integrated System of Instruction?

New Perspectives textbooks are part of a truly Integrated System of Instruction: text, graphics, video, sound, animation, and simulations that are linked and that provide a flexible, unified, and interactive system to help you teach and help your students learn. Specifically, the *New Perspectives Integrated System of Instruction* includes a Course Technology textbook in addition to some or all of the following items: Course Labs, Course Test Manager, Online Companions, and Course Presenter. These components—shown in the graphic on the back cover of this book—have been developed to work together to provide a complete, integrative teaching and learning experience.

How is the New Perspectives Series different from other microcomputer concepts and applications series?

The **New Perspectives Series** distinguishes itself from other series in at least four substantial ways: sound instructional design, consistent quality, innovative technology, and proven pedagogy. The applications texts in this series consist of two or more tutorials, which are based on sound instructional design. Each tutorial is motivated by a realistic case that is meaningful to students. Rather than learn a laundry list of features, students learn the features in the context of solving a problem. This process motivates all concepts and skills by demonstrating to students *why* they would want to know them.

Instructors and students have come to rely on the high quality of the **New Perspectives Series** and to consistently praise its accuracy. This accuracy is a result of Course Technology's unique multi-step quality assurance process that incorporates student testing at least two stages of development, using hardware and software configurations appropriate to the product. All solutions, test questions, and other supplements are tested using similar procedures. Instructors who adopt this series report that students can work through the tutorials independently with minimum intervention or "damage control" by instructors or staff. This consistent quality has meant that if instructors are pleased with one product from the series, they can rely on the same quality with any other New Perspectives product.

The **New Perspectives Series** also distinguishes itself by its innovative technology. This series innovated Course Labs, truly *interactive* learning applications. These have set the standard for interactive learning.

How do I know that the New Perspectives Series will work?

Some instructors who use this series report a significant difference between how much their students learn and retain with this series as compared to other series. With other series, instructors often find that students can work through the book and do well on homework and tests, but still not demonstrate competency when asked to perform particular tasks outside the context of the text's sample case or project. With the **New Perspectives Series**, however, instructors report that students have a complete, integrative learning experience that stays with them. They credit this high retention and competency to the fact that this series incorporates critical thinking and problem-solving with computer skills mastery.

How does this book I'm holding fit into the New Perspectives Series?

New Perspectives applications books are available in the following categories:

Brief books are typically about 150 pages long, contain two to four tutorials, and are intended to teach the basics of an application.

Introductory books are typically about 300 pages long and consist of four to seven tutorials that go beyond the basics. These books often build out of the Brief editions by providing two or three additional tutorials. The book you are holding is an Introductory book.

Comprehensive books are typically about 600 pages long and consist of all of the tutorials in the Introductory books, plus four or five more tutorials covering higher-level topics. Comprehensive books also include two Windows tutorials and three or four Additional Cases.

Advanced books cover topics similar to those in the Comprehensive books, but go into more depth. Advanced books present the most high-level coverage in the series.

Custom Books The New Perspectives Series offers you two ways to customize a New Perspectives text to fit your course exactly: *CourseKits*™, two or more texts packaged together in a box, and *Custom Editions*®, your choice of books bound together. Custom Editions offer you unparalleled flexibility in designing your concepts and applications courses. You can build your own book by ordering a combination of titles bound together to cover only the topics you want. Your students save because they buy only the materials they need. There is no minimum order, and books are spiral bound. Both CourseKits and Custom Editions offer significant price discounts. Contact your Course Technology sales representative for more information.

New Perspectives Series Microcomputer Applications

Brief Titles or Modules	Introductory Titles or Modules	Intermediate Tutorials	Advanced Titles or Modules	Other Modules
Brief	**Introductory**	**Comprehensive**	**Advanced**	**Custom Editions**
2 to 4 tutorials	6 or 7 tutorials, or Brief + 2 or 3 more tutorials	Introductory + 4 or 5 more tutorials. Includes Brief Windows tutorials and Additional Cases	Quick Review of basics + in-depth, high-level coverage	Choose from any of the above to build your own Custom Editions® or CourseKits™

In what kind of course could I use this book?

This book can be used in any course in which you want students to learn all the most important topics of Microsoft Excel, including creating, editing, and formatting worksheets and charts, working with Excel lists and pivot tables, integrating worksheet data with various programs and the World Wide Web, and creating and using macros to automate tasks. It is ideal as part of a microcomputer applications course or a short course on Microsoft Excel 97. This book assumes that students have learned basic Windows 95 navigation and file management skills from Course Technology's *New Perspectives on Microsoft Windows 95—Brief* or an *equivalent* book.

This book has been approved by Microsoft as courseware for the Certified Microsoft Office User (CMOU) program. After completing the tutorials and exercises in this book, you will be prepared to take the Proficient level CMOU Exam for Microsoft Excel 97. By passing the certification exam for a Microsoft software program you demonstrate your proficiency in that program to employers. CMOU exams are offered at participating test centers, participating corporations, and participating employment agencies. For more information about certification, please visit the CMOU program World Wide Web site at http://www.microsoft.com/office/train_cert/.

How do the Windows 95 editions differ from the Windows 3.1 editions?

Sessions We've divided the tutorials into sessions. Each session is designed to be completed in about 45 minutes to an hour (depending, of course, upon student needs and the speed of your lab equipment). With sessions, learning is broken up into more easily assimilated portions. You can more accurately allocate time in your syllabus, and students can better manage the available lab time. Each session begins with a "session box," which quickly describes the skills students will learn in the session. Furthermore, each session is numbered, which makes it easier for you and your students to navigate and communicate about the tutorial. Look on page E 2.18 for the session box that opens Session 2.2.

Quick Checks Each session concludes with meaningful, conceptual Quick Check questions that test students' understanding of what they learned in the session. Answers to the Quick Check questions in this book are provided on pages E 4.38 through E 4.40, and E 7.51 through E 7.52

New Design We have retained the best of the old design to help students differentiate between what they are to *do* and what they are to *read*. The steps are clearly identified by their shaded background and numbered steps. Furthermore, this new design presents steps and screen shots in a larger, easier to read format. Some good examples of our new design are pages E 1.12 and E 1.13.

What features are retained in the Windows 95 editions of the New Perspectives Series?

"Read This Before You Begin" Page This page is consistent with Course Technology's unequaled commitment to helping instructors introduce technology into the classroom. Technical considerations and assumptions about software are listed to help instructors save time and eliminate unnecessary aggravation. See pages E 1.2 and E 5.2 for the "Read This Before You Begin" pages in this book.

Tutorial Case Each tutorial begins with a problem presented in a case that is meaningful to students. The problem turns the task of learning how to use an application into a problem-solving process. The problems increase in complexity with each tutorial. These cases touch on multicultural, international, and ethical issues—so important to today's business curriculum. See page E 1.3 for the case that begins Tutorial 1.

1.
2.
3.

Step-by-Step Methodology This unique Course Technology methodology keeps students on track. They enter data, click buttons, or press keys always within the context of solving the problem posed in the tutorial case. The text constantly guides students, letting them know where they are in the course of solving the problem. In addition, the numerous screen shots include labels that direct students' attention to what they should look at on the screen. On almost every page in this book, you can find an example of how steps, screen shots, and labels work together.

TROUBLE?

TROUBLE? Paragraphs These paragraphs anticipate the mistakes or problems that students are likely to have and help them recover and continue with the tutorial. By putting these paragraphs in the book, rather than in the Instructor's Manual, we facilitate independent learning and free the instructor to focus on substantive conceptual issues rather than on common procedural errors. Some representative examples of TROUBLE? paragraphs appear on page E 1.6 and E1.11.

Reference Windows Reference Windows appear throughout the text. They are succinct summaries of the most important tasks covered in the tutorials. Reference Windows are specially designed and written so students can refer to them when doing the Tutorial Assignments and Case Problems, and after completing the course. Page E 2.19 contains the Reference Window for Using the Paste Function Button.

Task Reference The Task Reference contains a summary of how to perform common tasks using the most efficient method, as well as references to pages where the task is discussed in more detail. It appears as a table at the end of the book.

Tutorial Assignments, Case Problems, and Lab Assignments Each tutorial concludes with Tutorial Assignments, which provide students with additional hands-on practice of the skills they learned in the tutorial. See pages E 1.32 and E 1.33 for examples of Tutorial Assignments. The Tutorial Assignments are followed by four Case Problems that have approximately the same scope as the tutorial case. In the Windows 95 applications texts, the last Case Problem of each tutorial typically requires students to solve the problem independently, either "from scratch" or with minimum guidance. See pages E 1.33 through E 1.35 for examples of Case Problems. Finally, if a Course Lab accompanies a tutorial, Lab Assignments are included after the Case Problems. See page E 1.35 for examples of Lab Assignments.

Exploration Exercises The Windows environment allows students to learn by exploring and discovering what they can do. Exploration Exercises can be Tutorial Assignments or Case Problems that challenge students, encourage them to explore the capabilities of the program they are using, and extend their knowledge using the Help facility and other reference materials. Page E 1.33 contains Exploration Exercises for Tutorial 1.

What supplements are available with this textbook?

Course Labs: Now, Concepts Come to Life Computer skills and concepts come to life with the New Perspectives Course Labs—highly-interactive tutorials that combine illustrations, animations, digital images, and simulations. The Labs guide students step-by-step, present them with Quick Check questions, let them explore on their own, test their comprehension, and provide printed feedback. Lab icons at the beginning of the tutorial and in the tutorial margins indicate when a topic has a corresponding Lab. Lab Assignments are included at the end of each relevant tutorial. The Lab available with this book and the tutorial in which it appears is:

TUTORIAL 1

Spreadsheets

Course Test Manager: Testing and Practice at the Computer or on Paper
Course Test Manager is cutting-edge, Windows-based testing software that helps instructors design and administer practice tests and actual examinations. This full-featured program allows students to randomly generate practice tests that provide immediate on-screen feedback and detailed study guides. Instructors can also use Course Test Manager to produce printed tests. Course Test Manager can automatically grade the tests students take at the computer and can generate statistical information on individual as well as group performance.

Course Presenter: This lecture presentation tool allows instructors to create electronic slide shows or traditional overhead transparencies using the figure files from the book. Instructors can customize, edit, save, and display the figures from the text in order to illustrate key topics or concepts in class.

Online Companions: Dedicated to Keeping You and Your Students Up-To-Date When you use a New Perspectives product, you can access Course Technology's faculty sites and student sites on the World Wide Web. You can browse the password-protected Faculty Online Companions to obtain online Instructor's Manuals, Solution Files, Student Files, and more. Please see your Instructor's Manual or call your Course Technology customer service representative for more information. Student and Faculty Online Companions are accessible by clicking the appropriate links on the Course Technology home page at **http://www.course.com.**

Student Files Student Files contain all of the data that students will use to complete the tutorials, Tutorial Assignments, and Case Problems. A Readme file includes technical tips for lab management. See the inside covers of this book and the "Read This Before You Begin" pages for more information on Student Files.

Instructor's Manual New Perspectives Series Instructor's Manuals contain instructor's notes and printed solutions for each tutorial. Instructor's notes provide tutorial overviews and outlines, technical notes, lecture notes, and extra Case Problems. Printed solutions include solutions to Tutorial Assignments, Case Problems, and Lab Assignments.

Solution Files Solution Files contain every file students are asked to create or modify in the tutorials, Tutorial Assignments, and Case Problems.

The following supplements are included in the Instructor's Resource Kit that accompanies this textbook:

- Instructor's Manual
- Solution Files
- Student Files
- Spreadsheets Course Lab
- Course Test Manager Release 1.1 Test Bank
- Course Test Manager Release 1.1 Engine
- Course Presenter

Some of the supplements listed above are also available over the World Wide Web through Course Technology's password-protected Faculty Online Companions. Please see your Instructor's Manual or call your Course Technology customer service representative for more information.

Acknowledgments

Many thanks to the New Perspectives team at Course Technology, particularly Mac Mendelsohn, Associate Publisher; Susan Solomon, Series Consulting Editor; Mark Reimold, Acquisitions Editor; Donna Gridley, Product Manager; Nancy Ray, Production Editor; Greg Bigelow, QA Supervisor; Brian McCooey and John McCarthy, Quality Assurance testers; and Patty Stephan, Production Manager.

In addition, I would like to thank Kim Crowley, Developmental Editor, for all her help in transforming a rough manuscript into a polished text.

Finally, special thanks to Hilda Allred for all her support and encouragement while this text was being written.

Also, thank you to Calleen Coorough, Skafit Valley College, Nancy Alderice, Murray State, Patrick Carey and Jean Smelowitz for their reviews of the manuscript.

Roy Ageloff

Reference Windows

Microsoft®
Excel 97

LEVEL I

TUTORIALS

Read This **Before You Begin**

STUDENT DISK

To complete Excel 97 Tutorials 1-4, you need two Student Disks. Your instructor will either provide you with Student Disks or ask you to make your own.

If you are supposed to make your own Student Disks, you will need **two** blank, formatted high-density disks. You will need to copy a set of folders from a file server or standalone computer onto your disks. Your instructor will tell you which computer, drive letter, and folders contain the files you need. The following table shows you which folders go on your disks:

Student Disk	Write this on the disk label	Put these folders on the disk
1	Student Disk 1: Excel 97 Tutorials 1-3	Tutorial.01, Tutorial.02, Tutorial.03
2	Student Disk 2: Excel 97 Tutorial 4	Tutorial.04

See the inside front or inside back cover of this book for more information on Student Disk files, or ask your instructor or technical support person for assistance.

COURSE LAB

Tutorial 1 features an interactive Course Lab to help you understand spreadsheet concepts. There are Lab Assignments at the end of the tutorial that relate to this Lab. To start the Lab, click the Start button on the Windows 95 Taskbar, point to Programs, point to Course Labs, point to New Perspectives Applications, and click Spreadsheets.

USING YOUR OWN COMPUTER

If you are going to work through this book using your own computer, you need:

■ **Computer System** Microsoft Excel 97 and Windows 95 or Windows NT Workstation 4.0 must be installed on your computer. This book assumes a typical installation of Microsoft Excel 97.

■ **Student Disks** Ask your instructor or technical support person for details on how to get the Student Disks. You will not be able to complete the tutorials or exercises in this book using your own computer until you have Student Disks. The Student Files may also be obtained electronically over the Internet. See the inside front or inside back cover of this book for more details.

■ **Course Lab** See your instructor or technical support person to obtain the Course Lab software for use on your own computer.

To complete Excel 97 Tutorials 1-4, your students must use a set of student files on two Student Disks. These files are included in the Instructor's Resource Kit, and they may also be obtained electronically over the Internet. See the inside front or inside back cover of this book for more details. Follow the instructions in the Readme file to copy the files to your server or standalone computer. You can view the Readme file using WordPad. Once the files are copied, you can make Student Disks for the students yourself, or you can tell students where to find the files so they can make their own Student Disks.

COURSE LAB SOFTWARE

The Course Lab software is distributed on a CD-ROM included in the Instructor's Resource Kit. To install the Course Lab software, follow the setup instructions in the Readme file on the CD-ROM. Refer also to the Readme file for essential technical notes related to running the Lab in a multi-user environment. Once you have installed the Course Lab software, your students can start the Lab from the Windows 95 desktop by following the instructions in the Course Lab section above.

COURSE TECHNOLOGY STUDENT FILES AND COURSE LAB SOFTWARE

You are granted a license to copy the Student Files and Lab software to any computer or computer network used by students who have purchased this book.

Using Worksheets to Make Business Decisions

Evaluating Sites for an Inwood Design Group Golf Course

In this tutorial you will:

- Start and exit Excel

- Discover how Excel is used in business

- Identify the major components of the Excel window

- Navigate an Excel workbook and worksheet

- Open, save, print, and close a worksheet

- Enter text, numbers, formulas, and functions

- Correct mistakes

- Perform what-if analysis

- Clear contents of cells

- Use the Excel Help system

LAB

Spreadsheets

CASE

Inwood Design Group

In Japan, golf is big business. Spurred by the Japanese passion for the sport, golf enjoys unprecedented popularity. But because Japan is a small, mountainous country, the 12 million golfers have fewer than 2,000 courses from which to choose. Fees for 18 holes on a public course average between $200 and $300; golf club memberships are bought and sold like stock shares. The market potential is phenomenal, but building a golf course in Japan is expensive because of inflated property values, difficult terrain, and strict environmental regulations.

Inwood Design Group plans to build a world-class golf course, and one of the four sites under consideration is Chiba Prefecture, Japan. Other possible sites are Kauai, Hawaii; Edmonton, Canada; and Scottsdale, Arizona. You and Mike Nagochi are members of the site selection team for Inwood Design Group. The team is responsible for collecting information on the sites, evaluating that information, and recommending the best site for the new golf course.

Your team identified five factors likely to determine the success of a golf course: climate, competition, market size, topography, and transportation. The team has already collected information on these factors for three of the four potential golf course sites. Mike has just returned from visiting the last site in Scottsdale, Arizona.

Using Microsoft Excel 97 for Windows 95, Mike has created a worksheet that the team can use to evaluate the four sites. He needs to complete the worksheet by entering the data for the Scottsdale site. He then plans to bring the worksheet to the group's next meeting so that the team can analyze the information and recommend a site to management.

In this tutorial you will learn how to use Excel as you work with Mike to complete the Inwood site selection worksheet and work with the Inwood team to select the best site for the golf course.

Using the Tutorials Effectively

These tutorials are designed to be used at a computer. Each tutorial is divided into sessions. Watch for the session headings, such as "Session 1.1" and "Session 1.2." Each session is designed to be completed in about 45 minutes, but take as much time as you need. When you've completed a session, it's a good idea to exit the program and take a break. You can exit Microsoft Excel by clicking the Close button in the top-right corner of the program window.

Before you begin, read the following questions and answers. They are designed to help you use the tutorials effectively.

Where do I start?

Each tutorial begins with a case, which sets the scene for the tutorial and gives you background information to help you understand what you will be doing in the tutorial. Read the case before you go to the lab. In the lab, begin with the first session of the tutorial.

How do I know what to do on the computer?

Each session contains steps that you will perform on the computer to learn how to use Microsoft Excel. The steps are numbered and are set against a colored background. Read the text that introduces each series of steps, and read each step carefully and completely before you try it.

How do I know if I did the step correctly?

As you work, compare your computer screen with the corresponding figure in the tutorial. Don't worry if your screen display is somewhat different from the figure. The important parts of the screen display are labeled in each figure. Check to make sure these parts are on your screen.

What if I make a mistake?

Don't worry about making mistakes—they are part of the learning process. Paragraphs labeled **TROUBLE?** identify common problems and explain how to get back on track. Follow the steps in a **TROUBLE?** paragraph *only* if you are having the problem described. If you run into other problems, carefully consider the current state of your system, the position of the pointer, and any messages on the screen.

How do I use the Reference Windows?

Reference Windows summarize the procedures you learn in the tutorial steps. Do not complete the actions in the Reference Windows when you are working through the tutorial. Instead, refer to the Reference Windows while you are working on the assignments at the end of the tutorial.

How can I test my understanding of the material I learned in the tutorial?

At the end of each session, you can answer the Quick Check Questions. If necessary, refer to the Answers to Quick Check Questions to check your work.

After you have completed the entire tutorial, you should complete the Tutorial Assignments and Case Problems. These exercises are carefully structured so you will review what you have learned and then apply your knowledge to new situations.

What if I can't remember how to do something?

You should refer to the Task Reference at the end of the book; it summarizes how to accomplish commonly performed tasks.

What is the Spreadsheets Course Lab, and how should I use it?

This interactive Lab helps you review spreadsheet concepts and practice skills that you learn in Tutorial 1. The Lab Assignments section at the end of Tutorial 1 includes instructions for using the Lab.

Now that you've seen how to use the tutorials effectively, you are ready to begin.

In this session you will learn what a spreadsheet is and how it is used in business. You will learn what Excel is and about the Excel window and its elements, how to move around a worksheet using the keyboard and the mouse, and how to open a workbook.

Spreadsheets

What Is Excel?

Excel is a computerized spreadsheet. A **spreadsheet** is an important business tool that helps you analyze and evaluate information. Spreadsheets are often used for cash flow analysis, budgeting, decision making, cost estimating, inventory management, and financial reporting. For example, an accountant might use a spreadsheet like the one in Figure 1-1 for a budget.

Figure 1-1 ◄
Budget
spreadsheet

Cash Budget Forecast		
	January	*January*
	Estimated	*Actual*
Cash in Bank (Start of Month)	$1,400.00	$1,400.00
Cash in Register (Start of Month)	100.00	100.00
Total Cash	$1,500.00	$1,500.00
Expected Cash Sales	$1,200.00	$1,420.00
Expected Collections	400.00	380.00
Other Money Expected	100.00	52.00
Total Income	$1,700.00	$1,852.00
Total Cash and Income	$3,200.00	$3,352.00
All Expenses (for Month)	$1,200.00	$1,192.00
Cash Balance at End of Month	$2,000.00	$2,160.00

To produce the spreadsheet in Figure 1-1, you could manually calculate the totals and then type your results, or you could use a computer and spreadsheet program to perform the calculations and print the results. Spreadsheet programs are also referred to as electronic spreadsheets, computerized spreadsheets, or just spreadsheets.

In Excel 97, the document you create is called a **workbook**. Each workbook is made up of individual worksheets, or **sheets**, just as a spiral-bound notebook is made up of sheets of paper. You will learn more about using multiple sheets later in this tutorial. For now, just keep in mind that the terms *worksheet* and *sheet* are often used interchangeably.

Starting Excel

Mike arrives at his office early because he needs to work with you to finish the worksheet and get ready for your meeting with the design team.

Start Excel and complete the worksheet that Mike will use to help the design team decide about the golf course site.

To start Microsoft Excel:

1. Make sure Windows 95 is running on your computer and the Windows 95 desktop appears on your screen.

TROUBLE? If you're running Windows NT Workstation 4.0 (or a later version) on your computer or network, don't worry. Although the figures in this book were created while running Windows 95, Windows NT 4.0 and Windows 95 share the same interface, and Microsoft Excel 97 runs equally well under either systems.

2. Click the **Start** button on the taskbar to display the Start menu, and then point to **Programs** to display the Programs menu.

3. Point to **Microsoft Excel** on the Programs menu. See Figure 1-2.

Figure 1-2 ◄
Starting
Microsoft Excel

position mouse
pointer here
to display
Programs menu

Office
Shortcut
Bar (might
not appear
on your
screen)

click here to
start Excel

Start button

TROUBLE? If you don't see the Microsoft Excel option on the Programs menu, ask your instructor or technical support person for assistance.

TROUBLE? The Office Shortcut Bar, which appears along the top border of the desktop in Figure 1-2, might look different on your screen or it might not appear at all, depending on how your system is set up. The steps in these tutorials do not require that you use the Office Shortcut Bar; therefore, the remaining figures do not display the Office Shortcut Bar.

4. Click **Microsoft Excel**. After a short pause, the Microsoft Excel copyright information appears in a message box and remains on the screen until the Excel program window and a blank worksheet are displayed. See Figure 1-3.

TROUBLE? Depending on how your system is set up, the Office Assistant (see Figure 1-3) window might open when you start Excel. For now, click the Close button ☒ on the Office Assistant window to close it; you'll learn more about this feature later in this tutorial. If you've started Microsoft Excel immediately after installing it, you'll need to click the Start Using Microsoft Excel option, which the Office Assistant displays, before closing the Office Assistant window.

Figure 1-3
Excel Program
window
with blank
worksheet

title bar

Name box

active cell

mouse pointer

row headings

active sheet

status bar

sheet tab
scroll buttons

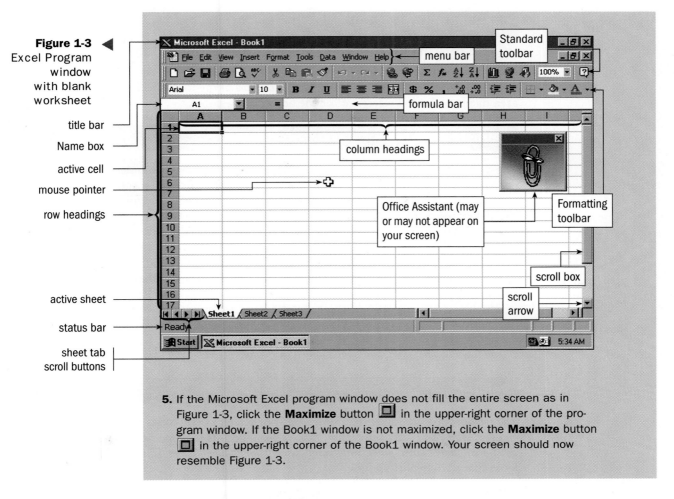

5. If the Microsoft Excel program window does not fill the entire screen as in Figure 1-3, click the **Maximize** button ☐ in the upper-right corner of the program window. If the Book1 window is not maximized, click the **Maximize** button ☐ in the upper-right corner of the Book1 window. Your screen should now resemble Figure 1-3.

The Excel Window

The Excel window layout is consistent with the layout of other Windows programs. It contains many common features, such as the title bar, menu bar, scroll bars, and taskbar. Figure 1-3 shows these elements as well as the main components of the Excel window. Take a look at each of these Excel components so you know their location and purpose.

Toolbars

Toolbars allow you to organize the commands in Excel. The menu bar is a special toolbar at the top of the window that contains menus such as File, Edit, and View. The Standard toolbar and the Formatting toolbar are located below the menu bar. The **Standard** toolbar contains buttons corresponding to the most frequently used commands in Excel. The **Formatting** toolbar contains buttons corresponding to the commands most frequently used to improve the appearance of a worksheet.

Formula Bar

The **formula bar**, located immediately below the toolbars, displays the contents of the active cell. A **cell's contents** is the data you enter into it. As you type or edit data, the changes appear in the formula bar. At the left end of the formula bar is the **Name box.** This area displays the cell reference for the active cell.

Worksheet Window

The document window, usually called the **worksheet window** or **workbook window,** contains the sheet you are creating, editing, or using. Each worksheet consists of a series of columns identified by lettered column headings and a series of rows identified by numbered row headings. Columns are assigned alphabetic labels from A to IV (256 columns). Rows are assigned numeric labels from 1 to 65,536 (65,536 rows).

A **cell** is the rectangular area where a column and a row intersect. Each cell is identified by a **cell reference,** which is its column and row location. For example, the cell reference B6 indicates the cell where column B and row 6 intersect. The column letter is always first in the cell reference. B6 is a correct cell reference; 6B is not. The **active cell** is the cell in which you are currently working. Excel identifies the active cell with a dark border that outlines one cell. In Figure 1-3, cell A1 is the active cell. Notice that the cell reference for the active cell appears in the reference area of the formula bar. You can change the active cell when you want to work elsewhere in the worksheet.

Pointer

The **pointer** is the indicator that moves on your screen as you move your mouse. The pointer changes shape to reflect the type of task you can perform at a particular location. When you click a mouse button, something happens at the pointer's location. In Figure 1-3 the pointer looks like a white plus sign ✛ .

Sheet Tabs

The **sheet tabs** let you move quickly between the sheets in a workbook; you can simply check the sheet tab of the sheet you want to move to. By default, a new workbook consists of three worksheets. If your workbook contains many worksheets, you can use the **sheet tab scroll buttons** to scroll through the sheet tabs that are not currently visible to find the sheet you want.

Moving Around a Worksheet

Before entering or editing the contents of a cell, you need to select that cell to make it the active cell. You can select a cell using either the keyboard or the mouse.

Using the Mouse

Using the mouse, you can quickly select a cell by placing the mouse pointer on the cell and clicking the mouse button. If you need to move to a cell that's not currently on the screen, use the vertical and horizontal scroll bars to display the area of the worksheet containing the cell you are interested in, and then select the cell.

Using the Keyboard

In addition to the mouse, Excel provides you with many keyboard options for moving to different cell locations within your worksheet. Figure 1-4 shows some of the keys you can use to select a cell within your worksheet.

Figure 1-4
Keys to move
around the
worksheet

Keystroke	Action
↑, ↓, ←, →	Moves up, down, left, or right one cell
PgUp	Moves the active cell up one full screen
PgDn	Moves the active cell down one full screen
Home	Moves the active cell to column A of the current row
Ctrl + Home	Moves the active cell to cell A1

Now, try moving around the worksheet using your keyboard and mouse.

To move around the worksheet:

1. Position the mouse pointer ▷ over cell E8, then click the **left mouse** button to make it the active cell. Notice that the cell is surrounded by a black border to indicate that it is the active cell and that the Name box on the formula bar displays E8.

2. Click cell **B4** to make it the active cell.

3. Press the → key to make cell C4 the active cell.

4. Press the ↓ key to make cell C5 the active cell. See Figure 1-5.

Figure 1-5
Cell C5 as
active cell

active cell

5. Press the **Home** key to move to cell A5, the first cell in the current row.

6. Press **Ctrl + Home** to make cell A1 the active cell.

So far you've moved around the portion of the worksheet you can see. Many worksheets can't be viewed entirely on one screen. Next, you'll use the keyboard and mouse to move beyond the worksheet window.

To move beyond the worksheet window:

1. Press the **Page Down** key to move the display down one screen. The active cell is now cell A17 (the active cell on your screen may be different). Notice that the row numbers on the left side of the worksheet indicate you have moved to a different area of the worksheet. See Figure 1-6.

Figure 1-6 ◀
Worksheet
screen after
moving to
different area
of worksheet

row headings
changed ⟩————▶

2. Press the **Page Down** key again to move the display down one screen. Notice that the row numbers indicate that you have moved to a different area of the worksheet.

3. Press the **Page Up** key to move the display up one screen. The active cell is now cell A17 (the active cell on your screen may be different).

4. Click the **vertical scroll bar arrow** until row 12 is visible. Notice that the active cell is still A17 (the active cell on your screen may be different). Using the scroll bar changes the portion of the screen you can view without changing the active cell.

5. Click cell **C12** to make it the active cell.

6. Click the blank area above the vertical scroll box to move up a full screen.

7. Click the blank area below the vertical scroll box to move down a full screen.

8. Click the **scroll box** and drag it to the top of the scroll area to again change the area of the screen you're viewing. Notice that the ScrollTip appears telling you where you will scroll to.

9. Click cell **E6** to make it the active cell.

As you know, a workbook can consist of one or more worksheets. Excel makes it easy to switch between them. Next, try moving from worksheet to worksheet.

Navigating in a Workbook

The sheet tabs let you move quickly between the different sheets in a workbook. If you can see the tab of the sheet you want, click the tab to activate the worksheet. You can also use the sheet tab scroll buttons to see sheet tabs hidden from view. Figure 1-7 describes the four tab scrolling buttons and their effects.

Figure 1-7 ◄
Sheet tab
scrolling
buttons

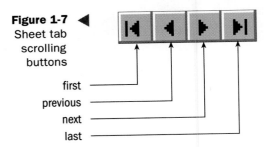

first ———
previous ———
next ———
last ———

Next, try moving to a new sheet.

To move to Sheet2:

1. Click the **Sheet2** tab. Sheet2, which is blank, appears in the worksheet window. Notice that the Sheet2 sheet tab is white and the name is bold, which means that Sheet2 is now the active sheet. Cell A1 is the active cell in Sheet2.

2. Click the **Sheet3** tab to make it the active sheet.

3. Click the **Sheet1** tab to make it the active sheet. Notice that cell E6 is the active cell.

Now that you have some basic skills navigating a worksheet and workbook, you can begin working with Mike to complete the golf site selection worksheet.

Opening a Workbook

When you want to use a workbook that you previously created, you must first open it. Opening a workbook transfers a copy of the workbook file from the hard drive or 3½-inch disk to the random access memory (RAM) of your computer and displays it on your screen. When the workbook is open, the file is both in RAM and on the disk.

After you open a workbook, you can view, edit, print, or save it again on your disk.

REFERENCE
window

OPENING A WORKBOOK

- Click the Open button on the Standard toolbar (or click File, and then click Open).
- Make sure the Look in list box displays the name of the folder containing the workbook you want to open.
- Click the name of the workbook you want to open.
- Click Open.

Mike created a workbook to help the site selection team evaluate the four potential locations for the golf course. The workbook, Inwood, is on your Student Disk.

To open an existing workbook:

1. Place your Excel Student Disk in the appropriate drive.

   TROUBLE? If you don't have a Student Disk, you need to get one before you can proceed. Your instructor or technical support person will either give you one or ask you to make your own by following the instructions on the "Read This Before You Begin" page before this tutorial. See your instructor or technical support person for information.

2. Click the **Open** button 🖼 on the Standard toolbar. The Open File dialog box opens. See Figure 1-8.

Figure 1-8 ◀
Open dialog
box

names and files
specified here
(yours may differ)

click here to
specify drive

3. Click the **Look in** list arrow to display the list of available drives. Locate the drive containing your Student Disk. In this text, we assume your Student Disk is a 3½-inch floppy in drive A.

4. Click the drive that contains your Student Disk. A list of documents and folders on your Student Disk appears in the list box.

5. In the list of document and folder names, double-click **Tutorial.01** to display that folder in the Look in list box, then click **Inwood**.

6. Click the **Open** button. (You could also double-click the filename to open the file.) The Inwood workbook opens and the first sheet in the workbook, Title Sheet, appears. See Figure 1-9.

TROUBLE? If you do not see Inwood listed, use the scroll bar to see additional names.

Figure 1-9 ◀
Title Sheet
sheet in Inwood
workbook

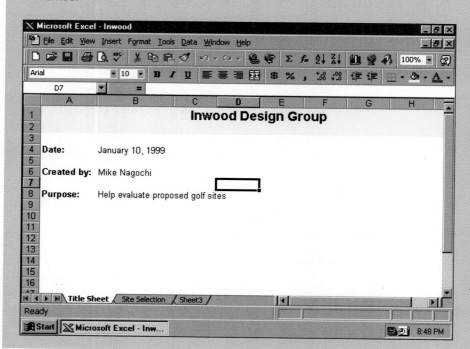

Layout of the Inwood Workbook

The first worksheet, Title Sheet, contains information about the workbook. The Title Sheet shows who created the workbook, the date when it was created, and its purpose.

Mike explains that whenever he creates a new workbook he makes sure he documents it carefully. This information is especially useful if he returns to a workbook after a long period of time (or if a new user opens it) because it provides a quick review of the workbook's purpose.

After reviewing the Title Sheet, Mike moves to the Site Selection worksheet.

To move to the Site Selection worksheet:

1. Click the **Site Selection** sheet tab to display the worksheet Mike is preparing for the site selection team. See Figure 1-10.

Figure 1-10
Site Selection
worksheet

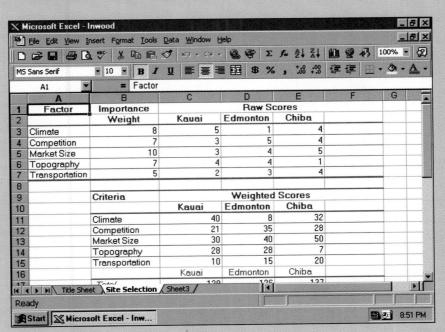

Mike explains the general layout of the Site Selection worksheet to you. He reminds you that to this point he has only entered data for three of the four sites. He will provide the missing Scottsdale information to you. Cells C2 through E2 list three of the four sites under consideration for which he has data. Cells A3 through A7 contain the five factors on which the team's decision will be based: Climate, Competition, Market Size, Topography, and Transportation. They assign scores for climate, competition, market size, topography, and transportation to each location. The team uses a scale of 1 to 5 to assign a raw score for each factor. Higher raw scores indicate strength; lower raw scores indicate weakness. Cells C3 through E7 contain the raw scores for the first three locations. For example, the raw score for Kauai's climate is 5; the two other locations have scores of 1 and 4, so Kauai, with its warm, sunny days all year, has the best climate for the golf course of the three sites visited so far. Edmonton, on the other hand, has cold weather and only received a climate raw score of 1.

The raw scores, however, do not provide enough information for the team to make a decision. Some factors are more important to the success of the golf course than others. The team members assigned an *importance weight* to each factor according to their knowledge of what factors contribute most to the success of a golf course. The importance weights are on a scale from 1 to 10, with 10 being most important. Mike entered the weights in cells B3 through B7. Market size, weighted 10, is the most important factor. The team believes the least important factor is transportation, so transportation is assigned a lower weight. Climate is important but the team considers market size most important. Therefore, they do not use the raw scores to make a final decision. Instead, they multiply each raw score by its importance weight to produce a weighted score. Which of the three sites already visited has the highest weighted score for any factor? If you look at the scores in cells C11 through E15, you see that Chiba's score of 50 for market size is the highest weighted score for any factor.

Cells C17 through E17 contain the total weighted scores for the three locations. With the current weighting and raw scores, Chiba is the most promising site, with a total score of 137.

Quick Check

1. A(n) _____ is the rectangular area where a column and a row intersect.

2. When you _____ a workbook, the computer copies it from your disk into RAM.

3. The cell reference _____ refers to the intersection of the fourth column and the second row.

4. To move the worksheet to the right one column:
   a. Press the Enter key
   b. Click the right arrow on the horizontal scroll bar
   c. Press the Escape key
   d. Press Ctrl + Home

5. To make Sheet2 the active worksheet, you would _____.

6. What key or keys do you press to make cell A1 the active cell?

You have now reviewed the layout of the worksheet. Now, Mike wants you to enter the data on Scottsdale. Based on his meeting with local investors and a visit to the Scottsdale site, he has assigned the following raw scores: Climate 5, Competition 2, Market Size 4, Topography 3, and Transportation 3. To complete the worksheet, you must enter the raw scores he has assigned to the Scottsdale site. You will do this in the next session.

SESSION 1.2

In this session you will learn how to enter text, values, formulas, and functions into a worksheet. You will use this data to perform what-if analysis using a worksheet. You'll also correct mistakes, and use the online Help system to determine how to clear the contents of cells. Finally, you'll learn how to print a worksheet, and how to close a worksheet and exit Excel.

Text, Values, Formulas, and Functions

As you have now observed, an Excel workbook can hold one or more worksheets, each containing a grid of 256 columns and 65,536 rows. The rectangular areas at the intersections of each column and row are called cells. A cell can contain a value, text, or a formula. To understand how the spreadsheet program works, you need to understand how Excel manipulates text, values, formulas, and functions.

Text

Text entries include any combination of letters, symbols, numbers, and spaces. Although text is sometimes used as data, it is more often used to describe the data contained in a worksheet. Text is often used to label columns and rows in a worksheet. For example, a projected monthly income statement contains the months of the year as column headings and income and expense categories as row labels. To enter text in a worksheet, you select the cell in which you want to enter the text by clicking the cell to select it, then typing the text. Excel automatically aligns the text on the left when it is displayed in a cell.

Mike's Site Selection worksheet contains a number of column heading labels. You need to enter the label for Scottsdale in the Raw Scores and Weighted Scores sections of the worksheet.

To enter a text label:

1. If you took a break after the last session, make sure Excel is running and make sure the Site Selection worksheet of the Inwood workbook is displayed.

2. Click cell **F2** to make it the active cell.

3. Type **Scottsdale**, then press the **Enter** key.

   TROUBLE? If you make a mistake while typing, you can correct the error with the Backspace key. If you realize you made an error after you press the Enter key, retype the entry by repeating Steps 2 and 3.

4. Click cell **F10** and type **S.** Excel completes the entry for you based on the entries already in the column. If your data involves repetitious text, this feature, known as **AutoComplete,** can make your data entry go more quickly.

5. Press the **Enter** key to complete the entry.

6. Click cell **F16**, type **S,** and press the **Enter** key to accept Scottsdale as the entry in the cell. See Figure 1-11.

Figure 1-11
Worksheet after text entered

Next, you need to enter the raw scores Mike assigned to Scottsdale.

Values

Values are numbers that represent a quantity of some type: the number of units in inventory, stock price, an exam score, and so on. Examples of values are 378, 25.2, and -55. Values can also be dates (11/29/99) and times (4:40:31). As you type information in a cell, Excel determines whether the characters you're typing can be used as values. For example, if you type 456, Excel recognizes it as a value and it is right-justified when displayed in the cell. On the other hand, Excel treats some data commonly referred to as "numbers" as text. For example, Excel treats a telephone number (1-800-227-1240) or a social security number (372-70-9654) as text that cannot be used for calculations.

You need to enter the raw scores for Scottsdale.

To enter a value:

1. If necessary, click the scroll arrow so row 2 is visible. Click cell **F3**, type **5** and then press the **Enter** key. The cell pointer moves to cell F4.

2. With the cell pointer in cell F4, type **2** and press the **Enter** key.

3. Enter the value **4** for Market Size in cell F5, the value **3** for Topography in cell F6, and the value **3** for Transportation in cell F7. See Figure 1-12.

Figure 1-12 ◀
Worksheet after numbers entered

Next, you enter the formulas to calculate Scottsdale's weighted score in each category.

Formulas

When you need to perform a calculation in Excel you use a formula. A **formula** is the arithmetic used to calculate values displayed in a worksheet. You can take advantage of the power of Excel by using formulas in worksheets. If you change one number in a worksheet, Excel recalculates any formula affected by the change.

An Excel formula always begins with an equal sign (=). Formulas are created by combining numbers, cell references, arithmetic operators, and/or functions. An **arithmetic operator** indicates the desired arithmetic operations. Figure 1-13 shows the arithmetic operators used in Excel.

Figure 1-13
Arithmetic
operators used
in formulas

Arithmetic Operation	Arithmetic Operator	Example	Description
Addition	+	=10+A5	Adds 10 to the value in cell A5
Subtraction	–	=C9–B9	Subtracts the value in cell B9 from the value in cell C9
Multiplication	*	=C9*B9	Multiplies the value in cell B9 by the value in cell C9
Division	/	=C9/B9	Divides the value in cell C9 by the value in cell B9
Exponentiation	^	=10^B5	Raises 10 to the value stored in cell B5

The result of the formula is displayed in the cell where you entered the formula. To view the formula that has been entered in a cell, you must first select the cell, then look at the formula bar.

REFERENCE window

ENTERING A FORMULA

- Click the cell where you want the result to appear.
- Type = and then type the rest of the formula.
- For formulas that include cell references, such as B2 or D78, you can type the cell reference or you can use the mouse or arrow keys to select each cell.
- When the formula is complete, press the Enter key.

You need to enter the formulas to compute the weighted scores for the Scottsdale site. The formula multiples the raw score for a factor by the importance weight assigned to the factor. Figure 1-14 displays the formulas you need to enter into the worksheet.

Figure 1-14
Formula to
calculate
Scottsdale's
weighted score

Cell	Formula	Explanation
F11	=B3*F3	Multiplies importance weight by raw score for climate
F12	=B4*F4	Multiplies importance weight by raw score for competition
F13	=B5*F5	Multiplies importance weight by raw score for market size
F14	=B6*F6	Multiplies importance weight by raw score for topography
F15	=B7*F7	Multiplies importance weight by raw score for transportation

To enter the formula to calculate each weighted score for the Scottsdale site:

1. Click cell **F11** to make it the active cell. Type **=B3*F3** to multiply the weight assigned to the climate category by the raw score assigned to Scottsdale for the climate category. Press the **Enter** key. The value 40 is displayed in cell F11.

   TROUBLE? If you make a mistake while typing, you can correct the error with the Backspace key. If you realize you made an error after you press the Enter key, repeat Step 1 to retype the entry.

2. Click cell **F12**, type **=B4*F4**, and then press the **Enter** key. This formula multiplies the weight assigned to competition (the contents of cell B4) by Scottsdale's raw score for competition (cell F4). The value 14 is displayed.

3. Enter the remaining formulas from Figure 1-14 into cells F13, F14, and F15. When completed, your worksheet will look like Figure 1-15.

Figure 1-15 ◄
Worksheet after entering formulas to calculate weighted score

You now have to enter the formula to calculate the total weighted score for Scottsdale into the worksheet. You can use the formula *=F11+F12+F13+F14+F15* to calculate the total score for the Scottsdale site. As an alternative, you can use a function to streamline this long formula.

Functions

A **function** is a special prewritten formula that's a shortcut for commonly used calculations. For example, the SUM function is a shortcut for entering formulas that total values in rows or columns. You can use the SUM function to create the formula =SUM(F11:F15) instead of typing the longer *=F11+F12+F13+F14+F15*. The SUM function in this example adds the range F11 through F15. A **range** can be a single cell or a rectangular block of cells, often rows or columns. The range reference in the function SUM(F11:F15) refers to the rectangular block of cells beginning at F11 and ending at F15. Figure 1-16 shows several examples of ranges.

Figure 1-16
Examples of
ranges

range D4:I4

range B3:B9

range D14:D14

range F8:H16

REFERENCE
window

ENTERING THE SUM FUNCTION

- Type = to begin the function.
- Type SUM in either uppercase or lowercase letters, followed by an opening parenthesis (( ). Do not put a space between "SUM" and the parenthesis.
- Type the range of cells you want to sum, separating the first and last cells in the range with a colon, as in B9:B15, or drag the pointer to outline the cells you want to sum.
- Press the Enter key.

You use the SUM function to compute the total score for the Scottsdale site.

To enter the formula using a function:

1. Click cell **F17** to make it the active cell.
2. Type **=SUM(F11:F15)**. Notice that the formula appears in the cell and the formula bar as you enter it. See Figure 1-17.

Figure 1-17 ◄
Viewing
the SUM
function before
completing
the entry

SUM function
appears in
formula bar

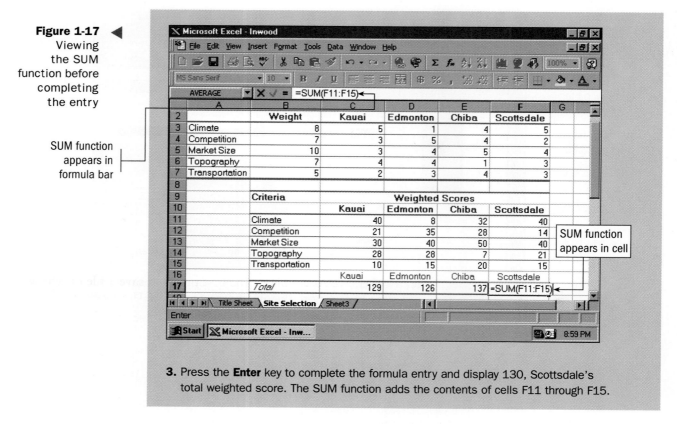

3. Press the **Enter** key to complete the formula entry and display 130, Scottsdale's total weighted score. The SUM function adds the contents of cells F11 through F15.

The worksheet for site selection is now complete. Mike's worksheet contains columns of information about the site selection and a chart displaying the weighted scores for each potential site. To see the chart you must scroll the worksheet.

To scroll the worksheet to view the chart:

1. Click the **scroll arrow** button on the vertical scroll bar until the section of the worksheet containing the chart is displayed. See Figure 1-18.

Figure 1-18 ◄
Scrolling the
worksheet to
view the chart

Chiba is leading site

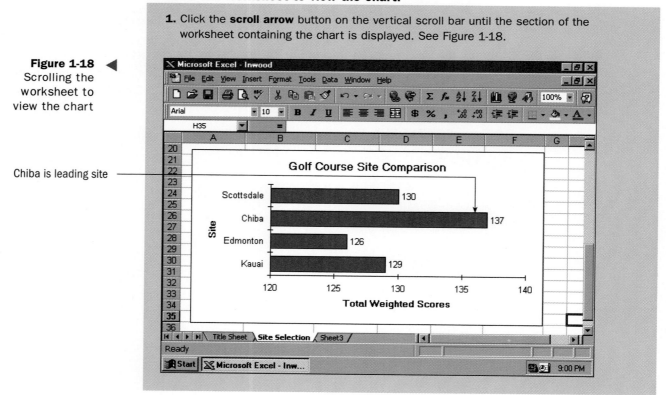

2. After you look at the chart, click and drag the **scroll box** to the top of the vertical scroll bar.

You have completed the worksheet; Mike decides to save it before showing it to the site selection team.

Saving the Workbook

To store a workbook permanently, so you can use it again without having to reenter the data and formulas, you must save it as a file on a disk. When you save a workbook, you copy it from RAM onto your disk. You'll use either the Save or the Save As command. The Save command copies the workbook onto a disk using its current filename. If a version of the file already exists, the new version replaces the old one. The Save As command asks for a filename before copying the workbook onto a disk. When you enter a new filename, you save the current file under that new name. The previous version of the file remains on the disk under its original name.

As a general rule, use the Save As command the first time you save a file or whenever you modify a file and want to save both the old and new versions. Use the Save command when you modify a file and want to save only the current version.

It is a good idea to save your file often. That way, if the power goes out or the computer stops working, you're less likely to lose your work. Because you use the Save command frequently, the Standard toolbar has a Save button , a single mouse-click shortcut for saving your workbook.

REFERENCE window	SAVING A WORKBOOK WITH A NEW FILENAME
	■ Click File and then click Save As.
	■ Change the workbook name as necessary.
	■ Make sure the Save in box displays the folder in which you want to save your workbook.
	■ Click the Save button.

Mike's workbook is named Inwood. On your screen is a version of Inwood that you modified during this work session. Save the modified workbook under the new name Inwood 2. This way if you want to start the tutorial from the beginning, you can open the Inwood file and start over.

To save the modified workbook under a new name:

1. Click **File** on the menu bar, and then click **Save As**. The Save As dialog box opens with the current workbook name in the File name text box.

2. Click at the end of the current workbook name, press the **spacebar**, and then type **2**. *(Do not press the Enter key.)*

Before you proceed, check the other dialog box specifications to ensure that you save the workbook on your Student Disk.

3. If necessary, click the **Save in** list arrow to display the list of available drives and folders. Click **Tutorial.01**.

4. Confirm that the Save as type text box specifies "Microsoft Excel Workbook."

5. When your Save As dialog box looks like the one in Figure 1-19, click the **Save** button to close the dialog box and save the workbook. Notice that the new workbook name, Inwood 2, now appears in the title bar.

Figure 1-19 ◀
Saving the
worksheet with
a new filename

new filename ⟶

You now have two versions of the workbook: the original file—Inwood—and the modified workbook—Inwood 2.

Changing Values and Observing Results

The worksheet for site selection is now complete. Mike is ready to show it to the group. As the team examines the worksheet, you ask if the raw scores take into account recent news that a competing design group has announced plans to build a $325-million golf resort just 10 miles away from Inwood's proposed site in Chiba. Mike admits that he assigned the values before the announcement, so the raw scores do not reflect the increased competition in the Chiba market. You suggest revising the raw score for the competition factor to reflect this market change in Chiba.

When you change a value in a worksheet, Excel recalculates the worksheet and displays updated results. The recalculation feature makes Excel an extremely useful decision-making tool because it lets you quickly and easily factor in changing conditions. When you revise the contents of one or more cells in a worksheet and observe the effect this change has on all the other cells, you are performing a **what-if analysis**. In effect, you are saying, what if I change the value assigned to this factor? What effect will it have on the outcomes in the worksheet?

Since another development group has announced plans to construct a new golf course in the Chiba area, the team decides to lower Chiba's competition raw score from 4 to 2.

To change Chiba's competition raw score from 4 to 2:

1. Click cell **E4**. The black border around cell E4 indicates that it is the active cell. The current value of cell E4 is 4.

2. Type **2**. Notice that 2 appears in the cell and in the formula bar, along with a formula palette of three new buttons. The buttons shown in Figure 1-20—the Cancel button ⊠, the Enter button ✓, and the Edit Formula button ▪—offer alternatives for canceling, entering, and editing data and formulas.

Figure 1-20 ◀
Changing a
cell's contents

edit formula

cancel typing

same as pressing
the Enter key

new competition
raw score

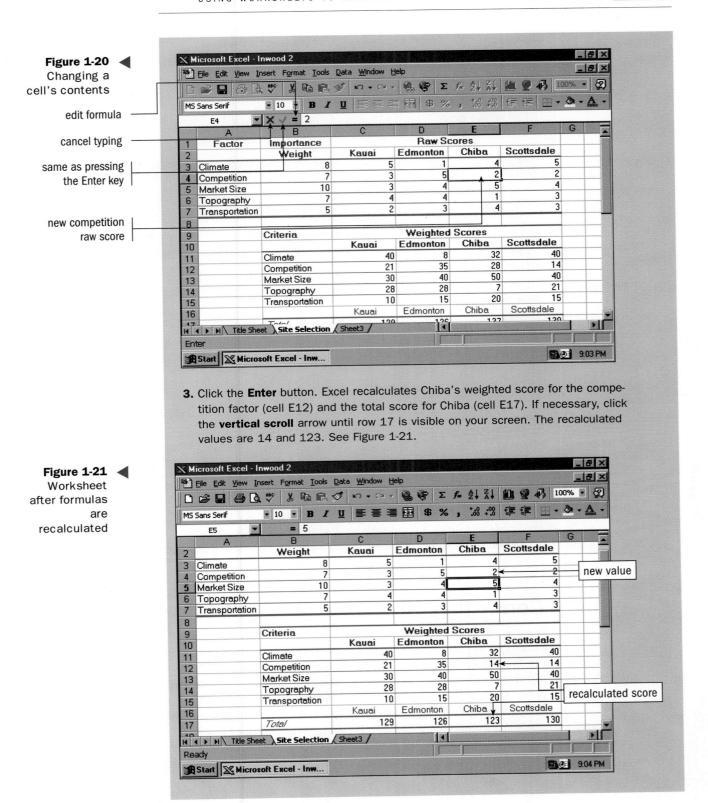

3. Click the **Enter** button. Excel recalculates Chiba's weighted score for the competition factor (cell E12) and the total score for Chiba (cell E17). If necessary, click the **vertical scroll** arrow until row 17 is visible on your screen. The recalculated values are 14 and 123. See Figure 1-21.

Figure 1-21 ◀
Worksheet
after formulas
are
recalculated

new value

recalculated score

The team takes another look at the total weighted scores in row 17. Scottsdale is now the top-ranking site, with a total weighted score of 130. Chiba's total weighted score is now 123.

As the team continues to discuss the worksheet, several members express concern over the importance weight used for transportation. In the current worksheet, transportation is weighted 5 (cell B7). You remember that the group agreed to use an importance weight of 2 at a previous meeting. You ask Mike to change the importance weight for transportation.

To change the importance weight for transportation:

1. Click cell **B7** to make it the active cell.

2. Type **2** and press the **Enter** key. Cell B7 now contains the value 2 instead of 5. Cell B8 becomes the active cell. See Figure 1-22. Notice that the weighted scores for transportation (row 15) and the total weighted scores for each site (row 17) have all changed.

Figure 1-22 ◄
Worksheet
after change
made to the
transportation
importance
weight

new value

all transportation
scores recalculated

all total scores
recalculated

The change in the transportation importance weight puts Kauai ahead as the most favorable site, with a total weighted score of 123.

As you enter and edit a worksheet, there are many data entry errors that can occur. The most commonly made mistake on a worksheet is a typing error. Typing mistakes are easy to correct.

Correcting Mistakes

It is easy to correct a mistake as you are typing information in a cell, before you press the Enter key. If you need to correct a mistake as you are typing information in a cell, press the Backspace key to back up and delete one or more characters. When you are typing information in a cell, don't use the cursor arrow keys to edit because they move the cell pointer to another cell. One of the team members suggests changing the label "Criteria" in cell B9 to "Factors." The team members agree and you make the change to the cell.

To correct a mistake as you type:

1. Click cell **B9** to make it the active cell.

2. Type **Fak**, intentionally making an error, but don't press the Enter key.

3. Press the **Backspace** key to delete "k."

4. Type **ctors** and press the **Enter** key.

Now the word "Factors" is in cell B9. Mike suggests changing "Factors" to "Factor." The team agrees. To change a cell's contents after you press the Enter key, you use a different method. Double-clicking a cell or pressing the F2 key puts Excel into Edit mode, which lets you use the Backspace key, the ← and → keys, and the mouse to change the text in the formula bar.

REFERENCE window

CORRECTING MISTAKES USING EDIT MODE

- Double-click the cell you want to edit to begin Edit mode and display the contents of the cell in the formula bar (or click the cell you want to edit, then press F2).
- Use Backspace, Delete, ←, →, or the mouse to edit the cell's contents either in the cell or in the formula bar.
- Press the Enter key when you finish editing.

You use Edit mode to change "Factors" to "Factor" in cell B9.

To change the word "Factors" to "Factor" in cell B9:

1. Double-click cell **B9** to begin Edit mode. Note that "Edit" appears in the status bar, reminding you that Excel is currently in Edit mode.

2. Press the **End** key if necessary to move the cursor to the right of the word "Factors," then press the **Backspace** key to delete the "s."

3. Press the **Enter** key to complete the edit.

You ask if the team is ready to recommend a site. Mike believes that based on the best information they have, Kauai should be the recommended site and Scottsdale the alternative site. You ask for a vote, and the team unanimously agrees with Mike's recommendation.

Mike wants to have complete documentation to accompany the team's written recommendation to management, so he wants to print the worksheet.

As he reviews the worksheet one last time, he thinks that the labels in cells C16 through F16 (Kauai, Edmonton, Chiba, Scottsdale) are unnecessary and decides he wants you to delete them before printing the worksheet. You ask how you delete the contents of a cell or a group of cells. Mike is not sure, so he suggests using the Excel Help system to find the answer.

Getting Help

If you don't know how to perform a task or forget how to carry out a particular task, Excel provides an extensive Help system. The Excel Help system provides the same options as the Help system in other Windows programs—the Help Contents, the Help Index, and the Find feature. The Excel Help system also provides additional ways to get help as you work. One way to get help is to use the Office Assistant, which you may have seen on your screen when you first started Excel, and which you hid earlier in this tutorial. The Office Assistant, an animated object, pops up on the screen when you click the Office Assistant button on the Standard toolbar. The Office Assistant answers questions, offers tips, and provides help for a variety of Excel features. In addition to the Office Assistant, Figure 1-23 identifies several other ways you can get help.

Figure 1-23 ◀
Alternative ways
to get help

Action	Results in
On Help menu, click Contents and Index, click Contents tab	Displays an outline of topics and subtopics on which you can get information
On Help menu, click Contents and Index, click Index tab	Displays alphabetical listings of topics; enter first few letters in the box to scroll to an entry
On Help menu, click Contents and Index, click Find tab	Provides capability to find all topics that contain a particular word or words
Press F1	Activates the Office Assistant
On Help menu, click ▨ What's This?	Pointer changes to the Help pointer, which you use to click any object or option on the screen to see a description of the object

REFERENCE **window**

USING THE OFFICE ASSISTANT

- Click the Office Assistant button on the Standard toolbar (or choose Microsoft Excel Help from the Help menu) to display the Office Assistant.
- Click Tips for information on using features more effectively.
  or
- Type an English-language question on an area where you need help, and then click Search.
- Click the suggested Help topic.
- To hide the Office Assistant, click its Close button.

Use the Office Assistant to get information on how to clear the contents of cells.

To get Help using the Office Assistant:

1. Click the Office Assistant ▨ button to display an animated object and an information box. See Figure 1-24.

Figure 1-24 ◀
Office
Assistant with
information box

enter question here ───

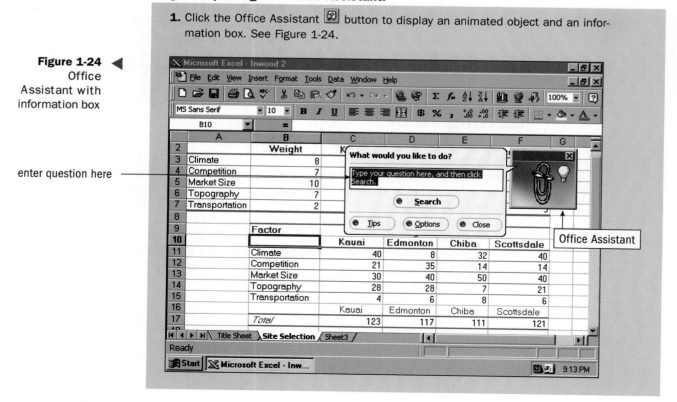

The Office Assistant can respond to an English-language question.

2. Type **how do I clear cells**, and then click **Search** to display several possible Help topics. See Figure 1-25.

Figure 1-25 ◀
Office Assistant with several suggested Help topics

click this topic

suggested Help topics

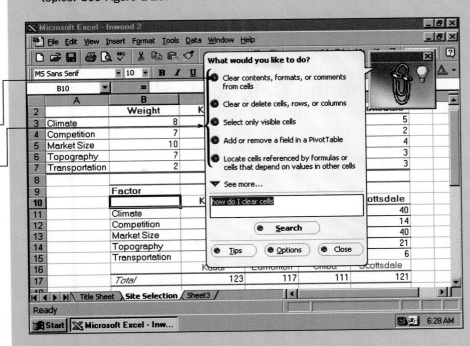

3. Click the first suggestion, **Clear contents, formats, or comments from cells**, to open a How To window on this topic. See Figure 1-26.

Figure 1-26 ◀
How To window on Clear contents, formats, or comments from cells

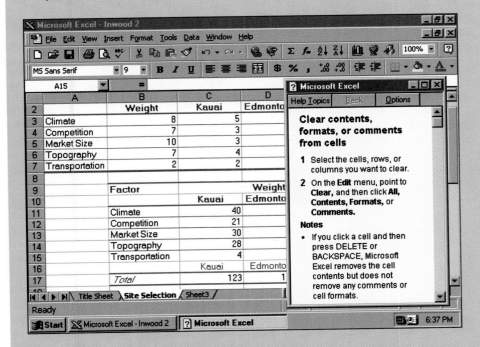

You can print the contents of the How To window, or you can click the Keep Help On Top command from the Options menu to keep the How To window on the screen where you can refer to it as you go through each step.

4. After reviewing the information, click the **Close** button ☒ on the How To window.

5. Click the **Close** button ☒ in the upper-right corner of the Office Assistant to hide the Assistant.

After reviewing the information from the Office Assistant, you are ready to remove the labels from the worksheet.

Clearing Cell Contents

As you are building or modifying your worksheet, you may occasionally find that you have entered a label, number, or formula in a cell that you want to be empty. To erase the contents of a cell, you use either the Delete key or the Clear command on the Edit menu. Removing the contents of a cell is known as clearing a cell. Do not press the spacebar to enter a blank character in an attempt to clear a cell's content. Excel treats a blank character as text, so even though the cell appears to be empty, it is not.

REFERENCE window

CLEARING CELL CONTENTS

- Click the cell you want to clear, or select a range of cells you want to clear.
- Press the Delete key.
  or
- Click Edit, point to Clear, and then click Contents to erase only the contents of a cell, or click All to completely clear the cell contents, formatting, and notes.

You are ready to clear the labels from cells C16 through F16.

To clear the labels from cells C16 through F16:

1. Click cell **C16**. This will be the upper-left corner of the range to clear.

2. Position the cell pointer over cell C16. With the cell pointer the shape of ✛, click and drag the cell pointer to F16 to select the range C16:F16.
If your pointer changes to a crosshair + *, or an arrow* ↖ *, do not drag the cell pointer to F16, until pointer changes to* ✛ . Note that when you select a range, the first cell in that range, cell C16 in this example, remains white and the other cells in the range are highlighted. See Figure 1-27.

Figure 1-27 ◀
Highlighted cell
range

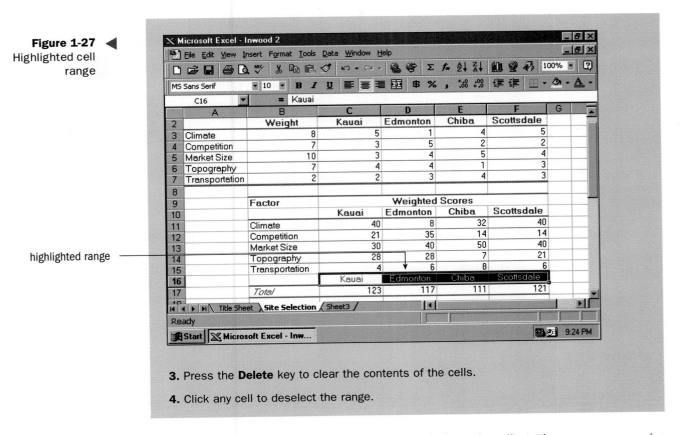

highlighted range ⎯⎯⎯⎯⎯

3. Press the **Delete** key to clear the contents of the cells.

4. Click any cell to deselect the range.

Now that you have cleared the unwanted labels from the cells, Mike wants you to print the site selection worksheet.

Printing the Worksheet

You can print an Excel worksheet using either the Print command on the File menu or the Print button on the Standard toolbar. If you use the Print command, Excel displays a dialog box where you can specify which worksheet pages you want to print, the number of copies you want to print, and the print quality (resolution). If you use the Print button, you do not have these options; Excel prints one copy of the entire worksheet using the current print settings.

REFERENCE
window

PRINTING A WORKSHEET

- Click File and then click Print.
- Adjust any settings you want in the Print dialog box.
- Click the OK button.
  or
- Click the Print button on the Standard toolbar.

Mike wants a printout of the entire Site Selection worksheet. You decide to select the Print command from the File menu instead of using the Print button so you can check the Print dialog box settings.

To check the print settings and then print the worksheet:

1. Make sure your printer is turned on and contains paper.

2. Click **File** on the menu bar, and then click **Print** to display the Print dialog box. See Figure 1-28.

Figure 1-28 ◀
Print dialog box

identifies printer (your
entry may be
different)

prints selected range
in worksheet

prints active sheet

Now you need to select what to print. You could print the complete workbook, which would be the Title Sheet and the Site Selection sheet. To do this, you would click the Entire workbook option button. You could also choose to print just a portion of a worksheet. For example, to print only the weighted scores data of the Site Selection worksheet, first select this range with your mouse pointer, and then select the Selection option button in the Print dialog box. In this case, Mike needs just the Site Selection worksheet.

3. If necessary, click the **Active sheet(s)** option button in the Print what section of the dialog box to print just the Site Selection worksheet, and not the Title Sheet.

4. Make sure "1" appears in the Number of copies text box, as Mike only needs to print one copy of the worksheet.

5. Click the **OK** button to print the worksheet. See Figure 1-29.

TROUBLE? If the worksheet does not print, see your technical support person for help.

Figure 1-29 ◄
Printed
worksheet

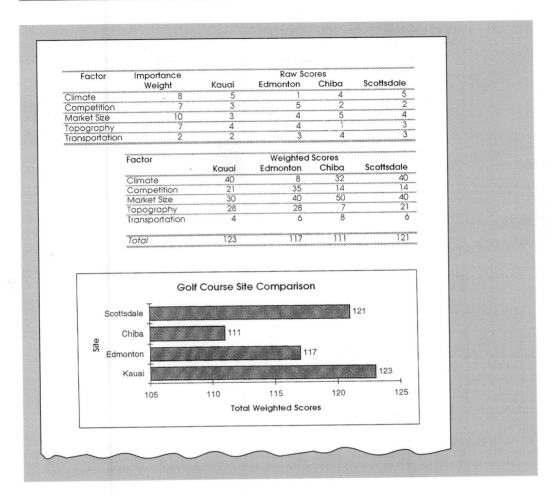

Factor	Importance Weight	Raw Scores			
		Kauai	Edmonton	Chiba	Scottsdale
Climate	8	5	1	4	5
Competition	7	3	5	2	2
Market Size	10	3	4	5	4
Topography	7	4	4	1	3
Transportation	2	2	3	4	3

Factor	Weighted Scores			
	Kauai	Edmonton	Chiba	Scottsdale
Climate	40	8	32	40
Competition	21	35	14	14
Market Size	30	40	50	40
Topography	28	28	7	21
Transportation	4	6	8	6
Total	123	117	111	121

Golf Course Site Comparison

Scottsdale 121
Chiba 111
Edmonton 117
Kauai 123

Site

105   110   115   120   125

Total Weighted Scores

Mike volunteers to put together the report with the team's final recommendation, and the meeting adjourns. You and Mike are finished working with the worksheet and are ready to close the workbook.

Closing the Workbook

Closing a workbook removes it from the screen. If a workbook contains changes that have not been saved, Excel asks if you want to save your modified worksheet before closing the workbook. You can now close the workbook.

To close the Inwood 2 workbook:

1. Click **File** on the menu bar, and then click **Close**. A dialog box displays the message "Do you want to save the changes you made to 'INWOOD 2'?"

2. Click the **Yes** button to save the Inwood 2 workbook before closing it.

The Excel window stays open so you can open or create another workbook. You do not want to, so your next step is to exit Excel.

Exiting Excel

To exit Excel, you can click the Close button on the title bar, or you can use the Exit command on the File menu.

To exit Excel:

1. Click the Close button ⊠ on the title bar. Excel closes and you return to the Windows desktop.

Quick Check

1. The formula =SUM(D1:K1) adds how many cells? Write an equivalent formula without using the SUM function.

2. What cells are included in the range B4:D6?

3. Indicate whether Excel treats the following cell entries as a value, text, or a formula:
   a. Profit
   b. 11/09/95
   c. 123
   d. =B9*225
   e. 1-800-227-1240
   f. =SUM(C1:C10)
   g. 123 N. First St.

4. To print the entire worksheet, you select the _____ option button from the _____ dialog box.

5. To print a copy of your worksheet, you use the _____ command on the _____ menu.

6. You can get Excel Help in any of the following ways except:
   a. clicking Help on the menu bar
   b. clicking the Help button on the Standard toolbar
   c. closing the program window
   d. pressing the F1 key

7. Why do you need to save a worksheet? What command do you use to save the worksheet?

8. What key do you press to clear the contents of a cell from a worksheet?

9. Explain the term *what-if analysis*.

The Inwood site selection team has completed its work. Mike's worksheet helped the team analyze the data and recommend Kauai as the best site for Inwood's next golf course. Although the Japanese market was a strong factor in favor of locating the course in Japan's Chiba Prefecture, the mountainous terrain and competition from nearby courses reduced the site's desirability.

Tutorial Assignments

The other company that had planned a golf course in Chiba, Japan, has run into financial difficulties. Rumors are that the project may be canceled. A copy of the final Inwood Design team workbook is on your Student Disk. Do the Tutorial Assignments to change this worksheet to show the effect of the other project's cancellation on your site selection.

1. If necessary, start Excel and make sure your Student Disk is in the appropriate disk drive.
   Open the Inwood 3 file in the TAssign folder for Tutorial 1 on your Student Disk.

2. Use the Save As command to save the workbook as Inwood4 in the TAssign folder for Tutorial 1. That way you won't change the original workbook.

3. In the Inwood4 worksheet, change the competition raw score for Chiba from 2 to 3. What site is ranked first?

4. The label "Transportation" in cell A9 was entered incorrectly as "Transportion." Use Edit mode to insert "ta" into the label.

5. Save the worksheet.

6. Print the worksheet.

7. Use the Contents and Index command on the Help menu to access the Help Topics dialog box. From the Contents tab, learn how to insert an additional worksheet into your workbook. (*Hint*: Choose Working with workbook and worksheets topic, then managing worksheets.) Write the steps to insert a worksheet.

8. Use the Office Assistant to learn how to delete a sheet from a workbook. Write the steps to delete a sheet.

9. Enter the text "Scores if the competing project in Chiba, Japan, is canceled" in cell A1.

10. Remove the raw scores for Chiba, cells E5 through E9. Print the worksheet.

11. Use the Index command on the Help menu to learn about the AutoCalculate feature. Write a brief explanation of this feature.

12. You are considering dropping transportation as a factor in the site selection decision. Use AutoCalculate to arrive at a revised total weighted score for each of the three remaining sites. Write the response.

13. Print the worksheet data without the chart. (*Hint*: Select the worksheet data before checking out the options in the Print dialog box.)

14. Use the What's This button. Learn more about the following Excel window components:
    a. Name box
    b. Sheet tabs
    c. Tip Wizard
    (*Hint*: Click , then click each item with the Help pointer.)

15. Close the workbook and exit Excel without saving the changes.

Case Problems

1. Market Share Analysis at Aldon Industries Helen Shalala is assistant to the regional director for Aldon Industries, a manufacturer of corporate voice mail systems. Helen has analyzed the market share of the top vendors with installations in the region. She's on her way to a meeting with the marketing staff where she will use her worksheet to plan a new marketing campaign. Help Helen and her team evaluate the options and plan the best advertising campaign for Aldon Industries. Write your responses to questions 4 through 10.

1. If necessary, start Excel and make sure your Student Disk is in the appropriate disk drive.

2. Open the workbook Aldon in the Case folder for Tutorial 1.

3. Use the Save As command to save the workbook as Aldon 2 in the Case folder for Tutorial 1. That way you won't change the original workbook for this case.

4. Take a moment to look over the Market Share worksheet. Do the following ranges contain text, values, or formulas?
    a. B13:G13
    b. C3:C10
    c. A3:A10
    d. G3:G10

5. What is Aldon Industries' overall market share?

6. Examine the worksheet to determine in which state Aldon Industries has the highest market share.

7. Which company leads the overall market?

8. What is Aldon Industries' overall ranking in total market share (1st, 2nd, 3rd, etc.)?

9. Which companies rank ahead of Aldon Industries in total market share?

10. What formula was used to calculate Total Installations in Illinois? Develop an alternative formula to calculate Total Installations in Illinois without using the SUM function.

11. Save and print the worksheet.

2. Selecting a Hospital Laboratory Computer System for Bridgeport Medical Center David Choi is on the Laboratory Computer Selection Committee for the Bridgeport Medical Center. After an extensive search, the committee has identified three vendors whose products appear to meet its needs. The Selection Committee has prepared an Excel worksheet to help evaluate the three potential vendors' strengths and weaknesses. The raw scores for two of the vendors, LabStar and Health Systems, have already been entered. Now raw scores must be entered for the third vendor, MedTech. Which vendor's system is best for the Bridgeport Medical Center? Complete these steps to find out:

1. If necessary, start Excel and make sure your Student Disk is in the appropriate disk drive.

2. Open the workbook Medical in the Case folder for Tutorial 1.

3. Use the Save As command to save the workbook as Medical 2 in the Case folder for Tutorial 1. That way you won't change the original workbook for this case.

4. Examine the Evaluation Scores worksheet, and type the following raw scores for MedTech: Cost = 6, Compatibility = 5, Vendor Reliability = 5, Size of Installed Base = 4, User Satisfaction = 5, Critical Functionality = 9, Additional Functionality = 8.

5. Use the Save command to save the modified worksheet.

6. Print the worksheet.

7. Based on the data in the worksheet, which vendor would you recommend? Why?

8. Assume you can adjust the value for only one importance weight (cells B6 through B12). Which factor would you change and what would its new weight be in order for LabStar to have the highest weighted score? (*Hint*: Remember that the value assigned to any importance weight cannot be higher then 10.)

9. Save and print the modified worksheet.

3. Enrollments in the College of Business You work 10 hours a week in the Dean's office at your college. The Assistant Dean has a number of meetings today and has asked you to complete a worksheet she needs for a meeting with Department Chairs this afternoon.

1. Open the workbook Enroll in the Case folder for Tutorial 1 on your Student Disk.

2. Use the Save As command to save the workbook as Enrollment.

3. Complete the workbook by performing the following tasks:

a. Enter the title "Enrollment Data for College of Business" in cell A1.

b. Enter the label "Total" in cell A8.

c. Calculate the total enrollment in the College of Business for 1999 in cell B8.

d. Calculate the total enrollment in the College of Business for 1998 in cell C8.

e. Calculate the change in enrollments from 1998 to 1999. Place the results in column D. Label the column heading "Change" and use the following formula: *Change = 1999 enrollment – 1998 enrollment*

4. Save the workbook.

5. Print the worksheet.

4. Krier Marine Services Vince DiOrio is an Information Systems major at a local college. To help pay for tuition, he works part-time three days a week at a nearby marina, Krier Marine Services. Vince works in the business office, and his responsibilities range from making coffee to keeping the company's books.

Recently, Jim Krier, the owner of the marina, asked Vince if he could help computerize the payroll for their part-time employees. He explained that the employees work a different number of hours each week for different rates of pay. Jim does the payroll manually now and finds it time-consuming. Moreover, whenever he makes an error, he is embarrassed and annoyed at having to take the additional time to correct it. Jim was hoping Vince could help him.

Vince immediately agrees to help. He tells Jim that he knows how to use Excel and that he can build a spreadsheet that will save him time and reduce errors. Jim and Vince meet. They review the present payroll process and discuss the desired outcomes of the payroll spreadsheet. Figure 1-30 is a sketch of the output Jim wants to get.

Figure 1-30 ◀
Sketch of worksheet

Krier Marine Services Weekly Payroll
Week Ending 10/15

Employee	Hours	Pay Rate	Gross Pay
Bramble	15	7	formula
Juarez	28	5	"
Smith	30	7	"
DiOrio	22	6	"
Total			formula

1. Open the workbook Payroll in the Cases folder for Tutorial 1 on your Student Disk.
2. Use the Save As command to save the workbook as Payroll 2.
3. Complete the worksheet by performing the following tasks:
   a. Enter the employee hours in column B.
   b. Enter the employee pay rate in column C.
   c. In column D, enter the formulas to compute gross pay for each employee. (*Hint*: Use Hours times Pay Rate.)
   d. In cell D9, enter the SUM function to calculate total gross pay.
4. Save the workbook.
5. Print the worksheet.
6. Remove the hours for the four employees.
7. Enter the following hours: 18 for Bramble, 25 for Juarez, 35 for Smith, and 20 for DiOrio.
8. Print the new worksheet.

Lab Assignments

Spreadsheets

These Lab Assignments are designed to accompany the interactive Course Lab called Spreadsheets. To start the Spreadsheets Lab, click the Start button on the Windows 95 taskbar, point to Programs, point to Course Labs, point to New Perspectives Applications, and click Spreadsheets. If you do not see Course Labs on your Programs menu, see your instructor or technical support person.

Spreadsheets Spreadsheet software is used extensively in business, education, science, and the humanities to simplify tasks that involve calculations. In this Lab you will learn how spreadsheet software works. You will use spreadsheet software to examine and modify worksheets, as well as to create your own worksheets.

1. Click the Steps button to learn how spreadsheet software works. As you proceed through the Steps, answer all of the Quick Check questions that appear. After you complete the Steps, you will see a Quick Check Summary report. Follow the instructions on the screen to print this report.
2. Click the Explore button. Click OK to display a new worksheet. Click File, and then click Open to display the Open dialog box. Click the file Income, then press the Enter key to open the Income and Expense Summary worksheet. Notice that the worksheet contains labels and values for income from consulting and training. It also contains labels and values for expenses such as rent

and salaries. The worksheet does not, however, contain formulas to calculate Total Income, Total Expenses, or Profit. Do the following:

a. Calculate the Total Income by entering the formula =SUM(C4:C5) in cell C6.

b. Calculate the Total Expenses by entering the formula =SUM(C9:C12) in cell C13.

c. Calculate Profit by entering the formula =C6-C13 in cell C15.

d. Manually check the results to make sure you entered the formulas correctly.

e. Print your completed worksheet that shows your results.

3. You can use a spreadsheet to keep track of your grade in a class. Click the Explore button to display a blank worksheet. Click File and then click Open to display the Open dialog box. Click the file Grades to open the Grades worksheet. This worksheet contains all the labels and formulas necessary to calculate your grade based on four test scores.

Suppose you receive a score of 88 out of 100 on the first test. On the second test, you score 42 out of 48. On the third test, you score 92 out of 100. You have not taken the fourth test yet. Enter the appropriate data on the Grade worksheet to determine your grade after taking three tests. Print out your worksheet.

4. Worksheets are handy for answering "what if" questions. For example, suppose you decide to open a lemonade stand. You're interested in how much profit you can make each day. What if you sell 20 cups of lemonade? What if you sell 100? What if the cost of lemons increases?

In Explore, open the file Lemons and use the worksheet to answer questions a through d, then print the worksheet for item e:

a. What is your profit if you sell 20 cups a day?

b. What is your profit if you sell 100 cups a day?

c. What is your profit if the price of lemons increases to $.07 and you sell 100 cups?

d. What is your profit if you raise the price of a cup of lemonade to $.30? (Lemons still cost $.07 and you assume you will sell 100 cups.)

e. Suppose your competitor boasts that she sold 50 cups of lemonade in one day and made exactly $12.00. On your worksheet, adjust the cost of cups, water, lemons, and sugar, and the price per cup to show a profit of exactly $12.00 for 50 cups sold. Print this worksheet.

5. It is important to make sure the formulas in your worksheet are accurate. An easy way to test this is to enter 1s for all the values on your worksheet, and then check the calculations manually. In Explore, open the worksheet Receipt, which calculates sales receipts. Enter 1 as the value for Item 1, Item 2, and Item 3. Enter .01 for the Sales Tax rate. Now, manually calculate what you would pay for three items that cost $1.00 each in a state where sales tax is 1% (.01). Do your manual calculations match those of the worksheet? If not, correct the formulas in the worksheet and print out a formula report of your revised worksheet.

6. In Explore, create your own worksheet showing your household budget for one month. Make sure you put a title on the worksheet. Use formulas to calculate your total income and your total expenses for the month. Add another formula to calculate how much money you were able to save. Print a formula report of your worksheet. Also, print your worksheet, showing realistic values for one month.

Creating a Worksheet

Producing a Sales Comparison Report for MSI

OBJECTIVES

In this tutorial you will:

- Plan, build, test, document, preview, and print a worksheet

- Enter labels, values, and formulas

- Calculate a total using the AutoSum button

- Copy formulas using the fill handle and Clipboard

- Learn about relative, absolute, and mixed references

- Use the AVERAGE, MAX, and MIN functions to calculate values in the worksheet

- Spell check the worksheet

- Insert a row

- Reverse an action using the Undo button

- Move a range of cells

- Format the worksheet using AutoFormat

- Center printouts on a page

- Customize worksheet headers

CASE

Motorcycle Specialties Incorporated

Motorcycle Specialties Incorporated (MSI), a motorcycle helmet and accessories company, provides a wide range of specialty items to motorcycle enthusiasts throughout the world. MSI has its headquarters in Atlanta, Georgia, but it markets its products in North America, South America, Australia, and Europe.

The company's Marketing and Sales Director, Sally Caneval, meets regularly with the regional sales managers who oversee global sales in each of the four regions in which MSI does business. This month, Sally intends to review overall sales in each region for the last two fiscal years and present her findings at her next meeting with the regional sales managers. She has asked you to help her put together a report that summarizes this sales information.

Specifically, Sally wants the report to show total sales for each region of the world for the two most recent fiscal years. Additionally, she wants to see the percentage change between the two years. She also wants the report to include the percentage each region contributed to the total sales of the company in 1999. Finally, she wants to include summary statistics on the average, maximum, and minimum sales for 1999.

SESSION

2.1

In this session you will learn how to plan and build a worksheet; enter labels, numbers, and formulas; and copy formulas to other cells.

Developing Worksheets

Effective worksheets are well planned and carefully designed. A well-designed worksheet should clearly identify its overall goal. It should present information in a clear, well-organized format, and include all the data necessary to produce the results that address the goal of the application.

Further, the process of developing a good worksheet includes the following planning and execution steps:

- Determine the worksheet's purpose, what it will include, and how it will be organized
- Enter the data and formulas into the worksheet
- Test the worksheet
- Edit the worksheet to correct any errors or make modifications
- Document the worksheet
- Improve the appearance of the worksheet
- Save and print the completed worksheet

Planning the Worksheet

Sally begins developing a worksheet that compares global sales by region over two years by first creating a planning analysis sheet. Her **planning analysis sheet** helps her answer the following questions:

1. What is the goal of the worksheet? This helps to define the problem to solve.

2. What are the desired results? This information describes the **output**—the information required to help solve the problem.

3. What data is needed to calculate the results you want to see? This information is the **input**—data that must be entered.

4. What calculations are needed to produce the desired output? These calculations specify the formulas used in the worksheet.

Sally's completed planning analysis sheet is shown in Figure 2-1.

Figure 2-1
Planning
analysis sheet

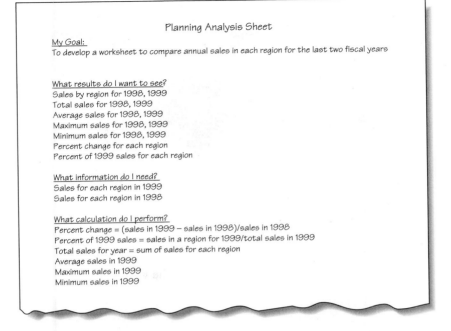

Planning Analysis Sheet

<u>My Goal:</u>
To develop a worksheet to compare annual sales in each region for the last two fiscal years

<u>What results do I want to see?</u>
Sales by region for 1998, 1999
Total sales for 1998, 1999
Average sales for 1998, 1999
Maximum sales for 1998, 1999
Minimum sales for 1998, 1999
Percent change for each region
Percent of 1999 sales for each region

<u>What information do I need?</u>
Sales for each region in 1999
Sales for each region in 1998

<u>What calculation do I perform?</u>
Percent change = (sales in 1999 – sales in 1998)/sales in 1998
Percent of 1999 sales = sales in a region for 1999/total sales in 1999
Total sales for year = sum of sales for each region
Average sales in 1999
Maximum sales in 1999
Minimum sales in 1999

Next, Sally makes a rough sketch of her design, including titles, column headings, row labels, and where data values and totals should be placed. Figure 2-2 shows Sally's sketch. With these two planning tools, Sally is now ready to enter the data into Excel and build the worksheet.

Figure 2-2
Sketch of
worksheet

Motorcycle Specialties Incorporated
Sales Comparison 1999 with 1998

Region	Year 1999	Year 1998	% Change	% of 1999 Sales
North America	365000	314330	0.16	0.28
South America	354250	292120	0.21	0.28
Australia	251140	262000	-0.04	0.19
Europe	310440	279996	0.11	0.24
Total	1280830	1148446	0.12	

Average	320207.5
Maximum	365000
Minimum	251140

Building the Worksheet

You will use Sally's planning analysis sheet, Figure 2-1, and the rough sketch shown in Figure 2-2 to guide you in preparing the sales comparison worksheet. You will begin by establishing the layout of the worksheet by entering titles and column headings. Next you will work on inputting the data and formulas that will calculate the results Sally needs.

To start Excel and organize your desktop:

1. Start Excel as usual.

2. Make sure your Student Disk is in the appropriate disk drive.

3. Make sure the Microsoft Excel and Book1 windows are maximized.

Entering Labels

When you build a worksheet, it's a good practice to enter the labels before entering any other data. These labels will help you identify the cells where you will enter data and formulas in your worksheet. As you type a label in a cell, Excel aligns the label at the left side of the cell. Labels that are too long to fit in a cell spill over into the cell or cells to the right, if those cells are empty. If the cells to the right are not empty, Excel displays only as much of the label as fits in the cell. Begin creating the sales comparison worksheet for Sally by entering the two-line title.

To enter the worksheet title:

1. If necessary, click cell **A1** to make it the active cell.

2. Type **Motorcycle Specialties Incorporated** and press the **Enter** key. Since cell A1 is empty, the title appears in cell A1 and spills over into cells B1, C1, and D1. Cell A2 is now the active cell.

   TROUBLE? If you make a mistake while typing, remember that you can correct errors with the Backspace key. If you notice the error only after you have pressed the Enter key, then double-click the cell to activate Edit mode, and use the edit keys on your keyboard to correct the error.

3. In cell A2 type **Sales Comparison 1999 with 1998** and press the **Enter** key.

Next, you will enter the column headings defined on the worksheet sketch in Figure 2-2.

To enter labels for the column headings:

1. If necessary, click cell **A3** to make it the active cell.

2. Type **Region** and press the → key to complete the entry. Cell B3 is the active cell.

3. In cell **B3** type **Year 1999** and press the → key.

   Sally's sketch shows that three more column heads are needed for the worksheet. Enter those next.

4. Enter the remaining column heads as follows:
   Cell C3: **Year 1998**
   Cell D3: **% Change**
   Cell E3: **% of 1999 Sales**
   See Figure 2-3.

   TROUBLE? If any cell does not contain the correct label, either edit the cell or retype the entry.

Figure 2-3
Worksheet
after titles and
column
headings
entered

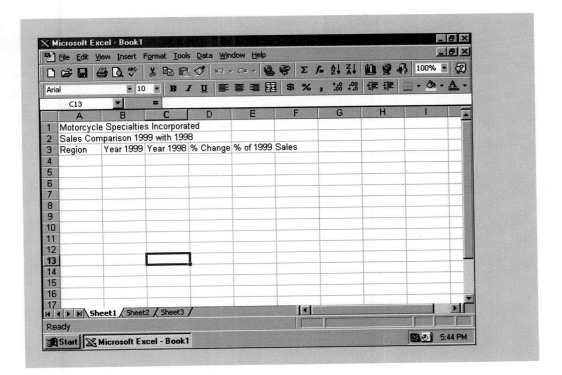

Recall that MSI conducts business in four different regions of the world, and the spreadsheet needs to track the sales information for each region. So Sally wants labels reflecting the regions entered into the worksheet. Enter these labels next.

To enter the regions:

1. Click cell **A4**, type **North America,** and press the **Enter** key.

2. In cell A5 type **South America,** and press the **Enter** key.

3. Type **Australia** in cell A6, and **Europe** in cell A7.

The last set of labels to be entered identify the summary information that will be included in the report.

To enter the summary labels:

1. In cell A8 type **Total** and press the **Enter** key.

2. Type the following labels into the specified cells:
   Cell A9: **Average**
   Cell A10: **Maximum**
   Cell A11: **Minimum**
   See Figure 2-4.

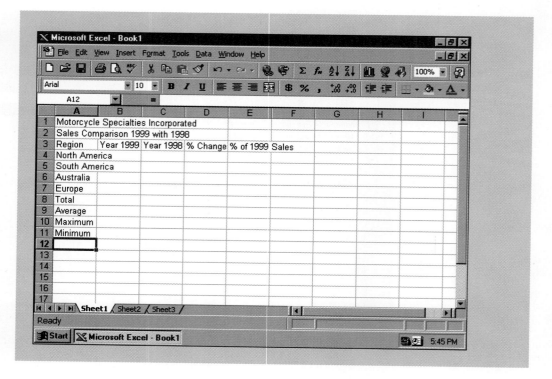

Figure 2-4 ◀
Worksheet
after all labels
have been
entered

The labels that you just entered into the worksheet will help to identify where the data and formulas need to be placed.

Entering Data

Recall that values can be numbers, formulas, or functions. The next step in building the worksheet is to enter the data, which in this case is the numbers representing sales in each region during 1998 and 1999.

To enter the sales values for 1998 and 1999:

1. Click cell **B4** to make it the active cell. Type **365000** and press the **Enter** key. See Figure 2-5. Notice that the region name, North America, is no longer completely displayed in cell A4 because cell B4 is no longer empty. Later in the tutorial you will learn how to increase the width of a column in order to display the complete contents of cells.

Excel

Figure 2-5 ◀
Worksheet with
label truncated
in cell

label truncated

label spills over
to cell B5

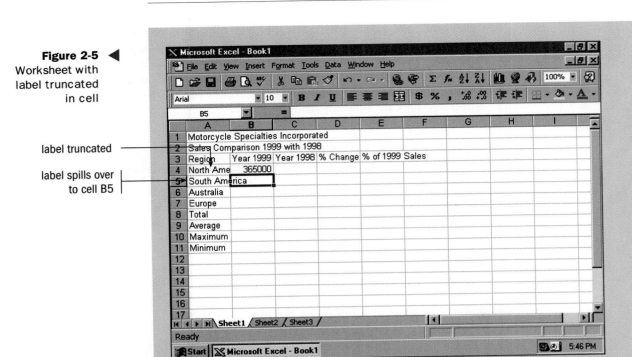

2. In cell B5 type **354250** and press the **Enter** key.

3. Enter the values for cells B6, **251140**, and B7, **310440**.

   Next, type the values for sales during 1998.

4. Click cell **C4**, type **314330**, and press the **Enter** key.

5. Enter the remaining values in the specified cells as follows:
   Cell C5: **292120**
   Cell C6: **262000**
   Cell C7: **279996**
   Your screen should now look like Figure 2-6.

Figure 2-6 ◀
Worksheet
after sales for
1998 and 1999
entered

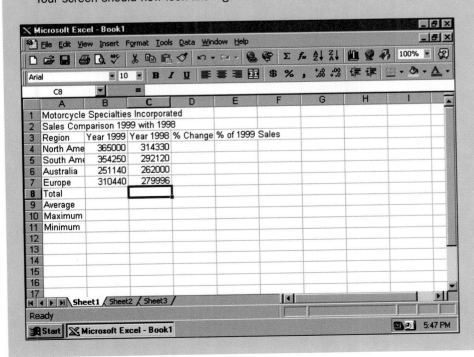

Now that you have entered the labels and data, you need to enter the formulas that will calculate the data to produce the output, or the results. The first calculation Sally wants to see is the total sales for each year. To determine total sales for 1999, you would simply sum the sales from each region for that year. In the previous tutorial you used the SUM function to calculate the weighted total score for the Scottsdale golf site by typing that function into the cell. Similarly, you can use the SUM function to calculate total sales for each year for MSI's comparison report.

Using the AutoSum Button

Since the SUM function is used more often than any other function, Excel includes the AutoSum button on the Standard toolbar. This button automatically creates a formula that contains the SUM function. To do this, Excel looks at the cells adjacent to the active cell, makes an assumption as to which cells you want to sum, and displays a formula based on its best determination about the range you want to sum. You can press the Enter key to accept the formula, or you can select a different range of cells to change the range in the formula. You will use the AutoSum button to calculate the total sales for each year.

To calculate total sales in 1999 using the AutoSum button:

1. Click cell **B8** because this is where you want to display the total sales for 1999.

2. Click the **AutoSum** button ∑ on the Standard toolbar. Excel enters a SUM function in the selected cell and determines that the range of cells to sum is B4:B7, the range directly above the selected cell. See Figure 2-7. In this case, that's exactly what you want to do.

Figure 2-7 ◄
Using the AutoSum tool

outline of cells to be summed

range of cells to be summed

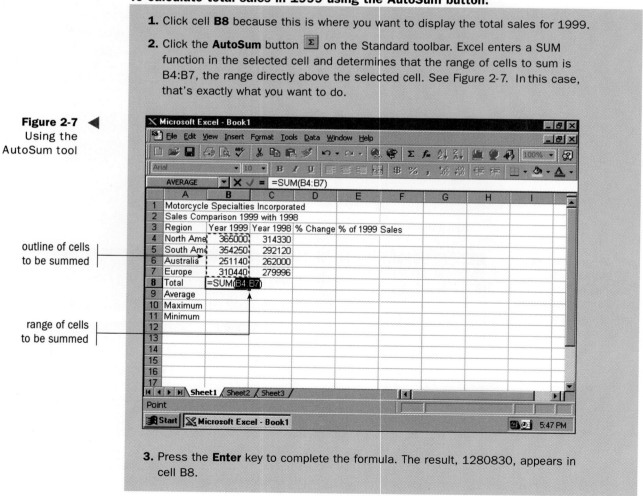

3. Press the **Enter** key to complete the formula. The result, 1280830, appears in cell B8.

Now use the same approach to calculate the total sales for 1998.

To calculate total sales in 1998 using the AutoSum button:

1. Click cell **C8** to make it the active cell.

2. Click the **AutoSum** button [Σ] on the Standard toolbar.

3. Press the **Enter** key to complete the formula. The result, 1148446, appears in cell C8.

Next, you need to enter the formula to calculate the percent change in sales for North America between 1999 and 1998.

Entering Formulas

Recall that a formula is an equation that performs calculations in a cell. By entering an equal sign (=) as the first entry in the cell, you are telling Excel that the numbers or symbols that follow constitute a formula, not just data. Reviewing Sally's worksheet plan, you note that you need to calculate the percent change in sales in North America. The formula is:

percent change in sales for North America =
(1999 sales in North America - 1998 sales in North America)/1998 sales in North America

So, in looking at the worksheet, the formula in Excel would be:

(B4-C4)/C4

If a formula contains more than one arithmetic operator, Excel performs the calculations in the standard order of precedence of operators shown in Figure 2-8. The **order of precedence** is a set of predefined rules that Excel uses to calculate a formula unambiguously by determining which part of the formula to calculate first, which part second, and so on.

Figure 2-8 ◀
Order of
precedence
operations

Order	Operator	Description
1	^	Exponentiation
2	* or /	Multiplication or division
3	+ or −	Addition or subtraction

Exponentiation has the highest rank, followed by multiplication and division, and finally addition and subtraction. For example, because multiplication has precedence over addition, in the formula =3+4*5 the result of the formula is 23.

When a formula contains more than one operator with the same order of precedence, Excel performs the operation from left to right. Thus, in the formula =4*10/8, Excel multiplies 4 by 10 before dividing the product by 8. The result of the calculation is 5. You can enter parentheses in a formula to make it easier to understand or to change the order of operations. Excel always performs any calculations contained in parentheses first. In the formula =3+4*5, the multiplication is performed before the addition. If instead you wanted the formula to add 3+4 and then multiply the sum by 5, you would enter the formula =(3+4)*5. The result of the calculation is 35.

Now enter the percent change formula as specified in Sally's planning sheet.

To enter the formula for the percent change in sales for North America:

1. Click cell **D4** to make it the active cell.

2. Type **=(B4-C4)/C4** and press the **Enter** key. Excel performs the calculations and displays the value 0.1612 in cell D4. The formula is no longer visible in the cell. If you select the cell, the result of the formula appears in the cell, and the formula you entered appears in the formula bar.

Next, you need to enter the percent change formulas for the other regions, as well as the percent change for the total company sales. You could type the formula =(B5-C5)/C5 in cell D5, the formula =(B6-C6)/C6 in cell D6, the formula =(B7-C7)/C7 in cell D7, and the formula =(B8-C8)/C8 in cell D8. However, this approach is time-consuming and error prone. Instead, you can copy the formula you entered in cell C4 (percent change in North American sales) into cells D5, D6, D7, and D8. **Copying** duplicates the underlying formula in a cell into other cells, automatically adjusting cell references to reflect the new cell address. Copying formulas from one cell to another saves time and reduces the chances of entering incorrect formulas when building worksheets.

Copying a Formula Using the Fill Handle

You can copy formulas using menu commands, toolbar buttons, or the fill handle. The **fill handle** is a small black square located in the lower-right corner of the selected cell, as shown in Figure 2-9. In this section you will use the fill handle to copy the formulas. In other situations you can also use the fill handle for copying values and labels from one cell or a group of cells.

Figure 2-9 ◄
Fill handle

fill handle ——

COPYING CELL CONTENTS WITH THE FILL HANDLE

REFERENCE
window

- Click the cell that contains the label, value, or formula you want to copy. If you want to copy the contents of more than one cell, select the range of cells you want to copy.
- To copy to adjacent cells, click and drag the fill handle to outline the cells where you want the copy or copies to appear, and then release the mouse button.

You want to copy the formula from cell D4 to cells D5, D6, D7, and D8.

To copy the formula from cell D4 to cells D5, D6, D7, and D8:

1. Click cell **D4** to make it the active cell.

2. Position the pointer over the fill handle (in the lower-right corner of cell D4) until the pointer changes to $+$.

3. Click and drag the pointer down the worksheet to outline cells D5 through D8. See Figure 2-10.

Figure 2-10 ◀
Copying a
formula

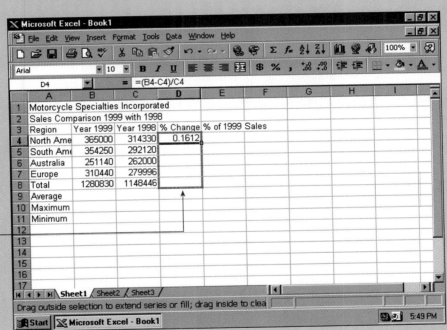

outline of cells
formula will
be copied to

4. Release the mouse button. Excel copies the formula from D4 to cells D5 to D8. Values now appear in cells D5 through D8.

5. Click any cell to deselect the range. See Figure 2-11.

Figure 2-11 ◀
Worksheet
after formula
copied

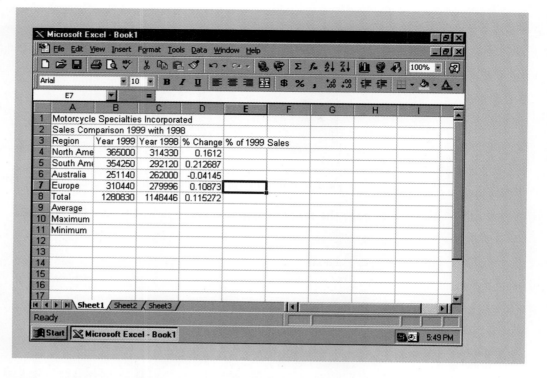

Notice that Excel didn't copy the formula =(B4-C4)/C4 exactly. Rather, it automatically adjusted the cell references for each new formula location. Why did that happen?

Copying a Formula Using Relative References

When you copy a formula that contains cell references, Excel automatically adjusts the cell references for the new locations. For example, when Excel copied the formula from cell D4, =(B4-C4)/C4, it automatically changed the cell references in the formula to reflect the formula's new position in the worksheet. So in cell D5 the cell references adjust to =(B5-C5)/C5. Cell references that change when copied are called **relative cell references**.

Take a moment to look at the formulas in cells D5, D6, D7, and D8.

To examine the formulas in cells D5, D6, D7, and D8:

1. Click cell **D5**. The formula =(B5-C5)/C5 appears in the formula bar.

When Excel copied the formula from cell D4 to cell D5, the cell references changed. The formula =(B4-C4)/C4 became =(B5-C5)/C5 when Excel copied the formula down one row to row 5.

2. Examine the formulas in cells D6, D7, and D8. Notice that the cell references were adjusted for the new locations.

Copying a Formula Using an Absolute Reference

According to Sally's plan, in the worksheet you need to display the percent that each region contributed to the total sales in 1999. For example, if the company's total sales were $100,000 and sales in North America were $25,000, then sales in North America would be 25% of total sales. To complete this calculation for each region you need to divide each region's sales by the total company sales, as shown in the following formulas:

Contribution by North America   =B4/B8
Contribution by South America   =B5/B8
Contribution by Australia   =B6/B8
Contribution by Europe   =B7/B8

First, enter the formula to calculate the percent North America contributed to total sales.

To calculate North America's percent of total 1999 sales:

1. Click cell **E4** to make it the active cell.

2. Type **=B4/B8** and press the **Enter** key to display the value .284971 in cell E4.

Cell E4 displays the correct result. Sales in North America for 1999 were 365,000, which is approximately .28 of the 1,280,830 in total sales in 1999. Next, you decide to copy the formula in cell E4 to cells E5, E6, and E7.

To copy the percent formula in cell E4 to cells E5 through E7:

1. Click cell **E4**, and then move the pointer over the fill handle in cell E4 until it changes to ➕ .

2. Click and drag the pointer to cell E7 and release the mouse button.

3. Click any blank cell to deselect the range. The message "#DIV/0!" appears in cells E5 through E7. See Figure 2-12.

Figure 2-12 ◀
Error message displayed in worksheet after copying formula

error message ——————

Something is wrong. Cells E5 through E7 display "#DIV/0!," a message that means that Excel was instructed to divide by zero. Take a moment to look at the formulas you copied into cells E5, E6, and E7.

To examine the formulas in cells E5 through E7:

1. Click cell **E5** and look at the formula displayed in the formula bar, =B5/B9. The first cell reference changed from B4 in the original formula to B5 in the copied formula. That's correct because the sales data for South America is entered in cell B5. The second cell reference changed from B8, in the original formula to B9, which is not correct. The correct formula should be =B5/B8 because the total sales are in cell B8, not cell B9.

2. Look at the formulas in cells E6 and E7 and see how the cell references changed in each formula.

As you observed, the cell reference to total company sales (B8) in the original formula was changed to B9, B10, and B11 in the copied formulas. The problem with the copied formulas is that Excel adjusted *all* the cell references relative to their new location.

Absolute Versus Relative References

Sometimes when you copy a formula, you don't want Excel to change all cell references automatically to reflect their new positions in the worksheet. If you want a cell reference to point to the same location in the worksheet when you copy it, you must use an absolute reference. An **absolute reference** is a cell reference in a formula that does not change when copied to another cell.

To create an absolute reference, you insert a dollar sign ($) before the column and row of the cell reference. For example, the cell reference $B$8 is an absolute reference, whereas the cell reference B8 is a relative reference. If you copy a formula that contains the absolute reference $B$8 to another cell, the cell reference to $B$8 does not change. On the other hand, if you copy a formula containing the relative reference B8 to another cell, the reference to B8 changes. In some situations, a cell might have a **mixed reference**, such as $B8; in this case, when the formula is copied, the row number changes but the column letter does not.

To include an absolute reference in a formula, you can type a dollar sign when you type the cell reference, or you can use the F4 key to change the cell reference type while in Edit mode.

REFERENCE window	**EDITING CELL REFERENCE TYPES**
	■ Double-click the cell that contains the formula you want to edit.
	■ Use the arrow keys to move the insertion point to the part of the cell reference you want to change.
	■ Press the F4 key until the reference is correct.
	■ Press the Enter key to complete the edit.

To correct the problem in your worksheet, you need to use an absolute reference, instead of a relative reference, to indicate the location of total sales in 1999. That is, you need to change the formula from =B4/B8 to =B4/$B$8. The easiest way to make this change is in Edit mode.

To change a cell reference to an absolute reference:

1. Click cell **E4** to move to the cell that contains the formula you want to edit.

2. Double-click the mouse button to edit the formula in the cell. Notice that each cell reference in the formula in cell E4 appears in a different color and the corresponding cells referred to in the formula are outlined in the same color. This feature is called Range Finder and is designed to make it easier for you to check the accuracy of your formula.

3. Make sure the insertion point is to the right of the division (/) operator, any-where in the cell reference B8.

4. Press the **F4** key to change the reference to $B$8.

   TROUBLE? If your reference shows the **mixed reference** B$8 or $B8, continue to press the F4 key until you see $B$8.

5. Press the **Enter** key to update the formula in cell E4.

Cell E4 still displays .284971, which is the formula's correct result. But remember, the problem in your original formula did not surface until you copied it to cells E5 through E7. To correct the error, you need to copy the revised formula and then check the results. Although you can again use the fill handle to copy the formula, you can also copy the formula using the Clipboard and the Copy and Paste buttons on the Standard toolbar.

Copying Cell Contents Using the Copy and Paste Method

You can duplicate the contents of a cell or range by making a copy of the cell or range and then pasting the copy into one or more locations in the same worksheet, another worksheet, or another workbook.

When you copy a cell or range of cells, the copied material is placed on the Clipboard. You can copy labels, numbers, dates, or formulas.

REFERENCE
window

COPYING AND PASTING A CELL OR RANGE OF CELLS

- Select the cell or range of cells to be copied.
- Click the Copy button on the Standard toolbar.
- Select the range into which you want to copy the formula.
- Click the Paste button on the Standard toolbar.
- Press the Enter key.

You need to copy the formula in cell E4 to the Clipboard and then paste that formula into cells E5 through E7.

To copy the revised formula from cell E4 to cells E5 through E7:

1. Click cell **E4** because it contains the revised formula that you want to copy.

2. Click the **Copy** button on the Standard toolbar. A moving dashed line surrounds cell E4, indicating that the formula has been copied and is available to be pasted into other cells.

3. Click and drag to select cells **E5** through **E7**.

4. Click the **Paste** button on the Standard toolbar. Excel adjusts the formula and pastes it into cells E5 through E7.

5. Click any cell to deselect the range and view the formulas' results. Press the **Escape** key to clear the Clipboard and remove the dashed line surrounding cell E4. See Figure 2-13.

Figure 2-13
Results of
copying the
formula with
an absolute
reference

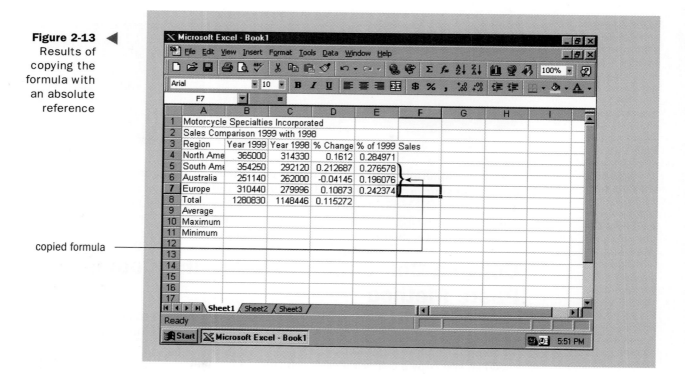

copied formula

Copying this formula worked. When you pasted the formula from cell E4 into the range E5:E7, Excel automatically adjusted the relative reference (B4), while using the cell reference ($B$8) for all absolute references. You have now implemented most of the design as specified in the planning analysis sheet. Now rename the worksheet to accurately describe its contents, then save the workbook to your Student Disk before entering the formulas to compute the summary statistics.

Renaming the Worksheet

Before saving the workbook, look at the sheet tab in the lower-left corner of the worksheet window: the sheet is currently named Sheet1—the name Excel automatically uses when it opens a new workbook. Now that your worksheet is taking shape, you want to give it a more descriptive name that better indicates its contents. Change the worksheet name to Sales Comparison.

To change a worksheet name:

1. Double-click the **Sheet1** sheet tab to select it.

2. Type the new name, **Sales Comparison**, over the current name, Sheet1. Click any cell in the worksheet. The sheet tab displays the name "Sales Comparison."

Saving the New Workbook

Now you want to save the workbook. Because this is the first time you have saved this workbook, you will use the Save As command and name the file MSI Sales Report.

To save the workbook as MSI Sales Report:

1. Click **File** on the menu bar, and then click **Save As** to display the Save As dialog box.

2. In the File name text box, type **MSI Sales Report** but don't press the Enter key yet. You still need to check some other settings.

3. Click the **Save in** list arrow, and then click the drive containing your Student Disk.

4. In the folder list, double-click the **Tutorial.02** folder to select the folder into which you want to save the workbook. Your Save As dialog box should look like the dialog box in Figure 2-14.

Figure 2-14 ◄
Saving the
worksheet as
MSI Sales
Report

enter name of
worksheet here

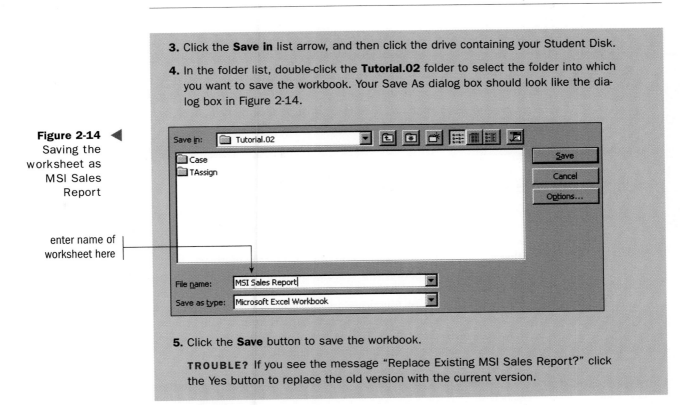

5. Click the **Save** button to save the workbook.

TROUBLE? If you see the message "Replace Existing MSI Sales Report?" click the Yes button to replace the old version with the current version.

Quick Check

1. Describe how AutoSum works.

2. In cell C5 you have the formula =A5+B5. After you copy this formula to cell C6, the formula in cell C6 would appear in the formula bar as _____.

3. In the formula =A5+B5, A5 and B5 are examples of _____ references.

4. In the formula =A8+(1+$C$1), $C$1 is an example of a(n) _____.

5. When you copy a formula using the Copy 📋 and Paste 📋 buttons on the Standard toolbar, Excel uses the _____ to temporarily store the formula.

6. The _____ is a small black square located in the lower-right corner of a selected cell.

7. Describe the steps you take to change the name of the sheet tab.

8. List the steps to follow to create a worksheet.

Now that you have planned and built the Sales Comparison worksheet by entering labels, values, and formulas, you need to complete the worksheet by entering some functions and format the worksheet. You will do this in Session 2.2.

In this session you will finish the worksheet as you learn how to enter several statistical functions, increase the column width, insert a row between the titles and column headings, move the contents of a range to another location, and apply one of the Excel predefined formats to the report. You will also spell check the worksheet, and preview and print it.

Excel Functions

According to Sally's planning analysis sheet, you still need to enter the formulas for the summary statistics. To enter these statistics you'll use three Excel functions, AVERAGE, MAX, and MIN. The many Excel functions help you enter formulas for calculations and other specialized tasks, even if you don't know the mathematical details of the calculations. As you recall, a function is a calculation tool that performs a predefined operation. You are already familiar with the SUM function, which adds the values in a range of cells. Excel provides hundreds of functions, including a function to calculate the average of a list of numbers, a function to find a number's square root, a function to calculate loan payments, and a function to calculate the number of days between two dates. Figure 2-15 shows how Excel organizes these functions into categories.

Figure 2-15 ◀
Excel function
categories

Function Category	Examples of Functions in This Category
Financial	Calculate loan payments, depreciation, interest rate, internal rate of return
Date & Time	Display today's date and/or time; calculate the number of days between two dates
Math & Trig	Round off numbers; calculate sums, logs, and least common multiple; generate random numbers
Statistical	Calculate average, standard deviation, and frequencies; find minimum, maximum; count how many numbers are in a list
Lookup & Reference	Look for a value in a range of cells; find the row or column location of a reference
Database	Perform crosstabs, averages, counts, and standard deviation for an Excel database
Text	Convert numbers to text; compare two text entries; find the length of a text entry
Logical	Perform conditional calculations
Information	Return information about the formatting, location, or contents of a range

Each function has a **syntax**, which specifies the order in which you must type the parts of the function and where to put commas, parentheses, and other punctuation. The general syntax of an Excel function is:

NAME(*argument1,argument2,...*)

The syntax of most functions requires you to type the function name followed by one or more arguments in parentheses. Function **arguments** specify the values that Excel must use in the calculation, or the cell references that Excel must include in the calculation. For example, in the function SUM(A1:A20) the function name is SUM and the argument is A1:A20, which is the range of cells you want to total.

You can use a function in a simple formula such as =SUM(A1:A20), or a more complex formula such as =SUM(A1:A20)*52. As with all formulas, you enter the formula that contains a function in the cell where you want to display the results. The easiest way to enter a function in a cell is to use the Paste Function button on the Standard toolbar, which leads you step-by-step through the process of entering a formula containing a function.

If you prefer, you can type the function directly into the cell. Although the function name is always shown in uppercase, you can type it in either uppercase or lowercase. Also, even though parentheses enclose the arguments, you need not type the closing parenthesis if the function ends the formula. Excel automatically adds the closing parenthesis when you press the Enter key to complete the formula.

According to Sally's planning analysis sheet, the next step is to calculate the average regional sales for 1999.

AVERAGE Function

AVERAGE is a statistical function that calculates the average, or the arithmetic mean. The syntax for the AVERAGE function is:

$$AVERAGE(number1, number2, ...)$$

Generally, when you use the AVERAGE function, *number* is a range of cells. To calculate the average of a range of cells, Excel sums the values in the range, then divides by the number of non-blank cells in the range.

REFERENCE window	USING THE PASTE FUNCTION BUTTON
	■ Click the cell where you want to display the results of the function. Then click the Paste Function button on the Standard toolbar to open the Paste Function dialog box.
	■ Click the type of function you want in the Function category list box.
	■ Click the function you want in the Function name list box.
	■ Click the OK button to open a second dialog box.
	■ Accept the default information or enter the information you want the function to use in its calculations.
	■ Click the OK button to close the dialog box and display the results of the function in the cell.

Sally wants you to calculate the average sales in 1999. You'll use the Paste Function button to enter the AVERAGE function, which is one of the statistical functions.

To enter the AVERAGE function using the Paste Function button:

1. Click cell **B9** to select the cell where you want to enter the AVERAGE function.

2. Click the **Paste Function** button on the Standard toolbar to display the Paste Function dialog box.

   TROUBLE? If the Office Assistant opens and offers help on this feature, click the No option button.

3. Click **Statistical** in the Function category list box.

4. Click **AVERAGE** in the Function name list box. See Figure 2-16. The syntax for the AVERAGE function, AVERAGE(*number1,number2,...*), is displayed beneath the Function category box.

Figure 2-16 ◀
Paste Function
dialog box

syntax for
AVERAGE Function

partial list of
statistical functions

5. Click the **OK** button to open the AVERAGE dialog box. Notice that the range B4:B8 appears in the Number1 text box, and =AVERAGE(B4:B8) appears in the formula bar. See Figure 2-17.

Figure 2-17 ◀
AVERAGE
dialog box

range includes
cell B8

Collapse Dialog
Box button

Excel has incorrectly included the total sales for 1999 (cell B8) in the range to calculate the average. The correct range is B4:B7.

6. Click the **Collapse Dialog Box** button to the right of the Number1 text box to collapse the dialog box to the size of one row. This makes it easier for you to identify and select the correct range.

7. Position the cell pointer over cell **B4**, click and drag to select the range **B4:B7**, and then click the **Collapse Dialog Box** button. The collapsed dialog box is restored and the correct range, B4:B7, is displayed in the Number1 text box. The formula =AVERAGE(B4:B7) is displayed in the formula bar.

8. Click the **OK** button to close the dialog box and return to the worksheet. The average, 320207.5, now appears in cell B9.

According to your plan, you need to enter a formula to find the largest regional sales amount in 1999. To do this, you'll use the MAX function.

MAX Function

MAX is a statistical function that finds the largest number. The syntax of the MAX function is:

$$MAX(number1, number2, ...)$$

In the MAX function, *number* can be a constant number such as 345, a cell reference such as B6, or a range of cells such as B5:B16. You can use the MAX function to simply display the largest number or to use the largest number in a calculation. Although you can use the Paste Function to enter the MAX function, this time you'll type the MAX function directly into cell B10.

To enter the MAX function by typing directly into a cell:

1. If necessary, click cell **B10** to select it as the cell into which you want to type the formula that uses the MAX function.

2. Type **=MAX(B4:B7)** and press the **Enter** key. Cell B10 displays 365000, the largest regional sales amount in 1999.

Next, you need to find the smallest regional sales amount in 1999. For that, you'll use the MIN function.

MIN Function

MIN is a statistical function that finds the smallest number. The syntax of the MIN function is:

$$MIN(number1, number2, ...)$$

You can use the MIN function to display the smallest number or to use the smallest number in a calculation.

You'll enter the MIN function directly into cell B11, using the pointing method.

Building Formulas by Pointing

Excel provides several ways to enter cell references into a formula. One is to type the cell references directly, as you have done so far in all the formulas you've entered. Another way to put a cell reference in a formula is to **point** to the cell reference you want to include while creating the formula. To use the pointing method to enter the formula, you click the cell or range of cells whose cell references you want to include in the formula. You may prefer to use this method to enter formulas, because it minimizes typing errors.

Now enter the formula to calculate the minimum sales by using the pointing method.

To enter the MIN function using the pointing method:

1. If necessary, click cell **B11** to move to the cell where you want to enter the formula that uses the MIN function.

2. Type **=MIN(** to begin the formula.

3. Position the cell pointer in cell **B4**, and then click and drag to select cells **B4** through **B7**. As you drag the mouse over the range, notice that the message "4Rx1C" appears in a ScreenTip, informing you that four rows and one column have been selected. Release the mouse button, and then press the **Enter** key. Cell B11 displays 251140, the smallest regional sales amount for 1999. See Figure 2-18.

Figure 2-18 ◄
Worksheet
after labels,
numbers,
formulas, and
functions
entered

Now that the worksheet labels, values, formulas, and functions have been entered, Sally reviews the worksheet.

Testing the Worksheet

Before trusting a worksheet and its results, you should test it to make sure you entered the correct formulas. You want the worksheet to produce accurate results.

Beginners often expect their Excel worksheets to work correctly the first time. Sometimes they do work correctly the first time, but even well-planned and well-designed worksheets can contain errors. It's best to assume that a worksheet has errors and test it to make sure it is correct. While there are no rules for testing a worksheet, here are some approaches:

■ Entering **test values**, numbers that generate a known result, to determine whether your worksheet formulas are accurate. For example, try entering a 1 into each cell. After you enter the test values, you compare the results in your worksheet with the known results. If the results on your worksheet don't match the known results, you probably made an error.

■ Entering **extreme values**, such as very large or very small numbers, and observing their effect on cells with formulas.

■ Working out the numbers ahead of time with pencil, paper, and calculator, and comparing these results with the output from the computer.

Sally used the third approach to test her worksheet. She had calculated her results using a calculator (Figure 2-2) and then compared them with the results on the screen (Figure 2-18). The numbers agree, so she feels confident that the worksheet she created contains accurate results.

Spell Checking the Worksheet

You can use the Excel spell check feature to help identify and correct spelling and typing errors. Excel compares the words in your worksheet to the words in its dictionary. If Excel finds a word in your worksheet not in its dictionary, it shows you the word and some suggested corrections, and you decide whether to correct it or leave it as is.

REFERENCE window	**CHECKING THE SPELLING IN A WORKSHEET**
	■ Click cell A1 to begin the spell check from the top of the worksheet.
	■ Click the Spelling button on the Standard toolbar.
	■ Change the spelling or ignore the spell check's suggestion for each identified word.
	■ Click the OK button when the spell check is complete.

You have tested your numbers and formulas for accuracy. Now you can check the spelling of all text entries in the worksheet.

To check the spelling in a worksheet:

1. Click cell **A1** to begin spell checking in the first cell of the worksheet.

2. Click the **Spelling** button ![spelling icon] on the Standard toolbar to check the spelling of the text in the worksheet. A message box indicates that Excel has finished spell checking the entire worksheet. No errors were found.

   TROUBLE? If the spell check does find a spelling error in your worksheet, use the Spelling dialog box options to correct the spelling mistake and continue checking the worksheet.

Improving the Worksheet Layout

Although the numbers are correct, Sally does not want to present a worksheet without a more polished appearance. She feels that there are a number of simple changes you can make to the worksheet that will improve its layout and make the data more readable. Specifically, she asks you to increase the width of column A so that the entire region names are displayed, insert a blank row between the titles and column headings, move the summary statistics down three rows from their current location, and apply one of the predefined Excel formats to the worksheet.

Changing Column Width

Changing the column width is one way to improve the appearance of the worksheet, making it easier to read and interpret data. In Sally's worksheet, you need to increase the width of column A so that the entire labels for North America and South America appear in their cells.

Excel provides several methods for changing column width. For example, you can click a column heading or click and drag the pointer to select a series of column headings and then use the Format menu. You can also use the dividing line between column headings in the column header row. When you move the pointer over the dividing line between two column headings, the pointer changes to ✛. You can then use the pointer to drag the dividing line to a new location. You can also double-click the dividing line to make the column as wide as the longest text label or number in the column.

REFERENCE window

CHANGING COLUMN WIDTH

- Click the column heading(s) whose width you want to change.
- Click Format, point to Column, and then click Width.
- In the Column Width dialog box, enter the new column width. Or click AutoFit Selection to make the column(s) as wide as the longest text label or number in the column(s).

  or

- Drag the column heading dividing line to the right to increase column width or to the left to decrease column width.

  or

- Double-click the column heading dividing line to make the column as wide as the longest text label or number in the column.

Sally has asked you to change column A's width so that the complete region name is displayed.

To change the width of column A:

1. Position the pointer ⊕ on the A in the column heading area.

2. Move the pointer to the right edge of the column heading dividing columns A and B. Notice that the pointer changes to the resize arrow ↔ .

3. Click and drag the resize arrow to the right, increasing the column width 12 characters or more, as indicated in the ScreenTip that pops up on the screen.

4. Release the mouse button. See Figure 2-19.

Figure 2-19 ◄
Worksheet after width of column A increased

now entire contents of cell displayed →

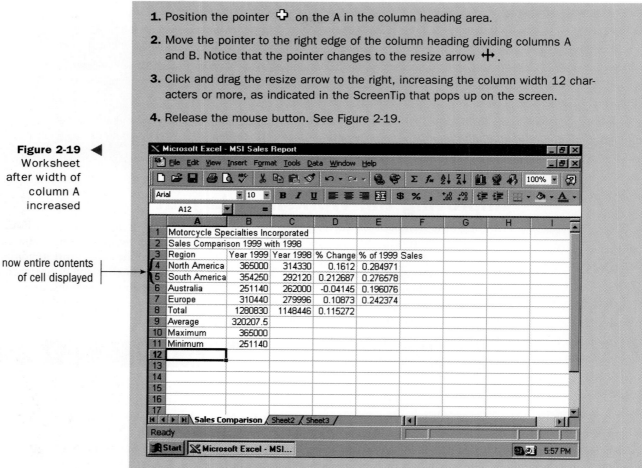

Next, you need to insert a row between the title and the column heading.

Inserting a Row into a Worksheet

At times, you may need to add one or more rows or columns to a worksheet to make room for new data or to make the worksheet easier to read. The process of inserting columns and rows is similar; you select the number of columns or rows you want to insert and then use the Insert command to insert the columns or rows. When you insert rows or columns, Excel repositions other rows and columns in the worksheet and automatically adjusts cell references in formulas to reflect the new location of values used in calculations.

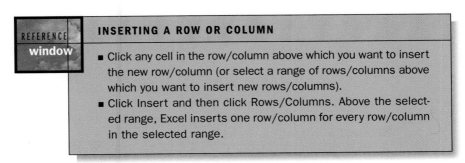

REFERENCE window

INSERTING A ROW OR COLUMN

- Click any cell in the row/column above which you want to insert the new row/column (or select a range of rows/columns above which you want to insert new rows/columns).
- Click Insert and then click Rows/Columns. Above the selected range, Excel inserts one row/column for every row/column in the selected range.

Sally wants one blank row between the titles and column headings in her worksheet.

To insert a row into a worksheet:

1. Click cell **A2**.

2. Click **Insert** on the menu bar, and then click **Rows**. Excel inserts a blank row above the original row 2. All other rows shift down one row. See Figure 2-20.

Figure 2-20 ◀
Worksheet after one row inserted above original row 2

row inserted in wrong position

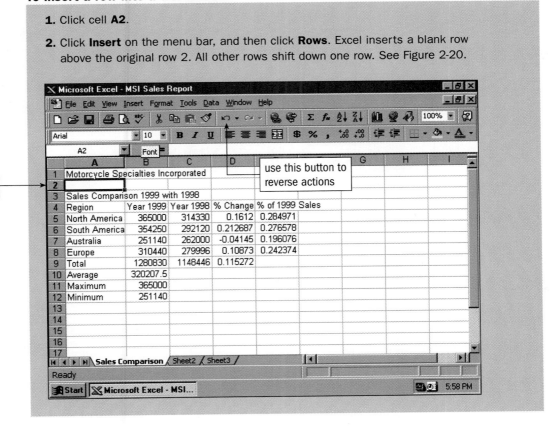

The blank row isn't really where you wanted it. You inserted a row between the two lines of the title instead of between the title and the column heading. To correct this error you can either delete the row or use the Undo button. If you need to delete a row or column, select the row(s) or column(s) you want to delete, then click Delete on the Edit menu, or press the Delete key on your keyboard. You use the Undo button because it is a feature you find valuable in many situations.

Using the Undo Button

The Excel Undo button lets you cancel recent actions one at a time. Click the Undo button to reverse the last command or delete the last entry you typed. To reverse more than one action, click the arrow next to the Undo button and click the action you want to undo on the drop-down list.

Now use the Undo button to reverse the row insertion.

To reverse the row insertion:

1. Click the **Undo** button 🔄 on the Standard toolbar to restore the worksheet to its status before the row was inserted.

Now you can insert the blank row in the correct place—between the second line of the worksheet title and the column heads.

To insert a row into a worksheet:

1. Click cell **A3** because you want to insert one row above row 3. If you wanted to insert several rows, you would select as many rows as you wanted to insert before using the Insert command.

2. Click **Insert** on the menu bar, and then click **Rows**. Excel inserts a blank row above the original row 3. All other rows shift down one row. See Figure 2-21.

Figure 2-21 ◀
Worksheet
after one row
inserted

row inserted in
desired location

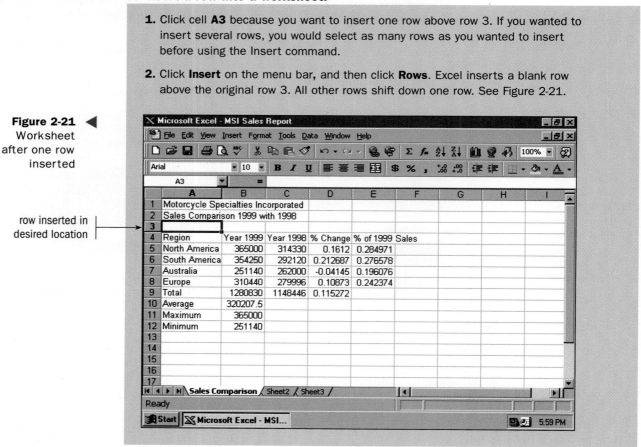

Adding a row changed the location of the data in the worksheet. For example, the percent change in North American sales, originally in cell D4, is now in cell D5. Did Excel adjust the formulas to compensate for the new row? Check cell D5 and any other cells you want to view to verify that the cell references were adjusted.

To examine the formula in cell D5 and other cells:

1. Click cell **D5**. The formula =(B5-C5)/C5 appears in the formula bar. You originally entered the formula =(B4-C4)/C4 in cell D4 to calculate percent change in North America. Excel automatically adjusted the cell reference to reflect the new location of the data.

2. Inspect other cells below row 3 to verify that their cell references were automatically adjusted when the new row was inserted.

Sally has also suggested moving the summary statistics down three rows from the present location to make the report easier to read. So, you will need to move the range of cells containing the average, minimum, and maximum sales to a different location in the worksheet.

Moving a Range Using the Mouse

To place the summary statistics three rows below the other data in the report, you could use the Insert command to insert three blank rows between the total and average sales. Alternatively, you could use the mouse to move the summary statistics to a new location. Since you already know how to insert a row, try using the mouse to move the summary statistics to a new location. This technique is called **drag-and-drop**. You simply select the cell range you want to move and use the pointer ⬉ to drag the cells' contents to the desired location.

REFERENCE window	**MOVING A RANGE USING THE MOUSE**
	■ Select the cell or range of cells you want to move.
	■ Place the mouse pointer over any edge of the selected range until the pointer changes to an arrow.
	■ Click and drag the outline of the range to the new worksheet location.
	■ Release the mouse button.

Sally has asked you to move the range A10 through B12 to the new destination area A13 through B15.

To move a range of cells using the drag-and-drop technique:

1. Select the range of cells **A10:B12**, which contains the sales summary statistics you want to move.

2. Place the mouse pointer over any edge of the selected range until the pointer changes to an arrow ⬉ . See Figure 2-22.

Figure 2-22 ◀
Range to
be moved

pointer shape
indicates you can
move selected range

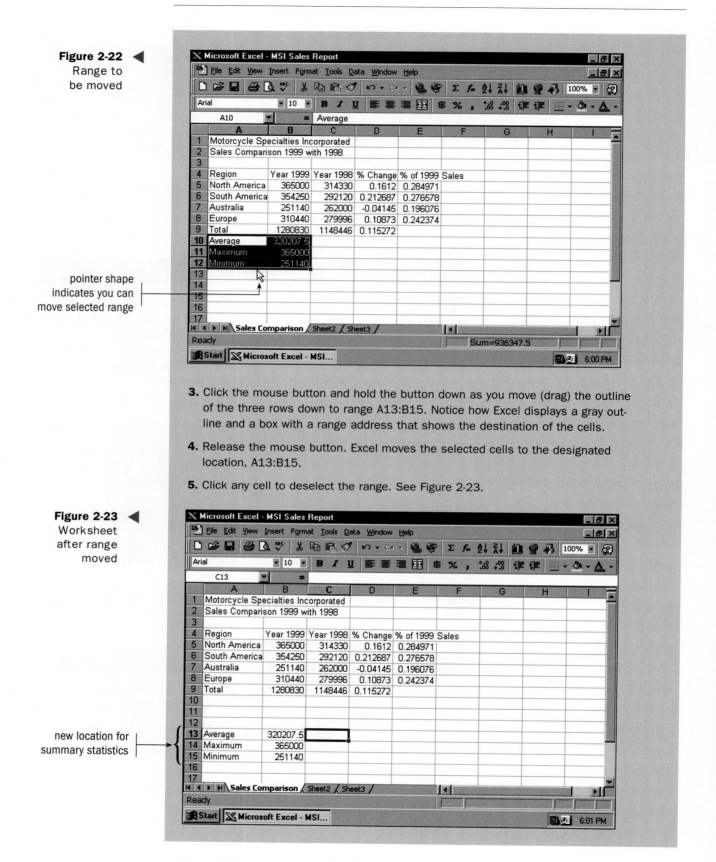

3. Click the mouse button and hold the button down as you move (drag) the outline of the three rows down to range A13:B15. Notice how Excel displays a gray outline and a box with a range address that shows the destination of the cells.

4. Release the mouse button. Excel moves the selected cells to the designated location, A13:B15.

5. Click any cell to deselect the range. See Figure 2-23.

Figure 2-23 ◀
Worksheet
after range
moved

new location for
summary statistics

Next, Sally wants you to use the Excel AutoFormat feature to improve the worksheet's appearance by emphasizing the titles and aligning numbers in cells.

Using AutoFormat

The **AutoFormat** feature lets you change your worksheet's appearance by selecting from a collection of predesigned worksheet formats. Each worksheet format in the AutoFormat collection gives your worksheet a more professional appearance by applying attractive fonts, borders, colors, and shading to a range of data. AutoFormat also adjusts column widths, row heights, and the alignment of text in cells to improve the worksheet's appearance.

REFERENCE window

USING AUTOFORMAT

- Select the cells you want to format.
- Click Format, and then click AutoFormat.
- Select a format style from the Table Format list.
- Click the OK button to apply the format.

Now you'll use AutoFormat's Simple format to improve the worksheet's appearance.

To apply AutoFormat's Simple format:

1. Select cells **A1:E9** as the range you want to format using AutoFormat.

2. Click **Format** on the menu bar, and then click **AutoFormat**. The AutoFormat dialog box opens. See Figure 2-24.

Figure 2-24 ◀
AutoFormat
dialog box

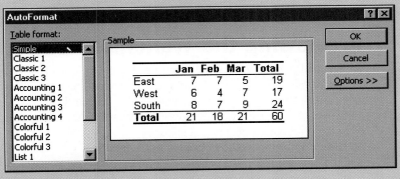

3. The Table format box lists the available formats. The format called "Simple" is selected and the Sample box shows how the Simple format looks when applied to a worksheet.

4. Click each of the formats from Simple down to Accounting 1. Notice the different font styles and colors of each format shown in the Sample box.

5. Click the **Simple** format, and then click the **OK** button to apply this format.

6. Click any cell to deselect the range. Figure 2-25 shows the newly formatted worksheet.

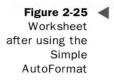

Figure 2-25
Worksheet
after using the
Simple
AutoFormat

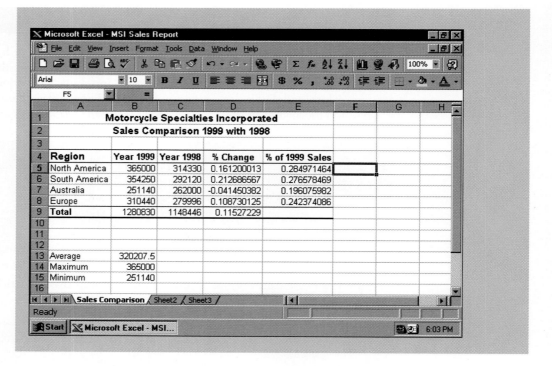

You show the worksheet to Sally. She's impressed with the improved appearance and decides to hand it out to the regional sales managers at their next meeting. She asks you to print it so she can make copies.

Previewing the Worksheet Using Print Preview

Before you print a worksheet, you can use the Excel Print Preview window to see how it will look when printed. The **Print Preview window** shows you margins, page breaks, headers, and footers that are not always visible on the screen. If the preview isn't what you want, you can close the Print Preview window and change the worksheet before printing it.

To preview the worksheet before you print it:

1. Click the **Print Preview** button on the Standard toolbar. After a moment Excel displays the worksheet in the Print Preview window. See Figure 2-26.

Figure 2-26 ◀
Print preview of
sales
comparison
worksheet

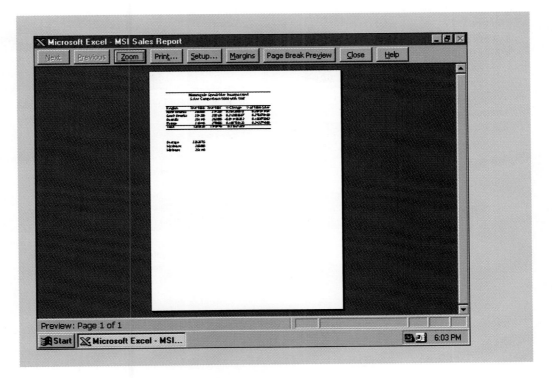

When Excel displays a full page in the Print Preview window, you might have difficulty seeing the text of the worksheet because it is so small. Don't worry if the preview isn't completely readable. One purpose of the Print Preview window is to see the overall layout of the worksheet and how it will fit on the printed page. If you want a better view of the text, you can use the Zoom button.

To display an enlarged section of the Print Preview window:

1. Click the **Zoom** button to display an enlarged section of the Print Preview.

2. Click the **Zoom** button again to return to the full-page view.

Notice that the Print Preview window contains several other buttons. Figure 2-27 describes each of these buttons.

Figure 2-27 ◀
Description of
Print Preview
buttons

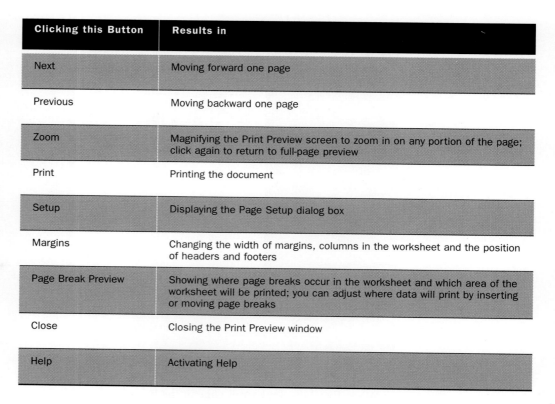

Clicking this Button	Results in
Next	Moving forward one page
Previous	Moving backward one page
Zoom	Magnifying the Print Preview screen to zoom in on any portion of the page; click again to return to full-page preview
Print	Printing the document
Setup	Displaying the Page Setup dialog box
Margins	Changing the width of margins, columns in the worksheet and the position of headers and footers
Page Break Preview	Showing where page breaks occur in the worksheet and which area of the worksheet will be printed; you can adjust where data will print by inserting or moving page breaks
Close	Closing the Print Preview window
Help	Activating Help

Looking at the worksheet in Print Preview, you observe that it is not centered on the page. By default, Excel prints a worksheet at the upper left of the page's print area. You can specify that the worksheet be centered vertically, horizontally, or both.

Centering the Printout

Worksheet printouts generally look more professional centered on the printed page. You decide that Sally would want you to center the sales comparison worksheet both horizontally and vertically on the printed page.

To center the printout:

1. Click the **Setup** button to display the Page Setup dialog box.

2. Click the **Margins** tab. See Figure 2-28. Notice that the preview box displays a worksheet positioned at the upper-left edge of the page.

Figure 2-28 ◀
Margins tab of
Page Setup
dialog box

indicates that
worksheet will be
displayed in upper-
left corner of page

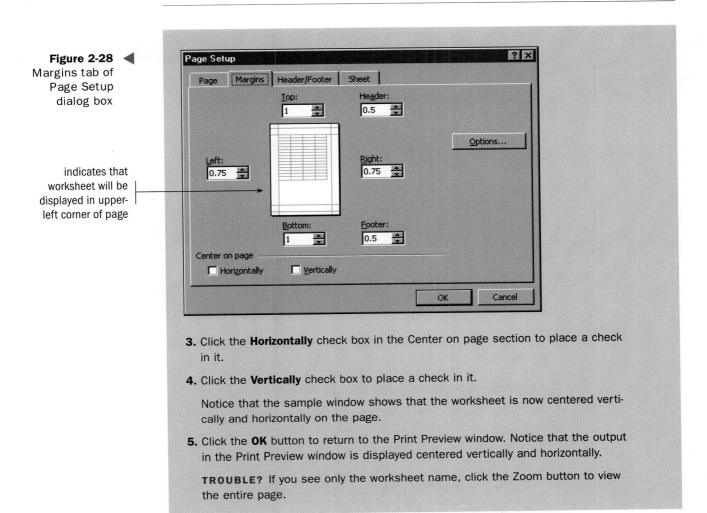

3. Click the **Horizontally** check box in the Center on page section to place a check in it.

4. Click the **Vertically** check box to place a check in it.

   Notice that the sample window shows that the worksheet is now centered vertically and horizontally on the page.

5. Click the **OK** button to return to the Print Preview window. Notice that the output in the Print Preview window is displayed centered vertically and horizontally.

   TROUBLE? If you see only the worksheet name, click the Zoom button to view the entire page.

Adding Headers and Footers

Headers and footers can provide you with useful documentation on your printed worksheet, such as the name of the person who created the worksheet, the date it was printed, and its filename. The **header** is text printed in the top margin of every worksheet page. A **footer** is text printed in the bottom margin of every page. Headers and footers are not displayed in the worksheet window. To see them, you must preview or print the worksheet.

Excel uses formatting codes in headers and footers to represent the items you want to print. Formatting codes produce dates, times, and filenames that you might want a header or footer to include. You can type these codes, or you can click a formatting code button to insert the code. Figure 2-29 shows the formatting codes and the buttons for inserting them.

Figure 2-29
Header
and footer
formatting
buttons

Button	Button Name	Formatting Code	Action
A	Font	none	Sets font, text style, and font size
#	Page Number	&[Page]	Inserts page number
	Total Pages	&[Pages]	Inserts total number of pages
	Date	&[Date]	Inserts current date
	Time	&[Time]	Inserts current time
	Filename	&[File]	Inserts filename
	Sheet name	&[Tab]	Inserts name of active worksheet

Sally asks you to add a header that includes the filename and today's date. She also wants you to add a footer that displays the page number.

To add a header and a footer to your worksheet:

1. In the Print Preview window, click the **Setup** button to open the Page Setup dialog box, and then click the **Header/Footer** tab.

2. Click the **Custom Header** button to display the Header dialog box.

3. With the insertion point in the Left section box, click the **Filename** button . The code &[File] appears in the Left section box.

   TROUBLE? If you clicked the wrong code, double-click the code, press the Delete key, then repeat Steps 2 and 3.

4. Click the **Right section** box to move the insertion point to the Right section box.

5. Click the **Date** button . The code &[Date] appears in the Right section box. See Figure 2-30.

Figure 2-30
Inserting
formatting
codes into
the Header
dialog box

formatting code to
display workbook
filename

   TROUBLE? If you clicked the wrong code, double-click the code, press the Delete key, then repeat Step 5.

6. Click the **OK** button to complete the header and return to the Page Setup dialog box. Notice that the header shows the filename on the left and the date on the right.

7. Click the **Custom Footer** button to display the Footer dialog box.

8. Click the **Center section** box to move the insertion point to the Center Section box.

9. Click the **Page Number** button [#]. The code &[Page] appears in the Center section box.

10. Click the **OK** button to complete the footer and return to the Page Setup dialog box. Notice that the footer shows the page number in the bottom center of the page.

11. Click the **OK** button to return to the Print Preview window. The changed header appears in the Print Preview window.

12. Click the **Close** button to exit the Print Preview window and return to the worksheet.

You'll use the Print button on the Standard toolbar to print one copy of the worksheet with the current settings. First, save the worksheet before printing it.

To save your page setup settings:

1. Click the **Save** button [icon] on the Standard toolbar.

2. Click the **Print** button [icon] on the Standard toolbar. See Figure 2-31.

   TROUBLE? If you see a message that indicates that you have a printer problem, click the Cancel button to cancel printing. Check your printer to make sure it is turned on and is online; also make sure it has paper. Then go back and try Step 2 again. If you have no printer available, click the Cancel button.

Figure 2-31 ◀
Printed
worksheet

Motorcycle Specialties Incorporated
Sales Comparison 1999 with 1998

Region	Year 1999	Year 1998	% Change	% of 1999 Sales
North America	365000	314330	0.161200013	0.284971464
South America	354250	292120	0.212686567	0.276578469
Australia	251140	262000	-0.041450382	0.196075982
Europe	310440	279996	0.108730125	0.242374086
Total	1280830	1148446	0.11527229	

Average	320207.5
Maximum	365000
Minimum	251140

Sally reviews the printed worksheet and is satisfied with its appearance. She will make four copies to be distributed to the regional managers at the next meeting.

Documenting the Workbook

Documenting the workbook provides valuable information to those using the workbook. Documentation includes external documentation as well as notes and instructions within the workbook. This information could be as basic as who created the worksheet and the date it was created, or it could be more detailed, summarizing formulas and layout.

Depending on the use of the workbook, the required amount of documentation varies. Sally's planning analysis sheet and sketch for the sales comparison worksheet are one form of external documentation. This information can be useful to someone who would need to modify the worksheet in any way because it states the goals, required input, output, and the calculations used.

One source of internal documentation would be a worksheet that is placed as the first worksheet in the workbook, such as the Title Sheet worksheet in the workbook you worked with in Tutorial 1 to determine the best location for the new Inwood golf course. In more complex workbooks, this sheet may also include an index of all worksheets in the workbook, instructions on how to use the worksheets, where to enter data, how to save the workbook, and how to print reports. This documentation method is useful because the information is contained directly in the workbook and can easily be viewed upon opening the workbook, or printed if necessary. Another source of internal documentation is the **Property dialog box**. This dialog box enables you to electronically capture information such as the name of the workbook's creator, the creation date, the number of revisions, and other information related to the workbook.

If you prefer, you can include documentation in each sheet of the workbook. One way is to attach notes to cells by using the Comments command to explain complex formulas and assumptions.

The worksheet itself can be used as documentation. Once a worksheet is completed, it is a good practice to print and file a "hard" copy of your work as documentation. This hard copy file should include a printout of each worksheet with the values displayed and another printout of the worksheet displaying the cell formulas.

Displaying and Printing Worksheet Formulas

You can document the formulas you entered in a worksheet by displaying and printing them. When you display formulas, Excel shows the formulas you entered in each cell instead of showing the results of the calculations. You want a printout of the formulas in your worksheet for documentation.

To display worksheet formulas:

1. Click **Tools** on the menu bar, and then click **Options** to open the Options dialog box.

2. Click the **View** tab, and then click the **Formulas** check box in the Window options section to place a check in it.

3. Click the **OK** button to return to the worksheet. The width of each column nearly doubles to accommodate the underlying formulas. See Figure 2-32.

Figure 2-32 ◀
Displaying
formulas in a
worksheet

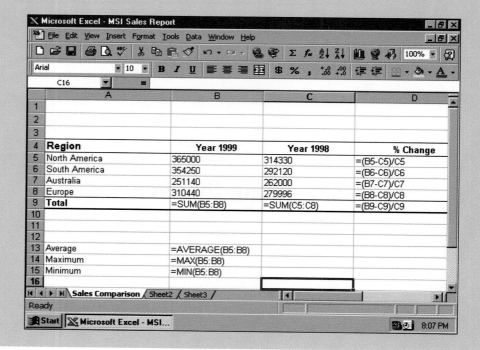

Now print the worksheet with the formulas displayed. Before printing the formulas you need to change the appropriate settings in the Page Setup dialog box to show the gridlines and the row/column headings, center the worksheet on the page, and fit the printout on a single page.

To adjust the print setups to display formulas:

1. Click **File** on the menu bar, and then click **Page Setup** to display the Page Setup dialog box.

2. Click the **Sheet** tab to view the sheet options. Click the **Row and Column Headings** check box to print the row numbers and column letters along with the worksheet results.

3. Click the **Gridlines** check box to place a check in it and select that option.

4. Click the **Page** tab, and then click the **Landscape** option button. This option prints the worksheet with the paper position so it is wider than it is tall.

5. Click the **Fit to** option button in the Scaling section of the Page tab. This option reduces the worksheet when you print it, so it fits on the specific number of pages in the Fit to check box. The default is 1.

6. Click the **Print Preview** button to open the Print Preview window.

7. Click the **Print** button. See Figure 2-33.

Figure 2-33 ◀
Printout of
worksheet
formulas

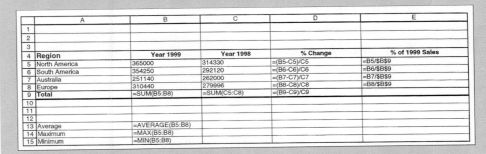

	A	B	C	D	E
1					
2					
3					
4	Region	Year 1999	Year 1998	% Change	% of 1999 Sales
5	North America	365000	314330	=(B5-C5)/C5	=B5/$B$9
6	South America	354250	292120	=(B6-C6)/C6	=B6/$B$9
7	Australia	251140	262000	=(B7-C7)/C7	=B7/$B$9
8	Europe	310440	279996	=(B8-C8)/C8	=B8/$B$9
9	Total	=SUM(B5:B8)	=SUM(C5:C8)	=(B9-C9)/C9	
10					
11					
12					
13	Average	=AVERAGE(B5:B8)			
14	Maximum	=MAX(B5:B8)			
15	Minimum	=MIN(B5:B8)			

After printing the formulas, return the worksheet so it displays the worksheet values.

To turn off the formulas display:

1. Click **Tools** on the menu bar, and then click **Options** to open the Options dialog box.

2. Click the **View** tab if necessary, and then click **Formulas** to remove the check mark next to that option to deselect it.

3. Click the **OK** button to return to the worksheet. The formulas are no longer displayed.

4. Close the workbook and exit Excel.

Quick Check

1   To move a range of cells, you must _____ the range first.

2   A _____ is text that is printed in the top margin of every worksheet page.

3   _____ is a command that lets you change your worksheet's appearance by selecting a collection of predesigned worksheet formats.

4   Describe how to insert a row or a column.

5   To reverse your most recent action, which button should you click?
a. 🖫
b. 📂
c. ↺

6   Describe how you use the pointing method to create a formula.

7   To display formulas instead of values in your worksheet, you choose what command?

8   If your worksheet has too many columns to fit on one printed page, you should try _____ orientation.

You have planned, built, formatted, and documented Sally's sales comparison worksheet. It is ready for her to present to the regional sales managers at their next meeting.

Tutorial Assignments

After Sally meets with the regional sales managers for MSI, she decides it would be a good idea to provide the managers with their own copy of the sales comparison worksheet, so they can update the report with next year's sales data, and also modify it to use for their own sales tracking purposes. Before passing it on to them, she wants to provide more documentation, and add some additional information that the managers thought would be useful to them. Complete the following for Sally:

1. Start Windows and Excel, if necessary. Insert your Student Disk into the appropriate disk drive. Make sure the Excel and Book1 windows are maximized.

2. Open the workbook MSI1 in the TAssign folder for Tutorial 2 on your Student Disk.

3. Save your workbook as MSI Sales Report 2 in the TAssign folder for Tutorial 2 on your Student Disk.

4. Make Sheet2 the active sheet. Use Sheet2 to include information about the workbook. Insert the information in Figure 2-34 into Sheet2. Increase the width of column A as necessary.

Figure 2-34 ◄

Cell	Text Entry
A1	Motorcycle Specialties Incorporated
A3	Created By:
A4	Date created:
A6	Purpose:
B3	enter your name
B4	enter today's date
B6	Sales report comparing sales by region for 1999 with 1998

5. Change the name of the worksheet from Sheet2 to Title Sheet.

6. Print the Title Sheet sheet.

7. Make Sales Comparison the active sheet.

8. Open the Office Assistant and enter the search phrase "Insert a column" to obtain instruction on inserting a new column into a worksheet. Insert a new column between columns C and D.

9. In cell D4 enter the heading "Change."

10. In cell D5 enter the formula to calculate the change in sales for North America from 1998 to 1999. (*Hint*: Check that the figure in cell D5 is 50670.)

11. Copy the formula in D5 to the other regions and total (D6 through D9) using the fill handle.

12. Calculate summary statistics for 1998. In cell C13 display the average sales, in cell C14 display the maximum, and in cell C15 display the minimum.

13. Save the workbook.

14. Print the sales comparison worksheet.

15. a. Use the Office Assistant to learn how to attach comments to a cell. List the steps.
    b. Insert the following comment into cell F4: "Divide 1999 sales in each region by total sales in 1999."

16. Open the MSI3 workbook and save it as MSI Report 4.
    a. Use the AutoSum button to compute the totals for 1998 and 1999. Print the worksheet. Are the results correct?
    b. Replace the values in the range B5:C8 with "1". Print the worksheet. Are the results correct? Why do you think this problem occurred?
    c. Use the pointing method to correct the formula. Print the worksheet.

17. a. Use the Office Assistant to learn how to use row and column headers in your formulas to create formulas (enter the search phrase "labels as formulas").
    b. Open the MSI5 workbook and save it as MSI Report 6.
    c. In cell D5, calculate the change in sales in North America from 1998 to 1999 using the labels in columns B and C.
    d. Copy the formula in D5 to the other regions and total (D6 through D9) using the fill handle.
    e. Print the worksheet.
    f. Print the formulas.
    g. Save the worksheet.

18. Open the MSI7 workbook and save it as MSI Report 8.
    a. Activate the Sales Comparison sheet and select the range A1:E9. Copy the selected range to the Clipboard. Activate Sheet2 and paste the selected range to the corresponding cells in Sheet2. Apply the Classic 1 AutoFormat to this range. Print Sheet2.
    b. Insert a new sheet using the Worksheet command from the Insert menu. Return to the Sales Comparison sheet and copy the range A1:E9 to the corresponding cells in the new sheet. Apply the 3D Effects 2 AutoFormat to this range. Print this sheet.
    c. Use the Delete Sheet command from the Edit menu to delete the Title Sheet sheet.
    d. Move the Sales Comparison sheet so it is the third sheet in the workbook.
    e. Save the workbook.

Case Problems

1. Magazine Circulation Report You are a research analyst in the marketing department of a large magazine publisher. You have been assigned the task of compiling circulation data on the company's competition. Circulation statistics for the top six magazines appear in Figure 2-35.

Figure 2-35 ◄

Magazine	Prior Year	Current Year
Better Homes & Gardens	8000	8002
Family Circle	5138	5108
Good Housekeeping	4975	5101
National Geographic	9925	9787
Reader's Digest	16300	16256
TV Guide	15337	14920

1. Open a new workbook and enter the data from Figure 2-35 in a worksheet.

2. Use the AutoSum button to compute total circulation for all six magazines listed for both the current year and the prior year.

3. Use the Paste Function dialog box to compute the average circulation for all six magazines for both the current and the prior year.

4. For each magazine, create and enter a formula to compute the increase/decrease in circulation compared to the prior year.

5. Use AutoFormat to improve the appearance of the worksheet. Use Classic 1 as the format.

6. Rename the sheet Total Circulation.

7. Use a sheet in the workbook to enter your name, the date created, and the purpose of this sheet. Rename the sheet Title Sheet.

8. Save the worksheet as Magazine in the Case folder for Tutorial 2.

9. Print both the worksheets.

2. Compiling Data on the U.S. Airline Industry The editor of *Aviation Week and Space Technology* has asked you to research the current status of the U.S. airline industry. You collect information on the revenue-miles and passenger-miles for each major U.S. airline (Figure 2-36).

Figure 2-36 ◀

Revenue-Miles and Passenger-Miles for Major U.S. Airlines		
Airline	Revenue-Miles (in 1000s of miles)	Passenger-Miles (in 1000s of miles)
American	26851	2210871
Continental	9316	622543
Delta	21515	1862276
Northwest	20803	1924288
US Air	9855	1542800
Trans World	16228	1188124
United	35175	3673152

You want to calculate the following summary information to use in the article:

- total revenue-miles for the U.S. airline industry
- total passenger-miles for the U.S. airline industry
- each airline's share of the total revenue-miles
- each airline's share of the total passenger-miles
- average revenue-miles for U.S. airlines
- average passenger-miles for U.S. airlines

Complete these steps:

1. Open a new workbook and enter the labels and data from Figure 2-36.

2. In cell A2, insert a second line to the title that reads:

    Compiled by: *XXXX*

    where *XXXX* is your name.

3. Enter the formulas to compute the total and average revenue-miles and passenger-miles. Use the SUM and AVERAGE functions where appropriate. Remember to include row labels to describe each statistic.

4. Add a column to display each airline's share of the total revenue-miles. Remember to include a column heading. You decide the appropriate location for this data.

5. Add a column to display each airline's share of the total passenger-miles. Remember to include a column heading. You decide the appropriate location for this data.

6. Name the worksheet Mileage Data.

7. Save the worksheet as Airline in the Case folder for Tutorial 2.

8. Print the worksheet. Center the report, no gridlines, and place the date in the upper-right corner of the header.

9. Select an AutoFormat to improve the appearance of your output.

10. Save your workbook.

11. Print the worksheet, centered on the page, no gridlines or row and column headings.

12. Print the formulas for the worksheet. Include row and column headings in the output.

3. Fresh Air Sales Incentive Program Carl Stambaugh is assistant sales manager at Fresh Air Inc., a manufacturer of outdoor and expedition clothing. Fresh Air sales representatives contact retail chains and individual retail outlets to sell the Fresh Air line.

This year, to spur sales, Carl has decided to run a sales incentive program for sales representatives. Each sales representative has been assigned a sales goal 15% higher than his or her total sales last year. All sales representatives who reach this new goal will be awarded an all-expenses-paid trip for two to Cozumel, Mexico.

Carl wants to track the results of the sales incentive program with an Excel worksheet. He has asked you to complete the worksheet by adding the formulas to compute:

- actual sales in 1999 for each sales representative

- sales goal in 1999 for each sales representative

- percent of goal reached for each sales representative

He also wants a printout before he presents the worksheet at the next sales meeting. Complete these steps:

1. Open the workbook Fresh (in the Case folder for Tutorial 2 on your Student Disk). Maximize the worksheet window and save the workbook as Fresh Air Sales Incentives in the Case folder for Tutorial 2.

2. Complete the worksheet by adding the following formulas:
   a. 1999 Actual for each employee = Sum of Actual Sales for each quarter
   b. Goal 1999 for each employee = 1998 Sales X (1 + Goal % increase)
   c. % Goal reached for each employee = 1999 Actual / 1999 Goal

   (*Hint:* Use the Copy command. Review relative versus absolute references.)

3. Make the formatting changes using an AutoFormat to improve the appearance of the worksheet.

4. Print the worksheet, centered horizontally and vertically, and add an appropriate header. Add your name and date in the footer.

5. At the bottom of the worksheet (three rows after the last sales rep) add the average, maximum, and minimum statistics for columns C through I.

6. Save the workbook.

7. Print the worksheet.

8. As you scroll down the worksheet, the column headings no longer appear on the screen, making it difficult to know what each column represents. Use the Help system to look up "Freezing Panes." Implement this feature in your worksheet. Save the workbook. Explain the steps you take to freeze the panes.

4. Stock Portfolio for Juan Cortez Your close friend, Juan Cortez, works as an accountant at a local manufacturing company. While in college, with a double major in accounting and finance, Juan dabbled in the stock market and expressed an interest in becoming a financial planner and running his own firm. To that end, he has continued his professional studies in the evenings with the aim of becoming a certified financial planner. He has already begun to provide financial planning services to a few clients. Because of his hectic schedule as a full-time accountant, part-time student taking evening classes, and part-time financial planner with client visits on the weekends, Juan finds it difficult to keep up with the data processing needs for his clients. You have offered to assist him until he completes his studies for the certified financial planner exams.

Juan asks you to set up a worksheet to keep track of a stock portfolio for one of his clients.

Open a new workbook and do the following:

1. Figure 2-37 shows the data you will enter into the workbook. For each stock, you will enter the name, number of shares purchased, and purchase price. Periodically, you will also enter the current price of each stock so Juan can review the changes with his clients.

2. In addition to entering the data, you need to make the following calculations:
   a. Cost = No of shares * Purchase price
   b. Current Value = No of shares * Current price
   c. Gains/Losses = Current value minus Cost
   d. Totals for Cost, Current value, and Gains/Losses

   Enter the formulas to calculate the Cost, Current Value, Gains/Losses, and Totals.

3. Save the workbook as Portfolio in the Case folder for Tutorial 2.

Figure 2-37 ◀

Stock	No. Of Shares	Purchase Price	Cost	Current Price	Current Value	Gains/ Losses
PepsiC	100	50.25		52.50		
FordM	250	31		30		
AT&T	50	60		61.25		
IBM	100	90.25		95.75		
Xerox	50	138		134		
Total						

4. Print the worksheet. Center the worksheet horizontally and vertically. Add an appropriate header.

5. Apply an AutoFormat that improves the appearance of the worksheet. Save the worksheet as Portfolio 2. Print the worksheet.

6. Print the formulas for the worksheet. Include row and column headings in the printed output.

7. Clear the prices in the Current price column of the worksheet.

8. Enter the following prices:

   PepsiC   55
   FordM   29.5
   AT&T   64
   IBM   91.25
   Xerox   125

   Print the worksheet.

9. From the financial section of your newspaper, look up the current price of each stock (all these stocks are listed on the New York Stock Exchange). Enter these prices in the worksheet. Print the worksheet.

Developing a Professional-Looking Worksheet

Producing a Projected Sales Report for the Pronto Salsa Company

OBJECTIVES

In this tutorial you will:

▨ Format data using the Number, Currency, and Percentage formats

▨ Align cell contents

▨ Center text across columns

▨ Change fonts, font style, and font size

▨ Use borders and color for emphasis

▨ Add comments and graphics to a worksheet using the Drawing toolbar

▨ Remove gridlines from the worksheet

▨ Print in landscape orientation

Pronto Salsa Company

Anne Castelar owns the Pronto Salsa Company, a successful business located in the heart of Tex-Mex country. She is working on a plan to add a new product, de Chili Guero Medium, to Pronto's gourmet salsa line.

Anne wants to take out a bank loan to purchase additional food-processing equipment to handle the production increase the new salsa requires. She has an appointment with her bank loan officer at 2:00 this afternoon. To prepare for the meeting, Anne creates a worksheet to show the projected sales of the new salsa and the expected effect on profits. Although the numbers and formulas are in place on the worksheet, Anne has no time to format the worksheet for the best impact. She planned to do that now, but an unexpected problem with today's produce shipment requires her to leave the office for a few hours. Anne asks you to complete the worksheet. She shows you a printout of the unformatted worksheet and explains that she wants the finished worksheet to look very professional—like those you see in business magazines. She also asks you to make sure that the worksheet emphasizes the profits expected from sales of the new salsa.

SESSION 3.1

In this session you will learn how to make your worksheets easier to understand through various formatting techniques. You will format values using Currency formats, Number formats, and Percentage formats. You will also change font styles and font sizes, and change the alignment of data within cells and across columns. As you perform all these tasks, you'll find the Format Painter button an extremely useful tool.

Opening the Workbook

After Anne leaves, you develop the worksheet plan in Figure 3-1 and the worksheet format plan in Figure 3-2.

Figure 3-1 ◀
Planning
analysis sheet

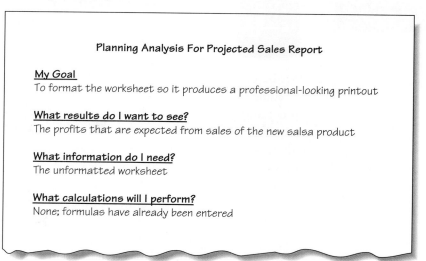

Planning Analysis For Projected Sales Report

My Goal
To format the worksheet so it produces a professional-looking printout

What results do I want to see?
The profits that are expected from sales of the new salsa product

What information do I need?
The unformatted worksheet

What calculations will I perform?
None; formulas have already been entered

Figure 3-2 ◀
Format plan

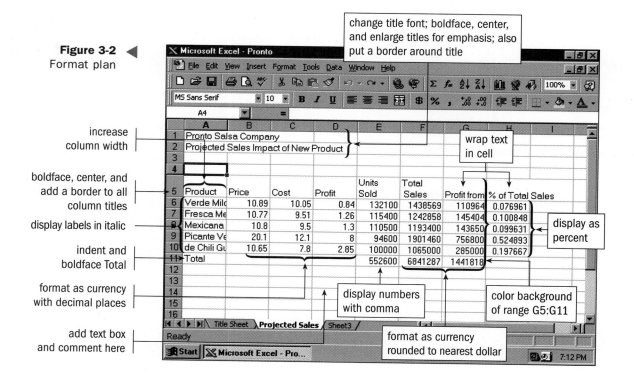

Anne has already entered all the formulas, numbers, and labels. Your main task is to format this information so it is easy to read and understand, and appears professional. This can be accomplished on two levels—by formatting the detailed data in the worksheet and by enhancing the appearance of the worksheet as a whole.

On the data level, you decide that the numbers should be formatted according to their use. For example, the product prices need to appear as dollar values. Secondly, the column and row labels need to fit within their cells. Also, the labels need to stand out more. To enhance the worksheet as a whole, you need to structure it so that related information is visually grouped together using lines and borders. Anne also wants certain areas of the worksheet that contain key information to stand out, and color may be a useful tool for this.

With all that needs to be done before Anne's 2:00 meeting, you decide that the best place to begin is with formatting the data within the worksheet. Once that is done, you will work to improve the worksheet's overall organization and appearance.

Now that the planning is done, you are ready to start Excel and open the workbook of unformatted data that Anne created.

To start Excel and organize your desktop:

1. Start Excel as usual.

2. Make sure your Student Disk is in the appropriate disk drive.

3. Make sure the Microsoft Excel and Book1 windows are maximized.

Now you need to open Anne's file and begin formatting the worksheet. Anne stored the workbook as Pronto, but before you begin to change the workbook, save it using the filename Pronto Salsa Company. This way, the original workbook, Pronto, remains unchanged in case you want to work through this tutorial again.

To open the Pronto workbook and save the workbook as Pronto Salsa Company:

1. Click the **Open** button 🖼 on the Standard toolbar to display the Open dialog box.

2. Open the **Pronto** workbook in the Tutorial.03 folder on your Student Disk.

3. Click **File** on the menu bar, and then click **Save As** to display the Save As dialog box.

4. In the File name text box, change the filename to **Pronto Salsa Company**.

5. Click the **Save** button to save the workbook under the new filename. The new filename, Pronto Salsa Company, appears in the title bar.

   TROUBLE? If you see the message "Replace existing file?" click the Yes button to replace the old version of Pronto Salsa Company with your new version.

6. Click the **Projected Sales** sheet tab. See Figure 3-3.

Figure 3-3
Pronto Salsa
Company
workbook

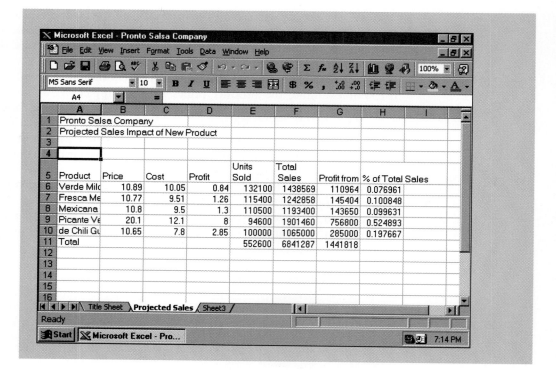

Studying the worksheet, you notice that the salsa names do not fit in column A. It is easy to widen column A, but if you do, some of the worksheet will scroll off the screen. Other formatting tasks are easier if you can see the entire worksheet, so you decide to do these tasks first.

Formatting Worksheet Data

Formatting is the process of changing the appearance of the data in worksheet cells. Formatting can make your worksheets easier to understand, and draw attention to important points.

In the previous tutorial you used AutoFormat to improve the appearance of your worksheet. AutoFormat applies a predefined format to your entire workbook. AutoFormat is easy to use, but its predefined format might not suit every worksheet. If you decide to customize a workbook's format, you can use the extensive Excel formatting options. When you select your own formats, you can format an individual cell or a range of cells.

Formatting changes only the appearance of the worksheet; it does not change the text or numbers stored in the cells. For example, if you format the number .123653 using a Percentage format that displays only one decimal place, the number appears in the worksheet as 12.4%; however, the original number, .123653, remains stored in the cell. When you enter data into cells, Excel applies an automatic format, referred to as the General format. The **General format** aligns numbers at the right side of the cell, uses a minus sign for negative values, and displays numbers without trailing zeros to the right of the decimal point. You can change the General format by using AutoFormat, the Format menu, the Shortcut menu, or toolbar buttons.

There are many ways to access the Excel formatting options. The Format menu provides access to all formatting commands. See Figure 3-4.

Figure 3-4 ◀
Format menu

The Shortcut menu provides quick access to the Format dialog box. See Figure 3-5. To display the Shortcut menu, make sure the pointer is positioned within the range you have selected to format, and then click the right mouse button.

Figure 3-5 ◀
Shortcut menu

The Formatting toolbar contains formatting buttons, including the style and alignment buttons, and the Font Style and Font Size boxes. See Figure 3-6.

Figure 3-6 ◀
Formatting
toolbar buttons

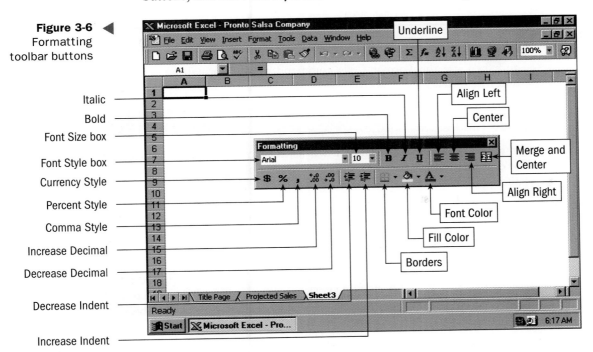

Most experienced Excel users develop a preference for which menu or buttons they use to access the Excel formatting options; however, most beginners find it easy to remember that all formatting options are available from the Format menu.

Looking at Anne's worksheet, you decide to change the appearance of the data first.

Changing the Appearance of Numbers

When the data in the worksheet appears as numbers, you want each number to appear in a style appropriate for what it is representing. The Excel default General format is often not the most appropriate style. For example, dollar values may require the dollar symbol ($) and thousand markers, and these can be applied to numerical data simply by changing the data's format. You can also standardize the number of decimal places displayed in a cell through formatting. Excel has a variety of predefined number formats. Figure 3-7 describes some of the most commonly used formats.

Figure 3-7 ◀
Commonly used
number formats

Category	Display Option
General	Excel default Number format; displays numbers without dollar signs, commas, or trailing decimal places
Number	Sets decimal places, negative number display, and comma separator
Currency	Sets decimal places and negative number display, and inserts dollar signs and comma separators
Accounting	Specialized monetary value format used to align dollar signs, decimal places, and comma separators
Date	Sets date or date and time display
Percentage	Inserts percent sign to the right of a number with a set number of decimal places

To change the number formatting, you select the cell or range of cells to be reformatted, and then use the Format Cells command or the Formatting toolbar button to apply a different format.

Currency Formats

In reviewing Anne's unformatted worksheet, you recognize that there are several columns of data that reflect currency. You decide to apply the Currency format to the Cost, Price, and Profit columns.

You have several options when formatting values as currency. You need to decide the number of decimal places you want displayed; whether or not you want to see the dollar sign; and how you want negative numbers to look. Keep in mind that if you want the currency symbols and decimal places to line up within a column, you should choose the Accounting format, rather than the Currency format.

In the Pronto Salsa Company worksheet, you want to apply the Currency format to the values in columns B, C, and D. The numbers will be formatted to include a dollar sign with two decimal places. You also decide to display negative numbers in the worksheet in parentheses.

To format columns B, C, and D using the Currency format:

1. Select the range **B6:D10**.

2. Click **Format** on the menu bar, and then click **Cells** to display the Format Cells dialog box.

3. If necessary, click the **Number** tab. See Figure 3-8.

Figure 3-8 ◀
Number tab of
Format Cells
dialog box

4. Click **Currency** in the Category list box. The Number tab changes to display the Currency formatting options, as shown in Figure 3-9. Notice that a sample of the selected format appears near the top of the dialog box. As you make further selections, the sample automatically changes to reflect your choices.

Figure 3-9 ◀
Selecting a
Currency
format

Notice that 2 decimal places is the default setting. A dollar sign ($) appears in the Symbol list box, indicating that the dollar sign will be displayed. If you are using a different currency, click the down arrow in the Symbol list box to select the currency symbol you want to display. Given the current options selected, you only need to select a format for negative numbers.

5. Click the third option **($1,234.10)** in the Negative numbers list box.

6. Click the **OK** button to format the selected range.

7. Click any cell to deselect the range and view the new formatting. See Figure 3-10.

Figure 3-10
Currency
formats in
columns B, C,
and D

amounts displayed as
currency with two
decimal places

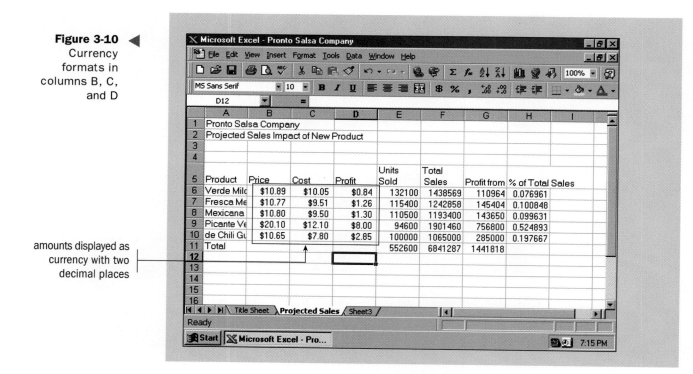

When your worksheet has large dollar amounts, you might want to use a Currency format that does not display any decimal places. To do this you use the Decrease Decimal button on the Formatting toolbar, or change the decimal places setting in the Format Cells dialog box. Currency values displayed with no decimal places are rounded to the nearest dollar: $15,612.56 becomes $15,613; $16,507.49 becomes $16,507; and so on.

You decide to format the Total Sales column as currency rounded to the nearest dollar.

To format cells F6 through F11 as currency rounded to the nearest dollar:

1. Select the range **F6:F11**.

2. Click **Format** on the menu bar, and then click **Cells** to display the Format Cells dialog box.

3. If necessary, click the **Number** tab.

4. Click **Currency** in the Category list box.

5. Click the **Decimal places** spin box down arrow twice to change the setting to 0 decimal places. Notice that the sample format changes to reflect the new settings.

6. Click the **OK** button to apply the format. Notice that Excel automatically increased the column width to display the formatted numbers.

7. Click any cell to deselect the range.

After formatting the Total Sales figures in column F, you realize you should have used the same format for the numbers in column G. To save time, you simply copy the formatting from column F to column G.

The Format Painter Button

The Format Painter button on the Standard toolbar lets you copy formats quickly from one cell or range to another. You simply click a cell containing the formats you want to copy, click the Format Painter button, and then use the click-drag technique to select the range to which you want to apply the copied formats.

To copy the format from cell F6:

1. Click cell **F6** because it contains the format you want to copy.

2. Click the **Format Painter** button 🖌 on the Standard toolbar. As you move the pointer over the worksheet cells, notice that the pointer turns to ⊕🖌.

3. Position ⊕🖌 over cell G6, and then click and drag to select cells **G6:G11**. When you release the mouse button, the cells appear in the Currency format, rounded to the nearest dollar—the same format used in cells F6 through F11.

4. Click any cell to deselect the range and view the formatted Profit from Sales column. See Figure 3-11.

Figure 3-11 ◄
Worksheet after Format Painter used to copy formats

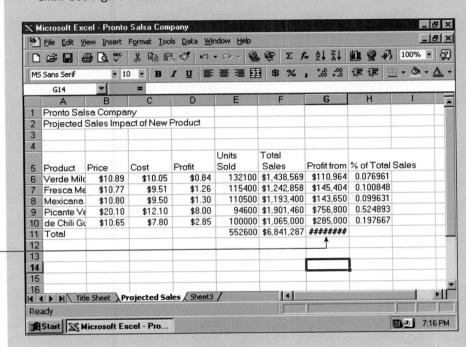

number symbols indicate column width needs to increase

As you review the changes on the screen, you notice that cell G11 contains number symbols (######) instead of values. This is because the formatting change has caused the data to exceed the width of the cell.

Number Symbol (###) Replacement

If a number is too long to fit within a cell's boundaries, Excel displays a series of number symbols (###) in the cell. The number symbols indicate that the number of digits in the value exceeds the cell's width. The number or formula is still stored in the cell, but the current cell width is not large enough to display the value. To display the value, you just need to increase the column width. One way you can do this is to use the Shortcut menu.

To replace the number symbols by increasing the column width:

1. Position the pointer on the column heading for column G.

2. Right-click the mouse button to display the Shortcut menu.

3. Click **Column Width** to display the Column Width dialog box.

4. Type **9** in the Column Width box.

5. Click the **OK** button to view the total sales, $1,441,818.

6. Click any cell to view the formatted data.

Now the cells containing price, cost, profit, total sales, and profit from sales are formatted as currency. Next, you want to apply formats to the numbers in columns E and H so that they are easier to read.

Number Formats

Like Currency formats, the Excel Number formats offer many options. You can select Number formats to specify

- the number of decimal places displayed
- whether to display a comma to delimit thousands, millions, and billions
- whether to display negative numbers with a minus sign, parentheses, or red numerals

REFERENCE window

FORMATTING NUMBERS

- Select the cells you want the new format applied to.
- Click Format, click Cells, and then click the Numbers tab in the Format Cells dialog box.
- Select a format category from the Category list box.
- Select the desired options for the selected format.
- Click the OK button.

To access all Excel Number formats, you can use the Number tab in the Format Cells dialog box. You can also use the Comma Style button, the Increase Decimal button, and the Decrease Decimal button on the Formatting toolbar to select some Number formats.

Looking at your planning sheet and sketch, you can see that the numbers in column E need to be made easier to read by changing the format to include commas.

To format the contents in column E with a comma and no decimal places:

1. Select the range **E6:E11**.

2. Click the **Comma Style** button on the Formatting toolbar to apply the Comma Style. The default for the Comma Style is to display numbers with two places to the right of the decimal. Use the Decrease Decimal button on the Formatting toolbar to decrease the number of decimal places displayed in cells formatted with the Comma Style to zero.

3. Click the **Decrease Decimal** button on the Formatting toolbar twice to display the number with no decimal places.

4. Click any cell to deselect the range and view the formatted Units Sold column. See Figure 3-12.

Figure 3-12
Cells formatted with Number format

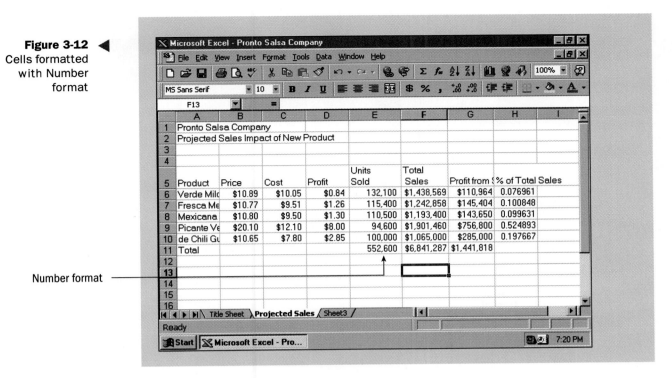

Number format

Looking at the numbers in column H, you realize that they are difficult to interpret and decide that you do not need to display so many decimal places. What are your options for displaying percentages?

Percentage Format

When formatting values as percentages, you need to select how many decimal places you want displayed. The Percentage format with no decimal places displays the number 0.18037 as 18%. The Percentage format with two decimal places displays the same number as 18.04%. If you want to use the Percentage format with two decimal places, you select this option using the Number tab in the Format Cells dialog box. You can also use the Percent Style button on the Formatting toolbar, and then click the Increase Decimal button twice to add two decimal places.

Your format sketch specifies a Percentage format with no decimal places for the values in column H. You could use the Number tab to choose this format. But it's faster to use the Percent Style button on the Formatting toolbar.

To format the values in column H as a percentage with no decimal places:

1. Select the range **H6:H10**.

2. Click the **Percent Style** button ![%] on the Formatting toolbar.

3. Click any cell to deselect the range and view the Percent Style. See Figure 3-13.

Figure 3-13 ◀
Percent of total
sales formatted
with Percent
Style

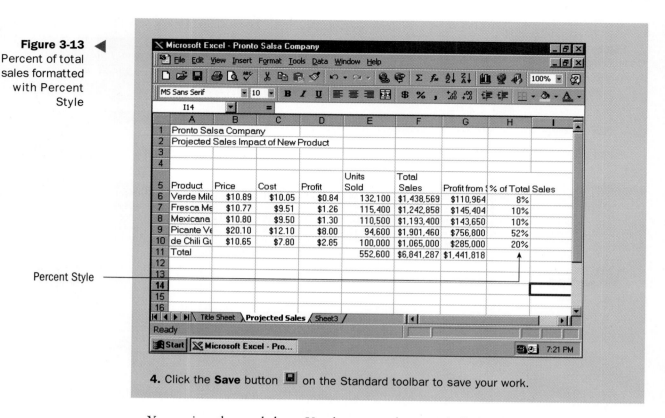

Percent Style ——

4. Click the **Save** button 🖫 on the Standard toolbar to save your work.

You review the worksheet. You have now formatted all the numbers in the worksheet appropriately. The next step in formatting Anne's worksheet is to improve the alignment of the data in the cells.

Aligning Cell Contents

The **alignment** of data in a cell is the position of the data relative to the right and left edges of the cell. Cell contents can be aligned on the left or right side of the cell, or centered in the cell. When you enter numbers and formulas, Excel automatically aligns them on the cell's right side. Excel automatically aligns text entries on the cell's left side. The default Excel alignment does not always create the most readable worksheet. Figure 3-14 shows a worksheet with the column titles left-aligned and the numbers in the columns right-aligned.

Figure 3-14 ◀
Poorly
formatted
worksheet

column titles
left-aligned

numbers
right-aligned

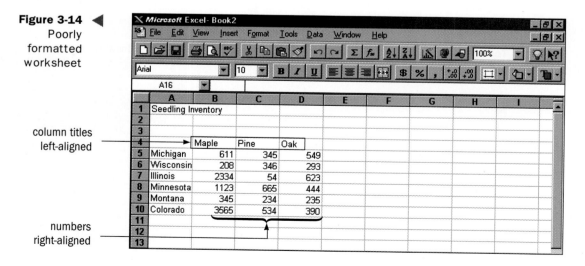

Notice how difficult it is to figure out which numbers go with each column title. Centering or right-aligning column titles would improve the readability of the worksheet in Figure 3-14. As a general rule, you should center column titles, format columns of numbers so that the decimal places are in line, and leave columns of text aligned on the left. You can change the alignment of cell data using the four alignment tools on the Formatting toolbar, or you can access additional alignment options by selecting the Alignment tab in the Format Cells dialog box.

To center the column titles:

1. Select the range **A5:H5**.

2. Click the **Center** button ≣ on the Formatting toolbar to center the cell contents.

3. Click any cell to deselect the range and view the centered titles. See Figure 3-15.

Figure 3-15 ◀
Worksheet with
centered
column titles

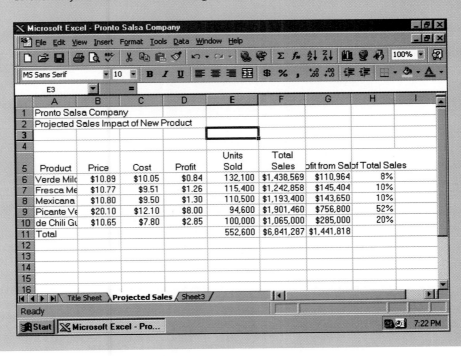

Notice that the column titles in columns G and H are not fully displayed. Although you could widen the column widths of these two columns to display the entire text, the Excel Wrap Text option enables you to display a label within a cell.

Wrapping Text in a Cell

As you know, if you enter a label that's too wide for the active cell, Excel extends the label past the cell border and into the adjacent cells—provided those cells are empty. If you select the Wrap Text option, Excel will display your label entirely within the active cell. To accommodate the label, the height of the row in which the cell is located is increased, and the text is "wrapped" onto the additional lines.

Now wrap the column titles in columns G and H.

To wrap text within a cell:

1. Select the range **G5:H5**.

2. Click **Format** on the menu bar, and then click **Cells** to display the Format Cells dialog box.

3. Click the **Alignment** tab. See Figure 3-16.

Figure 3-16 ◀
Alignment tab
of Format Cells
dialog box

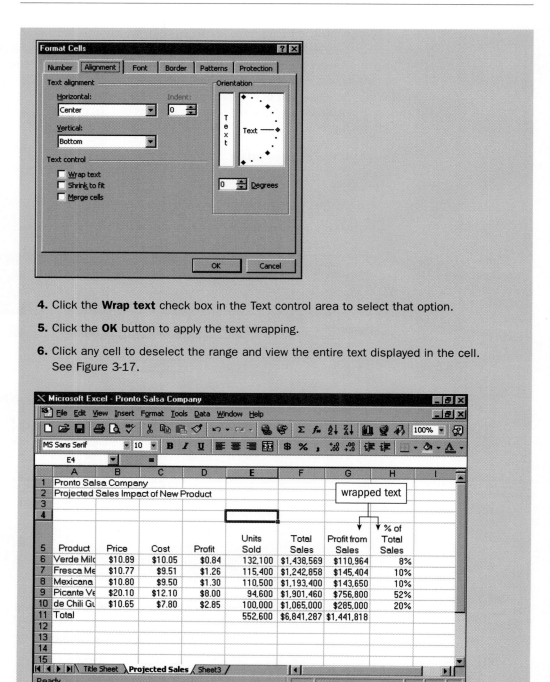

4. Click the **Wrap text** check box in the Text control area to select that option.

5. Click the **OK** button to apply the text wrapping.

6. Click any cell to deselect the range and view the entire text displayed in the cell. See Figure 3-17.

Figure 3-17 ◀
Wrapping text
in a cell

Now you will center the main worksheet titles.

Centering Text Across Columns

Sometimes you might want to center a cell's contents across more than one column. This is particularly useful for centering titles at the top of a worksheet. Now you will use the Center Across Selections option from the Format Cells dialog box to center the worksheet titles in cells A1 and A2 across columns A through H.

To center the worksheet titles across columns A through H:

1. Select the range **A1:H2**.

2. Click **Format**, click **Cells**, and if necessary click the **Alignment** tab in the Format Cells dialog box.

3. Click the arrow next to the Horizontal text alignment list box to display the horizontal text alignment options.

4. Click the **Center Across Selection** option to center the title lines across columns A through H.

5. Click the **OK** button.

6. Click any cell to deselect the range. See Figure 3-18.

Figure 3-18 ◀
Worksheet with titles centered across several columns

cell contents centered across columns A through H

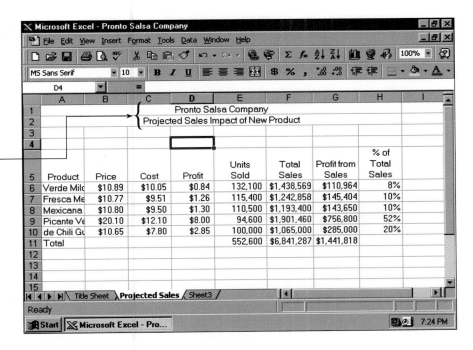

Indenting Text Within a Cell

When you type text in a cell it is left-aligned. You can indent text from the left edge by using the Increase Indent button on the Formatting toolbar or the Index spinner button in the Alignment tab of the Format Cells dialog box. You decide to indent the word "Total" to provide a visual cue of the change from detail to summary information.

To indent text within a cell:

1. Click cell **A11** to make it the active cell.

2. Click the **Increase Indent** button ⊞ on the Formatting toolbar to indent the word "Total" within the cell.

3. Click the **Save** button ⊟ on the Standard toolbar to save the worksheet.

You check your plan and confirm that you selected formats for all worksheet cells containing data, and that the data within the cells is aligned properly. The formatting of the worksheet contents is almost complete. Your next task is to improve the appearance of the labels by changing the font style of the title and the column headings.

You decide to use the Bold button on the Formatting toolbar to change some titles in the worksheet to boldface.

Changing the Font, Font Style, and Font Size

A **font** is a set of letters, numbers, punctuation marks, and symbols with a specific size and design. Figure 3-19 shows some examples. A font can have one or more of the following **font styles**: regular, italic, bold, and bold italic.

Figure 3-19 ◄
Selected fonts

Font	Regular Style	Italic Style	Bold Style	Bold Italic Style
Times	AaBbCc	*AaBbCc*	**AaBbCc**	***AaBbCc***
Courier	AaBbCc	*AaBbCc*	**AaBbCc**	***AaBbCc***
Garamond	AaBbCc	*AaBbCc*	**AaBbCc**	***AaBbCc***
Helvetica Condensed	AaBbCc	*AaBbCc*	**AaBbCc**	***AaBbCc***

Most fonts are available in many sizes, and you can also select font effects, such as strikeout, underline, and color. The Formatting toolbar provides tools for changing font style by applying boldface, italics, underline, and increasing or decreasing font size. To access other font effects, you can open the Format Cells dialog box from the Format menu.

REFERENCE window

CHANGING FONT, FONT STYLE, AND FONT SIZE

- Select the cells you want the new format to apply to.
- Click Format, click Cells, and then click the Font tab in the Format Cells dialog box.
- Select a typeface from the Font list box.
- Select a font style from the Font style list box.
- Select a type size from the Size list box.
- the OK button.
  or
- Select the cells you want the new format to apply to.
- Select the font, font size, and font style using the buttons on the Formatting toolbar.

You begin by formatting the word "Total" in cell A11 in boldface letters.

To apply the boldface font style:

1. If necessary, click cell **A11**.

2. Click the **Bold** button **B** on the Formatting toolbar to set the font style to bold-face. Notice that when a style like bold is applied to a cell's content, the toolbar button appears depressed to indicate that the style is applied to the active cell.

You also want to display the column titles in boldface. To do this, first select the range you want to format, and then click the Bold button to apply the format.

To display the column titles in boldface:

1. Select the range **A5:H5**.

2. Click the **Bold** button B on the Formatting toolbar to apply the boldface font style.

3. Click any cell to deselect the range.

Next, you decide to display the salsa products' names in italics.

To italicize the row labels:

1. Select the range **A6:A10**.

2. Click the **Italic** button I on the Formatting toolbar to apply the italic font style.

3. Click any cell to deselect the range and view the formatting you have done so far. See Figure 3-20.

Figure 3-20 ◀
Bold and Italic
formats applied

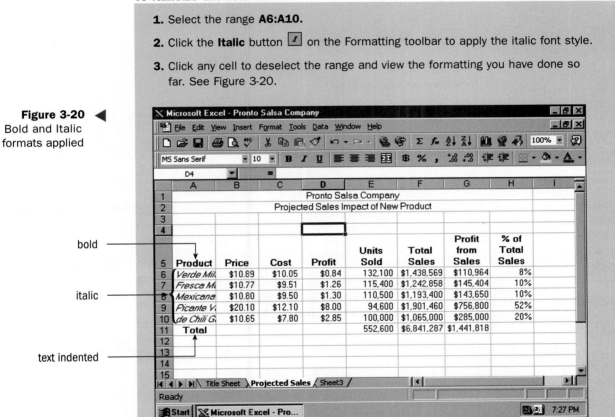

Next, you want to change the font and size of the worksheet titles for emphasis. You use the Font dialog box (instead of the toolbar) so you can preview your changes. Remember, although the worksheet titles appear to be in columns A through F, they are just spilling over from column A. To format the titles, you need to select only cells A1 and A2—the cells where the titles were originally entered.

To change the font and font size of the worksheet titles:

1. Select the range **A1:A2**.

2. Click **Format** on the menu bar, and then click **Cells** to display the Format Cells dialog box.

3. Click the **Font** tab. See Figure 3-21.

Figure 3-21 ◀
Font tab in
Format Cells
dialog box

select new
font here

change font
size here

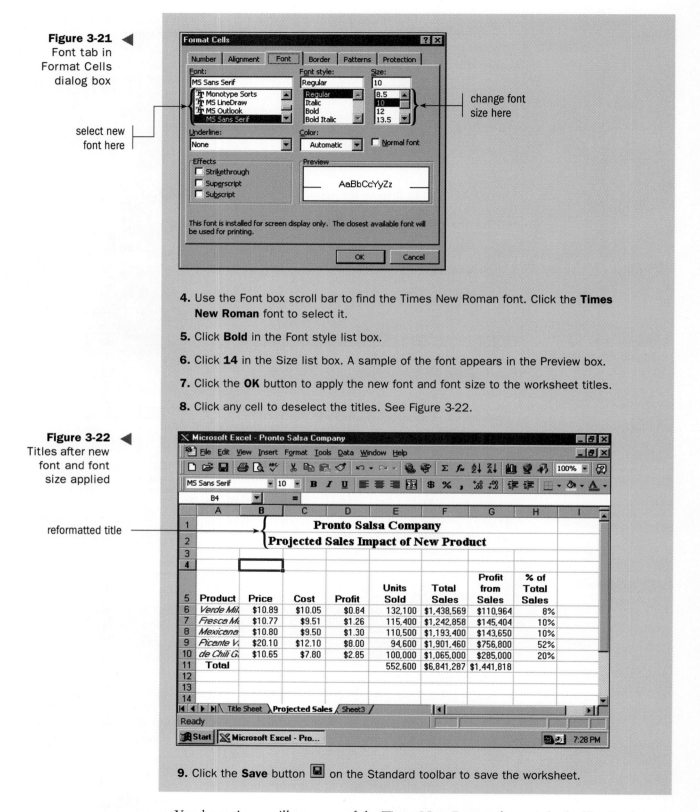

4. Use the Font box scroll bar to find the Times New Roman font. Click the **Times New Roman** font to select it.

5. Click **Bold** in the Font style list box.

6. Click **14** in the Size list box. A sample of the font appears in the Preview box.

7. Click the **OK** button to apply the new font and font size to the worksheet titles.

8. Click any cell to deselect the titles. See Figure 3-22.

Figure 3-22 ◀
Titles after new
font and font
size applied

reformatted title

9. Click the **Save** button 🖫 on the Standard toolbar to save the worksheet.

You hope Anne will approve of the Times New Roman font—it looks like the font on the Pronto salsa jar labels.

Quick Check

1 If the number .128912 is in a cell, what will Excel display if you:
  a. Format the number using the Percentage format with no decimal places
  b. Format the number using the Currency format with 2 decimal places and the dollar sign

2 List three ways you can access formatting commands, options, and tools.

3 Explain why Excel might display 3,045.39 in a cell, but 3045.38672 in the formula bar.

4 List the options available on the Formatting toolbar for aligning data.

5 What are the general rules you should follow for aligning column headings, numbers, and text labels?

6 Explain two ways to completely display a label that currently is not entirely displayed.

7 The _____ copies formats quickly from one cell or range to another.

8 A series of ####### in a cell indicates _____.

Now that you have finished formatting the data in the worksheet, you need to enhance the worksheet's appearance and readability as a whole. You will do this in Session 3.2 by applying borders, colors, and a text box.

SESSION 3.2

In this session you learn how to enhance a worksheet's overall appearance by adding borders and color. You will use the Drawing toolbar to add a text box and graphic to the worksheet, and use landscape orientation to print the worksheet.

Adding and Removing Borders

A well-constructed worksheet is clearly divided into zones that visually group related information. Figure 3-23 shows the zones on your worksheet. Lines, called **borders**, can help to distinguish different zones of the worksheet and add visual interest.

Figure 3-23 ◀
Information zones

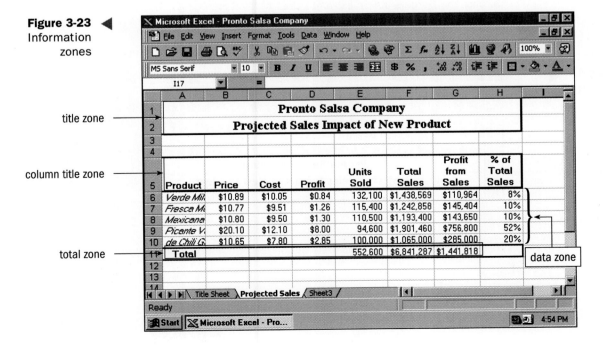

You can create lines and borders using either the Borders button on the Formatting toolbar, or the Border tab in the Format Cells dialog box. You can place a border around a single cell or a group of cells using the Outline option. To create a horizontal line, you place a border at the top or bottom of a cell. To create a vertical line, you place a border on the right or left side of a cell.

The Border tab lets you choose from numerous border styles, including different line thicknesses, double lines, dashed lines, and colored lines. With the Borders button, your choice of border styles is more limited.

To remove a border from a cell or group of cells, you can use the Border tab in the Format Cells dialog box. To remove all borders from a selected range of cells, select the None button in the Presets area.

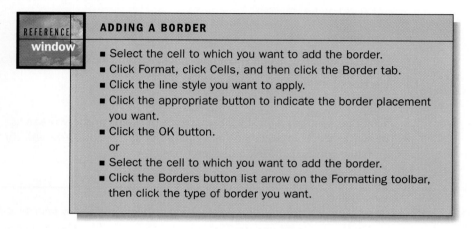

REFERENCE window

ADDING A BORDER

- Select the cell to which you want to add the border.
- Click Format, click Cells, and then click the Border tab.
- Click the line style you want to apply.
- Click the appropriate button to indicate the border placement you want.
- Click the OK button.
  or
- Select the cell to which you want to add the border.
- Click the Borders button list arrow on the Formatting toolbar, then click the type of border you want.

You decide that a thick line under all column titles will separate them from the data in the columns. To do this, you use the Borders button on the Formatting toolbar.

To underline column titles:

1. If you took a break after the last session, make sure Excel is running and the Projected Sales worksheet of the Pronto Salsa Company workbook is open.

2. Select the range **A5:H5**.

3. Click the **Borders** button list arrow on the Formatting toolbar. The Borders palette appears. See Figure 3-24.

Figure 3-24 ◄
Borders palette

medium thick underline

double-ruled line

thick outline

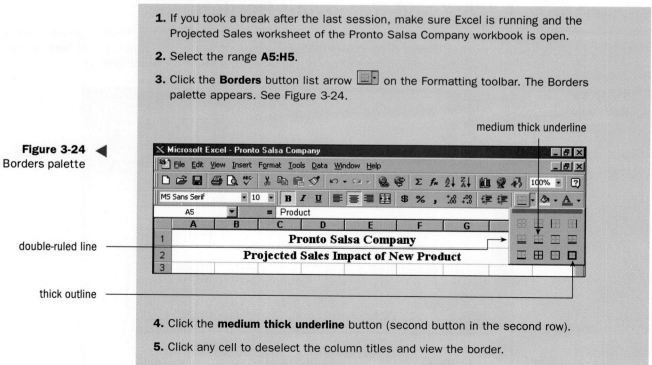

4. Click the **medium thick underline** button (second button in the second row).

5. Click any cell to deselect the column titles and view the border.

You also want a line to separate the data from the totals in row 11, and a double-ruled line below the totals. This time you use the Border tab in the Format Cells dialog box to apply borders to cells.

To add a line separating the data and the totals and a double-ruled line below the totals:

1. Select the range **A11:H11**.

2. Click **Format** on the menu bar, click **Cells**, and then click the **Border** tab in the Format Cells dialog box. See Figure 3-25.

Figure 3-25 ◀
Border tab from
Format Cells
dialog box

applies selected line
style to top border

applies selected line
style to bottom border

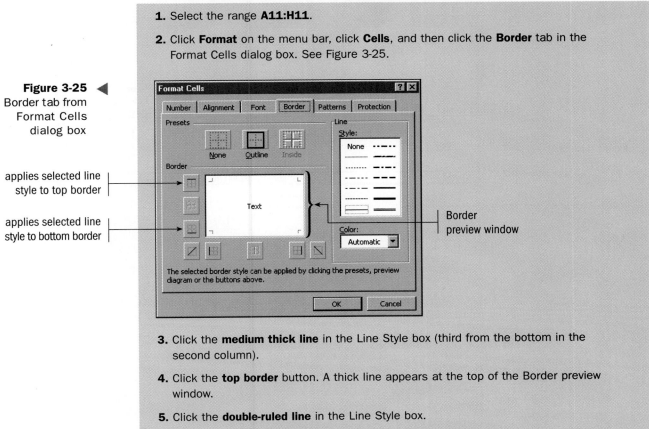

Border
preview window

3. Click the **medium thick line** in the Line Style box (third from the bottom in the second column).

4. Click the **top border** button. A thick line appears at the top of the Border preview window.

5. Click the **double-ruled line** in the Line Style box.

6. Click the **bottom border** button. A double-ruled line appears at the bottom of the Border preview window.

7. Click the **OK** button to apply the borders.

8. Click any cell to deselect the range and view the borders. See Figure 3-26.

Figure 3-26 ◄
Borders applied
to worksheet

medium thick line ———

double-ruled line ———

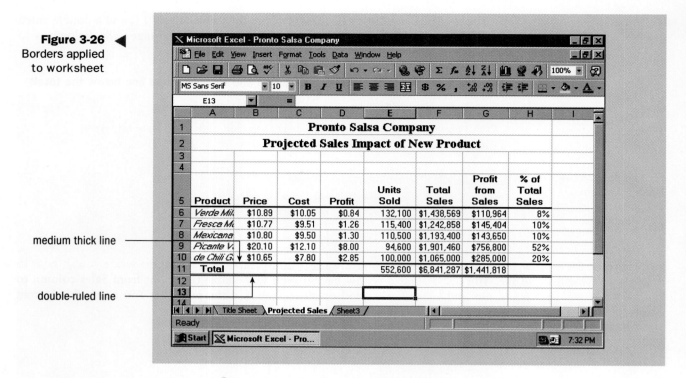

You consult your format sketch and see that you planned a border around the title zone to add a professional touch. You decide to add this border next.

To place an outline border around the title zone:

1. Select the range **A1:H2**.

2. Click the **Borders** button list arrow on the Formatting toolbar to display the Borders palette.

3. Click the **thick outline** button in the last row.

4. Click any cell to deselect the titles and view the border.

5. Click the **Save** button on the Standard toolbar to save the worksheet.

In addition to a border around the title zone, you want to add color to emphasize the Profit from Sales column.

Using Color for Emphasis

Patterns and colors provide visual interest, emphasize worksheet zones, or indicate data-entry areas. You should base the use of patterns or colors on the way you intend to use the worksheet. If you print the worksheet in color and distribute a hard copy of it, or if you plan to use a color projection device to display your worksheet on screen, you can take advantage of the Excel color formatting options. If you do not have a color printer, you can use patterns. It is difficult to predict how colors you see on your screen will be translated into gray shades on your printout.

APPLYING PATTERNS AND COLOR

REFERENCE **window**

- Select the cells you want to fill with a pattern or color.
- Click Format, click Cells, and then click the Patterns tab in the Format Cells dialog box.
- Select a pattern from the Pattern drop-down list. If you want the pattern to appear in a color, select a color from the Pattern palette, too.
- If you want a colored background, select it from the Cell shading color palette. You can also select colors by clicking the Color button on the Formatting toolbar and then clicking the color you want.

You want your worksheet to look good when you print it in black and white on the office laser printer, but you also want it to look good on the screen when you show it to Anne. You decide that a yellow background will enable the Profit from Sales column to stand out and looks fairly good on the screen and the printout. You apply this format using the Patterns tab in the Format Cells dialog box.

To apply a color to the Profit from Sales column:

1. Select the range **G5:G11**.

2. Click **Format** on the menu bar, click **Cells**, and then click the **Patterns** tab in the Format Cells dialog box. See Figure 3-27.

Figure 3-27 ◀
Color palette in the Patterns tab of the Format Cells dialog box

3. Click the **yellow square** in the fourth row (third square from the left) of the Cell shading Color palette.

4. Click the **OK** button to apply the color.

5. Click any cell to deselect the range and view the color in the Profit from Sales column. See Figure 3-28.

Figure 3-28 ◄
Worksheet
after applying
color to
a column

yellow background ——

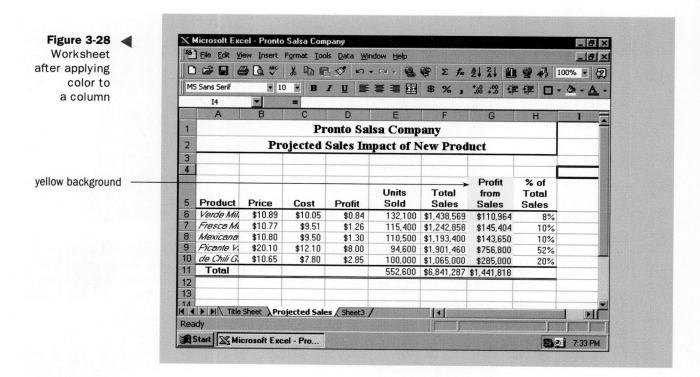

You delayed changing the width of column A because you knew that doing so would cause some columns to scroll off the screen, forcing you to scroll around the worksheet to format all the labels and values. Now that you have finished formatting labels and values, you can change the width of column A to best display the information in that column. To do this, you can use the Shortcut menu to change the column width.

To change the column width using the Shortcut menu:

1. Position the pointer on the column heading for column A.

2. Right-click the mouse button to display the Shortcut menu.

3. Click **Column Width** to display the Column Width dialog box.

4. Type **25** in the Column Width text box.

5. Click the **OK** button.

6. Click any cell to deselect the column and view the results of the column width change. See Figure 3-29.

Figure 3-29 ◀
Results of
changing
column width

column width
increased to 25

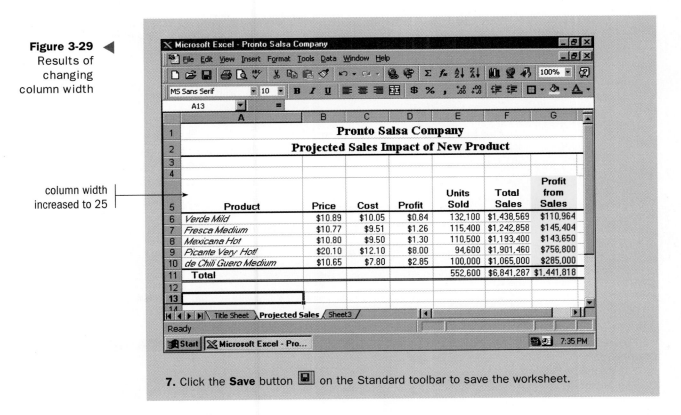

7. Click the **Save** button 🔲 on the Standard toolbar to save the worksheet.

Adding Comments to the Worksheet

The Excel Text Box feature lets you display a comment in a worksheet. A comment is like an electronic Post-It note that you paste inside a rectangular text box in the worksheet.

To add a comment to your worksheet, you first create a text box, then you simply type the text in the box. You create a text box using the Text Box button, which is located on the Drawing toolbar.

Activating a Toolbar

Excel provides many toolbars. You have been using two: the Standard toolbar and the Formatting toolbar. Some of the other toolbars include the Chart toolbar, the Drawing toolbar, and the Visual Basic toolbar. To activate a toolbar, it's usually easiest to use the toolbar Shortcut menu, but to activate the Drawing toolbar you can simply click the Drawing button on the Standard toolbar. When you finish using a toolbar, you can easily remove it from the worksheet.

REFERENCE
window

ACTIVATING AND REMOVING TOOLBARS

- To activate a toolbar, click any toolbar with the right mouse button to see the toolbar Shortcut menu. Then click the name of the toolbar you want to use.
- To remove a toolbar, click any toolbar with the right mouse button to see the toolbar Shortcut menu. Then click the name of the toolbar you want to remove.
  or
- Click the Drawing toolbar's Close button.

You need the Drawing toolbar to accomplish your next formatting task. (If your Drawing toolbar is already displayed, skip the following step.)

To display the Drawing toolbar:

1. Click the **Drawing** button ⊞ on the Standard toolbar.

The toolbar might appear in any location in the worksheet window; this is called a **floating toolbar**. You don't want the toolbar obstructing your view of the worksheet, so drag it to the bottom of the worksheet window, to **anchor** it there. (If your toolbar is already anchored at the bottom of the worksheet window, or at the top, skip the next set of steps.)

To anchor the Drawing toolbar to the bottom of the worksheet window:

1. Position the pointer on the title bar of the Drawing toolbar.

2. Click and drag the toolbar to the bottom of the screen.

3. Release the mouse button to attach the Drawing toolbar to the bottom of the worksheet window. See Figure 3-30.

Figure 3-30 ◄
Drawing toolbar
attached
to bottom
of window

Drawing toolbar ——

Text Box tool ——

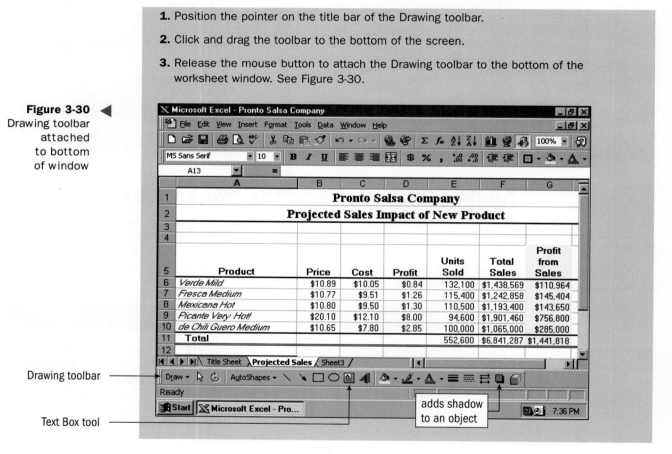

Now that the Drawing toolbar is where you want it, you proceed with your plan to add a comment to the worksheet.

Adding a Text Box

A **text box** is a block of text that sits in the worksheet. It is useful for adding comments to worksheets and charts. The text box is one example of a graphic object. With Excel you can create a variety of graphic objects, such as boxes, lines, circles, arrows, and text boxes. To move, modify, or delete an object, you first select it by moving the pointer over the object until the pointer changes to ↖ , then clicking. Small square handles indicate that the object is selected. Use these handles to adjust the object's size, change its location, or delete it.

Excel

REFERENCE window

ADDING A TEXT BOX AND COMMENT

- Click the Text Box button on the Drawing toolbar.
- Position the pointer where you want the text box to appear in the worksheet.
- Click and drag to outline the size and shape of the text box.
- Type the comment text for the text box.
- Click any cell outside the text box when you complete the comment.

You want to draw attention to the new salsa product's low price and high profit margin. To do this, you plan to add a text box to the bottom of the worksheet that contains a comment about expected profits.

To add a comment in a text box:

1. Scroll the worksheet so you can see rows 7 through 21.

2. Click the **Text Box** button 📧 on the Drawing toolbar. As you move the pointer inside the worksheet area, the pointer changes to ↓. Position the crosshair of the pointer at the top of cell **A13** to mark the upper-left corner of the text box.

3. Click and drag ✛ to cell **C18**, and then release the mouse button to mark the lower-right corner of the text box. See Figure 3-31.

   You are ready to type the text into the text box.

Figure 3-31 ◀
Creating a text box

text box →

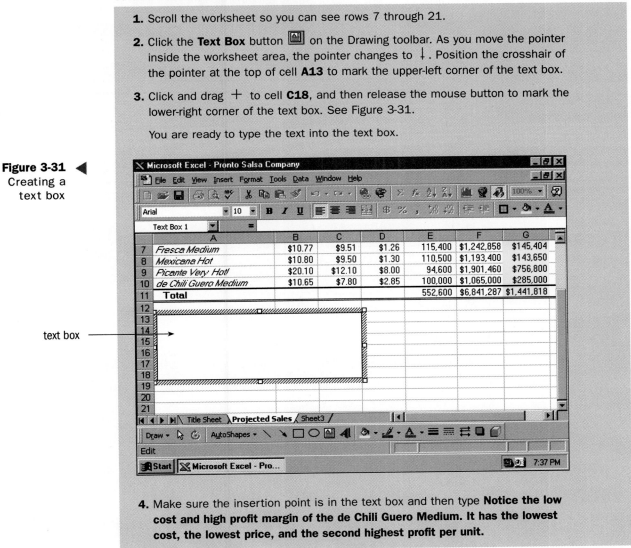

4. Make sure the insertion point is in the text box and then type **Notice the low cost and high profit margin of the de Chili Guero Medium. It has the lowest cost, the lowest price, and the second highest profit per unit.**

You want to use a different font style to emphasize the name of the new salsa product in the text box.

To italicize the name of the new salsa product:

1. Position I in the text box just before the word "de Chili."

2. Click and drag I to the end of the word "Medium", and then release the mouse button.

   TROUBLE? Don't worry if the text in your text box is not arranged exactly like the text in the figure. If the size of your text box differs slightly from the one in the figure, the lines of text might break differently.

3. Click the **Italic** button I on the Formatting toolbar.

4. Click any cell to deselect the product name, which now appears italicized. See Figure 3-32.

Figure 3-32 ◀
Italicizing text
in the text box

italicized text

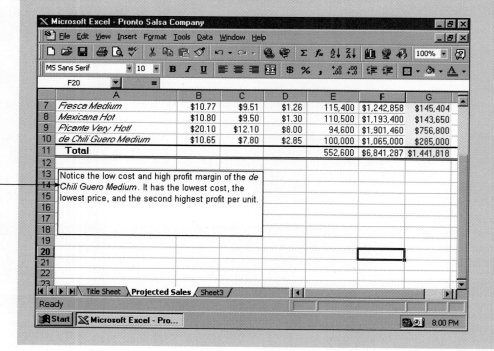

You decide to change the text box size so that there is no empty space at the bottom.

To change the text box size:

1. Click the **text box** to select it and display the patterned border with handles.

2. Position the pointer on the center handle at the bottom of the text box. The pointer changes to ↕ .

3. Click and drag ↕ up to shorten the box, and then release the mouse button.

You want to change the text box a bit more by adding a drop shadow to it.

To add a shadow to the text box:

1. Make sure the text box is still selected. (Look for the patterned border and handles.)

2. Click the **Shadow** button ▣ on the Drawing toolbar to display the gallery of Shadow options. See Figure 3-33.

Figure 3-33 ◄
Shadow
style options

reduced height
of text box

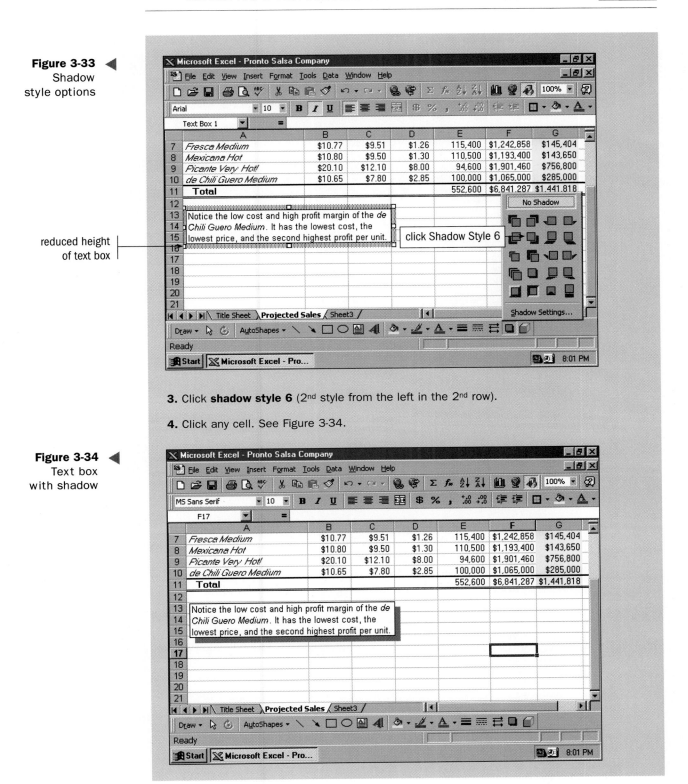

3. Click **shadow style 6** (2nd style from the left in the 2nd row).

4. Click any cell. See Figure 3-34.

Figure 3-34 ◄
Text box
with shadow

Adding an Arrow

You decide to add an arrow pointing from the text box to the row with information on the new salsa.

To add an arrow:

1. Click the **Arrow** button on the Drawing toolbar. As you move the mouse pointer inside the worksheet, the pointer changes to +.

2. Position + on the top edge of the text box in cell **B12**. To ensure a straight line, press and hold the **Shift** key as you drag + to cell **B10**, and then release the mouse button. See Figure 3-35.

Figure 3-35
Creating
an arrow

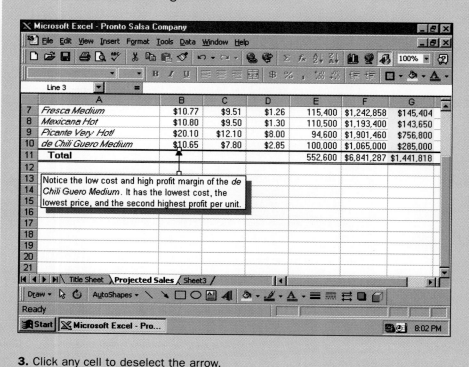

3. Click any cell to deselect the arrow.

You want the arrow to point to cell D10 instead of B10, so you need to reposition it. Like a text box, an arrow is an Excel object. To modify the arrow object, you must select it. When you do so, two small square handles appear on it. You can reposition either end of the arrow by dragging one of the handles.

To reposition the arrow:

1. Scroll the worksheet until row 5 appears as the first visible row in the window.

2. Move the pointer over the arrow object until the pointer changes to ✛.

3. Click the **arrow**. Handles appear at each end of the arrow.

4. Move the pointer to the top handle on the arrowhead until the pointer changes to ↖.

5. Click and drag + to cell **D10**, and then release the mouse button.

6. Click any cell to deselect the arrow object. See Figure 3-36.

Figure 3-36
Moving
the arrow ◄

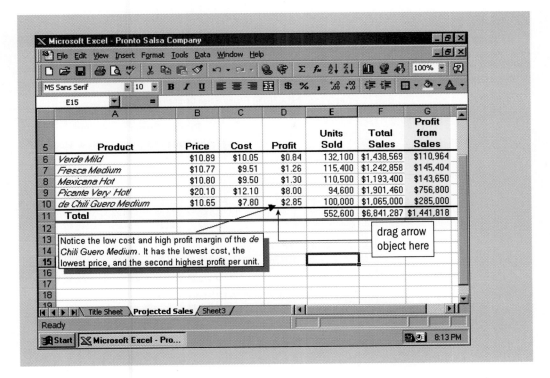

Now that the text box is finished, you can remove the Drawing toolbar from the worksheet.

To remove the Drawing toolbar:

1. Click the **Drawing** button 🔲 on the Standard toolbar. The Drawing toolbar is removed from the window, and the Drawing button 🔲 no longer appears depressed (selected).

2. Press **Ctrl + Home** to make cell A1 the active cell.

3. Click the **Save** button 🔲 on the Standard toolbar to save your work.

You have now made all the formatting changes and enhancements to Anne's worksheet. She has just returned to the office, and you show her the completed worksheet. She is very pleased with how professional the worksheet looks, but she thinks of one more way to improve the appearance of the worksheet. She asks you to remove the gridlines from the worksheet display.

Controlling the Display of Gridlines

Although normally the boundaries of each cell are outlined in black, Anne has decided that the appearance of your worksheet will be more effective if you remove the display of gridlines. To remove the gridline display, you deselect the Gridlines option in the View tab of the Options dialog box.

To remove the display of gridlines in the worksheet:

1. Click **Tools** on the menu bar, click **Options**, and if necessary, click the **View** tab in the Options dialog box.

2. Click the **Gridlines** check box in the Window option to remove the check and deselect the option.

3. Click the **OK** button to display the worksheet without gridlines. See Figure 3-37.

Figure 3-37 ◄
Worksheet
without
gridlines

no gridlines

Now you are ready to print the worksheet.

Printing the Worksheet

Before you print a worksheet, you can use the Excel Print Preview window to see how it will look when printed. Recall that the Print Preview window shows you margins, page breaks, headers, and footers that are not always visible on the screen.

To preview the worksheet before you print it:

1. Click the **Print Preview** button 📖 on the Standard toolbar to display the first worksheet page in the Print Preview window. See Figure 3-38.

Figure 3-38 ◄
Print Preview

active Next button
indicates more pages

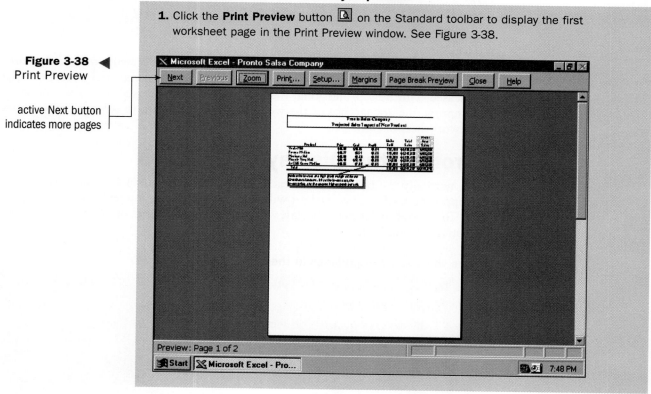

2. Click the **Next** button to preview the second worksheet page. Only one column appears on this page.

3. Click the **Previous** button to preview the first page again.

Looking at the Print Preview, you see that the worksheet is too wide to fit on a single page. You realize that if you print the worksheet lengthwise, however, it will fit on a single sheet of paper.

Portrait and Landscape Orientations

Excel provides two print orientations, portrait and landscape. **Portrait orientation** prints the worksheet with the paper positioned so it is taller than it is wide. **Landscape orientation** prints the worksheet with the paper positioned so it is wider than it is tall. Because some worksheets are wider than they are tall, landscape orientation is very useful.

You can specify print orientation using the Page Setup command on the File menu or using the Setup button in the Print Preview window. Use the landscape orientation for the Projected Sales worksheet.

To change the print orientation to landscape:

1. In the Print Preview window, click the **Setup** button to display the Page Setup dialog box. If necessary, click the **Page** tab.

2. Click the **Landscape** option button in the Orientation section to select this option.

3. Click the **OK** button to return to the Print Preview window. See Figure 3-39. Notice the Landscape orientation; that is, the page is wider than it is tall.

Figure 3-39 ◀
Landscape
orientation

Next button no
longer active

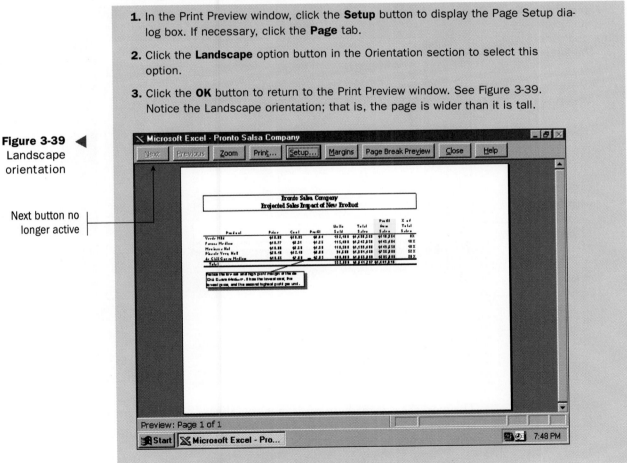

Before printing the worksheet, center the output on the page, and use the header/footer tab to document the printed worksheet.

To center the printed output:

1. Click the **Setup** button to display the Page Setup dialog box. Click the **Margins** tab.

2. Click the **Center on page Horizontally** check box to place a check in it and select that option.

Next, modify the printed footer by adding the date in the left section, and Anne's name in the right section.

To change the worksheet footer:

1. Click the **Header/Footer** tab, and then click the **Custom footer** to display the Footer dialog box.

2. In the Left section box, click the **Date** button 🖼 to display &Date in the Left section box.

3. Click the **Right section** box, then type **Prepared by Anne Castelar.**

4. Click the **OK** button to complete the footer and return to the Page Setup dialog box. See Figure 3-40.

Figure 3-40 ◄
Page Setup
after changing
the footer

from right section
of Custom Footer
dialog box

from left section
of Custom Footer
dialog box

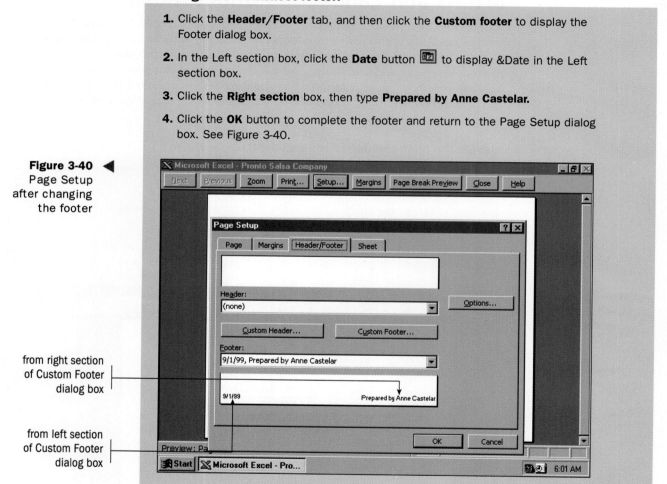

5. Click the **OK** button to return to the Print Preview window.

6. Click the **Close** button to return to the worksheet.

The worksheet is ready to print, but you always save your work before printing.

To save your page setup settings and print the worksheet:

1. Click the **Save** button 🖫 on the Standard toolbar.

2. Click the **Print** button 🖨 on the Standard toolbar. The worksheet prints. See Figure 3-41.

TROUBLE? If you see a message that indicates that you have a printer problem, click the Cancel button to cancel the printout. Check your printer to make sure it is turned on and is online; also make sure it has paper. Then go back and try Step 2 again. If you have no printer available, click the Cancel button.

Figure 3-41 ◀
Printed
worksheet

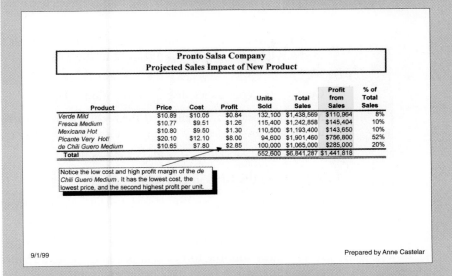

TROUBLE? If the title for the last two columns didn't print completely, you need to increase the row height for row 5. Select row 5. Drag the border below row 5 until the row height is 42.75 or greater (check the reference area of the formula bar). Click the Print button.

Now that you are done formatting the worksheet, close the workbook and exit Excel.

3. Close the workbook and exit Excel.

Quick Check

1 List two ways you can place a double-ruled line at the bottom of a range of cells.

2 Describe how to activate the Drawing toolbar.

3 To move, modify, or delete an object, you must _____ it first.

4 A _____ is a block of text that is placed in the worksheet.

5 _____ orientation prints the worksheet with the paper positioned so it is taller than it is wide.

6 If you are asked to remove the gridlines from the worksheet display, you will do what to the worksheet?

7 An arrow is an example of a _____.

You have completed formatting the Projected Sales worksheet and are ready to give it to Anne to check over before she presents it at her meeting with the bank loan officer.

Tutorial Assignments

After you show Anne the Projected Sales worksheet, the two of you discuss alternative ways to improve the worksheet's appearance. You decide to make some of these changes and give Anne the choice between two formatted worksheets. Do the following:

1. Start Windows and Excel, if necessary. Insert your Student Disk into the appropriate disk drive. Make sure the Excel and Book1 windows are maximized. Open the workbook Pronto2 in the TAssign folder for Tutorial 3 and save as Pronto3.

2. Center the percentages displayed in column H.

3. Make the contents of cells A10 through H10 bold to emphasize the new product. Make any necessary column-width adjustments.

4. Apply the color yellow to cells A1 through H2.

5. Right-align the label in cell A11.

6. Draw a vertical line to separate the product names from the rest of the data (the line begins in row 6 and continues to row 10).

7. Enter your name in the footer so that it appears on the printout of the worksheet. Make sure the footer also prints the date and filename. Remove any other information from the header and footer.

8. Make sure the Page Setup menu settings are set for centered horizontally and vertically, no row/column headings, and no cell gridlines.

9. Preview the printout to make sure it fits on one page. Save and print the worksheet.

 10. Fill the text box with the color yellow so that it appears as a "yellow sticky note."

 11. Change the color of the two-line title to red (the text, not the background color).

 12. In step 4 you applied the color yellow to the cells A1 through H2. Remove the yellow color so that the background is the same as the rest of your worksheet.

13. If you answered steps 10, 11, or 12, save the worksheet as Pronto4.

 14. a. Study the worksheet shown in Figure 3-42. Then open the Office Assistant and inquire about rotating and merging text in a cell.

Figure 3-42 ◄

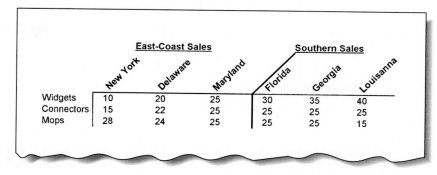

b. Open the workbook Explore3 and save it as Explore3 Solution.
c. Use the Rotate Text formatting feature to change the worksheet so it is similar to Figure 3-42. Make any other changes to make the worksheet as similar as possible to the one shown in Figure 3-42.
d. Save and print the worksheet.

Case Problems

1. Jenson Sports Wear Quarterly Sales Carl is the national sales manager for Jenson Sports Wear, a company that sells sports wear to major department stores. He has been using an Excel worksheet to track the results of a sales incentive program in which his sales staff has been participating. He has asked you to format the worksheet so it looks professional. He also wants a printout before he presents the worksheet at the next sales meeting. Complete these steps to format and print the worksheet:

1. Start Windows and Excel, if necessary. Insert your Student Disk into the appropriate disk drive. Make sure the Excel and Book1 windows are maximized. Open the workbook Running in the Case folder for Tutorial 3 on your Student Disk. Maximize the worksheet window and save the workbook as Running2 in the Case folder for Tutorial 3.

2. Complete the worksheet by doing the following:

   a. Calculating totals for each product
   b. Calculating quarterly subtotals for the Shoes and Shirts departments
   c. Calculating totals for each quarter and an overall total

3. Modify the worksheet so it is formatted as shown in Figure 3-43.

4. Use the Page Setup dialog box to center the output both horizontally and vertically.

5. Add the filename, your name, and the date in the footer section and delete the formatting code &[File] from the Center section of the header.

6. Save the worksheet.

7. Preview the worksheet and adjust the page setup as necessary for the printed results you want.

8. Print the worksheet.

9. Place the comment "Leading product" in a text box. Remove the border from the text box. (*Hint*: Use the Format Object dialog box.) Draw an oval object around the comment. (*Hint*: Use the Oval tool on the Drawing toolbar.) Draw an arrow from the edge of the oval to the number in the worksheet representing the leading product. Save and print the worksheet. Your printout should fit on one page.

Figure 3-43 ◀

Jenson Sports Wear
Quarterly Sales by Product

Shoes	Qtr 1	Qtr 2	Qtr 3	Qtr 4	Total
Running	1,750	2,050	2,125	2,200	8,125
Tennis	2,450	2,000	2,200	2,400	9,050
Basketball	1,150	1,300	1,450	1,500	5,400
Subtotal	5,350	5,350	5,775	6,100	22,575

Shirts	Qtr 1	Qtr 2	Qtr 3	Qtr 4	Total
Tee	900	1,100	1,000	1,050	4,050
Polo	2,000	2,100	2,200	2,300	8,600
Sweat	250	250	275	300	1,075
Subtotal	3,150	3,450	3,475	3,650	13,725
Total	8,500	8,800	9,250	9,750	36,300

2. Age Group Changes in the U.S. Population Rick Stephanopolous works for the U.S. Census Bureau and has been asked by his manager to prepare a report on changes in the U.S. population. Part of his report focuses on age group changes in the population from 1970 through 1980. Rick has created a worksheet that contains information from the U.S. Census reports from these years, and he is ready to format it. Complete these steps to format the worksheet:

1. Start Windows and Excel, if necessary. Insert your Student Disk into the appropriate disk drive. Make sure the Excel and Book1 windows are maximized. Open the workbook Census in the Case folder for Tutorial 3, and then save the workbook as US Population in the Case folder for Tutorial 3.

2. Make the formatting changes shown in Figure 3-44, adjusting column widths as necessary.

3. Use the Page Setup dialog box to modify the header so that the Right section consists of your name, a space, the current date, and the filename. Delete the contents of the Center section of the header.

4. Save the workbook.

5. Preview and print the worksheet. Your printout should fit on one page.

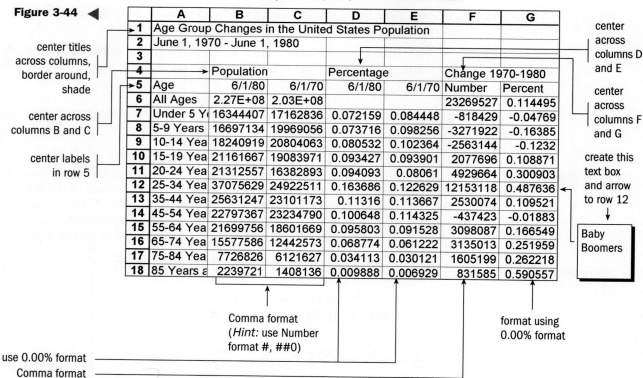

Figure 3-44

	A	B	C	D	E	F	G
1	Age Group Changes in the United States Population						
2	June 1, 1970 - June 1, 1980						
3							
4		Population		Percentage		Change 1970-1980	
5	Age	6/1/80	6/1/70	6/1/80	6/1/70	Number	Percent
6	All Ages	2.27E+08	2.03E+08			23269527	0.114495
7	Under 5 Y	16344407	17162836	0.072159	0.084448	-818429	-0.04769
8	5-9 Years	16697134	19969056	0.073716	0.098256	-3271922	-0.16385
9	10-14 Yea	18240919	20804063	0.080532	0.102364	-2563144	-0.1232
10	15-19 Yea	21161667	19083971	0.093427	0.093901	2077696	0.108871
11	20-24 Yea	21312557	16382893	0.094093	0.08061	4929664	0.300903
12	25-34 Yea	37075629	24922511	0.163686	0.122629	12153118	0.487636
13	35-44 Yea	25631247	23101173	0.11316	0.113667	2530074	0.109521
14	45-54 Yea	22797367	23234790	0.100648	0.114325	-437423	-0.01883
15	55-64 Yea	21699756	18601669	0.095803	0.091528	3098087	0.166549
16	65-74 Yea	15577586	12442573	0.068774	0.061222	3135013	0.251959
17	75-84 Yea	7726826	6121627	0.034113	0.030121	1605199	0.262218
18	85 Years a	2239721	1408136	0.009888	0.006929	831585	0.590557

add your name, date, and filename as header

center titles across columns, border around, shade

center across columns B and C

center labels in row 5

center across columns D and E

center across columns F and G

create this text box and arrow to row 12

Baby Boomers

Comma format (*Hint:* use Number format #, ##0)

format using 0.00% format

use 0.00% format
Comma format

EXPLORE

6. Change the border color of the text box from black to red. Change the color of the arrow to red. Save the workbook as US Population2. If you have access to a color printer, print the worksheet.

3. State Recycling Campaign Fred Birnbaum is working as an intern in the state's Waste Disposal Department. They have a pilot project on recycling for three counties (Seacoast, Metro, and Pioneer Valley). You have been asked to complete the worksheet and format it for presentation to their board of directors.

1. Start Windows and Excel, if necessary. Insert your Student Disk into the appropriate disk drive. Make sure the Excel and Book1 windows are maximized. Open the workbook Recycle in the Case folder on your Student Disk and save it as Recycle2.

2. Add two columns to calculate yearly totals for tons and a dollar value for each material in each county.

3. Insert three rows at the top of the worksheet to include:

   State Recycling Project
   Material Reclamation 1999
   <blank row>

4. Format the worksheet until you feel confident that the board of directors will be impressed with the appearance of the report.

5. Rename the worksheet Recycle Data.

6. Save the worksheet.

7. Print the worksheet centered horizontally and vertically on the page, using landscape orientation.

8. Remove the gridlines from the display. Use the Border tab of the Format Cells dialog box to place the recycle data, cells A6 to K20, in a grid. Save the workbook as Recycle3.

9. Change the magnification of the sheet so you can view the recycle data on the screen without having to scroll. (*Hint*: Use the Zoom control on the Standard toolbar.)

4. Cash Budgeting at Halpern's Appliances Fran Valence, the business manager for Halpern's Appliances, a small retail appliance store, is in the process of preparing a cash budget for January. The store has a loan that must be paid the first week in February. Fran wants to determine whether the business will have enough cash to make the loan payment to the bank.

Fran sketches the projected budget so that it will have the format shown in Figure 3-45.

Figure 3-45 ◀

```
              Halpern's Appliances Cash Budget
         Projected Cash Receipts and Disbursements
         January 1, 1999
         Cash balance, January 1, 1999                    xxxx
         Projected receipts during January:
              Cash sales during month           xxxx
              Collections from credit sales      xxxx
                   Total cash receipts                    xxxx
         Projected disbursements during January:
              Payments for goods purchased      xxxx
              Salaries                          xxxx
              Rent                              xxxx
              Utilities                         xxxx
                   Total cash disbursements              xxxx
         Cash balance, January 31, 1999                   xxxx
```

Do the following:

1. Start Windows and Excel, if necessary. Insert your Student Disk into the appropriate disk drive. Make sure the Excel and Book1 windows are maximized.

2. Use only columns A, B, and C to create the worksheet sketched in Figure 3-45.

3. Use the following formulas in your worksheet:

   a. Total cash receipts = Cash sales during month + Collections from credit sales
   b. Total cash disbursements = Payments for goods purchased + Salaries + Rent + Utilities
   c. Cash Balance, January 31, 1999 = Cash Balance, January 1, 1999 + Total cash receipts - Total cash disbursements

Figure 3-46 ◀

Budget Item	Amount
Cash balance at beginning of month	32000
Cash sales during month	9000
Collections from credit sales	17500
Payments for goods purchased	15000
Salaries	4800
Rent	1500
Utilities	800

4. Enter the data in Figure 3-46 into the worksheet.

5. Use the formatting techniques you learned in this tutorial to create a professional-looking worksheet.

6. Save the worksheet as Budget in the Case folder for Tutorial 3 on your Student Disk.

7. Print the projected cash budget.

8. After printing the budget Fran remembers that starting in January the monthly rent increases by $150. Modify the projected cash budget accordingly. Print the revised cash budget.

 EXPLORE

9. Add a footnote to the title Halpern's Appliances Cash Budget title line so it appears as

   Halpern's Appliances Cash Budget[1]
   Add the line
   [1]Prepared by <insert your name>

two rows after the last row. (*Hint*: Check out Superscript in the Font tab of the Format Cells dialog box.) Save the workbook as Budget1. Print the revised budget.

Creating Charts

Charting Sales Information for Cast Iron Concepts

OBJECTIVES

In this tutorial you will:

▨ Identify the elements of an Excel chart

▨ Learn which type of chart will represent your data most effectively

▨ Create an embedded chart

▨ Move and resize a chart

▨ Edit a chart

▨ Change the appearance of a chart

▨ Place a chart in a chart sheet

▨ Select nonadjacent ranges

▨ Work with 3-D chart types

▨ Add a picture to a chart

CASE

Cast Iron Concepts

The regional sales manager of Cast Iron Concepts (CIC), a distributor of cast iron stoves, Andrea Puest, is required to present information on how well the company's products are selling within her territory. Andrea sells in the New England region, which currently includes Massachusetts, Maine, and Vermont. She sells four major models—Star Windsor, Box Windsor, West Windsor, and Circle Windsor. The Circle Windsor is CIC's latest entry in the cast iron stove market. Due to production problems it was only available for sale the last four months of the year.

Andrea will make a presentation before the Director of Sales for CIC and the other regional managers next week when the entire group meets at corporate headquarters. Andrea gives you the basic data on sales in her territory for the past year. She must report on how well each model is moving in total for the region as well as within each state she covers. She knows that this kind of information is often understood best when it is presented in graphical form. So, she thinks she would like to show this information in a column chart as well as in a pie chart. You will help her prepare for her presentation by creating the charts she needs.

In this session you will learn about the variety of Excel chart types and learn to iden-tify the elements of a chart. You will learn how to create a column chart and learn a number of techniques for improving your chart, including moving and resizing it, adding and editing chart text, enhancing a chart title by adding a border, and using color for emphasis.

Excel Charts

Andrea's sales data is saved in a workbook named Concepts. You will generate the charts from the data in this workbook.

To start Excel, open the Concepts workbook, and rename it:

1. Start Excel as usual.

2. Open the **Concepts** workbook in the Tutorial.04 folder on your Student Disk.

   The Title Sheet sheet appears as the first sheet in the workbook. You can type your name and the current date and then save the workbook under a new name.

3. Type your name and the current date in the appropriate cells in the Title Sheet sheet.

4. Save the workbook as **Cast Iron Concepts**. After you do so, the new filename appears in the title bar.

5. Click the **Sales Data** tab to move to that sheet. See Figure 4-1.

Figure 4-1 ◄
Sales Data
worksheet in
Cast Iron
Concepts
workbook

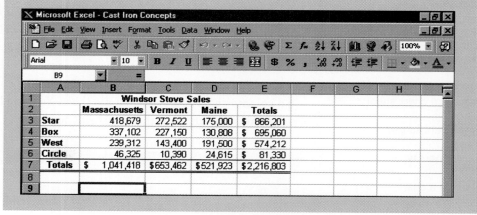

The worksheet shows the annual sales in dollars for each Windsor stove model by state. The total sales during the year for each model are in column E, and the total sales for each state appear in row 7.

It is easy to visually represent this kind of worksheet data. You might think of these graphical representations as "graphs"; however, in Excel they are referred to as **charts**. Figure 4-2 shows the 14 chart types within Excel that you can use to represent worksheet data.

Each chart type has two or more subtypes that provide various alternative charts for the selected chart type. For example, the Column chart type has seven subtypes, as shown in Figure 4-3. You can find more information on chart types and formats in the *Microsoft Excel User's Guide*, in the Excel Help facility, and in the Excel Chart Wizard.

Figure 4-2 ◀
Excel chart
types

Icon	Chart Type	Purpose
	Area	Shows magnitude of change over a period of time
	Column	Shows comparisons between the data represented by each column
	Bar	Shows comparisons between the data represented by each bar
	Line	Shows trends or changes over time
	Pie	Shows the proportion of parts to a whole
	XY (Scatter)	Shows the pattern or relationship between sets of (x,y) data points
	Radar	Shows change in data relative to a center point
	Surface chart	Shows the interrelationships between large amounts of data
	Bubble	A special type of XY (Scatter) that shows the pattern or relationship between sets of data points; compares three sets of data
	Stock	Compares high, low, open, and close prices of a stock
	Cylinder	Shows comparisons between the data represented by each cylinder
	Cone	Shows comparisons between the data represented by each cone
	Pyramid	Shows comparisons between the data represented by each pyramid
	Doughnut	Shows the proportion of parts to a whole

Figure 4-3 ◀
Chart subtypes
for Column
chart type

Chart Subtype Icon	Description
	Clustered column
	Stacked column
	100% Stacked column
	Clustered column with 3-D visual effect
	Stacked column with 3-D visual effect
	100% Stacked column with 3-D visual effect
	3-D column

Figure 4-4 shows the elements of a typical Excel chart. Understanding the Excel chart terminology is particularly important so you can successfully construct and edit charts.

Figure 4-4
Excel chart
elements

The entire chart and all its elements are contained in the **chart area**. The **plot area** is the rectangular area defined by the axis, with the Y-axis forming the left side and the X-axis forming the base; in Figure 4-4 the plot area is in gray. The **axis** is a line that borders one side of the plot area, providing a frame for measurement or comparison in a chart. Data values are plotted along the **value** or **Y-axis**, which is typically vertical. Categories are plotted along the **category** or **X-axis**, which is usually horizontal. Each axis in a chart can have a title that identifies the scale or categories of the chart data; in Figure 4-4 the **X-axis title** is "Territories" and the **Y-axis title** is "Sales ($U.S.)." The **chart title** identifies the chart.

A **tick mark label** identifies the categories, values, or series in the chart. **Tick marks** are small lines that intersect an axis like divisions on a ruler, and represent the scale used for measuring values in the chart. Excel automatically generates this scale based on the values selected for the chart. **Gridlines** extend the tick marks on a chart axis to make it easier to see the values associated with the data markers. The **category names** or **category labels**, usually displayed on the X-axis, correspond to the labels you use for the worksheet data.

A **data point** is a single value originating from a worksheet cell. A **data marker** is a graphic representing a data point in a chart; depending on the type of chart, a data marker can be a bar, column, area, slice, or other symbol. For example, sales of the Star Windsor stove in Massachusetts (value 418,679 in cell B3 of the worksheet on your screen) is a data point. Each column in the chart in Figure 4-4 that shows the sales of Windsor stoves is a data marker. A **data series** is a group of related data points, such as the Star Windsor sales shown as red column markers in the chart.

When you have more than one data series, your chart will contain more than one set of data markers. For example, Figure 4-4 has three data series, one for each Windsor stove. When you show more than one data series in a chart, it is a good idea to use a **legend** to identify which data markers represent each data series.

Charts can be placed in the same worksheet as the data; this type of chart is called an **embedded chart**, and enables you to place the chart next to the data so it can easily be reviewed and printed on one page. You can also place a chart in a separate sheet, called a **chart sheet**, which contains only one chart and doesn't have rows and columns. In this tutorial you will create both an embedded chart and a chart that resides in a separate chart sheet.

Planning a Chart

Before you begin creating a chart you should plan it. Planning a chart includes the following steps:

- identifying the data points to be plotted, as well as the labels representing each data series and categories for the X-axis

- choosing an appropriate chart type

- sketching the chart, including data markers, axes, titles, labels, and legend

- deciding on the location of the chart within the workbook

Remember, Andrea wants to compare sales for each model in each state in which she sells. She thinks that a column chart is the best way to provide her audience with an accurate comparison of sales of Windsor stoves in her New England territory. She also needs to show how total sales in her territory are broken down by stove model. When showing parts of a whole, a pie chart is most effective, so she will create a pie chart to use in her presentation as well.

Andrea sketched the column chart and pie chart shown in Figure 4-5.

Figure 4-5 ◄
Sketch of column and pie charts

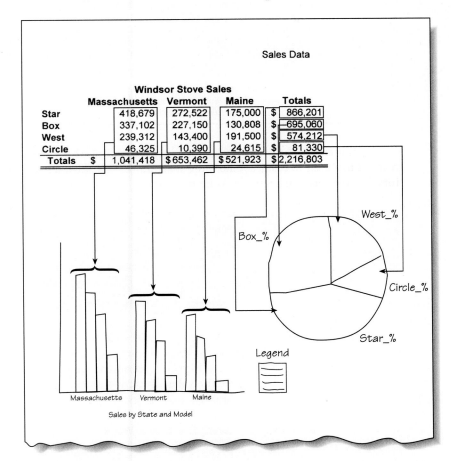

The sketches show roughly how Andrea wants the charts to look. It is difficult to envision exactly how a chart will look until you know how the data series looks when plotted; therefore, you don't need to incorporate every detail in the chart sketch. As you construct the charts, you can take advantage of Excel previewing capabilities to try different formatting options until your charts look just the way you want.

Create the column chart first. In looking at the sketch for this chart, note that Andrea wants to group the data by states; that is, the four models are shown for each of the three states. The names of the states in cells B2:D2 of the worksheet will be used as category labels. The names of each stove model, in cells A3:A6, will represent the legend text. The data series for the chart are in rows B3:D3, B4:D4, B5:D5, and B6:D6.

Creating a Column Chart

After studying Andrea's sketch for the column chart, you are ready to create it, using the Sales Data worksheet. When you create a chart, you first select the cells that contain the data you want to appear in the chart and then you click the Chart Wizard button on the Standard toolbar. The Chart Wizard consists of four dialog boxes that guide you through the steps required to create a chart. Figure 4-6 identifies the tasks you perform in each of the Chart Wizard dialog boxes.

Figure 4-6 ◀
Tasks
performed in
each step of
the Chart
Wizard

Dialog Box	Tasks Performed
Chart Type	Select the type of chart you want to create—displays a list of chart types available in Excel; for each chart type, presents you with several chart subtypes from which you can choose
Chart Source Data	Specify the worksheet cells that contain the data and labels that will appear in the chart
Chart Options	Change the look of the chart by changing options that affect the titles, axes, gridlines, legends, data labels, and data tables
Chart Location	Specify where to place the chart: embedded in a worksheet along with the worksheet data, or in a separate sheet called a chart sheet

You know that Andrea intends to create a handout of the worksheet and chart, so you want to embed the column chart in the same worksheet as the sales data, making it easier for her to create a one-page handout.

REFERENCE
window

CREATING A CHART

- Select the data you want to chart.
- Click the Chart Wizard button on the Standard toolbar.
- Follow the series of steps in the Chart Wizard dialog boxes.

Before activating the Chart Wizard you will need to select the cells containing the data the chart will display. If you want the column and row labels to appear in the chart, include the cells that contain them in your selection as well. For this chart, select the range A2 through D6, which includes the sales of each Windsor stove model in the three states as well as names of the stove models and states.

To create the column chart using the Chart Wizard:

1. Select cells **A2:D6**, making sure no cells are highlighted in column E or row 7.

   Now that you have selected the chart range, you use the Chart Wizard to create the column chart.

2. Click the **Chart Wizard** button 📊 on the Standard toolbar to display the Chart Wizard - Step 1 of 4 - Chart Type dialog box. See Figure 4-7.

   TROUBLE? If the Office Assistant appears on your screen, click the button next to the message "No, don't provide help now" to close the Office Assistant.

   This first dialog box asks you to select the type of chart you want to create. The Chart type list box displays each of the 14 chart types available in Excel. The default chart type is the Column chart type. To the right of the Chart type list box is a gallery of chart subtypes for the selected chart. Select the chart type you want to create.

Excel

Figure 4-7
Chart Wizard -
Step 1 of 4 -
Chart Type
dialog box

chart subtypes for
Column chart type

name and description
of selected chart
subtype

You want to create a column chart.

3. If necessary, click the **Column** chart type (the default) to select it. Seven Column
chart subtypes are displayed. The Clustered Column chart subtype is the default
subtype for the Column chart type. Click and hold the **Press and hold to view
sample** button to display a preview of the Clustered Column chart subtype. See
Figure 4-8. Release the mouse button.

To view any other Column chart subtype, select another subtype option and click
the Press and hold to view sample button.

Figure 4-8
Preview of
Clustered
Column chart
type

You decide to use the Clustered Column chart type, the default selection.

4. Click the **Next** button to display the Chart Wizard - Step 2 of 4 - Chart Source
Data dialog box. See Figure 4-9. In this step you confirm or specify the worksheet cells that contain the data and labels to appear in the chart.

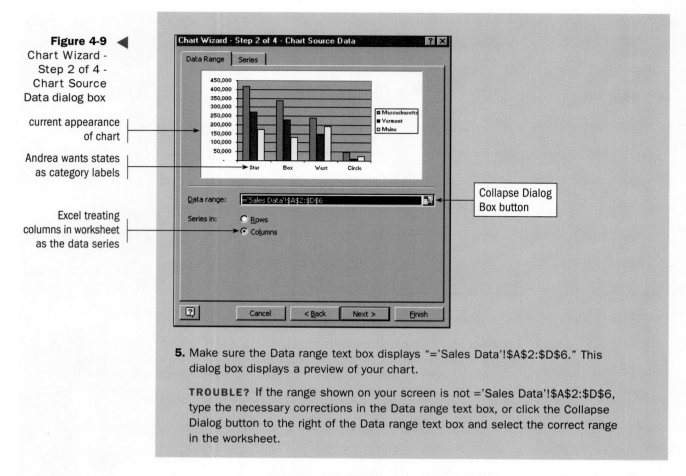

Figure 4-9 ◄
Chart Wizard -
Step 2 of 4 -
Chart Source
Data dialog box

current appearance
of chart

Andrea wants states
as category labels

Excel treating
columns in worksheet
as the data series

Collapse Dialog
Box button

5. Make sure the Data range text box displays "='Sales Data'!$A$2:$D$6." This
dialog box displays a preview of your chart.

TROUBLE? If the range shown on your screen is not ='Sales Data'!$A$2:$D$6,
type the necessary corrections in the Data range text box, or click the Collapse
Dialog button to the right of the Data range text box and select the correct range
in the worksheet.

In Step 2, you can also modify how the data series is organized—by rows or by
columns—using the **Series in** option. In Figure 4-9, the chart uses the columns in the
worksheet as the data series. To see how the chart would look if the rows in the worksheet were used as the data series, you can modify the settings in this dialog box.

Does the sample chart shown on your screen and in Figure 4-9 look like the sketch
Andrea prepared (Figure 4-5)? Not exactly. The problem is that the Chart Wizard
assumes that if the range to plot has more rows than columns (which is true in this case),
then the data in the columns (states) becomes the data series. Andrea wants the stove
models (rows) as the data series, so you need to make this change in the dialog box.

To change the data series and continue the steps in the Chart Wizard:

1. Click the **Rows** option button in the Series in area of the dialog box. The sample
chart now shows the stove models as the data series and the states as category
labels. See Figure 4-10.

Figure 4-10 ◀
Rows as data
series

2. Click the **Next** button to display the Chart Wizard - Step 3 of 4 - Chart Options
dialog box. See Figure 4-11. A preview area displays the current appearance of
the chart. This tabbed dialog box enables you to change various chart options,
such as titles, axes, gridlines, legends, data labels, and data tables. As you
change these settings, check the preview chart in this dialog box to make sure
you get the look you want.

Now add a title for the chart.

Figure 4-11 ◀
Chart Wizard -
Step 3 of 4 -
Chart Options
dialog box

3. If necessary click the **Titles** tab, click the **Chart title** text box, and then type **Sales
by State** for the chart title. Notice that the title appears in the preview area.

4. Click the **Next** button to display the Chart Wizard - Step 4 of 4 - Chart Location
dialog box. See Figure 4-12. In this fourth dialog box you decide where to place
the chart. You can place a chart in a worksheet, an embedded chart, or place it
in its own chart sheet. You want to embed this chart in the Sales Data worksheet, which is the default option.

Figure 4-12 ◄
Chart Wizard -
Step 4 of 4 -
Chart Location
dialog box

You have finished the steps in the Chart Wizard.

5. Click the **Finish** button to complete the chart and display it in the Sales Data worksheet. See Figure 4-13. Notice the selection handles around the chart; these handles indicate that the chart is selected. The Chart toolbar is automatically displayed when the chart is selected. Also, notice that the data and labels for the chart are outlined in blue, green, and purple in the worksheet. This enables you to quickly see which cells make up the chart.

TROUBLE? If you don't see the Chart toolbar, click View on the menu bar, click Toolbars, and then click the Chart check box to select that option.

Figure 4-13 ◄
Completed
column chart

indicates selected
chart element; click
list arrow to select
different element

Chart Type button;
click list arrow to
select chart type

formats selected
chart element

Chart toolbar (location
on your screen may be
different)

6. Click anywhere outside the chart to deselect it. Notice that the selection handles no longer surround the chart, indicating that the chart is no longer selected, and the Chart toolbar is no longer displayed. The Chart toolbar only appears when the chart is selected.

After reviewing the column chart, you think that the area outlined for the chart is too small to highlight the comparison between models. You also note that you need to move the chart so that it does not cover the worksheet data.

Moving and Resizing a Chart

When you use the Chart Wizard to create an embedded chart, Excel displays the chart in the worksheet. The size of the chart may not be large enough to accentuate relationships between data points or display the labels correctly. Since a chart is an object, you can move, resize, or copy it like any object in the Windows environment. However, before you can move, resize, or copy a chart, you must select, or **activate** it. You select a chart by clicking anywhere within the chart area. Small black squares, called **selection handles** or **sizing handles**, appear on the boundaries of the chart, indicating that it is selected. You will also notice that some of the items on the menu bar change to enable you to modify the chart instead of the worksheet.

You decide to move and resize the chart before showing it to Andrea.

To change the size and position of the chart:

1. Scroll the worksheet until row 8 appears as the first row in the window.

2. Click anywhere within the white area of the chart border to select the chart. Selection handles appear on the chart border. See Figure 4-14.

Figure 4-14 ◀
Selected chart

menu bar has changed because chart is activated

Name box indicates selected object

selection handles

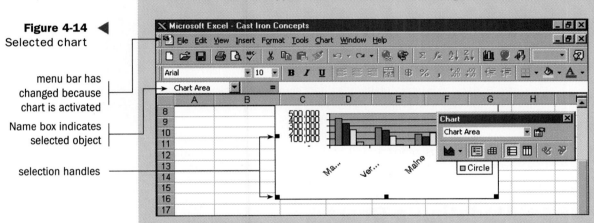

TROUBLE? If the Name box does not display the name "Chart Area," click the Chart Objects list box arrow on the Chart toolbar to display the list of chart objects. Select Chart Area.

TROUBLE? If the Chart toolbar is in the way, click and drag it to the bottom of the window to anchor it there.

3. Position the pointer anywhere on the chart border. The pointer changes to ↖. Click and hold down the mouse button as you drag the chart down and to the left until you see the upper-left corner of the dashed outline in column A of row 8. Release the mouse button to view the chart in its new position.

Now increase the width of the chart.

4. Position the pointer on the right center selection handle. When the pointer changes to ↔, hold down the mouse button and drag the selection handle to the right until the chart outline reaches the right edge of column G. Release the mouse button to view the resized chart. See Figure 4-15.

Figure 4-15 ◀
Chart after
being moved
and resized

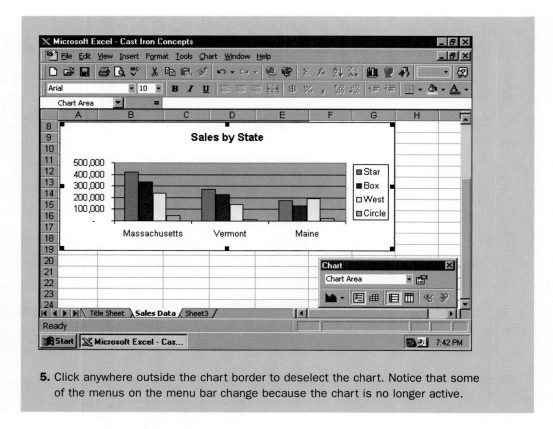

5. Click anywhere outside the chart border to deselect the chart. Notice that some of the menus on the menu bar change because the chart is no longer active.

The chart is repositioned and resized. You show Andrea the chart embedded in her Sales Data worksheet. As she reviews the chart, Andrea notices an error in the value entered for West Windsor stoves sold in Maine.

Updating a Chart

Every chart you create is linked to the worksheet data. As a result, if you change the data in a worksheet, Excel automatically updates the chart to reflect the new values. Andrea noticed that sales of West Windsor in Maine were entered incorrectly. She accidentally entered sales as 191,500, when the correct entry should have been 119,500. Correct this data entry error and observe how it changes the column chart.

To change the worksheet data and observe changes to the column chart:

1. Observe the height of the data marker for the West model in Maine (yellow data marker) in the column chart.

2. Scroll the worksheet until row 2 appears as the first row of the worksheet window.

3. Click cell **D5**, and then type **119500** and press the **Enter** key. See Figure 4-16. The total West sales (cell E5) and total sales for Maine (cell D7) automatically change. In addition, Excel automatically updates the chart to reflect the new source value. Now the data marker for the West Windsor sales in Maine is shorter.

Figure 4-16 ◀
Modified
column chart
after chart's
source data
changed

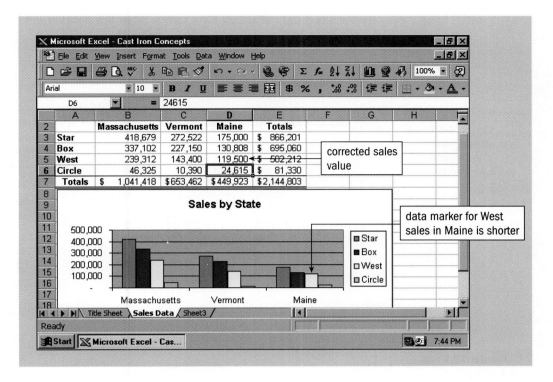

Now that the data for the West stove sales in Maine is corrected, you review the chart with Andrea for ways you can improve the presentation of the chart data.

Modifying an Excel Chart

You can make many modifications to a chart, including changing the type of chart, the text, the labels, the gridlines, and the titles. To make these modifications, you need to activate the chart. Selecting, or activating, a chart, as mentioned earlier, allows you to move and resize it. It also gives you access to the Chart commands on the menu bar and displays the Chart toolbar to use as you alter the chart.

After reviewing the column chart, Andrea believes that the Circle Windsor will distract the audience from the three products that were actually available during the entire period. Recall that the Circle Windsor was only on the market for four months and even then there were production problems. She wants to compare sales only for the three models sold during the entire year.

Revising the Chart Data Series

After you create a chart, you might discover that you specified the wrong data range, or you might decide that your chart should display different data series. Whatever your reason, you do not need to start over in order to revise the chart's data series.

REFERENCE
window

DELETING A DATA SERIES

- Click anywhere within the chart area to select the chart.
- Click a data marker within the series you want to delete.
- Press the Delete key.

Andrea asks you to remove the data series representing the Circle Windsor model from the column chart.

To delete the Circle Windsor data series from the column chart:

1. Click anywhere within the chart border to select the chart.

2. Click any data marker representing the Circle data series (any light blue data marker). Selection handles appear on each column of the Circle Windsor data series and a ScreenTip is displayed identifying the selected chart item. See Figure 4-17.

Figure 4-17 ◄
Chart with
Circle data
series selected

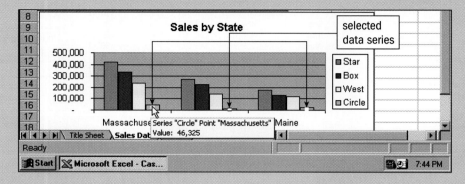

3. Press the **Delete** key. See Figure 4-18. Notice that the Circle Windsor data series is removed from the chart.

Figure 4-18 ◄
Column chart
after data
series removed

TROUBLE? If you deleted the wrong data series, click the Undo button ⟳ and repeat Steps 2 and 3.

Andrea reviews her sketch and notices that the chart title is incomplete; the intended title was "Sales by State and Model." She asks you to make this change to the chart.

Editing Chart Text

Excel classifies the text in your charts in three categories: label text, attached text, and unattached text. **Label text** includes the category names, the tick mark labels, the X-axis labels, and the legend. Label text often derives from the cells in the worksheet; you usually specify it using the Chart Wizard.

Attached text includes the chart title, X-axis title, and Y-axis title. Although attached text appears in a predefined position, you can edit it, and move it using the click-drag technique.

Unattached text includes text boxes or comments that you type in the chart after it is created. You can position unattached text anywhere in the chart. To add unattached text to a chart, you use the Text Box tool on the Drawing toolbar.

As noted earlier, you need to change the chart title to "Sales by State and Model." To do this you must select the chart, select the chart title, and then add "and Model" to the title.

To revise the chart title:

1. If the chart is not selected, click the **chart** to select it.

2. Click the **chart title** object to select it. Notice that the object name Chart Title appears in the Name box and as a ScreenTip; also, selection handles surround the Chart Title object.

3. Position the pointer in the chart title text box at the end of the title and click to remove the selection handles from the Chart Title object. The pointer changes to an insertion point I.

   TROUBLE? If the insertion point is not at the end of the title, press the End key to move it to the end.

4. Press the **spacebar** and type **and Model**, and then click anywhere within the chart border to complete the change in the title and deselect it.

Checking Andrea's sketch, you notice that the Y-axis title was not included. To help clarify what the data values in the chart represent, you decide to add "Sales ($U.S.)" as a Y-axis title. You use the Chart Option command on the Chart menu to add this title.

To add the Y-axis title:

1. Make sure that the chart is still selected.

2. Click **Chart** on the menu bar, and then click **Chart Options** to display the Chart Options dialog box. If necessary, click the **Titles** tab.

3. Click the **Value (Y) axis** text box, and then type **Sales ($U.S.)**.

4. Click the **OK** button to close the Chart Options dialog box.

5. If necessary, scroll the worksheet so that the entire chart is displayed.

6. Click anywhere within the chart border to deselect the Y-axis title. See Figure 4-19.

Figure 4-19
Chart after title
modified and
value axis label
inserted

Value axis title

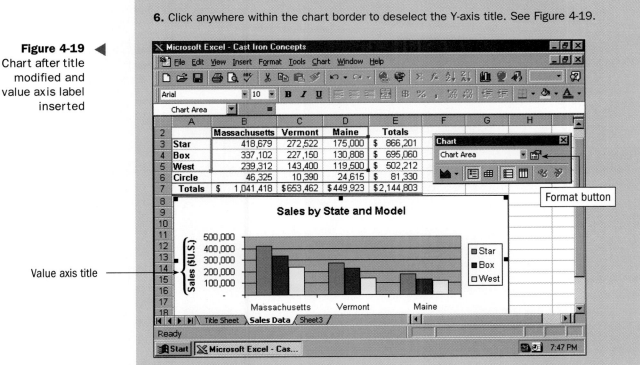

Now that the titles accurately describe the chart data, Andrea asks you to add data labels to show the exact values of the Star Windsor data series—CIC's leading model.

Adding Data Labels

A **data label** provides additional information about a data marker. Depending on the type of chart, data labels can show values, names of data series (or categories), or percentages. You can apply a label to a single data point, an entire data series, or all data markers in a chart.

REFERENCE window	**ADDING A DATA LABEL**

- Select the chart.
- Select a single data marker, entire data series, or all data markers in the chart.
- Click Chart, click Chart Options, and then click Data Labels.
- Click the option for the type of label you want to add.
- Click OK.

In this case, Andrea wants to add data labels to the Star model data series.

To apply data labels to a data series:

1. If the column chart is not selected, click anywhere within the chart border to select it.

2. Click any **Star Windsor data marker** (blue data marker) within the chart. Selection handles appear on all columns in the Star Windsor data series.

   To format any chart element, you can use the Format button on the Chart toolbar. The Format button's ToolTip name and function change depending on what chart element is selected for formatting. The list box that appears to the left of the Format button on the toolbar also displays the name of the currently selected chart element. In this case, the Star Windsor data series marker is selected, so the Format button on the Chart toolbar appears as the Format Data Series button, and when selected, opens the Format Data Series dialog box.

3. Click the **Format Data Series** button 🖼 on the Chart toolbar to display the Format Data Series dialog box. Click the **Data Labels** tab if necessary. See Figure 4-20.

Figure 4-20 ◄
Active Data
Labels tab in
Format Data
Series dialog
box

4. Click the **Show value** option button.

5. Click the **OK** button to display the column chart with data labels. See Figure 4-21.

Figure 4-21
Chart with data
labels

data labels

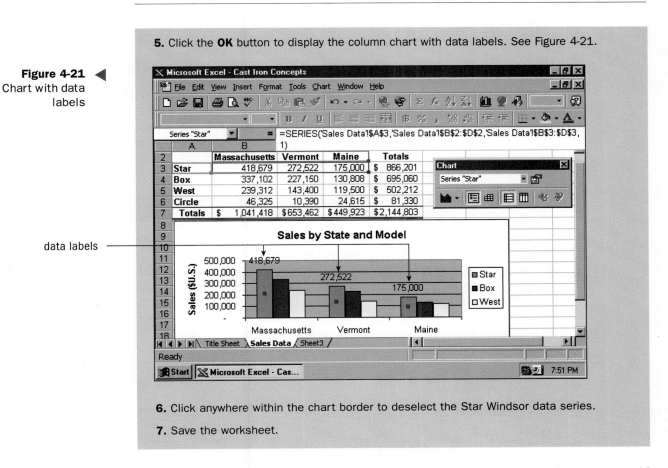

6. Click anywhere within the chart border to deselect the Star Windsor data series.

7. Save the worksheet.

Andrea is pleased with the changes in the chart's appearance. Now, she wants to add visual interest to the chart, making it look more polished.

Enhancing the Chart's Appearance

There are many ways to give charts a more professional look. The use of different font styles, types, and sizes can make chart labels and titles stand out. Also, using colors, borders, and patterns can make a chart more interesting to view.

Andrea thinks that a border and some color could accentuate the title of the chart.

Emphasizing the Title with Border and Color

The chart title is an object that you can select and format using the menu options or the toolbar buttons. Now make the changes to the chart title.

To display the title with border and color:

1. Click the **chart title** to select it and display selection handles. Now that the chart title is selected, notice that the Format button 📑 on the Chart toolbar becomes the Format Chart Title button, and the Format button list box displays "Chart Title."

2. Click the **Format Chart Title** button 📑 on the Chart toolbar to display the Format Chart Title dialog box, and then, if necessary, click the **Patterns** tab.

3. Click the **Weight** list arrow in the Border section to display a list of border weights.

4. Click the **second line** in the list.

5. Click the **gray** square in the Color palette (fourth row, last column) in the Area section.

6. Click the **OK** button to apply the format changes to the chart title, and then click anywhere within the chart area to deselect the title.

Andrea thinks that the chart looks better with its title emphasized. Now she wants you to work on making the data markers more distinctive. They certainly stand out on her computer's color monitor, but she is concerned that this will not be the case when she prints the chart on the office's black and white printer.

Changing Colors and Patterns

Patterns add visual interest to a chart and they can be useful when your printer has no color capability. Although your charts appear in color on a color monitor, if your printer does not have color capability, Excel translates colors to gray shades when printing. It's difficult to distinguish some colors, particularly darker ones, from one another when Excel translates them to gray shades and then prints them. To solve this potential problem, you can make your charts more readable by selecting a different pattern for each data marker.

To apply a different pattern to each data series you use the Patterns dialog box.

REFERENCE window

SELECTING A PATTERN FOR A DATA MARKER

- Make sure the chart is selected.
- Select the data marker or markers to which you want to apply a pattern.
- Click the Format Data Series button on the Chart toolbar to display the Format Data Series dialog box.
- Click the Patterns tab, click the Fill Effects button, and then click the Pattern tab to display a list of patterns.
- Click the pattern you want to apply, and then click the OK button twice to close the dialog boxes.

You want to apply a different pattern to each data series.

To apply a pattern to a data series:

1. Make sure the chart is selected.

2. Click any data marker for the Star data series (blue data marker) to display selection handles for all three data markers for that data series.

3. Click the **Format Data Series** button 🗃 on the Chart toolbar to display the Format Data Series dialog box.

4. If necessary, click the **Patterns** tab, and then click the **Fill Effects** button to display the Fill Effects dialog box. Click the **Pattern** tab to display the Pattern palette. See Figure 4-22.

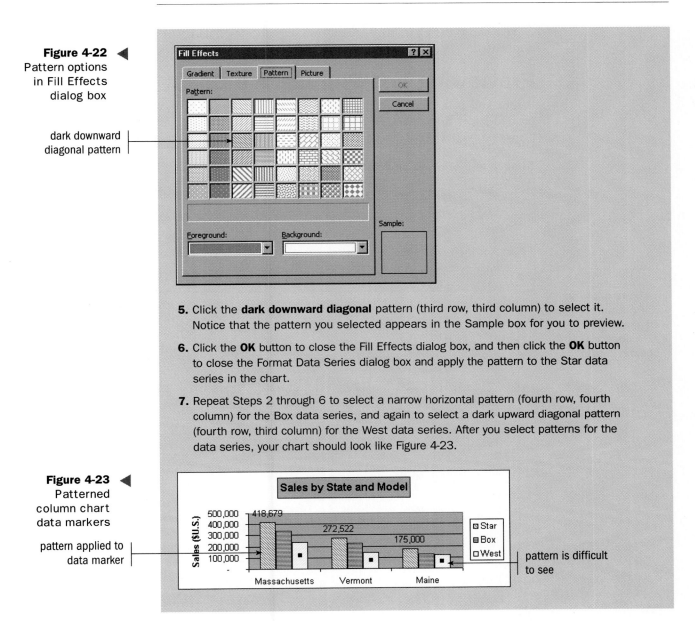

Figure 4-22 ◀
Pattern options
in Fill Effects
dialog box

dark downward
diagonal pattern

5. Click the **dark downward diagonal** pattern (third row, third column) to select it. Notice that the pattern you selected appears in the Sample box for you to preview.

6. Click the **OK** button to close the Fill Effects dialog box, and then click the **OK** button to close the Format Data Series dialog box and apply the pattern to the Star data series in the chart.

7. Repeat Steps 2 through 6 to select a narrow horizontal pattern (fourth row, fourth column) for the Box data series, and again to select a dark upward diagonal pattern (fourth row, third column) for the West data series. After you select patterns for the data series, your chart should look like Figure 4-23.

Figure 4-23 ◀
Patterned
column chart
data markers

pattern applied to
data marker

pattern is difficult
to see

You notice that the West markers appear to have no pattern applied because the pattern is very difficult to see when applied against the yellow color. You decide to change the color of the West markers to a darker color—green, so the pattern will be more visible.

To change the color of data markers:

1. If the West data markers are not selected, click any one of them to select the data markers for that data series.

2. Click the **Format Data Series** button 📑 on the Chart toolbar to display the Format Data Series dialog box.

3. If necessary, click the **Patterns** tab, click the **Fill Effects** button, and then click the **Pattern** tab in the Fill Effects dialog box to display the patterns palette.

4. In the Pattern tab, click the **Background** list arrow to display a color palette. Click the **green** square in the third row, third column, and click the **OK** button to close the Fill Effects dialog box and return to the Format Data Series dialog box.

5. Click the **OK** button to close the Format Data Series dialog box, and then click anywhere outside the chart border to deselect the chart.

You show the chart to Andrea, and she decides that it is ready to be printed and duplicated for distribution at the meeting.

Previewing and Printing the Chart

Before you print you should preview the worksheet to see how it will appear on the printed page. Remember, Andrea wants the embedded chart and the worksheet data to print on one page that she can use as a handout at the meeting.

To save and print an embedded chart:

1. Click the **Save** button 🖫 on the Standard toolbar to save the workbook.

2. Click the **Print Preview** button 🔍 on the Standard toolbar to display the Print Preview window.

3. Click the **Print** button to display the Print dialog box, and then click the **OK** button. See Figure 4-24.

Figure 4-24 ◀
Printout of worksheet with embedded column chart

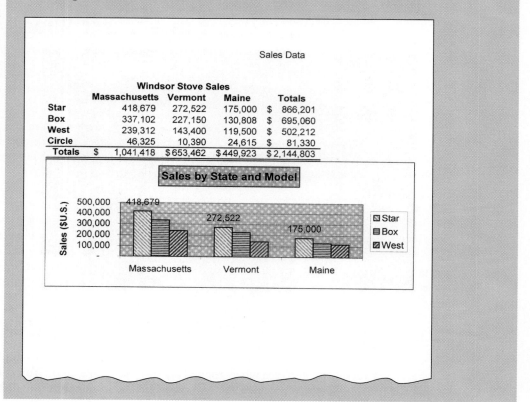

Quick Check

1. A column chart is used to show _____.

2. When you click an embedded chart, it is _____

3. Explain how to revise a chart's data series.

4. How do you move an embedded chart to a new location using the mouse?

5. Describe the action you're likely to take before beginning Step 1 of the Chart Wizard.

6. What happens when you change a value in a worksheet that is the source of data for a chart?

7   What is the purpose of a legend?

8   Explain the difference between a data point and a data marker.

You have finished creating the column chart showing stove sales by state and model for Andrea. Next, you need to create the pie chart showing total stove sales by model. You will do this in Session 4.2.

SESSION

4.2

In this session you will create a pie chart. You will also learn how to select nonadjacent ranges, how to change a 2-D pie chart to a 3-D pie chart, and how to "explode" a slice from a pie chart. You will also learn how to use chart sheets and how to add a border to a chart.

Creating a Chart in a Chart Sheet

Now Andrea wants to show the contribution of each Windsor model to the total stove sales. Recall from the planning sketch she did (Figure 4-5) that she wants to use a pie chart to show this relationship.

A pie chart shows the relationship, or proportions, of parts to a whole. The size of each slice is determined by the value of that data point in relation to the total of all values. A pie chart contains only one data series. When you create a pie chart, you generally specify two ranges. Excel uses the first range for the category labels and the second range for the data series. Excel automatically calculates the percentage for each slice, draws the slice to reflect the percentage of the whole, and gives you the option of displaying the percentage as a label in the completed chart.

Andrea's sketch (see Figure 4-5) shows estimates of each stove's contribution and how she wants the pie chart to look. The pie chart will have four slices, one for each stove model. She wants each slice labeled with the stove model's name and its percentage of total sales. Because she doesn't know the exact percentages until Excel calculates and displays them in the chart, she put "__%" on her sketch to show where she wants the percentages to appear.

Creating a Pie Chart

You begin creating a pie chart by selecting the data to be represented from the worksheet. You refer to your worksheet and note in the sketch that the data labels for the pie slices are in cells A3 through A6 and the data points representing the pie slices are in cells E3 through E6. You must select these two ranges to tell the Chart Wizard the data that you want to chart, but you realize that these ranges are not located next to each other in the worksheet. You know how to select a series of adjacent cells; now you need to learn how to select two separate ranges at once.

Selecting Nonadjacent Ranges

A **nonadjacent range** is a group of individual cells or ranges that are not next to each other. Selecting nonadjacent ranges is particularly useful when you construct charts because the cells that contain the data series and these that contain the data labels are often not side by side in the worksheet. When you select nonadjacent ranges, the selected cells in each range are highlighted. You can then format the cells, clear them, or use them to construct a chart.

SELECTING NONADJACENT RANGES

- Click the first cell or highlight the first range you want to select.
- Press and hold the Ctrl key while you click additional cells or highlight additional ranges.
- After you select all the cells you want to include, release the Ctrl key.

Now select the nonadjacent ranges to be used to create the pie chart.

To select range A3:A6 and range E3:E6 in the Sales Data sheet:

1. If you took a break after the last session, make sure that Excel is running, the Cast Iron Concepts workbook is open, and the Sales Data worksheet is displayed.

2. Click anywhere outside the chart border to make sure the chart is not activated. Press **Ctrl + Home** to make cell A1 the active cell.

3. Select cells **A3** through **A6**, and then release the mouse button.

4. Press and hold the **Ctrl** key while you select cells **E3** through **E6**, and then release the mouse and the Ctrl key. The two nonadjacent ranges are now selected: A3:A6 and E3:E6. See Figure 4-25.

   TROUBLE? If you don't select the cells you want on your first try, click any cell to remove the highlighting, then go back to Step 2 and try again.

Figure 4-25 ◄
Selecting nonadjacent cell ranges

nonadjacent ranges selected

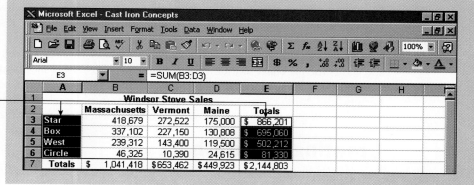

This time you'll place your new chart in a **chart sheet,** a special sheet that contains only one chart. It does not have the rows and columns of a regular worksheet. If you have many charts to create, you may want to place each chart in a separate chart sheet to avoid cluttering the worksheet. This approach also makes it easier to locate a particular chart because you can change the name on the chart sheet tab.

To create a pie chart in a chart sheet:

1. Click the **Chart Wizard** button 📊 on the Standard toolbar to display the Chart Wizard - Step 1 of 4 - Chart Type dialog box.

   TROUBLE? If the Office Assistant appears on your screen, click the button next to the message "No, don't provide help now" to close the Office Assistant.

   You want to create a pie chart.

2. Click the **Pie** chart type to select it. Six Pie chart subtypes are displayed. The Two-dimensional Pie chart subtype is the default subtype for the Pie chart type. Click the **Press and hold to view sample** button to display a preview of the Pie chart type.

You decide to use the default chart subtype.

3. Click the **Next** button to display the Chart Wizard - Step 2 of 4 - Chart Source Data dialog box. Make sure the Data range text box displays "='Sales Data'!$A$3:$A$6,'Sales Data'!$E$3:$E$6." This dialog box also displays a preview of your chart.

   TROUBLE? If the range shown on your screen is not "='Sales Data'!$A$3:$A$6, 'Sales Data'!$E$3:$E$6," type the necessary corrections in the Data range text box, or click the Collapse Dialog button located to the right of the Data range text box and select the correct range in the worksheet.

4. Click the **Next** button to display the Chart Wizard - Step 3 of 4 - Chart Options dialog box.

   Add a title for the chart.

5. If necessary, click the **Titles** tab, click the **Chart title** text box, and then type **Sales by Model** for the chart title. Notice that the title appears in the preview area.

6. Click the **Data Labels** tab, and then click the **Show label and percent** option button to place the label and percent next to each slice.

   Now remove the legend because it is no longer needed.

7. Click the **Legend** tab, and then click the **Show legend** check box to remove the check and deselect that option.

8. Click the **Next** button to display the Chart Wizard - Step 4 of 4 - Chart Location dialog box. Recall that in the fourth dialog box you decide where to place the chart. You can place a chart in a worksheet, or place it in its own chart sheet. You want to place this chart in a chart sheet.

9. Click the **As new sheet** option button to place the chart in the Chart1 chart sheet.

   You have finished the steps in the Chart Wizard.

10. Click the **Finish** button to complete the chart. The new chart, along with the Chart toolbar, appears in the chart sheet named Chart1. The chart sheet is inserted into the workbook before the worksheet on which it is based. If necessary, click the white portion of chart area to select the chart. See Figure 4-26.

Figure 4-26 ◄
Pie chart in a chart sheet

default name for first chart sheet

After reviewing the pie chart, Andrea asks you to change the current pie chart to a three-dimensional design to give the chart a more professional look.

Changing the Chart Type from 2-D to 3-D

As you recall, Excel provides 14 different chart types that you can choose from as you create a chart. You can also access these chart types after the chart is created and change from one type to another. To change the chart type, you can use the Chart Type command on the Chart menu or the Chart Type button on the Chart toolbar to make this change. You'll use the Chart toolbar to change this 2-D pie chart to a 3-D pie chart.

To change the pie chart to a 3-D pie chart:

1. Make sure the chart area is selected, and then click the **Chart Type** 📊 arrow on the Chart toolbar to display a palette of chart types. See Figure 4-27.

    TROUBLE? If the Chart toolbar is not displayed on the screen, click View on the menu bar, point to Toolbars, and click the Chart check box to display the Chart toolbar.

Figure 4-27 ◄
Palette of chart types

palette of chart types

3-D Pie Chart

2. Click the **3-D Pie Chart** sample 🍩 in the fifth row of the second column. The chart is redisplayed as a 3-D pie chart. See Figure 4-28.

Figure 4-28 ◀
3-D pie chart

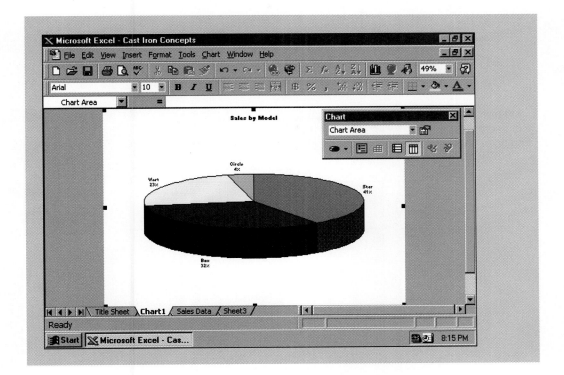

In her presentation, Andrea plans to emphasize the importance of the Star model because it is her best-selling model in the New England territory. She decides to "explode" the Star slice.

Exploding a Slice of a Pie Chart

When you create a pie chart, you may want to focus attention on a particular slice in the chart. You can present the data so a viewer can easily see which slice is larger or smaller—for example, which product sold the most. One method of emphasizing a particular slice over others is by separating the slice from the rest of the pie. The *cut* slice is more distinct because it is not connected to the other slices. A pie chart with one or more slices separated from the whole is referred to as an **exploded pie chart.**

REFERENCE
window

EXPLODING A SLICE OF A PIE CHART

- Click the pie chart, and then click the slice you want to explode.
- Drag the selected slice away from the center of the chart.

Andrea asks you to explode the slice that represents sales for the Star model.

To explode the slice that represents the Star model sales:

1. Click anywhere in the pie chart to select it. One selection handle appears on each pie slice and the Name box indicates that Series 1 is the selected chart object.

2. Now that you have selected the entire pie, you can select one part of it, the Star slice. Position the pointer over the slice that represents Star model sales. As you move the pointer over this slice, the ScreenTip "Series 1 Point: "Star" Value: $866,201 (41%)" is displayed. Click to select the slice. Selection handles now appear on only this slice.

3. With the pointer on the selected slice, click and hold down the mouse button while dragging the slice to the right, away from the center of the pie chart. As you drag the slice, an outline of the slice marks your progress.

4. Release the mouse button to leave the slice in the new position. See Figure 4-29.

Figure 4-29 ◀
Pie chart with
exploded slice

exploded slice ────

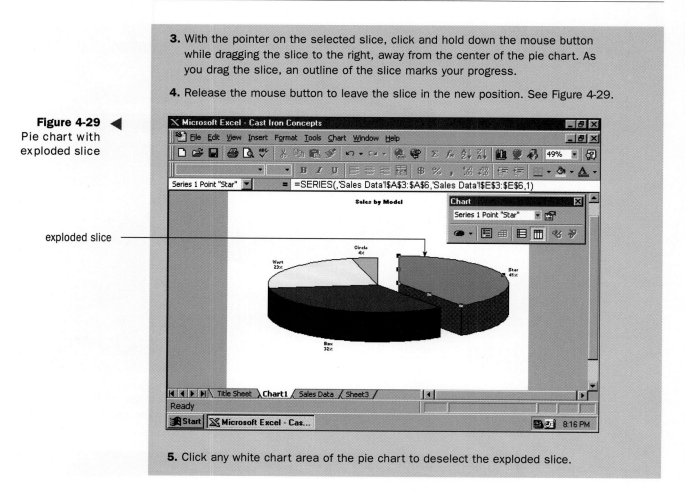

5. Click any white chart area of the pie chart to deselect the exploded slice.

The Star model now is exploded in the pie chart, but Andrea still isn't satisfied. You suggest moving the slice to the front of the pie.

Rotating a 3-D Chart

When working with a 3-D chart, you can modify the view of your chart to change its perspective, elevation, or rotation. You can change the elevation to look down on the chart or up from the bottom. You can also rotate the chart to adjust the placement of objects on the chart. Now rotate the chart so that the Star slice appears at the front of the chart.

To change the 3-D view of the chart:

1. Click **Chart** on the menu bar, and then click **3-D View** to display the 3-D View dialog box. See Figure 4-30.

Figure 4-30 ◀
3-D View dialog
box

clockwise rotation
arrow button

2. Click the **clockwise rotation arrow** button until the Rotation box shows 90; as you do this, notice that the pie chart sketch rotates to show the new position.

3. Click the **OK** button to apply the changes. See Figure 4-31.

Figure 4-31 ◀
3-D pie chart after view rotated to display cut slice in front

After looking over the chart, you decide to increase the size of the chart labels so that they are easier to read.

Formatting Chart Labels

You can change the font type, size, style, and the color of text in a chart using the Formatting toolbar buttons.

You look at the chart and decide that it will look better if you increase the size of the data labels from 10 to 14 points.

To change the font size of the chart labels:

1. Click any one of the four data labels to select all the data labels. Selection handles appear around all four labels, and the Name box displays "Series 1 Data Labels."

2. Click the **Font Size** list arrow on the Formatting toolbar, and then click **14**.

Now increase the font size of the title to 20 points.

To change the font size of the chart title:

1. Click the **chart title** to select it. Selection handles appear around the title.

2. Click the **Font Size** list arrow on the Formatting toolbar, and then click **20**.

3. Click any white area of the pie chart to deselect the title. See Figure 4-32.

Figure 4-32
3-D pie chart
after font size
of data labels
and title
increased

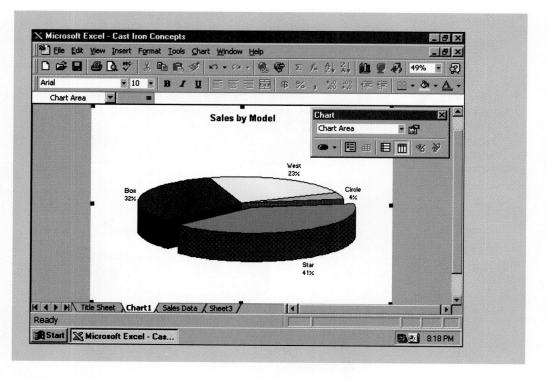

The pie chart looks good but Andrea has one last request. She asks you to apply a blue texture to the chart background.

Applying a Texture Fill Effect to the Chart Background

You can apply texture or gradient fill effects to chart walls, floors, bars, columns, and chart and plot background areas. These fill effects provide a professional look. You want to change the white chart area of the pie chart to a blue texture.

To apply a texture fill effect to the chart background:

1. Make sure the chart area is selected. If it is not, click the white area around the pie chart.

2. Click the **Format Chart Area** button 🔲 on the Chart toolbar to display the Format Chart Area dialog box.

3. If necessary, click the **Patterns** tab, click the **Fill Effects** button to display the Fill Effects dialog box, and then click the **Texture** tab. See Figure 4-33.

Figure 4-33 ◄
Texture options
in Fill Effects
dialog box

blue tissue
paper texture

4. Click the **Blue tissue paper** texture box (third row, first column).

5. Click the **OK** button twice to apply the texture to the chart area. See Figure 4-34.

Figure 4-34 ◄
Completed 3-D
pie chart

The chart is now complete. You decide to print it and show it to Andrea.

Printing the Chart from the Chart Sheet

When you create a chart in a separate sheet, you can print that sheet separately. If necessary, you can make page setup decisions for the chart sheet alone. In this case, the chart in the chart sheet is ready for printing. You don't need to change any setup options. Now that the 3-D pie chart is complete, save the workbook and print a copy of the chart.

To save the workbook and print the chart:

1. Click the **Save** button 🖫 on the Standard toolbar to save the workbook.

2. Click the **Print** button 🖨 on the Standard toolbar to print the chart.

Andrea is pleased with the printed chart and believes it will help her when she makes her presentation next week.

Creating a Bar Chart

Andrea decides to spend some time during her presentation reviewing sales of all stoves in each state in her territory. She recalls from one of her college classes that both the bar and column chart are useful for comparing data by categories. The bar chart may have an advantage if you have long labels, because the category labels in bar charts are easier to read. Andrea asks you to prepare a bar chart comparing sales of all stoves by state.

To prepare this chart, you will first select the cells containing the chart you will display. For this chart, select the range B2 through D2 for the category axis (states) and B7 through D7 for the data series (total sales in each state).

To select range B2:D2 and range B7:D7 in the Sales Data sheet:

1. Click the **Sales Data** tab to activate the Sales Data worksheet, and then press **Ctrl + Home** to make cell A1 the active cell.

2. Select cells **B2:D2**, and then release the mouse button.

3. Press and hold the **Ctrl** key while you select cells **B7:D7**, and then release the mouse and the Ctrl key. The two nonadjacent ranges are now selected: B2:D2 and B7:D7.

   TROUBLE? If you don't select the cells you want on your first try, click any cell to remove the highlighting, and then go back to Step 2 and try again.

Place the bar chart in a separate chart sheet so that Andrea can easily locate it.

To create a bar chart in a chart sheet:

1. Click the **Chart Wizard** button 📊 on the Standard toolbar to display the Chart Wizard - Step 1 of 4 - Chart Type dialog box.

   You want to create a bar chart.

2. Click the **Bar** chart type to select it. Six Bar chart subtypes are displayed. The Clustered Bar chart is the default subtype for the Bar chart. Click the **Press and hold to view sample** button to display a preview of the Clustered Bar chart subtype.

   You decide to use the Clustered Bar chart type.

3. Click the **Next** button to display the Chart Wizard - Step 2 of 4 - Chart Source Data dialog box. Make sure the Data range box displays "='Sales data'!$B$2:$D$2,'Sales Data'!$B$7:$D$7." This dialog box also displays a preview of your chart.

   TROUBLE? If the range shown on your screen is not "='Sales data'!$B$2:$D$2, 'Sales Data'!$B$7:$D$7," type the necessary corrections in the Data range text box, or click the Collapse Dialog button and select the correct range in the worksheet.

4. Click the **Next** button to display the Chart Wizard - Step 3 of 4 - Chart Options dialog box.

   Add a title for the chart.

5. If necessary, click the **Titles** tab, and then click the **Chart title** text box. Type **Sales by State** for the chart title. Notice that the title appears in the preview area. Click the **Category (X) axis** title box, and then type **Territories**. Click the **Value (Y) axis** title box, and then type **Sales ($U.S.)**.

   Since there is only one data series, remove the legend.

6. Click the **Legend** tab and then click the **Show legend** check box to remove the check and deselect that option.

7. Click the **Next** button to display the Chart Wizard - Step 4 of 4 - Chart Location dialog box. You want this chart to be placed in a chart sheet.

8. Click the **As new sheet** option button to place this chart in a chart sheet, and then type **Bar Chart** in the As new sheet text box to rename the chart sheet.

   You have finished the steps in the Chart Wizard.

9. Click the **Finish** button to complete the chart. The new chart, along with the Chart toolbar, appears in the chart sheet named Bar Chart. The chart sheet is inserted into the workbook before the worksheet on which it is based. See Figure 4-35.

Figure 4-35 ◀
Bar chart in a
chart sheet

categories are
organized vertically

values are displayed
horizontally

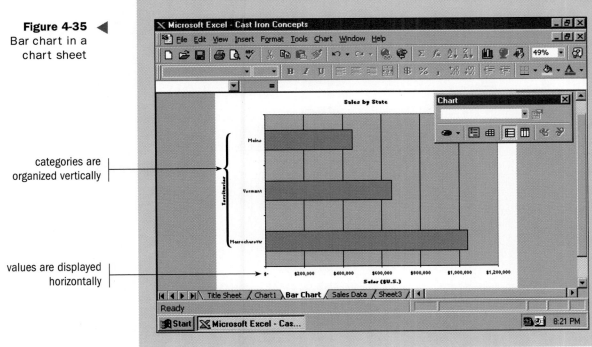

Andrea reviews the bar chart and believes it will focus the audience's attention on sales in each state.

Using Pictures in a Bar Chart

When making a presentation, an interesting way to enhance a bar or column chart is to replace the data markers with graphic images, thereby creating a picture chart. Any graphic image that can be copied to the Clipboard can serve as the basis for a picture chart. Andrea wants you to use a picture of the Windsor stove from CIC's latest catalog as the data marker in your bar chart.

REFERENCE
window

USING A PICTURE IN A BAR OR COLUMN CHART

- Create a bar or column chart using the Chart Wizard.
- Select all the bars or columns you want to replace with the picture.
- Click Insert, point to Picture, and then click From File to display the Insert Picture dialog box.
- Select the image file you want to use.
- Click Insert.

The graphic image of the Windsor stove is located in the Tutorial.04 folder on your Student Disk. The file is named Stove. To replace the plain bars with the graphic image, you need to select one bar or column of the chart and use the Picture command on the Insert menu.

To insert the picture into the bar chart:

1. Click any column in the chart so that all three data markers are selected.

2. Click **Insert** on the menu bar, point to **Picture,** and then click **From File** to display the Insert Picture dialog box.

3. Make sure Tutorial.04 is the folder shown in the Look In list box, and then click **Stove**.

4. Click the **Insert** button to insert the picture into the chart. The three bars are each filled by the picture of the stove. See Figure 4-36. Notice that each picture is "stretched" to fit the bar it fills.

Figure 4-36 ◀
Picture chart
with stretched
graphic

Stove graphic ——————

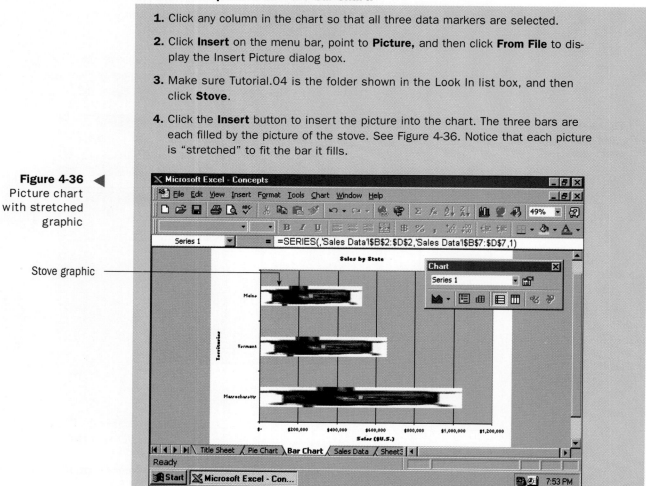

When you insert a picture into a bar or column chart, Excel automatically stretches the picture to fill the space formerly occupied by the marker. Some pictures stretch well, but others become distorted, and detract from, rather than add to, the chart's impact.

Stretching and Stacking Pictures

As an alternative to stretching a picture, you can stack the picture so that it appears repeatedly in the bar, reaching the height of the original bar in the chart. You'll stack the Windsor stove picture in your chart to improve its appearance.

The value axis has tick mark labels at 200000, 400000, 600000, and so on. To match the axis labels, you'll stack one stove each 200000 units.

To stack the picture:

1. If the handles have disappeared from the bars, click any bar in the chart to select all the bars.

2. Click the **Format Data Series** button on the Chart toolbar to display the Format Data Series dialog box, and if necessary, click the **Patterns** tab.

3. Click the **Fill Effects** button to display the Fill Effects dialog box, and then click the **Picture** tab.

4. Click the **Stack and scale to** option button. Accept the Units/Picture value.

5. Click the **OK** button to close the Fill Effects dialog box, and then click the **OK** button to close the Format Data Series dialog box and return to the chart sheet and display the data markers as stacked stoves.

6. Click the white area of the chart to deselect the data markers. See Figure 4-37.

Figure 4-37 ◄
Picture chart
with stacked
graphic

stacked graphic
image

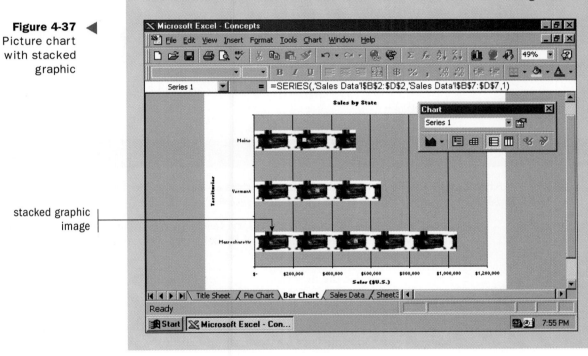

Andrea likes the picture chart, but is not sure how her audience will react to this type of chart. She wants to think about it. She asks you to save the workbook with the picture chart included and will let you know in the morning whether to print the picture chart or return to the bar chart. If Andrea asks you to remove the pictures and return to the original bars for the data markers, you will select the data series, click Edit, click Clear, and then click Formats.

Now save the workbook.

To save the workbook:

1. Click the **Title Sheet** tab to make it the active worksheet.

2. Click the **Save** button on the Standard toolbar.

3. Close the workbook and exit Excel.

Quick Check

1. Define the following terms in relation to a pie chart:
   a. data point
   b. data marker
   c. data series

2. Explain how to select cells A1, C5, and D10 at the same time.

3. What type of chart shows the proportion of parts to a whole?

4. When creating charts, why is it important to know how to select nonadjacent ranges?

5. Explain the difference between an embedded chart and a chart placed in a chart sheet.

6. Explain how to rotate a 3-D pie chart.

7. Explain how to explode a slice from a pie chart.

8. When you change a two-dimensional pie chart to a 3-D pie chart, you change the _____.

You have finished creating the column chart, pie chart, and bar chart that Andrea needs for her presentation.

Tutorial Assignments

After having the night to think about it, Andrea comes to work the next morning and asks you to create one more chart for her presentation. Do the following:

1. Start Windows and Excel, if necessary. Insert your Student Disk into the disk drive. Make sure that the Excel and Book1 windows are maximized. Open the file Concept2 in the TAssign folder for Tutorial 4.

2. Save the file under the new name Cast Iron Concepts 2 in the TAssign folder.

3. Type your name and the current date in the Title Sheet sheet.

4. In the Sales Data sheet select the nonadjacent ranges that contain the models (A3:A6) and the total sales for each model (E3:E6).

5. Use the Chart Wizard to create a clustered column chart with 3-D visual effect. Place the completed chart in a chart sheet.

6. As you are creating the chart, remove the legend and add "Total Stove Sales by State" as the chart title.

7. Rename the chart sheet "3D Column."

8. After the chart is completed, increase the font size of the title and axis labels so that they are easier to read.

 9. Put a box around the chart's title, using a thick line for a border. Add a drop shadow to the border.

10. Save the workbook. Print the chart. Include your name, the filename, and the date in the footer for the printed chart.

 11. Select the walls chart element and apply a 1-color gradient fill effect. You select an appropriate color.

 12. Select the value axis and change its scale so that the major unit is 150000.

13. Open the Office Assistant and learn how you can show the worksheet data in a data table, which is a grid at the bottom of the chart. (*Hint*: Search on "add data table to a chart.") Add a data table to your chart. Increase the font size associated with the data table.

14. Save the workbook, and then print the chart.

15. Switch to the Sales Data worksheet and do the following:

 a. Change the color of the West Windsor pattern to brown.

 b. Move the legend to the bottom of the chart. Increase the height of the chart, so it has a more professional look.

 c. Annotate the column chart with the note "Star model—best seller in Massachusetts!" by adding a text box and arrow using the tools on the Drawing toolbar.

 d. Save the workbook, and then print the Sales Data sheet with the embedded chart.

Case Problems

1. Illustrating Production Data at TekStar Electronics You are executive assistant to the President of TekStar Electronics, a manufacturer of consumer electronics. You are compiling the yearly manufacturing reports and have collected production totals for each of TekStar's four U.S. manufacturing plants. The workbook TekStar contains these totals. Now you need to create a 3-D pie chart showing the relative percentage of CD players each plant produced.

1. Open the workbook Tekstar in the Case folder for Tutorial 4 and add the necessary information to the Title Sheet sheet to create a summary of the workbook. Save the workbook as TekStar Electronics in the Case folder for Tutorial 4.

2. Activate the Units Sold sheet. Use the Chart Wizard to create a 3-D pie chart in a chart sheet that shows the percentage of CD players produced at each plant location. Use the Pie with 3-D Visual Effect subtype.

3. Enter "Production of CD Players" as the chart title. Show "Label" and "Percent" as the data labels. Remove the legend.

4. Pull out the slice representing the Chicago plant's CD player production.

5. Increase the font size of the title and data labels so that they are easier to read.

6. Name the chart sheet 3D Pie Chart.

7. Preview and print the chart sheet. Save your work.

8. Create an embedded chart comparing sales of all the products by city. Select the appropriate range and then use the Chart Wizard to create a clustered bar chart. Use the products as the data series and the cities as the X-axis (category) labels. Enter "Production by Product and Plant Location" as the title.

9. Move the bar chart under the table, and then enhance the chart in any way you think appropriate.

10. Preview and print the embedded bar chart. Save your work.

11. Create a clustered column chart with 3-D visual effect comparing the production of VCRs by city. Remove the legend. Place the chart in a chart sheet named "VCRs."

    a. Add a data table (a grid in a chart that contains the numeric data used to create the chart) to the chart. (*Hint*: Use the Office Assistant to find out how to add a data table to a chart.)

    b. Save the workbook, and then print the chart.

2. Dow Jones Charting You are working for a stock analyst who is planning to publish a weekly newsletter. One regular component of the newsletter will be a 15-week chart tracking the Dow Jones average. Create the chart that can be used for the newsletter.

1. Open the workbook DowJones in the Case folder for Tutorial 4. Save the workbook as Dow Jones 8-2-96 in the Case folder for Tutorial 4.

2. Use the Chart Wizard to create an embedded line chart (Line subtype) in the Data worksheet. Specify "Dow Jones Average" as the chart title and "Index" as the title for the Y-axis. Do not add a legend or X-axis title.

3. Place the chart to the right of the present worksheet data and resize it until you are satisfied with its appearance.

4. Edit the chart as follows:

    a. Change the line marker to a thick line.
    b. Apply a texture fill effect to the chart area. You decide the texture.
    c. Change the color of the plot area to a shade of yellow.
    d. Angle the text upward for the dates on the category axis.

5. Save your workbook. Preview and print the embedded chart.

6. Add the text box "Inflation Worries Wall Street" pointing to 7-26-96.

7. Save your workbook. Print the chart.

8. The Dow Jones average for the week ending 8-9-96 was 5500.

    a. Add this data to the last row of the worksheet.
    b. Modify the chart by plotting the 15-week period beginning 5-3-96 and ending 8-9-96.
    c. Save the workbook as Dow Jones 8-9-96. Preview your work and print only the chart. Center the chart vertically and horizontally on the page.

3. *New York Chronicle* You are working as an intern for Jeff Sindle, business economist, of the *New York Chronicle*—a New York newspaper with circulation in New York City and Long Island. The paper is planning to publish an economic profile of the region and you are assisting in this project.

1. Open the workbook NewYork in the Case folder for Tutorial 4. Save the workbook as New York Economic Data. Create three charts, each in its own chart sheet.

2. First, create a 3-D pie chart that compares the population of the six geographic areas in the study. Title the chart and enhance it as you think appropriate. Rename the chart sheet to reflect the chart it contains.

3. Create a clustered column chart that compares the number of establishments in retail and services by the six geographic areas. (*Hint*: Categorize by type of establishment; each geographic area is a data series.) Title the chart and enhance it as you think appropriate. Rename the chart sheet to reflect the chart it contains.

4. Create a clustered bar chart comparing sales/receipts by geographic area (categorize by geographic area; the data series is sales/receipts). Title the chart and enhance it as you think appropriate. Rename the chart sheet to reflect the chart it contains.

5. Add a title sheet that includes your name, date created, purpose, and a brief description of each sheet in the workbook.

6. Save the workbook.

7. Print the entire workbook (title and data worksheet and the three chart sheets).

4. Duplicating a Printed Chart Look through books, business magazines, or textbooks for your other courses to find an attractive chart. Select one, photocopy it, and create a worksheet that contains the data displayed in the chart. You can estimate the data values plotted in the chart. Do your best to duplicate the chart you found. You might not be able to duplicate the chart fonts or colors exactly, but choose the closest available substitutes. When your work is complete, save it as Duplicate Chart in the Case folder for Tutorial 4, preview it, and print it. Submit the photocopy of the original as well as the printout of the chart you created.

Answers to Quick Check Questions

SESSION 1.1

1 cell

2 open

3 D2

4 b

5 click the "Sheet2" sheet tab

6 press Ctrl + Home

SESSION 1.2

1 8; D1 + E1 + F1 + G1+ H1 + I1 + J1 + K1

2 B4, B5, B6, C4, C5, C6, D4, D5, D6

3 a. text
  b. value
  c. value
  d. formula
  e. text
  f. formula
  g. text

4 Active sheet(s), Print

5 Print, File

6 c

7 When you exit Excel, the workbook is erased from RAM. So if you want to use the workbook again you need to save it to disk. Click File, then click Save As.

8 press the Delete key

9 revising the contents of one or more cells in a worksheet and observing the effect this change has on all other cells in the worksheet

SESSION 2.1

1 Select the cell where you want the sum to appear. Click the AutoSum button. Excel suggests a formula which includes the SUM function. To accept the formula press the Enter key.

2 =A6+B6

3 cell references. If you were to copy the formula to other cells, these cells are relative references

4 absolute reference

5 Windows clipboard

6 fill-handle

7 double-click the sheet tab, then type the new name, then press the Enter key or click any cell in the worksheet to accept the entry

8 determine the purpose of the worksheet, enter the data and formulas, test the worksheet; correct errors, improve the appearance, document the worksheet, save and print

SESSION 2.2

1 select

2 header

3 Autoformat

4 Click any cell in the row above which you want to insert a row. Click Insert, then click Row

5 c

6 Assuming you are entering a formula with a function, first select the cell where you want to place a formula, type =, the function name and a left parenthesis, then click and drag over the range of cells to be used in the formula. Press the Enter key.

7 click Tools, click Options, then in the View tab, click the Formula check box

8 Landscape

SESSION 3.1

1 a. 13%; b. $0.13

2 Click Format, click Cells; right-click mouse in cell you want to format; use buttons on the Formatting toolbar

3 the data in the cell is formatted with the Comma style using two decimal places

4 Left Align button, Center button, Right Align button, and Merge and Center button

5 Center column headings, right-align numbers, and left-align text

6 Position the mouse pointer over the column header, right-click the mouse and click Column Width. Enter the new column width in the Column Width dialog box. Position the mouse pointer over the right edge of the column you want to modify, then click and drag to increase the column width.

7 Format Painter button

8 The column width of a cell is not wide enough to display the numbers, and you need to increase the column width

SESSION 3.2

1 use the Borders Tab on the Format Cells dialog box, or the Borders button on the Formatting toolbar

2 Click the Drawing button on the Standard toolbar

3 select

4 text box

5 Portrait

6 Click Tools, click View tab, then click the Gridlines check box to remove the check from the check box

7 Excel (graphic) object

SESSION 4.1

1 comparisons among items or changes in data over a period of time

2 selected; also referred to as activated

3 Select the appropriate chart, click Chart Menu, then click Source Data. Click the Collapse dialog box button, then select values to be included in the chart, press the Enter key, then click the OK button

4 Select the chart, move the pointer over the chart area until the pointer changes to an arrow then click and drag to another location on the worksheet

5 select the range of cells to be used as the source of data for the chart

6 the data marker that represents that data point will change to reflect the new value

7 identifies the pattern or colors assigned to the data series in a chart

8 A data point is a value in the worksheet, while the data marker is the symbol (pie slice, column, bar, and so on) that represents the data point in the chart

SESSION 4.2

1 a. a value that originates from a worksheet cell
b. a slice in a pie chart that represents a single point
c. a group of related data points plotted in a pie chart that originate from rows or columns in a worksheet

2 Select the A1, then press and hold down the CTRL key and select cells C5 and D10

3 pie chart

4 often, the data you want to plot is not in adjacent cells

5 an embedded chart is a chart object placed in a worksheet and saved with the worksheet when the workbook is saved; a chart sheet is a sheet in a workbook that contains only a chart

6 Select the pie chart you want to rotate, click Chart on the menu bar then click 3-D View to display the 3-D View dialog box. Click either rotate button to rotate the chart.

7 Select the slice you want to "explode," then click and drag the slice away from the center.

8 chart type

Microsoft® Excel 97

LEVEL II

TUTORIALS

Read This **Before You Begin**

STUDENT DISKS

To complete Excel 97 Tutorials 5–7 you need 2 Student Disks. Your instructor will either provide you with Student Disks or ask you to make your own.

If you are supposed to make your own Student Disks, you will need 2 blank, formatted high-density disks. You will need to copy a set of folders from a file server or standalone computer onto your disks. Your instructor will tell you which computer, drive letter, and folders contain the files you need. The following table shows you which folders go on each of your disks, so that you will have enough disk space to complete all the tutorials, Tutorial Assignments, and Case Problems:

Student Disk	Write this on the disk label	Put these folders on the disk
1	Student Disk 1: Tutorials 5 and 7	Tutorial.05 and Tutorial.07
2	Student Disk 2: Tutorial 6	Tutorial.06

Please note, the Tutorial.05 and Tutorial.07 folders must go on Student Disk 1.

When you begin each tutorial, be sure you are using the correct Student Disk. See the inside front or inside back cover of this book for more information on Student Disk files, or ask your instructor or technical support person for assistance.

COURSE LAB

Tutorial 1 features an interactive Course Lab to help you understand spreadsheet concepts. There are Lab Assignments at the end of the tutorial that relate to this Lab. To start the Lab, click the Start button on the Windows 95 Taskbar, point to Programs, point to Course Labs, point to New Perspectives Applications, and click Spreadsheets.

USING YOUR OWN COMPUTER

If you are going to work through this book using your own computer, you need:

■ **Computer System** Microsoft Windows 95 or Microsoft Windows NT Workstation 4.0 (or a later version) and Microsoft Excel 97 must be installed on your computer. This book assumes a typical installation of Microsoft Excel 97.

■ **Student Disks** Ask your instructor or lab manager for details on how to get the Student Disks. You will not be able to complete the tutorials or end-of-tutorial assignments in this book using your own computer until you have Student Disks. The Student Files may also be obtained electronically over the Internet. See the inside front or inside back cover of this book for more details.

■ **Course Lab** See your instructor or technical support person to obtain the Course Lab software for use on your own computer.

To complete Excel 97 Tutorials 5–7 your students must use a set of files on 2 Student Disks. These files are included in the Instructor's Resource Kit, and they may also be obtained electronically over the Internet. See the inside front or inside back cover of this book for more details. Follow the instructions in the Readme file to copy the files to your server or standalone computer. You can view the Readme file using WordPad. Once the files are copied, you can make Student Disks for the students yourself, or you can tell students where to find the files so they can make their own Student Disks.

COURSE LAB SOFTWARE

The Course Lab software is distributed on a CD-ROM included in the Instructor's Resource Kit. Refer to the Readme file for essential technical notes related to running the Lab in a multi-user environment. Once you have installed the Course Lab software, your students can start the Lab from the Windows 95 desktop by following the instructions in the Course Lab section above.

COURSE TECHNOLOGY STUDENT FILES AND LAB SOFTWARE

You are granted a license to copy the Student Files and Course Lab software to any computer or computer network used by students who have purchased this book.

Working with Excel Lists

Managing Faculty Data at North State University

OBJECTIVES

In this tutorial you will:

- Identify the elements of an Excel list

- Freeze rows and columns

- Sort data in a list

- Use a data form to enter, search for, edit, and delete records

- Filter data in a list using AutoFilters

- Apply conditional formatting to a range

- Create natural language formulas

- Insert subtotals into a list

- Use the subtotals outline view

- Insert page breaks using Page Break Preview

- Summarize a list using pivot tables

CASE

North State University

Janice Long is the dean of the College of Business Administration at North State University. The College of Business Administration has three academic departments: management, marketing, and accounting. Each faculty member holds an academic rank, such as professor or associate professor. Most faculty members are hired as instructors or assistant professors. After a period of time, he or she might be promoted to associate professor and then to full professor. Faculty salaries usually reflect the faculty member's rank and length of service in the department.

The dean frequently asks you to locate and summarize information about the College of Business Administration faculty. This week, she has several important budget and staffing meetings to attend for which she will need to produce detailed and specific information on her faculty. She asks for your help to compile the necessary data. She has provided an Excel worksheet that contains the name, academic rank, department, hire date, salary, and sex of each faculty member in the College of Business Administration. She asks you to use the worksheet to create several reports that will organize the information to produce the specific output she requires for each meeting.

SESSION

5.1

You already know how to use Excel to perform calculations using numeric data or values you enter into worksheet cells. In this lesson you will learn how to use Excel to manage lists of data. You will discover how easy it is to sort the information in a worksheet, to add and delete data, and to search for specific information. You will also learn how to filter the information to display only data meeting certain criteria.

Introduction to Lists

One of the more common uses of a worksheet is to manage lists of data, such as client lists, phone lists, and transaction lists. Excel provides you with the tools to manage such tasks. Using Excel, you can store and update data, sort data, search for and retrieve data, summarize and compare data, and create reports.

In Excel a **list** is a collection of similar data stored in a structured manner, in rows and columns. Figure 5-1 shows a portion of the College of Business Administration faculty list. Within an Excel list, each column represents a **field** that describes some attribute or characteristic of an object, person, place, or thing. In this situation, a faculty member's last name, the department in which the faculty member works, and the faculty member's annual salary are examples of fields. When related fields are grouped together in a row, they form a **record**, a collection of fields that describes a person, place, or thing. For example, the data for each faculty member—first name, last name, department, rank, year hired, sex, and salary—represents a record. A collection of related records makes up an Excel list.

Figure 5-1 ◄
Portion of
faculty list

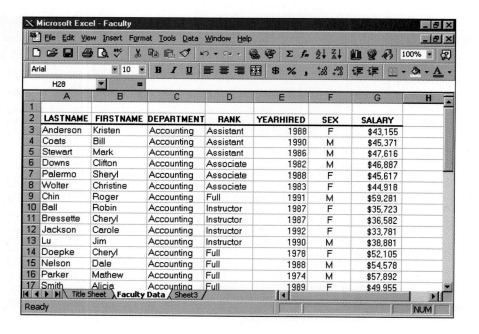

If you have worked with spreadsheets before, you may associate the term "database" with what Excel now calls a list. Since the introduction of Excel Version 5, Microsoft refers to database tables in Excel worksheets as lists. The term **database** refers to files created using database management software, such as dBASE, Access, and Paradox. In this tutorial we focus on Excel lists.

Planning and Creating a List

Before you create a list you will want to do some planning. As you spend time thinking about how you will use the list, consider the types of reports, queries, and searches you may need. This process should help you determine the kind of information to include for each record and the contents of each field. As with most projects, the planning you do will help you avoid redesigning the list later.

To create the faculty list she has given you to work with, the dean first determined her information requirements. As a way of documenting the information requirements of the faculty list, she developed a **data definition table** that describes the fields she plans to maintain for each faculty member at the College of Business Administration. Figure 5-2 shows the data definition table the dean developed to define her data requirements. She used this as a guide in creating the faculty list.

Figure 5-2 ◀
Data definition
table for
faculty list

Field Name	Description
LASTNAME	Faculty member's last name
FIRSTNAME	Faculty member's first name
DEPARTMENT	Name of department (accounting, finance, and management)
RANK	Faculty rank (instructor, assistant, associate, and full)
YEARHIRED	Year in which faculty member was hired
SEX	Female (F) or male (M)
SALARY	Annual salary

Once you determine the design of your list, you can create the list in a worksheet. You can use a blank worksheet, or one that already contains data.

When creating a list in Excel, use the following guidelines:

- The top row of the list should contain a **field name**, a unique label describing the contents of the data in the rows below it. This row of field names is sometimes referred to as the **field header row**.

- Field names can contain up to 255 characters. Usually a short name is easier to understand and remember. Short field names also enable you to display more fields on the screen at one time.

- You should boldface the field names, change the font, or use a different color to make it easier for Excel to distinguish between the data in the list and the field names.

- Each column should contain the same kind of information for each row in the list.

The list should be separated from any other information in the same worksheet by at least one blank row and one blank column because Excel automatically determines the range of the list by identifying blank rows and columns. For the same reason, you should avoid blank rows and columns within the list.

Now open the workbook the dean created to help you maintain the data on faculty at North State University's College of Business Administration.

To open the Faculty workbook:

1. Start Excel. Make sure your Student Disk is in the appropriate drive, and then open the workbook **Faculty** in the Tutorial.05 folder on your Student Disk, and immediately save it as **CBA Faculty**.

2. Switch to the **Faculty Data** sheet to display the faculty list. See Figure 5-3. The dean's worksheet contains the list of faculty at the College of Business Administration. Currently there are 41 faculty. Each faculty record is stored as a separate row (rows 3 through 43). There are seven fields for each faculty record (columns A through G). Notice that the field names have been boldfaced to make it easier for Excel to distinguish the field names from the data in the list.

To become familiar with the data, you decide to scroll the faculty list.

Figure 5-3 ◀
Faculty list

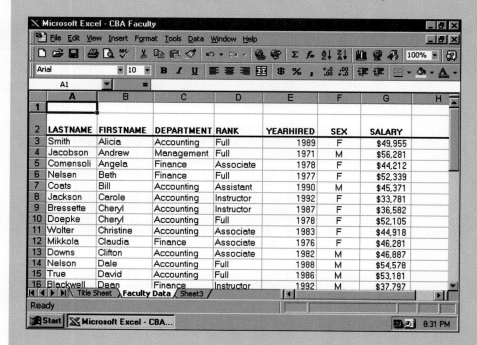

3. Click the **vertical scroll bar down arrow** to scroll to the bottom of the list (row 43). As you scroll, notice that the column headings are no longer visible.

4. After viewing the last record in the faculty list, press **Ctrl + Home** to return to cell A1.

You want to keep the column headings on the screen as you scroll the faculty list because not being able to see the column headings makes it difficult to know what the data in each column represents.

Freezing Rows and Columns

You can freeze rows and columns so they will not scroll off the screen as you move around the worksheet. This lets you keep headings on the screen as you work with the data in a large worksheet.

REFERENCE
window

FREEZING ROWS AND COLUMNS

■ Select the cell below and to the right of row(s) or column(s) you want to freeze.
■ Click Window, and then click Freeze Panes.

Excel

You decide to freeze the row with the column headings and the LASTNAME column so that they remain on the screen as you scroll the list.

To freeze rows and columns:

1. Click cell **B3** to make it the active cell.

2. Click **Window** on the menu bar, and then click **Freeze Panes** to freeze the rows above row 3 and the columns to the left of column B. Excel displays dark horizontal and vertical lines to indicate which rows and columns are frozen.

   Now scroll the list.

3. Click the **vertical scroll bar down arrow** to scroll down to the bottom of the list (row 43). As you scroll, notice that the column headings remain visible. See Figure 5-4.

dark horizontal and vertical lines indicate which columns and rows are frozen

Figure 5-4
Faculty list with column labels visible as you scroll

column labels remain on screen

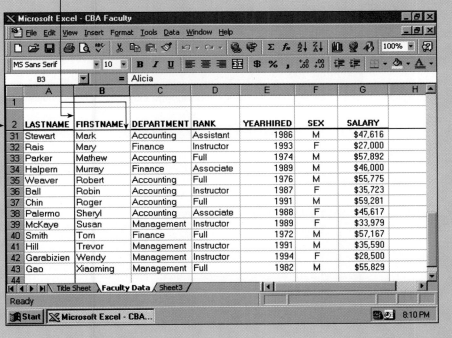

4. Click the **horizontal scroll bar right arrow**. As you scroll to the right, notice that column A, LASTNAME, remains visible.

5. Press **Ctrl + Home** to return to cell B3. Notice that Ctrl + Home no longer returns you to cell A1—instead it returns you to the cell directly below and to the right of the frozen row and column.

To unfreeze the rows and columns, you would select Unfreeze Panes from the Window menu.

Sorting Data

In preparation for her meetings this week, the dean wants a list of faculty members sorted by last name, so she can have quick access to faculty data when not near a computer. She asks you to prepare a list of all faculty, alphabetized by last name.

When you initially enter records into a list, each new record is placed at the bottom of the list. To rearrange records in a list, you sort based on the data in one or more of the fields (columns). The fields you use to order your data are called **sort fields** or **sort keys**.

For example, to sort the faculty list alphabetically by last name, you order the data using the values in the LASTNAME field. LASTNAME becomes the sort field. Because LASTNAME is the first sort field, and in this case the only sort field, it is the **primary** sort field.

Before you complete the sort, you will need to decide whether you want to put the list in ascending or descending order. **Ascending order** arranges labels alphabetically from A to Z, and numbers from smallest to largest. **Descending order** arranges labels in reverse alphabetical order from Z to A, and numbers from largest to smallest. In both ascending and descending order, any blank fields are placed at the bottom of the list. For the quick reference list of faculty, the dean wants to sort the list by last name in ascending order.

Sorting a List Using One Sort Field

To sort data in an Excel worksheet, you can use the Sort Ascending and Sort Descending buttons on the Standard toolbar, or you can use the Sort command on the Data menu. The easiest way to sort data when there is only one sort key is to use the Sort Ascending or Sort Descending buttons on the Standard toolbar. If you are sorting using more than one sort key, you should use the Sort command on the Data menu to specify the columns on which you want to sort.

REFERENCE window

SORTING USING A SINGLE SORT FIELD

- Click any cell in the column you want to sort by.
- Click the Sort Ascending or Sort Descending button on the Standard toolbar to sort the data.

Produce the dean's alphabetized list by sorting the faculty list using LASTNAME as the sort field.

To sort a list using a single sort field:

1. Click any cell in the LASTNAME column.

2. Click the **Sort Ascending** button on the Standard toolbar. The data is sorted in ascending order by last name. See Figure 5-5.

TROUBLE? If you selected the wrong column before sorting the list, and your data is sorted in the wrong order, you can undo it. To undo a sort, click the Undo button on the Standard toolbar.

Figure 5-5 ◀
Faculty list
sorted by
last name

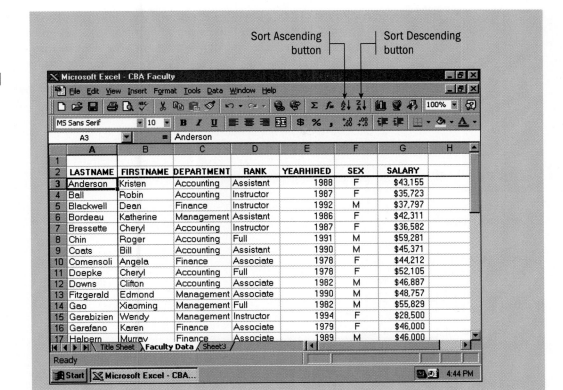

The dean also requests a list of faculty sorted alphabetically by department, and within each department, sorted alphabetically by last name.

Sorting a List Using More than One Sort Field

Sometimes sorting by one sort field results in ties. A **tie** occurs when more than one record has the same value for a field. For example, if you sort the faculty list on the DEPARTMENT field, all employees with the same department name would be grouped together. To break a tie you can sort the list on multiple fields. For example, you can sort the faculty list by department, and then by last name within each department. In this case, you specify the DEPARTMENT field as the **primary sort field** and the LASTNAME field as the **secondary sort field**.

REFERENCE
window

SORTING A LIST USING MORE THAN ONE SORT FIELD

- Click any cell in the list.
- Click Data, and then click Sort to display the Sort dialog box.
- Click the Sort By list arrow to display a list of column headings. Select the column you want to use as the primary sort field. Click the appropriate option button to specify sort order.
- Click the first Then By list box and use the list arrow to select the desired column heading for the secondary sort field. Click the appropriate option button to specify sort order.
- If you want to sort by a third column, click the second Then By list box and select the desired column heading. Click the appropriate option button to specify sort order.
- Click the OK button to sort the list.

The dean asked you to sort by department and then alphabetically by last name within each department. To prepare this second list, you will need to sort the data using two columns: DEPARTMENT will be the primary sort field and LASTNAME will be the secondary sort field. When you have more than one sort key, you should use the Sort command on the Data menu to specify the columns you want to sort.

Now sort the faculty list by department, and within department by last name.

To sort the records by department and within department by last name:

1. Click any cell in the list.

2. Click **Data** on the menu bar, and then click **Sort** to display the Sort dialog box. See Figure 5-6.

Figure 5-6 ◀
Sort dialog box

primary sort key ——

specify secondary
sort key here

specify third
sort key here

use to specify a
custom sort order

3. Click the **Sort By** list arrow to display the list of column headings, and then click **DEPARTMENT**.

4. If necessary, click the **Ascending** option button to specify that you want to sort the DEPARTMENT field in ascending order.

   Now specify the secondary sort field.

5. Click the first **Then By** list arrow to display the list of column headings, and then click **LASTNAME**.

6. Make sure the Ascending option button is selected.

7. Click the **OK** button to sort the records by department and within department by last name. See Figure 5-7.

Figure 5-7 ◀
Faculty list
sorted by
department
and within
department by
last name

sorted by last name
within accounting
department

sorted in ascending
order by department

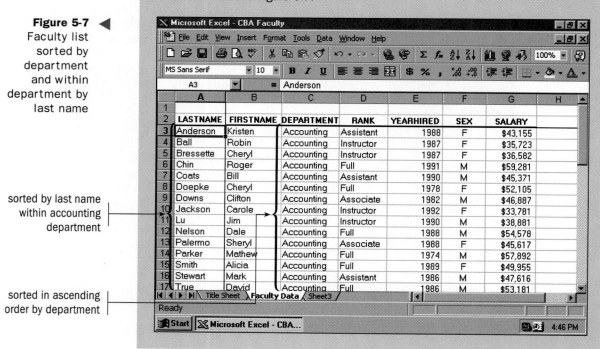

8. Scroll the list to view the data sorted by department and within department by last name.

9. Save the workbook.

Now the dean has a list of faculty members sorted by department and within department by last name. This will make finding information about faculty members much easier.

Maintaining a List Using a Data Form

The dean has several changes regarding the faculty status that need to be reflected in the faculty list. First, the accounting department has hired an instructor, Mary Hutch, to teach the introductory accounting courses. Her record needs to be added to the faculty list. Second, Kevin Mack just received official confirmation on his promotion to associate professor. Kevin's record must be updated to reflect his change in rank and new salary of $45,000. Finally, Wendy Garabizien retired at the end of the term; her record needs to be deleted from the faculty list. The dean asks you to update the faculty list to reflect these changes.

One of the easiest ways to maintain a list in Excel is to use a data form. A **data form** is a dialog box in which you can add, find, edit, and delete records in a list. A data form displays one record at a time, as opposed to the table of rows and columns you see in the worksheet. Although you can use the worksheet to make changes directly to the list, using the data form can help prevent mistakes that can occur if you accidentally enter data in the wrong column or in a row above or below the correct one.

REFERENCE window	**ADDING A RECORD USING A DATA FORM**
	■ Click any cell in the list.
	■ Click Data, and then click Form to display a data form.
	■ Click the New button to display a blank data form.
	■ Type the values for the new record, pressing the Tab key to move from field to field.
	■ Press the Enter key to add the record.
	■ When finished adding records, click the Close button.

Begin updating the faculty list by adding Mary Hutch's data, using the data form.

To add a new record using the data form:

1. Click any cell in the list.

2. Click **Data**, and then click **Form** to display the Faculty Data data form. The first record in the list appears. See Figure 5-8. Notice that Excel uses the worksheet name, Faculty Date, as the title of the data form.

indicates that first record
in list is displayed

indicates total number
of records in list

click here to display
blank data form

Figure 5-8
Faculty Data
data form

labels from
column headings
of faculty list

The names that appear on the left side of the data form are taken from the header row of the faculty list.

In the upper-right corner of the form, there is information on how many records are in the list and which row is currently selected.

Now add the new record.

3. Click the **New** button to display a blank data form. Notice that the label "New Record" appears in the upper-right corner of the data form. Enter the values for the record in the text boxes next to each field name.

4. Type **Hutch** in the LASTNAME text box, and then press the **Tab** key to move to the FIRSTNAME text box.

TROUBLE? If you pressed the Enter key instead of the Tab key, a blank data form appears. Click the Find Prev button to return to the previous record, the record you were entering, and continue entering the data.

5. Type **Mary** in the FIRSTNAME text box, and then press the **Tab** key to move to the DEPARTMENT text box.

6. Type **Accounting** in the DEPARTMENT text box, and then press the **Tab** key to move to the RANK text box. Continue entering the remaining data. Remember to press the Tab key after you complete each entry.

RANK:	**Instructor**
YEARHIRED:	**1999**
SEX:	**F**
SALARY:	**28000**

7. Press the **Enter** key to add the record to the bottom of the list.

The data form is blank again, ready for you to add a new record. But since you don't have any new records to add now, return to the worksheet.

8. Click the **Close** button to close the data form and return to the worksheet.

Confirm that the new record has been added to the faculty list. It should appear at the bottom of the list.

9. Click cell **A3** to make it the active cell.

> **10.** Press **End + ↓** to move to the last record in the list, in cell A44. Verify that the last record contains the data for Mary Hutch.
>
> **11.** Press **Ctrl + Home** to return to cell B3.

Now you can make the other updates to the faculty list. You still need to complete two tasks: change Kevin Mack's rank and salary, and delete Wendy Garabizien's record. Although you can manually scroll through the list to find a specific record, with larger lists of data this method is slow and prone to error. The quicker and more accurate way to find a record is to use the data form's search capabilities. You will use this method to make Kevin Mack's changes and delete Wendy Garabizien's record.

Using the Data Form to Search for Records

You can use the data form to search for a specific record or group of records. When you initiate a search, you specify the search criteria, or instructions for the search. Excel starts from the current record and moves through the list, searching for any records that match the search criteria. If Excel finds more than one record that matches the search criteria, it displays the first record that matches the criteria. You can use the Find Next button in the data form to display the next record that matches the search criteria.

You need to find Kevin Mack's record to change his salary. Use the data form to find this record.

To search for a record in a list using the data form:

1. Make sure the active cell is inside the faculty list.

2. Click **Data**, and then click **Form** to display the Faculty Data data form.

3. Click the **Criteria** button to display a blank data form. The label "Criteria" in the upper-right corner of the data form indicates that the form is ready to accept search criteria.

   Enter the search criteria in the appropriate field.

4. Click the **LASTNAME** text box, and then type **Mack**.

   If necessary, you can enter multiple criteria. If you enter multiple criteria, all criteria must be met for Excel to find a match.

5. Click the **Find Next** button to display the next record in the list that meets the specified criteria—LASTNAME equal to Mack. See Figure 5-9.

Figure 5-9 ◄
Data form after
Kevin Mack's
record found

Kevin Mack is the record you're looking for. However, if more than one employee were named Mack and this was not the record you were interested in, you could click the Find Next button again and the next record meeting the search criteria would be displayed.

If no records meet the search criteria, no message is displayed. Instead, the data form simply displays the current record.

Now update his record.

6. Double-click the **RANK** text box, and then type **Associate**.

7. Double-click the **SALARY** text box, and then type **45000**.

8. Click the **Close** button to return to the faculty list. The rank and salary for Kevin Mack have been updated.

9. Scroll the list to verify that Kevin Mack's salary is now $45,000, and then press **Ctrl + Home** to return to cell B3.

Now complete the final update to the list, deleting Wendy Garabizien's record.

Using the Data Form to Delete a Record

To delete Wendy Garabizien's record, you will again use the search criteria to find the record. If you enter the full name as the search criteria, the spelling must be absolutely correct; otherwise there will be no match and Wendy Garabizien's record won't be found. As an alternative, the data form allows you to use wildcard characters when you enter search criteria. A **wildcard character** is a symbol that stands for one or more characters. Excel recognizes two wildcards: the question mark (?) and the asterisk (*).

REFERENCE window

DELETING A RECORD USING A DATA FORM

- Click any cell in the list.
- Click Data, and then click Form to display a data form.
- Locate and display the record you want to delete.
- Click the Delete button, and then click the OK button to confirm the deletion.

You use the asterisk (*) wildcard to represent any group of characters. For example, if you use "Gar*" as the search criteria for LASTNAME, Excel will find all the records with a last name that begins with Gar, no matter what letters follow. You use the question mark (?) to substitute for a single character. For example, enter "Richm?n" as the search criteria and you might find Richman, Richmen, or Richmon.

Since there is a chance of entering Wendy Garabizien's name incorrectly, use the asterisk wildcard character to help find her record.

To search for a record using a wildcard character:

1. Click any cell in the list, click **Data**, and then click **Form** to display the Faculty Data data form.

2. Click the **Criteria** button to begin entering the search criteria.

Specify the new search criteria.

3. Click the **LASTNAME** text box, and then type **Gar***. See Figure 5-10.

Figure 5-10
Searching for
faculty member
using wildcard
character

4. Click the **Find Next** button to display the first record in the list that contains the letters Gar as the first three letters of the last name. Karen Garafano is not the record you want to delete.

   TROUBLE? If you did not retrieve Karen Garafano's record, click the Close button, click Data on the menu bar, and then click Form before repeating Steps 1 through 4.

5. Click the **Find Next** button to display the next record that contains the letters Gar at the beginning of the name. Wendy Garabizien is the record you're looking for.

6. Click the **Delete** button. A message box appears, warning you that the displayed record will be permanently deleted from the list.

7. Click the **OK** button to confirm the record deletion. Wendy Garabizien's record has been deleted from the list, and the next record in the list is displayed in the data form.

8. Click the **Close** button to close the data form and return to the worksheet.

9. Print the list so the dean has a printout of the most current faculty information.

Quick Check

1. A row within a data list is often called a _____.

2. A column within a data list is often called a _____.

3. In Excel, a _____ is a collection of similar data stored in a structured manner.

4. Explain how to order a student list so that all students in the same major appear together in alphabetical order by the student's last name.

5. The _____ button in the Data Form is used to add a record to a list.

6. You have a list of 250 employees. Explain how to find Jin Shinu's record using the data form.

7. A _____ sort key is a field used to arrange records in a list.

8. If you sort the faculty list from the most recent start date to the earliest start date, you have sorted the faculty in _____ order.

You have now provided the dean with a current list of all faculty members, sorted alphabetically by department. Now she requires specific information on only some of the faculty at different levels on her staff. She could work with the complete list to find this information, but a customized list limited to just the information she requires would be more useful to her. You can help the dean by filtering the faculty list to show just the information she requires. You will do this in Session 5.2.

SESSION

5.2

In this session you will learn to filter a list to display only specific information using AutoFilters, and you will learn how to customize filters to meet more complex criteria. You will use conditional formatting to highlight data in the list. You will also expand the list to include a new field using natural language formulas, and insert subtotals to display summary information in the list. Finally, you will use Page Break Preview to insert custom page breaks for printing the list.

Filtering a List Using AutoFilters

Now that the dean has the full list of faculty organized for easy reference, she is ready to use the list to prepare the reports she needs for her upcoming meetings. The first scheduled meeting is with the other deans at NSU—their task is to form a university-wide accreditation committee comprising faculty representatives from each of the individual colleges and departments at the university. The dean needs to select a faculty member from the College of Business Administration to serve on the committee. She wants to select a senior faculty member and asks you for a list of full professors.

To get a list of faculty members who are full professors you could scan the entire faculty list. However, with large lists locating the data you need can be difficult and time-consuming. Sorting can help because you group the data; however, you're still working with the entire list. You could use a data form, but if you use a data form to find records that meet specified criteria, you will only display one record at a time. A better solution is to have Excel find the specific records you want, displaying only these records in the worksheet. This process of "hiding" certain records and viewing the ones you want is called **filtering** your data. All records that do not meet your criteria are temporarily hidden from view.

REFERENCE window	**FILTERING A LIST WITH AUTOFILTER**
	■ Click any cell in the list. ■ Click Data, point to Filter, and then click AutoFilter to insert list arrows next to each column label in your list. ■ Click the list arrow in the column that contains the data you want to filter. ■ Click the criteria you want to filter.

The Excel AutoFilter feature allows you to filter your data so you view only the records you want. You will use this feature to create a list of full professors in the College of Business Administration.

To filter a list using the AutoFilter command:

1. If you took a break after the last session, make sure Excel is running, the CBA Faculty workbook is open, and the Faculty Data worksheet is displayed. Make sure the active cell is within the faculty list.

2. Click **Data**, point to **Filter**, and then click **AutoFilter**. See Figure 5-11. List arrows appear next to each column label in the list. To see a list of filtering criteria for a specific column, click the list arrow next to the column heading.

Figure 5-11 ◀
Faculty list after AutoFilter feature activated

filtering arrow next to each column heading

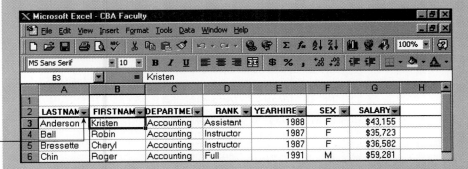

3. Click the **RANK column** list arrow in cell D2 to display a list of criteria you can use to filter the data. See Figure 5-12. Besides the unique values—Assistant, Associate, Full, and Instructor—in the RANK column, three other choices appear that apply to every column. Figure 5-13 describes these three options.

Figure 5-12 ◀
Filtering options for the RANK field

these options appear in all columns

list of filtering options

Figure 5-13 ◀
Default filtering options

Option	Description
All	Displays all items in the column and removes filtering for the column
Top 10	Displays the top or bottom *n* items in the list
Custom	Specifies more complex criteria

Now select your criteria for filtering the data.

4. Click **Full** to display only full professors. See Figure 5-14. In the status bar, Excel displays the number of records found out of the total records in the list. Review the list to verify that only records with a value equal to Full in the RANK column are visible. Excel hides all rows (records) that do not have the value Full in this column.

Figure 5-14
Faculty list displaying only full professors

blue arrow indicates column used to filter list

gaps in row numbers

indicates number of records found out of all records in list

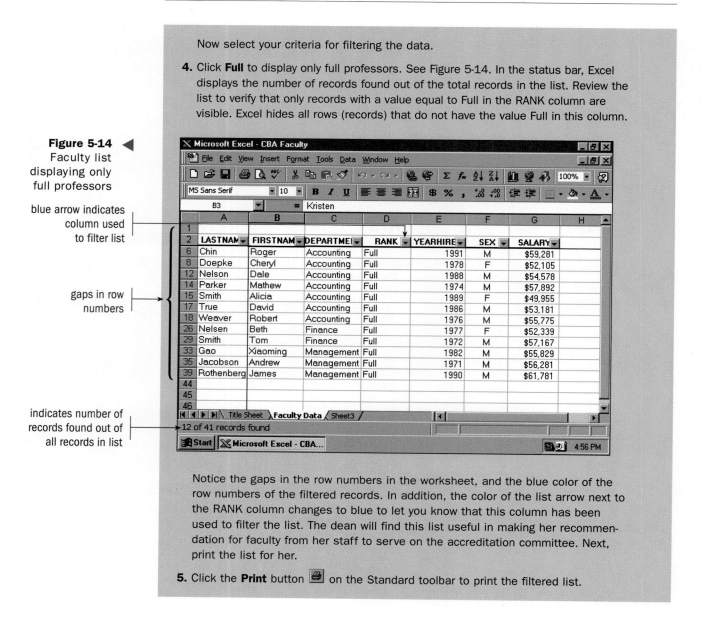

Notice the gaps in the row numbers in the worksheet, and the blue color of the row numbers of the filtered records. In addition, the color of the list arrow next to the RANK column changes to blue to let you know that this column has been used to filter the list. The dean will find this list useful in making her recommendation for faculty from her staff to serve on the accreditation committee. Next, print the list for her.

5. Click the **Print** button 🖨 on the Standard toolbar to print the filtered list.

If you need to, you can further restrict the records that appear in the filtered list by selecting entries from another drop-down list. For instance, if the dean wanted to select from a pool of female faculty with a rank of full professor, you could simply click the SEX column and then click F.

To filter by more than one criterion:

1. Click the **SEX column** list arrow, in cell F2, and then click **F** to display the female full professors. See Figure 5-15.

Figure 5-15 ◄
Faculty list
showing female
full professors

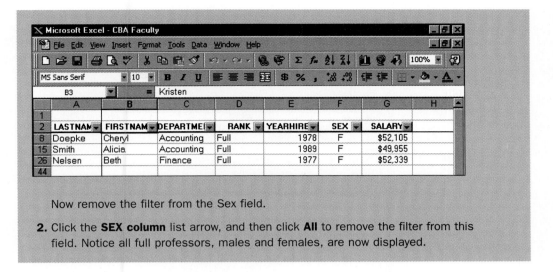

Now remove the filter from the Sex field.

2. Click the **SEX column** list arrow, and then click **All** to remove the filter from this field. Notice all full professors, males and females, are now displayed.

Now that you have provided the dean with the list of full professors, restore the list so all the records can be viewed again.

To restore all the data to the list:

1. Click **Data**, point to **Filter**, and then click **Show All**. All the records appear in the worksheet, but all the list arrows remain next to the column headings. Therefore, you can continue to customize the list by filtering it to show certain data.

Now that the list again shows all the faculty records, the dean has a more complex task, which requires you to provide specific information based on customized criteria.

Using Custom AutoFilters to Specify More Complex Criteria

Although you can often find the information you need by selecting a single item from a list of values in the filter list, there are times when you need to specify a custom set of criteria to find certain records. **Custom AutoFilters** allow you to specify relationships other than "equal to" to filter records. For instance, the dean will be meeting with the university's budget director, Bin Chi, later this week to review the College of Business Administration's budget needs for the next fiscal cycle. She received a memo today from the budget office asking for a list of faculty earning over $50,000 a year hired during the 1980s. The dean asks you to print this information. You can develop a custom set of criteria using the Custom option in the AutoFilter list to retrieve these records for the dean.

To use a custom AutoFilter to filter a list:

1. Click the **YEARHIRED** list arrow, and then click **Custom** to display the Custom AutoFilter dialog box. See Figure 5-16.

click here for a list of
comparison operators

criteria boxes

Figure 5-16
Custom
AutoFilter
dialog box

operator boxes

The operator list box, the first list box in the Show rows where section of the dialog box, lets you specify a comparison operator by selecting an item from a list.

The criteria list box, the list box to the right of the operator list box, lets you specify the field value by typing a value or selecting an item from a list.

The And and Or option buttons are used if you want to display rows that meet two conditions for the field. You select And to display rows that meet both criteria. You select Or to display rows that meet either criterion.

2. Click the **first operator** list arrow, and then click **is greater than or equal to**.

3. Click the **first criteria** list box, and then type **1980** in the list box.

4. If necessary, click the **And** option button.

5. Click the **second operator** list arrow, and then click **is less than**.

6. Click the **second criteria** list box, and then type **1990**. See Figure 5-17.

Figure 5-17
Custom
AutoFilter
dialog box
showing
custom criteria

Custom AutoFilter	? X
Show rows where:	
YEARHIRED	
is greater than or equal to ▼ 1980 ▼	OK
⦿ And ○ Or	
is less than ▼ 1990 ▼	Cancel
Use ? to represent any single character	
Use * to represent any series of characters	

7. Click the **OK** button to display the filtered list consisting of all faculty hired between 1980 and 1989.

You have only some of the information the dean requires, however, because she also needs to know all the faculty hired during the 1980s who earn more than $50,000. So, further restrict the filtered list to those faculty earning more than $50,000.

8. Click the **SALARY** list arrow, and then click **Custom** to display the Custom AutoFilter dialog box.

9. Click the **first operator** list arrow, click **is greater than** from the list of operators, click the **first criteria** list box, and then type **50000**.

10. Click the **OK** button to view the filtered list showing faculty hired between 1980 and 1989 earning more than $50,000. See Figure 5-18.

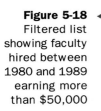

Figure 5-18
Filtered list
showing faculty
hired between
1980 and 1989
earning more
than $50,000

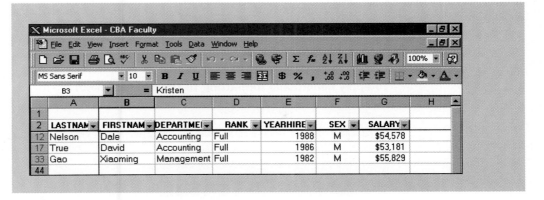

You show the list to the dean. She asks you to sort the list in descending order by salary.

To sort the filtered list, and then restore all the records to the list:

1. Click any field in the SALARY column.

2. Click the **Sort Descending** button on the Standard toolbar to sort the filtered list in descending order by salary.

3. Click the **Print** button on the Standard toolbar to print the list.

   After printing the list you give it to the dean. You can now remove all the filters to return to the original complete faculty list.

4. Click **Data**, point to **Filter**, and then click **AutoFilter** to remove all the filters. All the records are displayed and the list arrows no longer appear in the column headings.

The dean wants to be able to quickly identify faculty earning more than $50,000 and asks you to apply the new Excel conditional formatting feature to the SALARY field.

Using Conditional Formatting

Excel lets you apply **conditional formatting**—formatting that appears only when data in the cell meets conditions that you specify. Using this feature you can specify up to three conditions that apply to the value of a cell or the formula that produces the value. For each condition, you specify the formatting (font, font style, font color, border, etc.) that will be applied to the cell if the condition is true.

REFERENCE
window

APPLY CONDITIONAL FORMATS TO CELLS

- Select the cells you want to format.
- Click Format, then click Conditional Formatting to display the Conditional Formatting dialog box.
- Specify the condition on which to apply formatting.
- Click the Format button to display the Format Cells dialog box.
- Select the font style, font color, underlining, borders, shading, or patterns you want to apply, then click the OK button to return to the Conditional Formatting dialog box.
- Click the OK button to apply conditional formats to cells.

Since the dean wants to be able to quickly identify faculty earning more than $50,000, you decide to apply conditional formatting to any cell in the SALARY field containing a value exceeding $50,000, so that the background color of these cells is green.

Now apply the conditional formatting to the SALARY field.

To apply conditional formatting to the SALARY field:

1. Select the range **G3:G43**.

2. Click **Format** on the menu bar, and then click **Conditional Formatting** to display the Conditional Formatting dialog box. See Figure 5-19. First, specify the condition that will be applied to the salary range.

click here to see list
of comparison
operators

Figure 5-19 ◀
Conditional
Formatting
dialog box

3. Since the contents of the cells in the SALARY field are values, as opposed to formulas or text, make sure Cell Value Is appears in the Condition 1 list box.

   Next, choose the comparison operator to compare with the cell value.

4. Click the **list arrow** in the second list box to display a list of comparison operators, and then click **greater than**. Notice the number of boxes changes to reflect the comparison operator you should use.

   Now enter the value.

5. Click the **third** list box for Condition 1, and type **50000**. The condition has been defined. If you needed to, you could specify two additional conditions.

   Now define the formatting to be applied to the cell or range if the condition is true.

6. Click the **Format** button in the Conditional Formatting dialog box to display the Format Cells dialog box.

7. Click the **Patterns** tab, and then click the color **green** from the Cell Shading palette (fourth row, fourth column).

8. Click the **OK** button to return to the Conditional Formatting dialog box. Notice that green shading appears in the Preview box.

9. Click the **OK** button to apply the conditional formatting to the selected cells.

10. Click any cell to deselect the range. See Figure 5-20. Notice that the background color of several cells in the range is now green.

Figure 5-20 ◀
Faculty
list after
conditional
formatting
applied

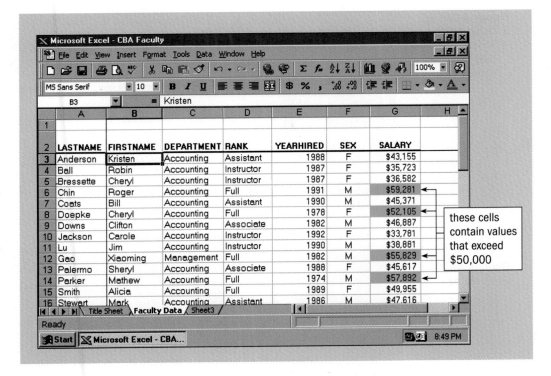

Note that if the value of the cell changes and no longer meets the specified condition(s), Excel temporarily suppresses the formats associated with that cell. However, the conditional formats remain applied to the cells until you remove them, even when none of the conditions are met and the specified cell formats are not displayed.

The dean has a request for information she needs for her meeting with the budget director, and she meets with you to discuss how the faculty list can be used in this task.

Creating Natural Language Formulas

Bin, the budget director, is getting ready to start the next budget cycle. He asks each college dean to provide him with a list of faculty and the proposed salary for each faculty member for next year. Currently, the plan is to increase each faculty member's salary by three percent to keep pace with inflation. The report requested by Bin should list each faculty member by department, and should include a departmental subtotal for the PROPOSED SALARY field.

You will need to add a new field to the faculty list—PROPOSED SALARY—a calculated field equal to each faculty member's current salary times 1.03.

Although you can use cell references to build this formula, Excel 97 has a feature, natural language formulas, which can be used to create such formulas. **Natural language formulas** allow you to use column headers and row labels in building formulas. For example, in Figure 5-21 you have two labels, Sales and Expenses, which identify the values in cells B1 and B2. These labels can be used to build the formula to compute net income. Instead of entering the formula =B1-B2, the natural language formula =*Sales - Expenses* was used to calculate net income.

Figure 5-21 ◀
Example of
natural
language
formula

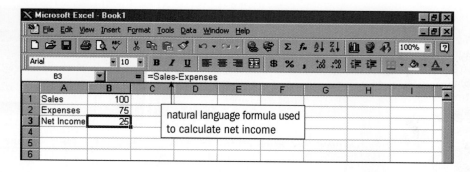

Now, add the PROPOSED SALARY field to the faculty list using a natural language formula.

To enter and format the column heading for proposed salary:

1. Click cell **H2**, and then type **PROPOSED SALARY**.

2. Click cell **G2**, click the **Format Painter** button, on the Standard toolbar, and then click ceil **H2** to copy the format in cell G2 to cell H2.

3. Click **Format** on the menu bar, and then click **Cells** to display the Format Cells dialog box.

4. Click the **Alignment** tab, click the **Wrap Text** check box, and then click the **OK** button to apply text wrapping to cell H2.

Now enter the formula to calculate the proposed salary.

To create a natural language formula:

1. In cell H3, type **=salary*1.03**, and then press the **Enter** key. "Salary" in the formula is the column heading. Excel uses the corresponding cell in the SALARY column (G3) to multiply times 1.03.

Apply the format used in the SALARY field to the PROPOSED SALARY field.

2. Format cell H3 using Currency style with zero decimal places.

3. Copy the formula in cell H3 to the range H4:H43. Scroll to the top of the list.

4. Click any cell to deselect the range. See Figure 5-22. Notice on Figure 5-22, column B is not visible, unless you scroll to the left. Depending on the size of your monitor, column B may or may not be visible.

Figure 5-22
Faculty list
with new field

natural language
formula

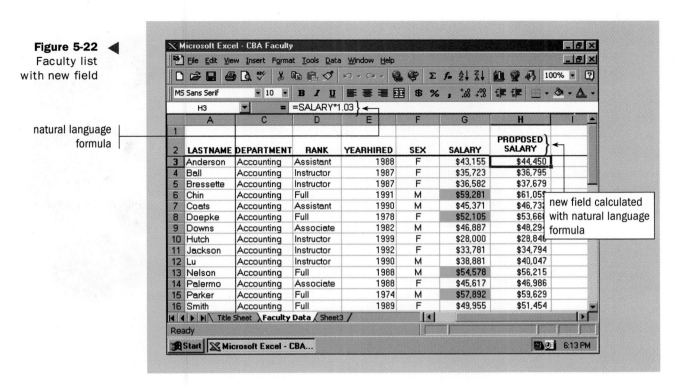

Now that the PROPOSED SALARY field has been added to the list, you can prepare the information for the dean. Remember, this report will list the faculty by department, followed by totals for each department.

Inserting Subtotals into a List

Excel can summarize data in a list by inserting subtotals. The Subtotals command offers many kinds of summary information, including counts, sums, averages, minimums, and maximums. The Subtotals command automatically inserts a subtotal line into the list for each group of data in the list. A grand total line is also added to the bottom of the list. Since Excel inserts subtotals whenever the value in a specified field changes, you need to sort the list so records with the same value in a specified field are grouped together before you can use the subtotals command.

REFERENCE
window

CALCULATING SUBTOTALS IN A LIST

- Sort the list by the column for which you want a subtotal.
- Click a cell in the list.
- Click Data, and then click Subtotals to display the Subtotal dialog box.
- In the At each change in list box, select the column containing the group you want to subtotal.
- In the Use function list box, select the function you want to use to summarize the data.
- In the Add subtotal to list box, select the column containing the values you want to summarize.
- Click the OK button.

To supply Bin with the information he requested, you will develop a list of faculty, sorted by department, with subtotals calculated for the PROPOSED SALARY field. Each subtotal will be inserted after each departmental grouping.

To calculate subtotals by department:

1. If the list is not sorted by department, click any cell in the DEPARTMENT column, and then click the **Sort Ascending** button ⬇ on the Standard toolbar. The list is sorted by department.

   Now calculate the subtotals in the list.

2. Click **Data** on the menu bar, and then click **Subtotals** to display the Subtotal dialog box. See Figure 5-23.

Figure 5-23 ◀
Subtotal dialog
box

3. Click the **At each change in** list arrow, and then click **DEPARTMENT** to select the column containing the field for which you want subtotals.

4. If necessary, click the **Use function** list arrow, and then click **Sum** to select the function you want to use to summarize the data.

   You want departmental subtotals for the PROPOSED SALARY field.

5. In the Add subtotal to list box, scroll the list and, if necessary, remove any check marks in the category check boxes, and then click the **PROPOSED SALARY** check box, the column containing the field you want to summarize.

6. Make sure the Replace current subtotals and the Summary below data check boxes are checked so that the subtotals appear below the related data.

7. Click the **OK** button to insert subtotals into the list. Subtotals are added to the PROPOSED SALARY column, showing the total salaries for each department.

8. Scroll through the list to be sure you can see all the subtotals and the grand total at the bottom. If necessary, increase the column width so you can view the subtotal values. See Figure 5-24. Notice the Outline buttons to the left of the worksheet, which show the levels of detail possible while the Subtotals command is active.

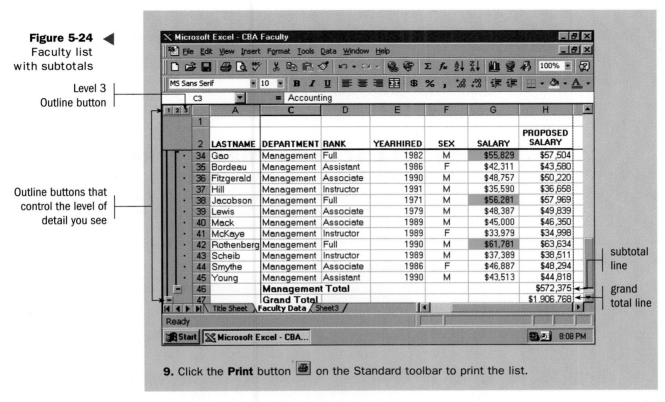

Figure 5-24
Faculty list
with subtotals

Level 3
Outline button

Outline buttons that
control the level of
detail you see

subtotal
line

grand
total line

9. Click the **Print** button 🖨 on the Standard toolbar to print the list.

The subtotals are useful for the dean to see, but she asks if there is a way to isolate the different subtotal sections so that she can focus on them individually.

Using the Subtotals Outline View

In addition to displaying subtotals, the Subtotals command "outlines" your worksheet so you can control the level of detail that is displayed. The three Outline buttons displayed at the top of the outline area in Figure 5-24 allow you to show or hide different levels of detail in your worksheet. By default, Level 3 is active. Level 3 displays the most detail—the individual faculty records, the subtotals, and the grand total. If you click the Level 2 Outline button, Excel displays the subtotals and the grand total but not the individual records. If you click the Level 1 Outline button, Excel displays only the grand total.

Now, use the Outline buttons to prepare a report that includes only subtotals and the grand total.

To use the Outline buttons to hide the details:

1. Click the **Level 2** Outline button. Scroll the worksheet until all subtotals are visible. See Figure 5-25. Notice that the worksheet hides the individual faculty records and shows only the subtotals for each department and the grand total.

Figure 5-25
Subtotals after
Level 2 Outline
button selected

Level 2 Outline button

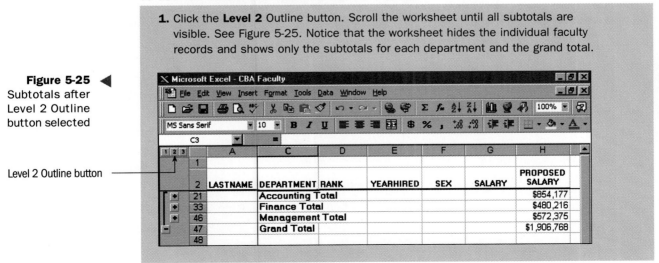

> **2.** Print the worksheet.
>
> **3.** Click the **Level 3 Outline** button to show all the records again.

The dean is very pleased with the way you have manipulated the faculty list to provide her with the data she needs. She now needs printouts she can hand out to the various department heads.

Printing the List Using Page Breaks

When you printed the faculty list, it printed on one page. The dean has asked that the data for each department be printed on a separate page so copies can be shared with each department head as well as the budget director. You can use the Page Break Preview button from the Print Preview window to view where Excel breaks pages in your worksheet and to change either a horizontal or a vertical page break.

To insert a page break to start a new page:

> **1.** Click the **Print Preview** button on the Standard toolbar to display the faculty list. Notice that only one page is needed to print the list.
>
> **2.** Click the **Page Break Preview** button to view a version of the worksheet that shows the entire print area with page breaks and page numbers superimposed on it. Excel is now in Page Break Preview view. See Figure 5-26.
>
> **TROUBLE?** If the message, "Welcome to Page Break View. You can adjust where the page breaks are by clicking and dragging with your mouse" is displayed, click the check box, and then click the OK button, so the message is not displayed again.

Figure 5-26 ◀
Page Break
Preview view

Select All button

click here to indicate
row where page break
will occur

Page Break Preview is different from Print Preview in that you can make some modifications to the worksheet in this mode.

> **3.** Click the **row selector** button to the left of column A at row 22, the row where you want to start a new page.
>
> **4.** Click **Insert** on the menu bar, and then click **Page Break**.
>
> **5.** Repeat Steps 3 and 4 to insert a page break at row 34. Notice that after you insert the page break, a thick blue line appears to indicate where the break is located.

6. Repeat Steps 3 and 4 to insert a page break at row 47 so that the grand total is *not* printed on the same page as the management department data.

7. If necessary, increase the column width of column H so that you can view the grand total.

8. Click the **Print** button 🖨 on the Standard toolbar to print the faculty list on separate pages for each department.

   Because you will not need these page breaks for future printouts of the faculty list, remove them now.

9. To remove all the page breaks, click the **Select All** button located at the intersection of the row and column headings of your worksheet (if necessary, refer to Figure 5-26), click **Insert** on the menu bar, and then click **Reset All Page Breaks**.

   Now return to normal view.

10. Click **View** on the menu bar, and then click **Normal**. The worksheet returns to normal view.

Now that you have prepared and printed the list with subtotals, you can remove the subtotals from the list.

To remove the subtotals from the list:

1. Click any cell in the list, click **Data**, and then click **Subtotals** to display the Subtotal dialog box.

2. Click the **Remove All** button to remove the subtotals from the list.

3. Click **Ctrl + Home** to return to the top of the list.

4. Save the worksheet.

Quick Check

1. Explain the relationship between the Sort and Subtotals commands.

2. If you have a list of students sorted by major and you wanted to print the students in each major on a separate page, you would use the _____.

3. If you had a worksheet with the column headings Shares and Cost Per Share, and entered the formula =*Shares * Cost Per Share* to compute Total Cost, you were using a _____ formula.

4. If you have a list of 300 students in the College of Business Administration and wanted to print only finance majors, you would use the _____ command from the _____ menu.

5. Explain how you can display a list of marketing majors with a GPA of 3.0 or greater from a list of 300 students.

6. Once subtotals are displayed, you can use the _____ button to control the level of detail displayed.

7. _____ enables formatting to appear only when the data in a cell meets a condition you specify.

You have supplied the dean with the information she needs for her meeting with the budget director to review financial plans for the next fiscal cycle. Now the dean needs to generate some information for a meeting with the affirmative action task force. You will work with the CBA faculty list in the next session to gather the information she needs for that meeting.

SESSION

5.3

In this session you will learn to summarize data from an Excel list in different formats using the PivotTable Wizard.

Creating and Using Pivot Tables to Summarize a List

An Excel list can contain a wealth of information, but because of the large amounts of detailed data, it is often difficult to form a clear overall view of the information. You can use a pivot table to help organize the information. A **pivot table** is a special type of table that enables you to group and summarize an Excel list into a concise, tabular format for easier reporting and analysis. A pivot table summarizes data in different categories using functions such as COUNT, SUM, AVERAGE, MAX, and MIN.

All pivot tables have similar elements. These include **column fields**, **row fields**, and **page fields**. Typically, the values in descriptive fields, such as department, rank, year hired, and sex, appear in pivot tables as rows, columns, or pages. In creating a pivot table, you also specify which fields you want to summarize. Salaries, sales, and costs are examples of fields that you usually summarize. In pivot table terminology these are known as **data fields**.

One advantage of pivot tables is that you can easily rearrange, hide, and display different categories in the pivot table to provide alternative views of the data. This ability to "pivot" your table—for example, change column headings to row positions and vice versa—gives the pivot table its name and makes it a powerful analytical tool.

The dean now wants some tabulated information for an affirmative action report. She first reviewed the data within the faculty list to try to get a feel for whether men and women in comparable positions are making comparable salaries. She became overwhelmed and asked you to set up a pivot table.

You consider the information that the dean wants and create a pivot table plan (Figure 5-27) and a pivot table sketch (Figure 5-28). Your plan and sketch will help you work with the PivotTable Wizard to produce the pivot table you want.

Figure 5-27 ◀
Pivot table plan for calculating average salaries

> Pivot Table Plan
>
> **My Goal:**
> Create a table that compares female and male average salary for each academic rank
>
> **What results do I want to see?**
> Average female salary for each rank
> Average male salary for each rank
> Overall average female salary
> Overall average male salary
> The average at each rank for males and females combined
>
> **What information do I need?**
> The table rows will show the data for each rank
> The table columns will show the data for each sex
> The table will summarize salary data
>
> **What calculation method will I use?**
> The salary data will be averaged for each rank and sex

Figure 5-28 ◀
Sketch of table
to compare
average
salaries

Average Salaries by Rank for Females and Males

Rank	Females	Males	Totals
Instructor	xx	xx	xx
Assistant	xx	xx	xx
Associate	xx	xx	xx
Full	xx	xx	xx
Totals	xx	xx	xx

Now you are ready to create a pivot table summarizing average faculty salaries of men and women by rank.

Creating a Pivot Table

To create the pivot table for the dean, you can use the Excel PivotTable Wizard to guide you through a four-step process. Although the PivotTable Wizard will prompt you for the information necessary to create the table, the preliminary plan and sketch you created will be helpful in achieving the layout the dean wants.

Defining the Layout of the Pivot Table

In the third step of the PivotTable Wizard you specify which fields contain the data you want to summarize, and specify how the data will be summarized by selecting from functions such as COUNT, SUM, AVERAGE, MAX, and MIN. In addition to identifying the data to be summarized, you also specify how the data is to be arranged; that is, what fields will appear as column, row, and page headings in the pivot table.

In this step the fields are represented by a set of field buttons. You create the layout by dragging the field buttons into any of the four areas of the sample pivot table: ROW, COLUMN, PAGE, or DATA.

In the pivot table you are creating, you will compute average salaries for each rank and sex. The values in the RANK field will appear as row labels, the values in the SEX field will appear as column headings, and the SALARY field will be the data that is summarized.

Now that you have done some planning, you are ready to create the pivot table for the dean.

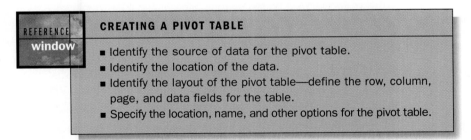

REFERENCE
window

CREATING A PIVOT TABLE

- Identify the source of data for the pivot table.
- Identify the location of the data.
- Identify the layout of the pivot table—define the row, column, page, and data fields for the table.
- Specify the location, name, and other options for the pivot table.

Most often when creating a pivot table, you begin with a list stored in a worksheet. In this case, you will use the faculty list in the Faculty Data worksheet to create the pivot table.

To create a pivot table:

1. Click any cell in the list, click **Data**, and then click **PivotTable Report** to display the PivotTable Wizard - Step 1 of 4 dialog box. See Figure 5-29. In this dialog box, you specify the source of the data that is to be used to create the pivot table. You can select from an Excel list; an external data source, such as a dBASE file; multiple consolidation ranges; or another pivot table. To develop the average salaries pivot table, you use the Excel list in the Faculty Data worksheet.

TROUBLE? If the Office Assistant appears, select the option "No, don't provide help now."

Figure 5-29 ◄
PivotTable
Wizard -
Step 1 of 4
dialog box

2. Make sure the Microsoft Excel list or database option is selected, and then click the **Next** button to display the PivotTable Wizard - Step 2 of 4 dialog box. See Figure 5-30.

Figure 5-30 ◄
PivotTable
Wizard - Step
2 of 4 dialog
box

Excel automatically
selects range of list

At this point, you need to identify the location of the data you are going to summarize in the pivot table.

Since the active cell is located within the range of the Excel list (Step 1), the Wizard automatically selects the range of the faculty list, 'Faculty Data'!$A$2:$H$43, as the source of data for the pivot table.

TROUBLE? If the Range box in the PivotTable Wizard - Step 2 of 4 displays "Database" instead of 'Faculty Data'!$A$2:$H$43 as the source of the data, click the Next button to go to Step 3 of the PivotTable Wizard. If an error message displays when you click the Next button, click the Collapse Dialog box button and select the range A2:H43, and then continue to Step 3.

3. Click the **Next** button to display the PivotTable Wizard - Step 3 of 4 dialog box. See Figure 5-31. In this dialog box you specify the layout of the pivot table. Notice the field buttons on the right side of the dialog box and the diagram to the left of the field buttons. They are used to specify the layout of the pivot table.

Figure 5-31 ◄
PivotTable
Wizard - Step
3 of 4 dialog
box

field buttons for
each field in list

4. Click the **RANK** field button and drag it to the ROW area of the sample pivot table. When you release the mouse button, the RANK button appears in the ROW area. See Figure 5-32. When the Wizard is finished, the pivot table will contain a row label for each unique value in the RANK field.

Figure 5-32 ◀
Sample pivot
table area

RANK button dragged
to ROW area

TROUBLE? If you moved the wrong field into the sample pivot table area, you can remove it by dragging it anywhere outside the diagram.

5. Click and drag the **SEX** field button to the COLUMN area of the sample pivot table. When you release the mouse button, the SEX button appears in the COLUMN area. When the Wizard is finished, the pivot table will contain a column label for each unique value in the SEX field.

6. Click and drag the **SALARY** field button to the DATA area of the sample pivot table. When you release the mouse button, a Sum of SALARY button appears in the DATA area. See Figure 5-33. When the Wizard is finished, the pivot table will contain the sum of the SALARY field entries for each combination of the SEX and RANK field entries.

Figure 5-33 ◀
Sample pivot
table area with
entries in ROW,
COLUMN, and
DATA areas

RANK field is
row label

SEX field is
column label

SALARY field to
be summarized

By default, the PivotTable Wizard uses the SUM function for calculations involving numeric values in the DATA area, and the COUNT function for nonnumeric values. If you want to use a different summary function, such as AVERAGE, MAX, or MIN, you can double-click the field button in the DATA area and select the summary function from a list of available functions in the PivotTable Field dialog box.

Now compute average salaries.

7. Double-click the **Sum of SALARY** button in the DATA area to display the PivotTable Field dialog box. See Figure 5-34.

Figure 5-34
PivotTable Field
dialog box

select this summary
function

8. Click **Average** in the Summarize by list box, and then click the **OK** button to return to the PivotTable Wizard - Step 3 of 4 dialog box. Notice that the summary button in the DATA area indicates Average of SALARY. The third step is complete.

9. Click the **Next** button to display the PivotTable Wizard - Step 4 of 4 dialog box. See Figure 5-35.

Figure 5-35
PivotTable
Wizard - Step
4 of 4 dialog
box

In this final dialog box of the PivotTable Wizard you decide where to place the pivot table—either in a new worksheet or in an existing worksheet. Place the pivot table in a new worksheet.

10. Make sure the New worksheet option button is selected, and then click the **Finish** button to create the pivot table. A new worksheet, Sheet1, containing the pivot table, appears to the left of the Faculty Data sheet. See Figure 5-36. Notice that the field buttons RANK and SEX appear as part of the pivot table. Additionally, the PivotTable toolbar is displayed. Figure 5-37 describes the tools available on this toolbar.

TROUBLE? If the PivotTable toolbar does not appear on your screen, click View on the menu bar, click Toolbars, and then click PivotTable.

Figure 5-36 ◄
Pivot table
showing
average
salaries for
males and
females by rank

SEX field button ──

RANK field button ──

PivotTable toolbar ──

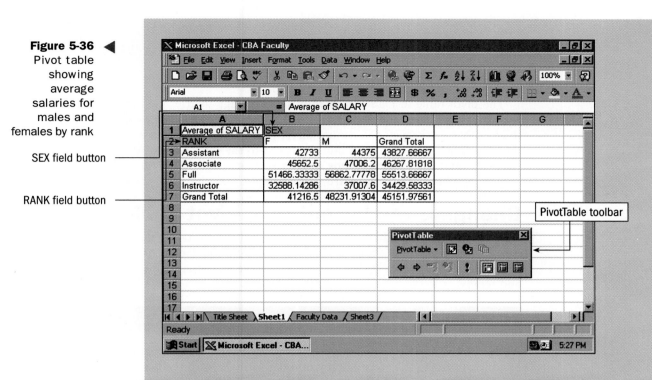

Figure 5-37 ◄
PivotTable
toolbar

Button	Name	Function
PivotTable	PivotTable	Shortcut menu of all pivot table commands
🖼	PivotTable Wizard	Accesses the PivotTable Wizard so you can create or modify a pivot table
🖼	PivotTable Field	Displays the PivotTable Field dialog box so you can modify the options for the selected field
🖼	Show Pages	Displays each page of a pivot table page field in a new worksheet in the same workbook
◆	Ungroup	Ungroups the values in a selected field
◆	Group	Groups selected items; lets you group numeric items, dates, or times into ranges
🖼	Hide Detail	Hides detail lines for a selected field in a pivot table
🖼	Show Detail	Shows detail lines for a selected field in a pivot table
!	Refresh Data	Updates the contents of the pivot table based on changes made to the source data
🖼	Select Label	Selects just the labels in the table for formatting
🖼	Select Data	Selects just the data in the table for formatting
🖼	Select Label and Data	Selects the data and the labels in the table for formatting

11. Rename the worksheet **AvgSalary**.

12. Save the workbook.

The pivot table in Figure 5-36 shows the average salaries paid to faculty members in each rank, by males and females. Although the data in a pivot table may look like data in any other worksheet, you cannot directly enter or change data in the DATA area of the pivot table, because the pivot table is linked to the source data. Any changes that affect the pivot table must first be made to the Excel list. Later in the tutorial you will update a faculty member's salary and learn how to reflect that change in the pivot table.

Changing the Layout of a Pivot Table

Although you cannot change the values inside the pivot table, there are many ways you can change the layout, formatting, and computational options of a pivot table. For example, once the pivot table is created, you have numerous ways of rearranging, adding, and removing fields.

Formatting Numbers in the Pivot Table

As the dean runs off to a meeting, she mentions to you that the numbers in the pivot table are difficult to read. You can apply number formats to the cells in the pivot table just as you would format any cell in a worksheet. You will format the average salary using the Currency style.

To specify the number format for pivot table values:

1. Select the range **B3:D7**.

2. Click the **Currency Style** button 🕭 on the Formatting toolbar. Click the **Decrease Decimal** button 🕮 on the Formatting toolbar twice to reduce the number of decimal places to zero. The pivot table is displayed with the Currency format applied to the cells in the DATA area of the table.

3. Click any cell to deselect the range and view the newly formatted pivot table. See Figure 5-38.

Figure 5-38 ◄
Pivot table
after formatting

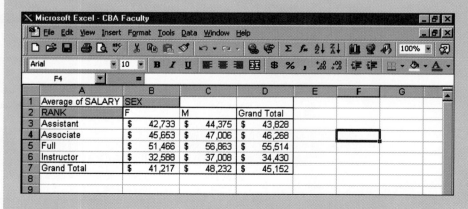

With the numbers formatted, the data in the pivot table is much easier to interpret.

Repositioning a Field in the Pivot Table

Recall that the benefit of a pivot table is that it summarizes large amounts of data into a readable format. Once you have created the table, you can also choose to view the same data from different angles. At the top of the pivot table's ROW and COLUMN areas are field buttons that enable you to change, or pivot, the view of the data by dragging these buttons to different locations in the pivot table.

The dean reviews the tabular format of the pivot table you have created, and decides it might be more useful if it displayed males and females as row classifications under rank. Reposition the column headings for the SEX field (females and males) as row labels.

To move a column field to a row field in the pivot table:

1. Click and drag the **SEX** field button below the RANK field button. See Figure 5-39. Notice that when you click and drag in the COLUMN area, your mouse pointer changes to 🖑. After you drag into the ROW area, the mouse pointer changes to 🖑.

Figure 5-39 ◀
Repositioning
SEX field
button in pivot
table

indicates pivot table
is being rearranged

2. Release the mouse button. See Figure 5-40. The pivot table is reordered so that the SEX field is treated as a row field instead of a column field.

   TROUBLE? If the SEX field appears to the left of the RANK field, click the Undo button 🔄 on the Standard toolbar to undo the last step and then repeat Step 1. When you drag the SEX field button, just drag the button into the blank area under the RANK button. If you drag the button much further to the left, you will change the order of the fields.

Figure 5-40 ◀
Rearranged
pivot table

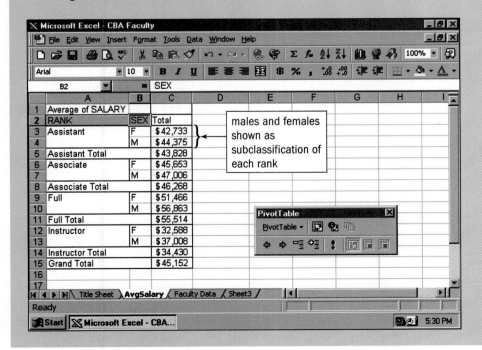

After viewing the pivot table in the new arrangement, the dean decides she prefers the original layout.

3. Click the **SEX** field button and drag it above the RANK field button. The pivot table again looks like Figure 5-38.

Sorting Items Within the Pivot Table

After reviewing the pivot table the dean asks you to rearrange it so that it displays the rank with the highest average salary first. To complete this task, you can sort the data in the pivot table.

To sort a pivot table:

1. Click cell **D3** to place the cell pointer in the cell that contains the field you want to sort.

2. Click the **Sort Descending** button ![icon] on the Standard toolbar. See Figure 5-41. The full professor rank is now the first rank in the pivot table.

Figure 5-41 ◄
Pivot table after values sorted

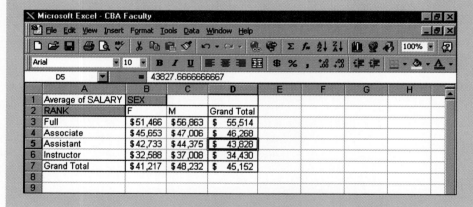

Adding a Field to a Pivot Table

You can expand a pivot table by adding columns, rows, page fields, and data fields; this creates a more informative table. For example, the dean believes that a more accurate comparison of average salaries would include the DEPARTMENT field. Adding this field to the pivot table enables you to calculate average salaries based on an additional breakdown—one that categorizes faculty in each rank into departmental classifications as well as by sex. The dean thinks the additional information will be useful in her discussion with the affirmative action task force, and she asks you to add it to the pivot table.

To add a field to the pivot table:

1. Click any cell in the pivot table.

2. Click the **PivotTable Wizard** button ![icon] on the PivotTable toolbar to display the PivotTable Wizard - Step 3 of 4 dialog box.

   TROUBLE? If the PivotTable toolbar is in the way, drag it to a different location on your screen.

3. Click and drag the **DEPARTMENT** field button into the ROW area, immediately below the RANK field button, and release the mouse button. See Figure 5-42.

Figure 5-42 ◀
PivotTable
Wizard – Step 3
of 4 after
adding
DEPARTMENT
field button

DEPARTMENT field
added

4. Click the **Finish** button. Excel adds the new field and redisplays the pivot table. See Figure 5-43. The pivot table adds department subcategories (accounting, management, and marketing) for each rank.

Figure 5-43 ◀
Pivot table
after
DEPARTMENT
field added

field added
to pivot table

	A	B	C	D	E
1	Average of SALARY		SEX		
2	RANK	DEPARTMENT	F	M	Grand Total
3	Full	Accounting	$51,030	$56,141	$ 54,681
4		Finance	$52,339	$57,167	$ 54,753
5		Management		$57,964	$ 57,964
6	Full Total		$51,466	$56,863	$ 55,514
7	Associate	Accounting	$45,268	$46,887	$ 45,807
8		Finance	$45,498	$46,000	$ 45,623
9		Management	$46,887	$47,381	$ 47,258
10	Associate Total		$45,653	$47,006	$ 46,268
11	Assistant	Accounting	$43,155	$46,494	$ 45,381
12		Finance		$41,000	$ 41,000
13		Management	$42,311	$43,513	$ 42,912
14	Assistant Total		$42,733	$44,375	$ 43,828
15	Instructor	Accounting	$33,522	$38,881	$ 34,593
16		Finance	$30,026	$36,589	$ 33,308
17		Management	$33,979	$36,490	$ 35,653

Removing a Field from the Pivot Table

If you decide you want to remove a field from the pivot table, just drag the field button outside the pivot table. The dean reviews the pivot table showing the data arranged by rank, department, and sex. While she thinks this is important information, she feels the additional breakdown is not needed to show the difference in average salaries between men and women. She asks you to remove the DEPARTMENT field from the pivot table.

To remove a field from the pivot table:

1. Click and drag the **DEPARTMENT** field button outside the pivot table range. When the field button is outside the pivot table, it changes to ✖. See Figure 5-44.

Figure 5-44 ◄
DEPARTMENT
field button
outside pivot
table range

remove this field
button

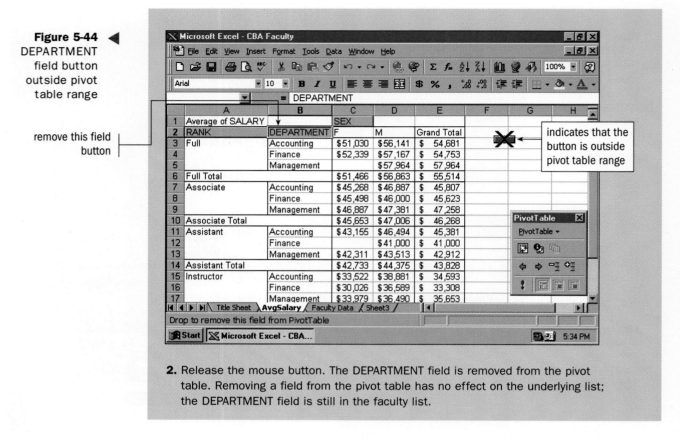

2. Release the mouse button. The DEPARTMENT field is removed from the pivot table. Removing a field from the pivot table has no effect on the underlying list; the DEPARTMENT field is still in the faculty list.

Recall that you cannot change the data in the pivot table; you can simply rearrange it, or format it. So if you were to receive updated information, how would you update the values in the pivot table?

Refreshing a Pivot Table

Recall that in order to change the data in the pivot table, you must make the changes to the original list first; then you need to update the pivot table. To update a pivot table so it reflects the current state of the faculty list, you need to update, or "refresh," the pivot table using the Refresh command.

You receive a memo from the dean informing you that Jodie Weeks, a faculty member in the finance department, will receive an additional $3,000 in salary because her merit increase was approved. Her new salary is $36,052. Update her record in the faculty list and see how this affects the pivot table. (Make a note at this point that the average salary for female instructors is $32,588.) Observe whether there is any change in the pivot table after you update Jodie Weeks' salary.

To update Jodie Weeks' salary:

1. Activate the **Faculty Data** worksheet, and then click any cell in the list.

2. Click **Data** on the menu bar, and then click **Form** to display the Faculty Data data form dialog box.

3. Click the **Criteria** button to display a blank data form.

Enter the search criteria in the appropriate field.

4. Click the **LASTNAME** text box, and then type **Weeks**.

5. Click the **Find Next** button to display the next record in the list that meets the specified criteria—LASTNAME equal to Weeks.

6. Change Jodie Weeks' salary to **$36,052**.

7. Click the **Close** button. The salary for Jodie Weeks has been updated.

Now return to the pivot table to observe whether there is any change in the average salary for female instructors.

8. Switch to the **AvgSalary** worksheet. Notice that the average salary for female instructors remains at $32,588.

Because the pivot table is not automatically updated when data in the source list is updated, the pivot table must be "refreshed."

To refresh a pivot table:

1. Select any cell inside the pivot table.

2. Click the **Refresh Data** button ![!] on the PivotTable toolbar to update the pivot table. See Figure 5-45. The new average salary for female instructors is $33,017.

Figure 5-45 ◄
Pivot table
after being
refreshed

this average changed —————

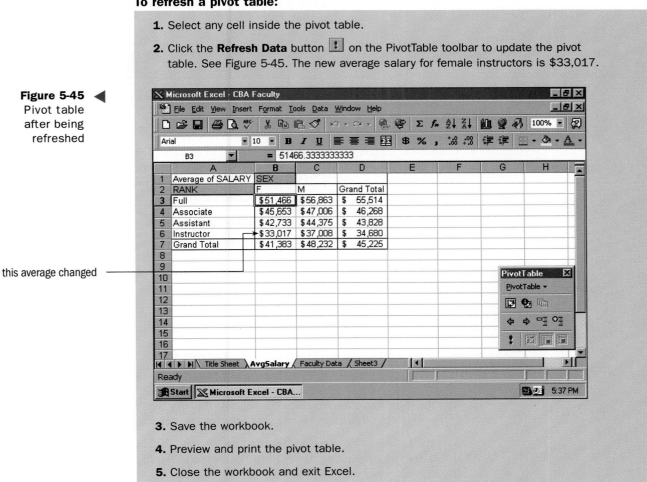

3. Save the workbook.

4. Preview and print the pivot table.

5. Close the workbook and exit Excel.

The dean is pleased with the appearance of the pivot table. The table shows that the average salary paid to females is lower in every rank than the average salary paid to males.

 Quick Check

1 What is the default calculation method for numeric data in a pivot table?

2 After the data in a list has been updated, you would have to _____ the pivot table in order to see an updated version of it.

3. Fields such as region, state, country, and zip code are most likely to appear as
_____ in a pivot table.

4. Assume that you have a list of students, and included in the list is a code for males and
females and a field identifying the student major. Which tool, AutoFilter or pivot table,
would you use in each of the following situations:
a. You want a list of all females majoring in history.
b. You want a count of the number of males and females in each major at your institution.

You have modified and added data to an Excel list. You have also filtered the data in the
list in numerous ways to highlight certain budget information that the dean of the College
of Business Administration needs for her meeting with the university's budget director.
Finally, you have created pivot tables from the list to further organize the information into
specialized reports that the dean can use in her upcoming meetings with the affirmative
action task force.

Tutorial Assignments

The dean has asked for more information about the College of Business Administration
faculty.
  To provide the answers she asks you to complete the following:

1. If necessary, start Excel and make sure your Student Disk is in the appropriate
disk drive. Open the workbook Faculty2 in the TAssign folder for Tutorial.05
on your Student Disk, and save it as CBA Faculty 2. Type your name and date
in the title sheet, then move to the Faculty Data sheet.

2. Add the following information for a new faculty member.

   Last name = Gerety

   First name = Estelle

   Department = Management

   Rank = Assistant

   Year hired = 1999

   Sex = F

   Salary = 42500

3. Use the data form to determine how many faculty members hold the rank of
full professor. Explain the steps you followed to get your answer.

4. Sort the faculty list by sex, within sex by rank, and within rank by salary. Arrange
the salaries in descending order. Print the sorted list so that males and females
print on separate pages.

5. Use the Subtotals command to count how many males and how many females
are on the faculty. Print the faculty list with the subtotals.

6. Use the AutoFilter command to display all females in the accounting department. Sort by last name. Print the filtered list.

7. Further refine the list from question 6 so you display all female accounting faculty hired after 1990. Print the list.

8. Use the AVERAGE function to determine the average faculty salary. Based on
this information, print a list of all faculty earning above the average salary.

9. Use conditional formatting to boldface the YEARHIRED field for faculty hired before 1980. Print the faculty list.

10. Use the Subtotals command to compute the average salary paid by department.

11. Based on question 10, use the appropriate Outline button to display only the subtotals and the grand total. Print the result.

12. Create a pivot table to show the maximum salary by rank and sex. Place your pivot table in a blank worksheet, leaving room for a title. Format your pivot table to produce an attractive printout. Add an appropriate title. Rename the pivot table sheet using an appropriate name. Print the pivot table.

13. Modify the pivot table in question 12 to also display the minimum salary by rank and sex. Print the modified pivot table. (*Hint:* Check out the top 10 option in the list of available AutoFilters.)

14. Use AutoFilters to produce and then print the faculty with the top five salaries in descending order.

15. Print a list of faculty sorted by department and within department by last name. Include only the last name, department, year hired, and gender in the output. (*Hint:* Use the Office Assistant to learn about hiding columns.) After printing the report, unhide the columns.

16. When you used the Page Break command in the tutorial to print each department's faculty on a separate page, you may have noticed that the column headings appeared only on the first page. Use the Print Area and Print Title sections of the Page Setup dialog box (Sheet tab), along with the Page Break command, to print the column headings on each page.

17. In column I, create a new calculated field using a natural language formula reflecting an alternative Proposed Salary of a 4 1/2% increase.

18. Save and close the workbook.

Case Problems

1. Inventory at OfficeMart Business Supplies You are an assistant buyer at OfficeMart Business Supplies, a retail business supply store. Your boss, Ellen Kerrigan, created an Excel workbook containing product and pricing information for inventory items purchased from each primary vendor. Ellen is preparing her monthly order for EB Wholesale Office Supplies, one of OfficeMart's suppliers. She has asked you to print a list of all back-ordered EB Wholesale products so you can include them in the order. She would also like a list of all discontinued items so you can remove those items from the catalog. Do the following:

1. If necessary, start Excel and make sure your Student Disk is in the appropriate disk drive. Open the workbook Office in the Case folder for Tutorial.05 on your Student Disk and save it as Office Supplies.

2. Freeze the panes so the column headings and the Part number row labels remain on the screen as you scroll the office supplies list.

3. Print the items in each status category on a separate page.

4. Display only the records for back-ordered items (Status = B). Sort the back-ordered items by part description. Print the records for back-ordered items.

5. Apply conditional formatting to all discontinued products (Status = D) so that for each discontinued product the status code appears in red.

6. Add a new field to the list. Name the field Retail Value and format appropriately. For each inventory item, calculate the value at retail (quantity on hand multiplied by retail) using a natural language formula. Format the numbers in the new field. Print the list so it prints on one page.

7. Use the Subtotals command to compute the total retail value of the inventory by status category (B, D, and S). Print the list with subtotals.

8. Prepare the same list with subtotals as in question 7, but exclude all records whose retail value is zero.

9. Prepare a pivot table to summarize the retail value of inventory by status category. For each status category, include a count of the number of different items (this is not the sum of the quantity on hand), the total retail value, and the average retail value. Place the pivot table in a new sheet. Assign a descriptive name to the sheet. Print the pivot table.

10. Display only the discontinued items (Status = D). Copy these records to a blank worksheet. Rename the worksheet Discontinued. Print the list of discontinued items.

11. Save and close the workbook.

2. Creating a Current Membership List for Shih Tzu Fanciers of America Jennifer Santarelli is the membership coordinator for the Shih Tzu Fanciers of America, a nonprofit organization for owners, fanciers, and breeders of Shih Tzu dogs. The organization maintains a membership list. The list includes the first name, last name, address, city, state, and zip code for approximately 100 current members.

The board of the Shih Tzu Fanciers of America (STFA) has asked Jennifer to prepare a report on the current membership, showing the number of members in each state and the total current membership.

It has been some time since Jennifer used the list features in Excel. She has tried to create the report but has run into trouble, so she asks you to help her use the PivotTable Wizard to create a pivot table.

Do the following:

1. If necessary, start Excel and make sure your Student Disk is in the appropriate drive. Open the Members workbook in the Case folder for Tutorial.05 on your Student Disk and save it as Current Members.

2. Freeze the column headings and last name row labels.

3. Add the following record. After you add this record, how many records are in the list? How did you determine this?

    Last name = CLEMENTE

    First name = HELEN

    Address = 111 ANGEL WAY

    City = PHOENIX

    State = AZ

    Zip code = 85628 (format as appropriate)

4. Explain how you can quickly find the last record in the list.

5. Explain how you can quickly find Nelson Cruz's record.

6. Sort the list by state, and within state by last name. Print the list so all the fields appear on one page. (*Hint*: You will still have more than one page of output.)

7. Prepare a pivot table to summarize the number of members in each state. Print the pivot table. Name the worksheet StateCount.

8. Use the Subtotals command to count the number of members in each state. Print the list with subtotals for each state, with each state on a separate page.

9. Print a list of all members in Florida and Colorado, sorted by state and within state by last name. Again, all fields should appear on one page.

10. Print the same data as question 8, but include only last name, city, and state in the output. (*Hint*: Use the Office Assistant, if necessary, to learn how to hide columns.)

11. Modify the output from question 10 so the column headings appear on each page. Use the Print Area and Print Title sections of the Page Setup dialog box (Sheet tab) along with the Page Break command, to print Column headings on each page.

12. Save and close the workbook.

3. Sales Analysis at Medical Technology, Inc. Medical Technology, Inc. distributes supplies to hospitals, medical laboratories, and pharmacies. Records of all customer and accounts receivable data are available to department managers on the company's mainframe computer. Tom Benson, the manager of credit and collections, was reviewing this data and noticed that the outstanding balances of several customers in Rhode Island and Massachusetts appeared to be higher than the average customer balances. He believes the average customer balance to be approximately $4,000. He wants to study these accounts in more detail with the goal of creating a plan to bring these accounts closer to the average balance.

Tom was able to download the necessary data from the company's mainframe, and he set up an Excel list.

Do the following:

1. If necessary, start Excel and make sure your Student Disk is in the appropriate disk drive. Open the workbook Medical in the Case folder for Tutorial.05, and then save it as Med Tech.

2. Sort the list by sales rep (ascending) and within sales rep by year-to-date (YTD) sales (descending). Print the sorted list.

3. Insert subtotals (SUM) on YTD sales by type of customer. Print the list with only subtotals and grand total included. After printing, remove the subtotals.

4. Use conditional formatting to display all customers with YTD sales above 50000 in blue text, and apply boldface.

5. Display all customers with a balance owed above $25000 who are from Rhode Island. Sort the list in descending order by balance owed. How many customers are in this list? Which customer owes the most? Print the list.

6. Print a list of customers that have the word "lab" anywhere in the customer name. Explain how you got your results.

7. Prepare a pivot table summarizing total YTD sales by sales rep. Format the pivot table, and then print it. Name the pivot table sheet Sales Rep.

8. Using the pivot table you prepared in question 7, sort total YTD sales in descending order. Print the modified pivot table.

9. There appears to be a problem in the collection of money (balance) owed for one state and one type of customer. Identify the state and customer type that has the highest average outstanding balance. Print a report that supports your observation.

10. Save and close the workbook.

4. Revenue at the Tea House Arnold Tealover, sales manager for Tea House Distributors, is getting ready for a semi-annual meeting at the company headquarters. At this meeting, Arnold plans to present summary data on his product line. The data he has accumulated consists of revenues by product, by month, and by region for the last six months. Help him summarize and analyze the data. Do the following:

1. If necessary, start Excel and make sure your Student Disk is in the appropriate drive. Open the workbook TeaHouse in the Case folder for Tutorial.05 on your Student Disk, and save it as TeaHouse Revenue.

2. Improve the formatting of the revenue field.

3. Freeze the column headings so they remain on the screen as you scroll the worksheet.

4. Revenue for Duke Gray Tea for June in the West region was $51,100. Use the data form to enter Duke Gray Tea, June, West, 51100.

5. Sort the tea list by product and within product by month. Insert subtotals by product and also by month for each product. Print the information for each product on a separate page.

6. Use conditional formatting to display revenue below $25000 hired.

7. Use the Subtotals command to display total sales by product. Print the list with subtotals.

8. Use the Outline buttons to display only the subtotals and grand total. Print this information.

9. Sort the data by month and within month by region. The months should appear in January through December sequence. (*Hint*: Click the Options button in the sort dialog box to customize your sort options.) Print the list.

10. Determine which product was the company's best seller during May or June in the West region. Print the list that supports your answer.

11. You want to determine which month had the highest sales and which region had the lowest sales. Prepare one pivot table that provides you with the information you can use to determine the answer to both questions. Use a text box to place the answer in the sheet with the pivot table. Name the sheet with the pivot table MaxMin. Print the pivot table.

12. Summarize each product's revenue using a pivot table. Use the data in the pivot table to create a pie chart of total revenue by product. Print the pivot table and pie chart on one page. Name the sheet Product Summary.

13. Sort the list by region. Print the data for each region on a separate page. Use Page Break Preview to drag the automatic page breaks to the appropriate locations. (*Hint*: You may also need to insert additional page breaks manually.)

14. Sort the data by region. The region should appear in the following sequence: North, South, East, West. Print the list. (*Hint*: Use online Help to search on customizing, sort order.)

15. Save and close the workbook.

Integrating Excel with Other Windows Programs and the World Wide Web

Creating Integrated Documents for Country Gardens

OBJECTIVES

In this tutorial you will:

- Learn about Object Linking and Embedding (OLE)

- Paste a graphic object into an Excel worksheet

- Embed a WordArt object in Excel

- Link an Excel worksheet to a Word document

- Update linked documents

- Embed an Excel chart in a Word document

- Complete a mail merge using an Excel list and a Word document

- View documents from a mail merge

- Preview and print a mail-merged document

- Create hyperlinks to connect files

- Convert worksheet data to HTML format

CASE

Country Gardens

Nearly fifteen years ago, Sue Dickinson began growing and selling plants and herbs from her 15-acre farm in Bristol, New Hampshire. At the urging of her customers, she opened a small shop in her barn and originally called the shop The Country Gardener. Today, Sue's business, renamed Country Gardens, has grown to include three shops, located in Derry, New Hampshire; Dunstable, Massachusetts; and the newest one in Burlington, Vermont.

The customer base has grown from townspeople and neighbors to include garden centers, nurseries, and landscaping companies throughout the Northeast who purchase products in bulk to stock their own greenhouses. This year, Country Gardens has received the much-prized recognition as the largest grower and greens supplier in New England, a title established by the New England Growers and Horticultural Association (NEGHA).

Sue has decided to offer her products through a mail-order catalog. The catalog will give Sue's customers an opportunity to better plan their own stock and gardening needs by previewing the available products, prices, and quantities a few months before the products are needed. This approach will also allow her to better monitor market trends and customer needs as she tracks orders—products, dollar volume, and purchase dates.

Sue wants to display a flyer at the checkout counter announcing the year's new products to the customers who visit the three stores. In addition to inserting the company logo, she can use WordArt, a shared program that comes with all Microsoft Office 97 programs, to dress up the new products table.

Sue also has drafted the body of a letter to her customers, highlighting the company's recent award from NEGHA, introducing the mail-order catalog, and previewing ten new products that will be available this year. To show this information in an easy-to-understand format, she plans to include a table outlining the ten new products to be offered in the catalog. In addition, she wants the letter to include a chart that NEGHA has supplied depicting the company's status as the top area grower. She will then merge an Excel list containing her customer addresses to the list.

Lastly, Sue wants her customers who use the Internet and the World Wide Web to have access to the new products information online. She will create a Web page showing the new products information.

You'll complete the flyer, the letter, and the Web page for Sue using the integration features of Excel, which allow you to easily incorporate information from documents created in other programs.

SESSION

6.1

In this session you will learn about the different methods of integrating information between Windows programs to create compound documents. You will paste a logo into an Excel worksheet, create WordArt, link an Excel workbook to a Word document, and embed an Excel chart into a Word document.

Methods of Integration

Like Sue, you may occasionally need to copy data between two or more programs to produce the type of document you require. This type of document is referred to as a **compound document**—a document made up of parts created in more than one program. For example, you may want to incorporate data from a worksheet, a graphic design, or a chart, and insert it into a word-processed report.

Excel is part of a suite of programs called Microsoft Office 97. In addition to Excel, the Office programs consist of Word, a word processing program; Access, a database program; PowerPoint, a program used for creating presentations; and Outlook, a personal information manager. Microsoft Office also contains some auxiliary programs, such as WordArt, that allow you to customize your documents even further. All of these programs can share information, which saves time and ensures consistency.

There are essentially three ways to copy data between Windows programs; you can use pasting, linking, or embedding. Regardless of the method used, a copy of the data appears in the compound document. Figure 6-1 provides a description of each of these methods, and examples of when each method would be appropriate.

Figure 6-1 ◀
Comparison of methods of integrating information

Method of Sharing	Description	Use When
Copying and pasting	Places a copy of the information in a document	You will be exchanging the data between the two documents only once, and it doesn't matter if the data changes.
Linking	Displays an object in the destination document but doesn't store it there—only the location of the source document is stored in the destination document	You want to use the same data in more than one document, and you need to ensure that the data will be current and identical in each document. Any changes you make to the source document will be reflected in the destination document(s).
Embedding	Displays and stores an object in the destination document	You want the source data to become a permanent part of the destination document, or the source data will no longer be available to the destination document. Any changes you make to either the destination document or the source document will not affect the other.

Pasting Data

You can **paste** an object, such as a range of cells or a chart, from one program to another using copy-and-paste operations. This creates a static copy of the data. For example, you can paste a range of cells from an Excel worksheet into a Word document, and use it as part of your Word document.

Once you paste an object from one program into another, that data is now part of the new document, and can only be altered in that document's program. The pasted data has no connection to the source document. For example, if you paste a range of cells from Excel into a Word document, you can only edit or change that data using the Word commands and features. The pasted data becomes a table of text and numbers, just as if you had entered it directly from the keyboard. There is no connection to the Excel worksheet. Once you have pasted the range of cells, any changes in the Excel worksheet are not reflected in the Word document. In order for changes in the worksheet to appear in the Word document, you need to repeat the copy-and-paste operation. Pasting is used when you need to perform a one-time exchange of information between programs.

Object Linking and Embedding

There are situations when copying and pasting information into a document is not the best solution. Excel supports a technology called **Object Linking and Embedding** (OLE). This technology enables you to copy and paste objects—a graphic file, a worksheet range, a chart, or a sound file—in such a way that the data is associated with its source. For example, using OLE (pronounced oh-lay) you can insert a worksheet or chart into a Word document as either a linked object or an embedded object.

OLE involves the exchange of information between two programs, called the **source** or **server program** and the **destination** or **client program**. The source is the program in which the data was created. The destination is the program that receives the data. For example, if you insert an Excel pivot table into a Word document, Excel is the source program and Word is the destination program.

Using OLE, you can share data between programs by creating a **link** between files. Linking files lets information created in one file be displayed in another file. When an object is linked, the data is stored in the original source file. For example, you can link a chart from a worksheet to a Word document. Although the chart appears in the Word document, it actually exists as a separate file. The destination document simply displays the object. In effect, the destination document stores a **reference** (location and name of the source file) to the object in the source file. Thus, only one copy of the original, or source, object exists. If you make changes to the original object, changes also appear in the destination document. With only one version of the object, every document containing a link to the source object uses the same copy of the object.

Embedding lets you store data from multiple programs—for example, a worksheet or chart—directly in the destination document. The information is totally contained in one file. The copied object, which is embedded, exists as a separate object within the destination document. To make changes to the embedded object, you edit the embedded object directly from within the destination document. The embedded object has no link to the original source document, which means that changes to the embedded object do not alter the original object. This also means that the changes you make to the original source data do not appear in the embedded document.

The main differences between objects that are linked and objects that are embedded are where the data is stored and how it is updated after you place it in the destination document. Figure 6-2 illustrates the differences between linking and embedding.

Figure 6-2 ◄
Embedding
contrasted
with linking

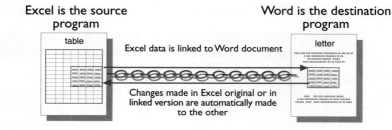

Planning the Integration

Recall that Sue has two documents she wants to create. First, she wants to create a flyer to be placed next to each cash register in the three stores. The flyer will describe the ten new products being offered. The table of the products and their prices is contained in an Excel file, Products. To create the flyer, Sue needs to paste the company logo at the top, which she can do using Excel's Insert command, as this will be a one-time exchange of data. Then, she will use WordArt to insert a visually pleasing title above the product table.

In the case of the customer letter, Sue has already created the body of the letter in Word. However, the Excel new products table must be linked to the Word document because the prices of some of the products might change, and both customer letter and product worksheet will need to show the latest prices. The NEGHA pie chart depicting Country Gardens as the leading area grower needs to be integrated into the customer letter as well. Sue knows the data in the chart will not change, but she might need to modify the chart's size and appearance once it is integrated into the letter. To do this, Sue will want to use the Excel commands for modifying a chart; therefore she decides to embed the chart. Figure 6-3 shows Sue's plan for integrating these pieces to create the flyer and the customer letter.

Figure 6-3
Sue's
Integration
plans for the
flyer and
customer letter

Creating the New Products Flyer

Sue wants to complete the flyer first. To create this document, she needs to insert the Country Gardens logo, a graphic file, into the Excel worksheet, Products, that contains the table of new products. She also needs to create and then insert a WordArt image in the Excel worksheet.

To open the products table:

1. Start Excel as usual. Make sure your Student Disk is in the appropriate disk drive.

2. Open the Excel workbook named **Products** in the Tutorial.06 folder on your Student Disk. Use the Save As command to save the file as **New Products**.

3. Activate the **New Products** sheet. See Figure 6-4.

Figure 6-4 ◄
New Products
worksheet

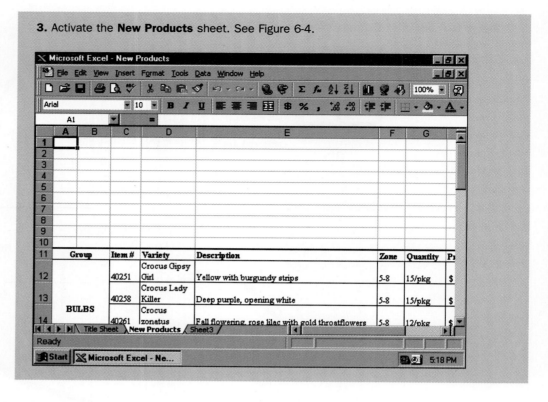

You are now ready to insert the Country Gardens logo at the top of the new products table.

To insert the company logo into the worksheet:

1. Make sure cell A1 is selected.

2. Click **Insert** on the menu bar, point to **Picture**, and then click **From File** to display the Insert Picture dialog box.

3. Make sure the Look in list box displays the Tutorial.06 folder, click **Country** in the list of available fonts, and then click the **Insert** button to paste the company logo into the worksheet. See Figure 6-5. Notice that the Picture toolbar appears on the screen while the graphic object is selected. The Picture toolbar contains tools you can use to change the characteristics of a graphic image. For example, you can crop the image, or adjust its brightness.

Figure 6-5 ◀
Worksheet
after company
logo inserted

company logo ────

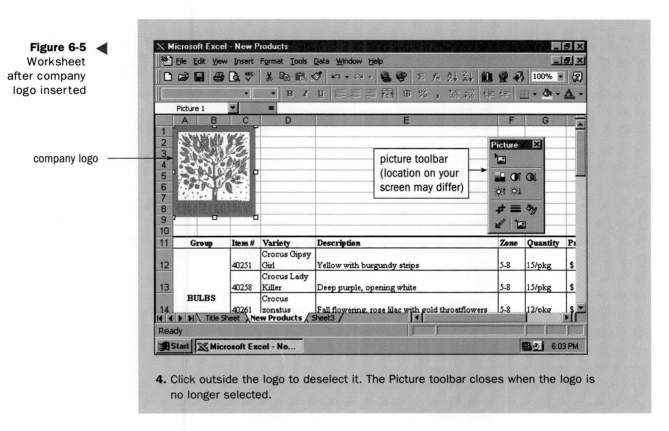

> **4.** Click outside the logo to deselect it. The Picture toolbar closes when the logo is no longer selected.

Sue still needs to add a title to the new products table.

Inserting WordArt into an Excel Worksheet

When Sue reviews her work so far, she knows that her table shows the basic data but it does nothing to attract her customers' attention. To add some pizzazz, she would like you to use WordArt, a shared application available to all Office programs. WordArt enables you to add special graphic effects to your documents. You can bend, rotate, and stretch the text, and insert the graphic object in other documents, such as an Excel worksheet.

To prepare Sue's flyer, you will start WordArt while in Excel, create the graphic object, and then return to Excel to insert the object into the Excel worksheet.

To create a WordArt graphic object:

> **1.** If necessary, click the **Drawing** button 🖉 on the Standard toolbar to display the Drawing toolbar. You can access the WordArt program from the Drawing toolbar.
>
> **2.** Click the **Insert WordArt** button ◀ on the Drawing toolbar to display a gallery of WordArt special effects styles. See Figure 6-6.

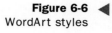

Figure 6-6 ◀
WordArt styles

— select this style

3. Click the WordArt style in the third row, fifth column, and then click the **OK** button to open the Edit WordArt Text dialog box. See Figure 6-7. In this dialog box, you specify the text you want to appear in the WordArt style you selected. If you want, you can also change the font, font size, and font style in the dialog box. For now, just type the text you want as the title of the worksheet. You will adjust the font size and style as necessary after you see how it appears in the worksheet.

Figure 6-7 ◀
Edit WordArt
Text dialog box

4. Type **New Products & Prices** and then click the **OK** button to place the WordArt graphic on your worksheet. See Figure 6-8. Notice that the WordArt toolbar is displayed while the WordArt object is selected. Figure 6-9 describes each button on the WordArt toolbar.

TROUBLE? If the WordArt toolbar is not displayed on your screen, click View on the menu bar, point to Toolbars, and then click WordArt to place a check next to this option and display the WordArt toolbar on your screen.

Figure 6-8 ◀
WordArt
graphic in
worksheet

handles indicate
WordArt object
is selected

WordArt graphic

WordArt toolbar

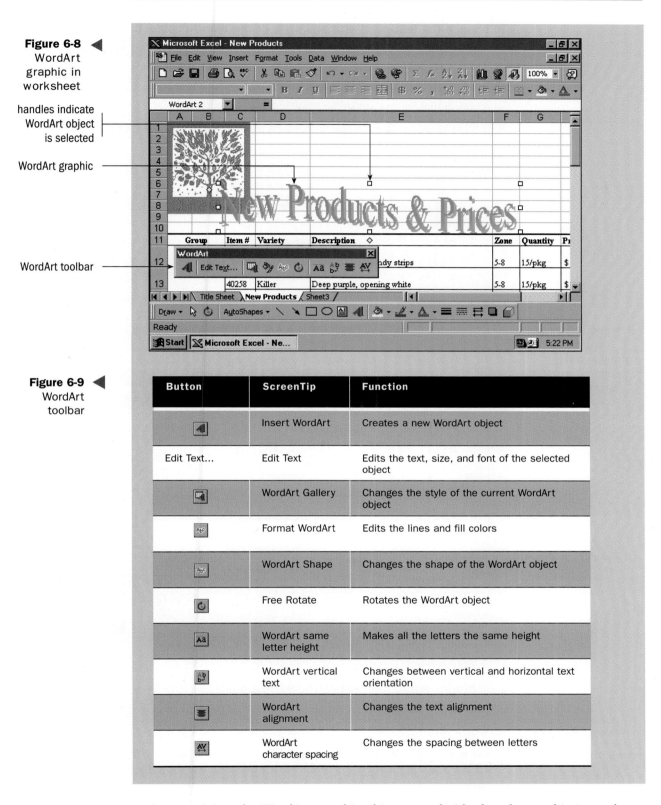

Figure 6-9 ◀
WordArt
toolbar

Button	ScreenTip	Function
	Insert WordArt	Creates a new WordArt object
Edit Text...	Edit Text	Edits the text, size, and font of the selected object
	WordArt Gallery	Changes the style of the current WordArt object
	Format WordArt	Edits the lines and fill colors
	WordArt Shape	Changes the shape of the WordArt object
	Free Rotate	Rotates the WordArt object
	WordArt same letter height	Makes all the letters the same height
	WordArt vertical text	Changes between vertical and horizontal text orientation
	WordArt alignment	Changes the text alignment
	WordArt character spacing	Changes the spacing between letters

As you review the WordArt graphic object, you decide that the graphic is too large. You decide to change the point size from 36 to 24 points and apply a bold style to make the graphic stand out. To make these changes, you need to return to the WordArt program because when you insert WordArt into an Excel worksheet, the object is embedded. This means that in order to modify the object, you need access to its source program's commands and features.

To change the font point size and style of the WordArt object:

1. Make sure the graphic object is selected, and then click the **Edit Text** button on the WordArt toolbar to return to the Edit WordArt Text dialog box.

2. Click the **Size** list arrow and click **24**. Click the **Bold** button, and then click the **OK** button. You return to the New Products worksheet.

   Now move the graphic object above the new products table, and to the right of the logo.

3. Make sure the graphic object is selected, and then position the pointer over the graphic until the pointer changes to a four-headed arrow ⊕ .

4. Click and drag the WordArt object to the top of row 4 in column E. As you drag the object, an outline of the object indicates its placement on the worksheet. Release the mouse button.

   TROUBLE? If the Country Gardens logo moves instead of the WordArt object, click Undo, select the WordArt object, and repeat Steps 3 and 4.

5. Click anywhere outside the graphic so it is no longer selected. See Figure 6-10.

Figure 6-10 ◀
WordArt
graphic after
being moved
and edited

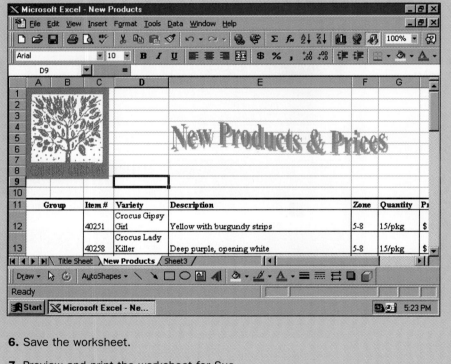

6. Save the worksheet.

7. Preview and print the worksheet for Sue.

8. Click the **Drawing** button 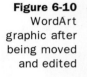 on the Standard toolbar to remove the Drawing toolbar.

Sue is pleased with how professional the worksheet looks with the company logo and WordArt. She can print copies of the table now, and distribute them as flyers at each store.

Linking an Excel Worksheet to a Word Document

Now Sue needs to link the new products table created in Excel and the customer letter created in Word. As you know, Sue maintains her new product and pricing information in an Excel workbook. She wants to include the new products table in a letter to her customers. Since the product and pricing information is always subject to change, the copy-and-paste method is not the appropriate method to integrate these documents. Recall that pasting only allows you to change or modify the pasted object from the destination program. Sue wants the most current pricing information to appear both in the original source file—the new products worksheet—and the destination document—the customer letter. Therefore, a better solution is to create a link between data copied from Excel to Word. When she creates a link between the documents, if the data changes in the source document, these changes automatically appear in the destination document. For example, Sue believes that the price of bulbs will most likely change when she receives a signed quote from her supplier. It's possible that she won't receive this quote until right before she plans to send out the letter. Therefore, you'll link the table from the New Products workbook to the Customer Letter document so that you can make changes to the Excel new products table and have these changes automatically reflected in the Word document.

REFERENCE window	**LINKING AN OBJECT**
	■ Start the source program, open the file containing the object to be linked, select the object or information you want to link to the destination program, and then click the Copy button on the Standard toolbar.
	■ Start the destination program, open the file that will contain the link to the copied object, position the insertion point where you want the linked object to appear, click Edit, and then click Paste Special.
	■ Click the Paste link option button, select the option you want in the As list box, and then click the OK button.

Sue has given you the Word file containing her letter. You need to link the new products table to the customer letter. First you need to select the new products table, which is the Excel object to be linked.

To link the new products table to the customer letter:

1. Make sure the New Products sheet is the active sheet. Select the range of cells **A11:H21** to select the new products table.

2. Click the **Copy** button 🔲 on the Standard toolbar to copy the data to the Clipboard.

Now, you need to start Word, and then open the customer letter document.

To start Word and open the customer letter document:

1. Make sure your Student Disk is in the appropriate disk drive. Click the **Start** button on the taskbar, point to **Programs**, and then click **Microsoft Word** to start this program.

2. Open the **Letter** document, which is located in the Tutorial.06 folder on your Student Disk. Sue's letter to the Country Gardens customers is displayed in the document window in page layout view. See Figure 6-11.

   TROUBLE? If your document does not show the nonprinting characters, click the Show/Hide button ¶ on the Standard toolbar.

   Next you'll save the file with a new name. That way, the original letter remains intact on your Student Disk, in case you want to restart the tutorial.

Figure 6-11 ◀
Beginning of
customer letter

3. Use the Save As command to save the file as **Customer Letter** in the Tutorial.06 folder on your Student Disk.

   Now link the Excel new products table to the customer letter.

4. Scroll the document and position the insertion point to the left of the paragraph mark above the paragraph that begins, "You will receive...." This is where you want the product and pricing data to appear. See Figure 6-12.

Figure 6-12 ◀
Placement of
product table in
customer letter

position insert point —

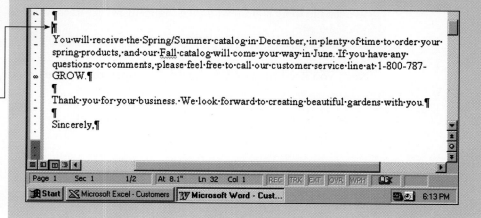

5. Click **Edit** on the menu bar, and then click **Paste Special**. The Paste Special dialog box opens. See Figure 6-13.

Figure 6-13 ◀
Paste Special
dialog box

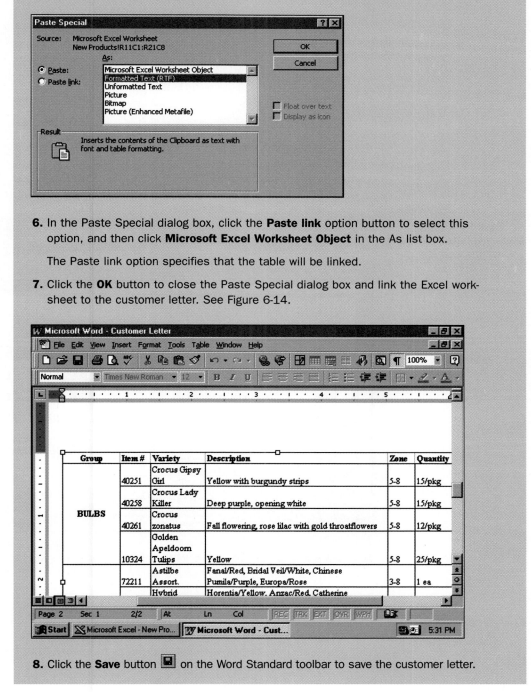

6. In the Paste Special dialog box, click the **Paste link** option button to select this option, and then click **Microsoft Excel Worksheet Object** in the As list box.

The Paste link option specifies that the table will be linked.

7. Click the **OK** button to close the Paste Special dialog box and link the Excel worksheet to the customer letter. See Figure 6-14.

Figure 6-14 ◀
New products
table in Word
document

8. Click the **Save** button 🖫 on the Word Standard toolbar to save the customer letter.

Sue has just received the signed quote from her bulb supplier. As she expected, some of the prices have changed. She would now like you to update the new products table.

Updating Linked Objects

Now that you have linked the new products table from Excel to the customer letter, you can make changes to the source document, the Excel new products table, and the changes will automatically be reflected in the destination file. When making changes, you can have one or both files open.

To update the new products table in Excel:

1. Click the **Microsoft Excel** button on the taskbar to switch to the New Products workbook. Make sure the New Products sheet is the active sheet.

2. Click any cell to deselect the table and press the **Esc** key to remove the data from the Clipboard.

   The price of Crocus Gipsy Girl bulbs has changed from $2.95 to $3.95 each.

3. Enter **3.95** in cell H12.

   Now check to see if this change is reflected in the customer letter.

4. Click the **Microsoft Word** button on the taskbar to switch to the customer letter, and then scroll to view the price of Crocus Gipsy Girl bulbs. Because you linked the table from Excel to Word, the change you just made to the price of product 40251, Crocus Gipsy Girl bulbs, also appears in the destination document. See Figure 6-15.

Figure 6-15 ◀
Customer letter
with updated
price

updated price ──────

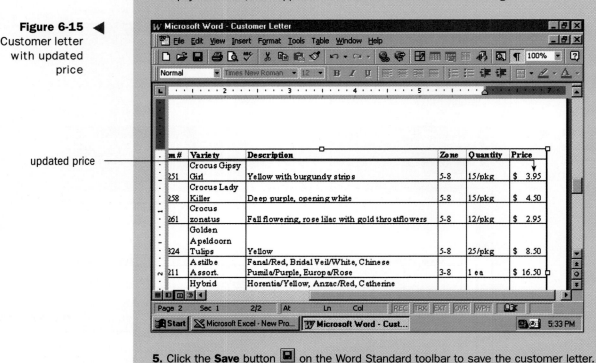

5. Click the **Save** button 🖫 on the Word Standard toolbar to save the customer letter.

What would happen if you were working on the new products table in Excel without the Word document open? Would the information still be updated in the customer letter? To find out, make the remaining changes to the prices for bulbs with the customer letter closed. You can then reopen the customer letter to ensure that the changes appear there as well.

To change the linked object with the Word document closed:

1. Click **File** on the Word menu bar, and then click **Close** to close the Customer Letter document.

2. Click the **Microsoft Excel** button on the taskbar to switch to the New Products workbook.

3. Enter **4.95** in cell H13, and then enter **3.25** in cell H14.

4. Click the **Save** button 🔲 on the Excel Standard toolbar.

5. Close the Excel workbook.

   Now reopen the customer letter to confirm that the prices have been updated in the linked new products table.

6. Click the **Microsoft Word** button on the taskbar. Click **File** on the menu bar, and then click **1 Customer Letter**.

7. Scroll the document to view the linked table. Notice that the new bulb prices appear in the linked table in Word. See Figure 6-16.

Figure 6-16 ◀
Linked table
after all prices
updated

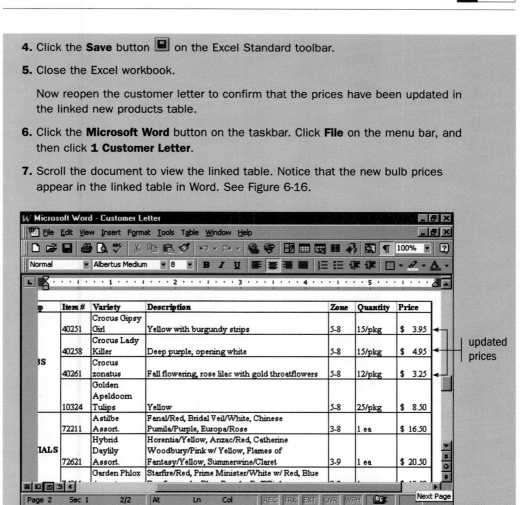

updated
prices

8. Save the letter.

The customer letter is almost complete. Now Sue just needs you to add the NEGHA pie chart.

Embedding an Excel Chart in a Word Document

Sue wants her letter to include the pie chart from NEGHA showing Country Gardens as the top grower in the area for 1999. Sue knows the data for the chart will not change, so there is no need for her to link the pie chart in her Word letter to the source file. Therefore, she decides to embed it. That way, if the pie chart needs to be resized or moved once it is in the customer letter, she can make these changes using Excel chart commands. (Recall that when you embed an object, you automatically have access to the object's source program's commands and features to manipulate it in the destination program.)

REFERENCE window

EMBEDDING AN OBJECT

- Start the source program, open the file containing the object to be embedded, select the object or information you want to embed in the destination program, and then click the Copy button on the Standard toolbar.
- Start the destination program, open the file that will contain the embedded object, position the insertion point where you want to place the object, click Edit, and then click Paste Special.
- Click the Paste option button, select the option you want in the As list box, and then click the OK button.

Now you can embed the pie chart in the customer letter.

To embed the Excel chart in the Word document:

1. Click the **Microsoft Excel** button on the taskbar to switch to Excel. Open the **NEGHA** workbook, which is located in the Tutorial.06 folder on your Student Disk. The workbook is displayed in the worksheet window. See Figure 6-17.

Figure 6-17 ◄
NEGHA pie chart

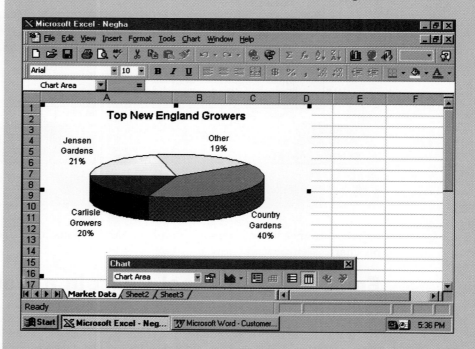

2. If necessary, click the **chart area** (the white area around the pie) to select the chart. When the chart is selected, handles appear on the chart area.

3. Click the **Copy** button ▦ on the Excel Standard toolbar to copy the chart to the Clipboard. The chart now appears with a rotating dashed line around its frame, indicating that it has been copied.

4. Click the **Microsoft Word** button on the taskbar to return to the Customer Letter document.

5. Scroll to page 1 of the Customer Letter document, and then click to the left of the paragraph mark immediately above the paragraph that begins "Since 1985 Country Gardens...." to position the insertion point where you need to embed the pie chart. See Figure 6-18.

Excel

Figure 6-18
Placement of
pie chart in
customer letter

position insertion
point here

6. Click **Edit** on the menu bar, and then click **Paste Special**. The Paste Special dialog box opens. See Figure 6-19.

Figure 6-19
Paste Special
dialog box with
settings for
paste

7. Make sure the Paste option button is selected. This option will embed the chart.

8. In the As list box, make sure Microsoft Excel Chart Object is selected as the object to be embedded.

TROUBLE? If the Microsoft Excel Chart Object option does not appear in the As list box, you might not have selected and copied the chart correctly. Click the Cancel button, and then repeat Steps 1 through 8, making sure that when you select the chart, handles appear around the chart area, and that when you copy the chart, a rotating dashed line appears around the chart area.

9. Click the **OK** button. The Paste Special dialog box closes, and after a few moments, the Excel pie chart appears embedded in the letter. See Figure 6-20.

Figure 6-20 ◀
Customer letter
with embedded
pie chart

embedded pie chart ——————

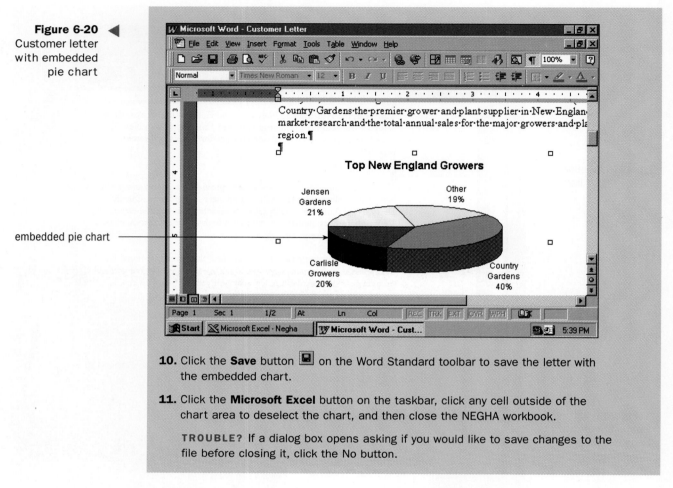

10. Click the **Save** button 🖫 on the Word Standard toolbar to save the letter with the embedded chart.

11. Click the **Microsoft Excel** button on the taskbar, click any cell outside of the chart area to deselect the chart, and then close the NEGHA workbook.

   TROUBLE? If a dialog box opens asking if you would like to save changes to the file before closing it, click the No button.

After reviewing the letter with the embedded pie chart, Sue decides that the Country Gardens slice should be "exploded" so the reader's attention is drawn to the fact that Country Gardens' percentage of the market is greatest. Because you embedded the chart (as opposed to just copying and pasting it), you can use Excel chart commands from within the Word document to modify the chart.

Modifying an Embedded Object

When you make changes to an embedded object within the destination program, the changes are made to the embedded object only; the original object in the source program is not affected. When you select an embedded object, the menu commands on the destination program's menu bar change to include the menu commands of the embedded object's source program. You can then use these commands to modify the embedded object.

Now that you have embedded the pie chart in Word, you can modify it by exploding the Country Gardens pie slice.

Excel

To edit the pie chart from within Word:

1. Click the **Microsoft Word** button on the taskbar.

2. Double-click the **chart** to select it. After a moment, a thick border appears around the chart, and the Excel Chart menu is displayed at the top of the Word window. See Figure 6-21. Notice that the embedded object appears within the Excel row and column borders. You can now edit this object in place using Excel commands. Thus, you have access to all of the Excel features while you are in Word.

Figure 6-21 ◄
Embedded object selected for editing

still in Word

Excel menus and toolbars

embedded object (pie chart) appears in Excel

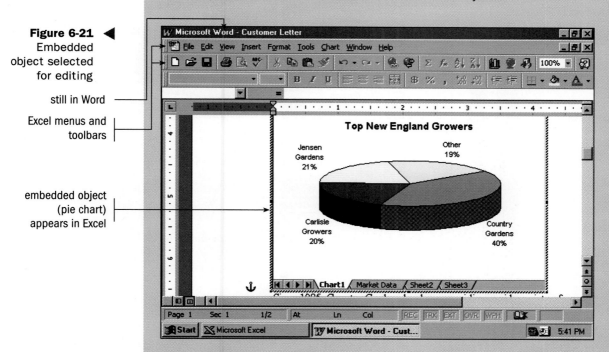

TROUBLE? If the floating Chart toolbar appears, click its Close button to close it.

Now you can modify the chart.

3. Click anywhere within the **chart** to select it, and then click the **Country Gardens slice** to select it. Selection handles now appear on only this slice.

4. With the pointer on the selected slice, click and drag the Country Gardens slice down and to the right, and then release the mouse button. The Country Gardens slice is exploded.

5. Click outside of the chart area to deselect the chart and return the window to the display of Word commands and features only. See Figure 6-22.

Figure 6-22 ◄
Pie chart in
Word document
after slice
exploded

exploded slice —

6. Click the **Save** button on the Word Standard toolbar to save the Customer Letter document.

Quick Check

1 When linking objects, you use the _____ command on the Edit menu.

2 OLE stands for _____ .

3 If two documents are _____ using OLE, changing the source document will automatically change the destination document.

4 You can create special text effects using _____ .

5 Updating an embedded object (has, has no) effect on the original source object.

6 You have embedded a range of cells in a Word document. Describe what happens when you double-click the embedded object.

7 When you _____ an object, that object is now part of the new document, and can only be altered from within that document's program.

8 You should _____ an object if you plan to use the same data in several documents and need to ensure that the data will be identical in each document.

Now that you have completed the body of the customer letter, Sue is ready for you to send it to the Country Gardens Vermont customers. You can do this through a mail merge. You will do this in Session 6.2.

SESSION

6.2

In this session, you will plan and complete a mail merge by inserting merge fields into a form letter that links to data in an Excel list.

Customizing a Form Letter Using an Excel List

Sue is ready to send out the completed promotional letter announcing the new mail-order catalog and introducing the new products. She has decided to customize the customer letter by inserting the customer's name and address into each letter. Using her customer list, which is maintained in Excel, she plans separate mailings to coincide with promotional events at each of her company's three stores. For instance, the store in Burlington, Vermont has an open house planned next month and Sue wants to send the letter to only those customers in Vermont so that they receive the letter in advance of the open house. Later, she will do a separate mailing for New Hampshire customers to coincide with a fall festival, and then a separate mailing to Massachusetts customers to coincide with the Dunstable store's participation in a town fair.

In this section, you'll complete the customer letter for Sue by merging it with the names and addresses of Country Gardens' Vermont customers. This data is stored as an Excel list. Therefore, you will again be integrating Excel data with a Word document.

Planning the Form Letter

Sue plans to use the Mail Merge feature of Word to send the customer letter you completed in the previous session to each Country Gardens customer in Vermont. She will be sending the same letter, a form letter, to each customer; only the name and address will change. A **form letter** is a Word document that contains standard paragraphs of text and a minimum of variable text, usually just the names and addresses of the letter recipients. The **main document** of a form letter contains the text that stays the same in each letter, as well as the **merge fields** that tell Word where to insert the variable information into each letter. The variable information, the information that changes from letter to letter, is contained in a **data source**, which can be another Word document, an Excel list, an Access database, or some other source. The main document and the data source work together—when you merge the main document with the data source, Word replaces the merge fields with the corresponding field values from the data source. The process of merging the main document with the data source is called a **mail merge**.

In this case, Sue's customer letter will be the main document and a customer list maintained in Excel containing the names and addresses of Country Gardens customers will be the data source. Figure 6-23 shows Sue's plan for the form letter.

Figure 6-23 ◀
Sue's plan for
the form letter

Note that the data source contains all Country Gardens customers. Sue first wants to send the letter to only the Vermont customers.

REFERENCE window

CREATING THE MAIN DOCUMENT

■ Click Tools, and then click Mail Merge to open the Mail Merge Helper.
■ Click the Create button and then select the type of document you are creating.
■ Click the Active Window button.
■ Click the Get Data button and select the source of data. For an Excel worksheet, specify the entire worksheet or the desired worksheet range.

To help simplify the mail merge process, you will use the Word Mail Merge Helper, which guides you through the steps of the mail merge.

Specifying a Main Document and a Data Source

A mail-merged main document can be a new or existing Word document. In this case, the main document is Sue's customer letter.

Now you need to specify the customer letter as the main document and the Excel customer list as the data source.

To specify the main document and the data source:

1. If you took a break after the last session, make sure that Excel and Word are running, and the Customer Letter document is open and displayed on your screen.

Excel

2. Scroll to the top of the letter, click **Tools** on the menu bar, and then click **Mail Merge**. The Mail Merge Helper dialog box opens. See Figure 6-24. The dialog box displays the three tasks you need to perform: creating the main document, creating or getting a data source, and merging the main document with the data source.

Figure 6-24 ◀
Mail Merge
Helper dialog
box

click to choose the
type of merge
document

The type of merge document you need to create is a form letter.

3. Click the **Create** button in the Main document section to display the list of main document types. Click **Form Letters**. Word displays a message box asking whether you want to use the active window as the main document or create a new main document. In this case, you want to use the open document, Customer Letter, as the main document.

4. Click the **Active Window** button. The area below the Create button now indicates the type of mail merge (Form Letters) and the file path and name of the main document (Customer Letter).

You have now established Customer Letter as the main document. Next you need to specify the data source, the source of the variable information that will be inserted into the main document during the merge process. The data source is an Excel workbook named Customers.

5. Click the **Get Data** button in the Data source section of the Mail Merge Helper dialog box, and then click **Open Data Source**. The Open Data Source dialog box opens.

The Customers workbook is located in the Tutorial.06 folder on your Student Disk.

6. Make sure that the Tutorial.06 folder is displayed in the Look in list box.

Because the dialog box currently shows only the Word documents in the selected folder, you need to change the entry in the Files of type list box to show the Excel files.

7. Click the **Files of type** list arrow, and then click **MS Excel Worksheets**. The dialog box now shows a list of all the Excel files in the Tutorial.06 folder on your Student Disk.

8. Click **Customer** and then click the **Open** button. A Microsoft Excel dialog box opens, in which you can choose the data source—either the entire spreadsheet or the range containing the customer list. In this case, you need to specify the range Customers. See Figure 6-25.

Figure 6-25 ◀
Choose data
source

click this data source ────

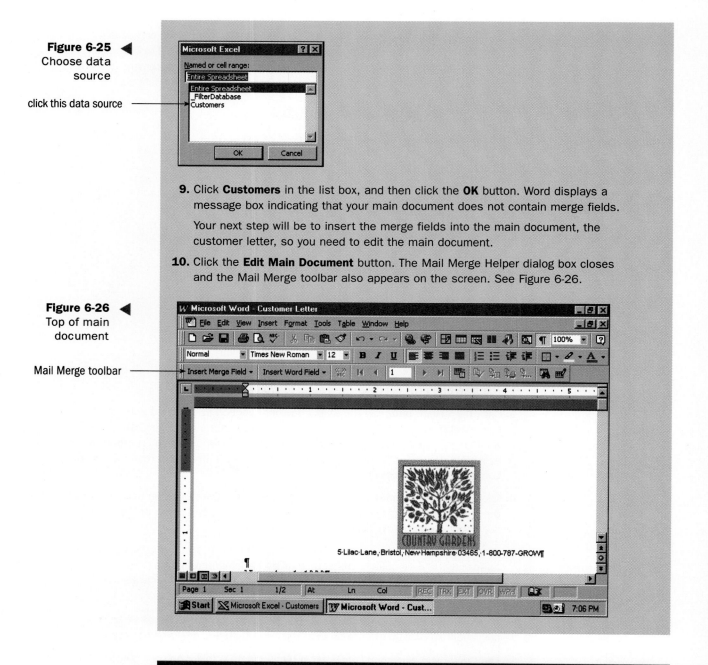

9. Click **Customers** in the list box, and then click the **OK** button. Word displays a message box indicating that your main document does not contain merge fields.

Your next step will be to insert the merge fields into the main document, the customer letter, so you need to edit the main document.

10. Click the **Edit Main Document** button. The Mail Merge Helper dialog box closes and the Mail Merge toolbar also appears on the screen. See Figure 6-26.

Figure 6-26 ◀
Top of main
document

Mail Merge toolbar ────

Inserting the Merge Fields

Because you now have a data source to use with the main document, you can go back to the main document and identify which fields to pull into the document and where to place each. This process is called **inserting merge fields**. As noted earlier, a merge field is a special instruction that tells Word where to insert the variable information from the data source into a form letter.

REFERENCE window

INSERTING MERGE FIELDS INTO A MAIN DOCUMENT

■ Position the insertion point where you want the merge field to appear in the main document.
■ Click the Insert Merge Field button on the Mail Merge toolbar.
■ Click the name of the field you want to insert.

To complete Sue's form letter, you need to insert seven merge fields, one for each of the following pieces of information: customer name, company name (if any), street, city, state, and zip code—all for the inside address—and customer name again in the salutation of the letter.

To insert the merge fields into the customer letter document:

1. Scroll the document window and position the insertion point in the blank paragraph directly above the salutation ("Dear,"). This is where the customer's name and address will appear.

2. Press the **Enter** key to insert a blank line, and then click the **Insert Merge Field** button on the Mail Merge toolbar. A list of the available merge fields is displayed. See Figure 6-27.

Figure 6-27 ◀
Inserting
merge fields
into main
document

available fields from
customer list

3. Click **CustomerName** to select this field. See Figure 6-28. Word inserts the field name into the document, enclosed in chevron symbols (<< >>). The chevrons distinguish the merge fields from the rest of the text in the main document.

Figure 6-28 ◀
Main document
after one merge
field inserted

merge field

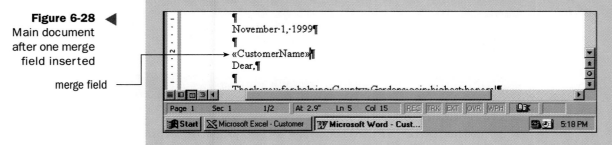

The company name (if any) should appear on the line below the customer name.

4. Press the **Enter** key to move the insertion point to the next line, click the **Insert Merge Field** button on the Mail Merge toolbar, and then click **Company**. Word inserts the Company merge field into the document.

5. Repeat Step 4 to insert the **Street** field on the third line of the inside address.

6. Repeat Step 4 to insert the **City** field on the fourth line of the inside address. The State and ZipCode fields must appear on the same line as the City field, with a comma and a space separating the city and state, and a space separating the state and zip code.

7. Type **,** (a comma), press the **Spacebar**, click the **Insert Merge Field** button on the Mail Merge toolbar, and then click **State**.

8. Press the **Spacebar**, click the **Insert Merge Field** button on the Mail Merge toolbar, and then click **ZipCode**.

9. Press the **Enter** key to insert a blank line between the inside address and the salutation. The final merge field you need to insert is the CustomerName field again, after the word "Dear" in the salutation of the letter.

10. Position the insertion point between the "r" in the word "Dear" and the comma following it, press the **Spacebar**, click the **Insert Merge Field** button on the Mail Merge toolbar, and then click **CustomerName**. The merge fields are now complete. See Figure 6-29.

Figure 6-29 ◀
All merge fields
inserted into
main document

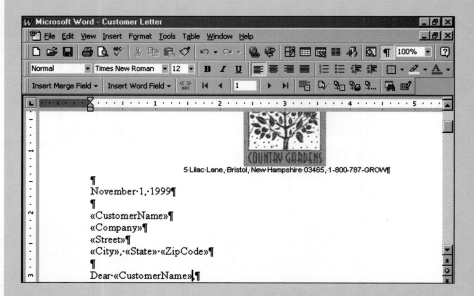

TROUBLE? Compare your screen with Figure 6-29 and make sure there are no extra spaces or punctuation around the merge fields. If you need to delete a merge field, highlight the entire field, and then press the Delete key.

11. Click the **Save** button 🖫 on the Word Standard toolbar to save the letter.

Performing the Mail Merge

With the main document and merge fields in place, you're ready to merge the main document with the data source—the Excel customer list—to produce the customized letter.

PERFORMING A MAIL MERGE

- Display the completed main document (with all merge fields inserted) in the Word document window.
- Click the Mail Merge Helper button on the Mail Merge toolbar.
- Click the Merge button.
- In the Merge to list box of the Merge dialog box, specify the destination for the merge results (document, printer, or electronic mail). Change any other settings, as necessary.
- Click the Merge button.

In this case, Sue wants the merge results placed in a new document, so that she can check the merged form letters before printing them. First she needs to specify the records that are to be included in the mail merge—customers in Vermont.

To specify selection criteria for records to retrieve from the data source:

1. Click the **Mail Merge Helper** button 🖳 on the Mail Merge toolbar. The Mail Merge Helper dialog box opens.

2. Click the **Merge** button to display the Merge dialog box. See Figure 6-30.

Figure 6-30
Merge dialog box

specify destination of merged results

click here to specify selection options

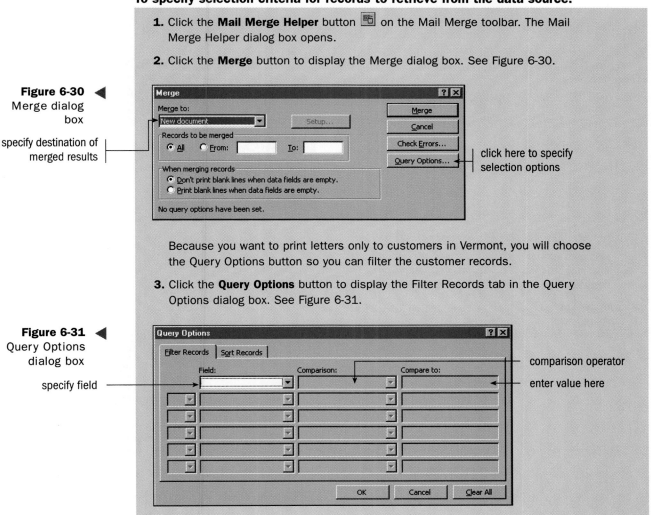

Because you want to print letters only to customers in Vermont, you will choose the Query Options button so you can filter the customer records.

3. Click the **Query Options** button to display the Filter Records tab in the Query Options dialog box. See Figure 6-31.

Figure 6-31
Query Options dialog box

specify field

comparison operator

enter value here

4. Click the **Field** list arrow to display the list of fields from the customer list. Scroll the list until the State field appears. Click **State** to select the field you want to base your selection on. Notice that the Comparison operator box now displays the default operator—Equal to. Accept the default comparison operator and enter a value to compare the State field to.

5. Make sure the insertion point is in the Compare to text box and then type **VT**.

6. Click the **OK** button to return to the Merge dialog box.

You are now ready to merge the data with the letter. You can merge the data to a new document, or merge directly to the printer, electronic mail, or fax. Sue wants to check the merged document before printing, so you will merge to a new document.

7. Click the **Merge** button. The Excel data is merged with the Word form letter and placed in a new document named Form Letters1 (the default name supplied by Word). The form letter for each of the five Vermont customers is contained in the merged document, each separated by a section break.

8. Scroll the document until you can see the first merged address. Word replaced each merge field with the appropriate Excel data. See Figure 6-32.

Figure 6-32 ◀
Merged results
in new
document

first Vermont
customer in Excel
customer list

document contains 5
two-page letters

Notice that the merged document contains 10 pages. Each letter is two pages long, and there are five letters in all.

9. Use the buttons in the vertical scroll bar to page through the merged document. Notice that in addresses that do not include a company name, the blank line is suppressed. Also, notice that each two-page form letter is separated from the others by a section break.

Now you'll save the merged document and then close it.

10. Save the document as **Merged Customer Letters** in the Tutorial.06 folder on your Student Disk.

11. Close the Merged Customer Letters document. You return to the main document, the customer letter.

Excel

Viewing Merged Documents

When you're working with mail-merge documents, you don't have to open the document containing the merge results in order to view them. You can view the merged documents right from the main document.

The View Merged Data button on the Mail Merge toolbar lets you check the merge results quickly. When you click this button, Word displays information from the first data record in place of the merge fields. You can then use the navigation buttons on the Mail Merge toolbar to view the results for other data records. You'll practice using the navigation buttons to view the merge results.

To view the merge results from the main document:

1. Click the **View Merged Data** button ⟨⟩ on the Mail Merge toolbar. Word displays the information from the first merged letter in place of the merge fields. See Figure 6-33.

Figure 6-33 ◄
Viewing merged results from main document

View Merged Data button
first record
previous record

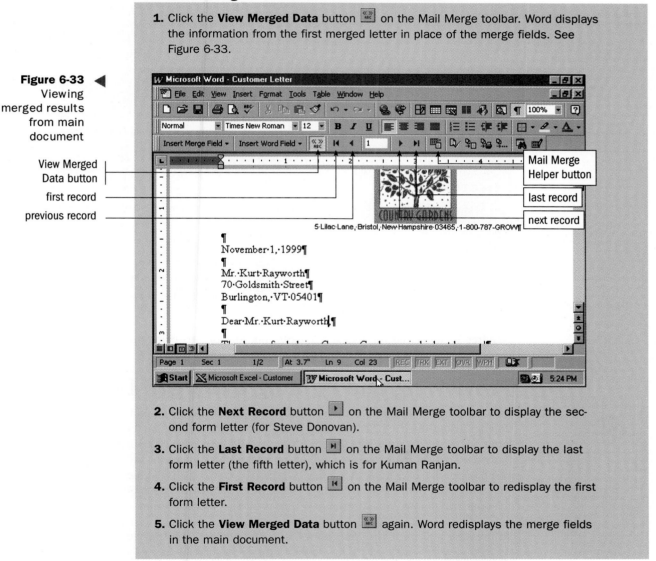

2. Click the **Next Record** button ▶ on the Mail Merge toolbar to display the second form letter (for Steve Donovan).

3. Click the **Last Record** button ▶| on the Mail Merge toolbar to display the last form letter (the fifth letter), which is for Kuman Ranjan.

4. Click the **First Record** button |◀ on the Mail Merge toolbar to redisplay the first form letter.

5. Click the **View Merged Data** button ⟨⟩ again. Word redisplays the merge fields in the main document.

Sue has just learned that one of her customers, Williston Lawn Services, has moved to a different location. She asks you to enter the new address for this customer in Excel and then re-merge the Word document with the data.

To change the address and then re-merge the document:

1. Click the **Microsoft Excel** button on the taskbar to switch to Excel.

2. Use the data form to locate Williston Lawn Services (customer number 192) and change the Street entry to **10 Main Street**.

3. Click the **Microsoft Word** button on the taskbar to switch back to Word.

4. Click the **View Merged Data** button 〔《》〕 on the Mail Merge toolbar. Word displays the information from the first merged letter.

The record for Williston Lawn Services is the second record (in the mail merge).

5. Click the **Next Record** button 〔▶〕 on the Mail Merge toolbar to select the next record. Word displays the record for Williston Lawn Services. Note that the data has been updated to show the new street address (10 Main Street).

Although the main document now shows the updated record data, the document containing the merge results—Merged Customer Letters—still contains the old address, because it contains only the results of the previous merge. In order to update the Merged Customer Letters document, you need to re-merge the main document with the data source and then save the updated merge results.

6. Click the **Mail Merge Helper** button 〔▦〕 on the Mail Merge toolbar. The Mail Merge Helper dialog box opens.

7. Click the **Merge** button to open the Merge dialog box, and then click the **Merge** button. The mail merge results are displayed in a new document window.

8. Scroll through the results until you find the address for Williston Lawn Services. Note that it now includes the updated street data.

Now you need to save the merge results as Merged Customer Letters to overwrite the existing document.

9. Use the Save As command to save the document containing the merge results as **Merged Customer Letters**, answer **Yes** to the prompt for overwriting the existing file, and then close the Merged Customer Letters document. You return to the main document, which still displays the data for Williston Lawn Services.

After viewing the merged documents, Sue decides to print just one of the letters to check its appearance and layout before printing all the letters.

Previewing and Printing a Merged Document

You can preview and print a merged document in the same way that you do any Word document—using the Print Preview and Print buttons on the Standard toolbar. For the sample letter Sue wants to print, she decides that it would be best to print one that includes a company name in the address. This will allow her to make sure that the additional line for the company name does not cause a bad page break across the two pages of the letter. Because the main document already displays the data for Williston Lawn Services, which includes the company name, you can preview and print this merged letter.

To preview and print the merged letter for Williston Lawn Services:

1. Click the **Print Preview** button 〔🔍〕 on the Standard toolbar. Both pages of the letter are displayed in Print Preview. See Figure 6-34.

Figure 6-34 ◀
Merged letter
for Williston
Lawn Services
in Print Preview

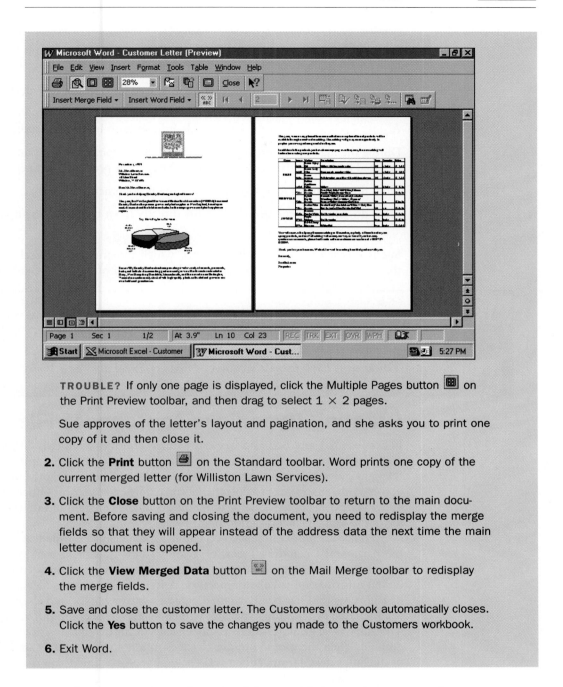

TROUBLE? If only one page is displayed, click the Multiple Pages button 🔲 on the Print Preview toolbar, and then drag to select 1 × 2 pages.

Sue approves of the letter's layout and pagination, and she asks you to print one copy of it and then close it.

2. Click the **Print** button 🖨 on the Standard toolbar. Word prints one copy of the current merged letter (for Williston Lawn Services).

3. Click the **Close** button on the Print Preview toolbar to return to the main document. Before saving and closing the document, you need to redisplay the merge fields so that they will appear instead of the address data the next time the main letter document is opened.

4. Click the **View Merged Data** button on the Mail Merge toolbar to redisplay the merge fields.

5. Save and close the customer letter. The Customers workbook automatically closes. Click the **Yes** button to save the changes you made to the Customers workbook.

6. Exit Word.

Sue plans on reviewing the printed letter with her assistants to make sure everyone approves of it before she prints and mails all the form letters.

Quick Check

1. The _____ document of a form letter contains the text that stays the same, as well as the _____ .

2. A _____ contains the variable information in a form letter.

3. During the mail merge process you updated the customer list in Excel and then observed the updated address in the merged customer letter. That process illustrates _____ .

4. How do you insert merge fields into a main document?

5. How do you view merged documents directly from the main document?

Sue is pleased with her finished letter, which integrates her Excel data. She is confident that it will contribute to the successful promotion of Country Gardens.

SESSION

6.3

In this session, you will create hyperlinks between documents so that you can easily access other information from a single document. You will learn how to navigate a series of hyperlinks using the Web toolbar. You will also learn how to convert an Excel worksheet to HTML format so you can display Excel data as a Web document.

Creating Hyperlinks to Connect Files

In Sessions 6.1 and 6.2, you worked with several files from two different programs, Excel and Word, that contained related information. To do this, you opened each program, and then navigated between the two using their program buttons on the taskbar. With Excel 97, you can now insert links to documents created using Microsoft Office programs. These links allow you to easily navigate to different documents created in different programs, without having to launch each program first.

To link various documents, you can use a hyperlink. A **hyperlink** is an object (computer file pathname or address, text, or graphic) in a document that you can click to access information in other locations in that document or in other documents. This system of linked information is called **hypertext**. A hyperlink can be a filename, a word, a phrase, or a graphic that has been assigned an address to a file located elsewhere. If the hyperlink is a filename or text, the hyperlink will be displayed in color and as underlined text. If the hyperlink is a graphic, there is no visual cue until you position your mouse over the graphic. Then the mouse pointer changes to a pointing hand 🖑 and displays the location of the link's destination. When you click a hyperlink, the destination document is brought into memory and displayed on the screen. This hyperlink may reference

- a document created in Word, Excel, PowerPoint, or Access
- a section farther down in the same document
- a document on the World Wide Web

Hyperlinks offer a new way of making information available. Files containing hyperlinks are called **hyperlink documents**. Using the hyperlinks available to you in a hyperlink document, you are able to jump from one topic to the next in whatever order you want, regardless of where they reside.

As more hyperlinks are added between and within various documents, a structure emerges that you can navigate, traveling from hyperlink to hyperlink, following a path of information and ideas. You have already worked with such a structure when you accessed the Excel online Help system. By clicking a keyword or phrase, you were able to access additional information on the topic you were interested in. The Excel online Help system is an example of a series of hyperlink documents.

Inserting a Hyperlink

Sue asks you to place a hyperlink in the New Products workbook to the Merged Customer Letters (Word file) and to the Customers workbook (Excel file). With the files connected she can easily jump to the other files if she wants to recall specific information. For instance, by including links to the customer list and the merged customer letter she can check a customer's name, or make sure she sent a letter to an important new client—while working in the New Products workbook.

INSERTING A HYPERLINK

- Select the text, graphic, or cell where you want to insert the hyperlink, and then click the Insert Hyperlink button on the Standard toolbar to display the Insert Hyperlink dialog box.
- Type the address of the Web page or file you want to jump to. If you are not sure of the filename, click the Browse button to display the Link to File dialog box. Find and select the file you want to link to.
- If you want to jump to a particular location within the file, enter the location in the Named location in file text box.
- Click the Use relative path for hyperlink check box if you want the Excel destination's relative file address.

To insert a hyperlink into an Excel worksheet:

1. If you took a break after the last session, make sure Excel is running and your Student Disk is in the appropriate disk drive.

2. Open the **New Products** workbook located in the Tutorial.06 folder on your Student Disk.

3. Make sure the Title Sheet sheet is active, and then click cell **A10**. The Title Sheet is where you want to insert the hyperlinks to the other files Sue works with when using this workbook.

4. Type **Cross Reference to Related Documents**, and then press the **Enter** key.

5. Click cell **A10**, and then click the **Bold** button on the Standard toolbar.

   Enter the text you want to use as a reference.

6. Click cell **A11**, type **Merged Customer Letters**, and press the **Enter** key.

7. In cell A12 type **Customer List**, and then press the **Enter** key.

   Now you need to specify the location of the destination file for each hyperlink. You do this using the Insert Hyperlink button on the Standard toolbar.

8. Click cell **A11** and then click the **Insert Hyperlink** button on the Standard toolbar to display the Insert Hyperlink dialog box. See Figure 6-35.

   TROUBLE? If the message "You should save this document before creating a hyperlink...." appears, click the Yes button and save the document before inserting the link.

Figure 6-35 ◀
Insert
Hyperlink
dialog box

enter destination
file for the link

click here to view contents
of selected drive

Enter the address of the merged customer letter, which is its filename.

9. Click the **Browse** button in the Link to file or URL section to open the Link to File dialog box. Make sure your Student Disk is in the appropriate disk drive, and the Tutorial.06 folder is specified in the Look in list box.

10. Click **Merged Customer Letters** and then click the **OK** button.

11. Make sure the Use relative path for hyperlink check box is checked so that the Path section of the dialog box will show only the name of the file and not the drive letters. Therefore, in the event that you decide at a later time to move the file to another folder, you will not have to insert a new address for the hyperlink to that file.

12. Click the **OK** button to close the dialog box. Notice that the hyperlink text is colored and underlined, which indicates the text is a hyperlink.

13. Click cell **A12** and repeat Steps 8-12 to create a hyperlink to the Customer workbook. See Figure 6-36.

Figure 6-36 ◀
Hyperlinks
inserted into
Title Sheet

hyperlinks

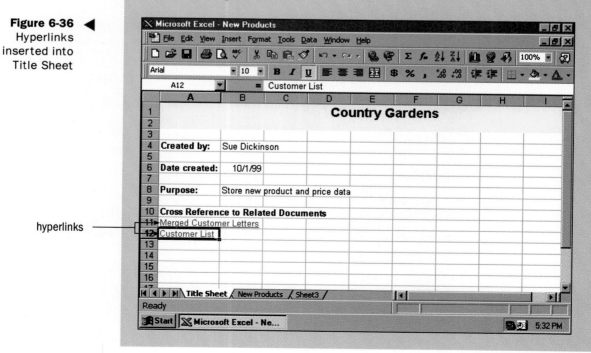

Now that you have created the hyperlinks, you should test them.

Testing Hyperlinks

Now that you have created the hyperlinks, you decide to test them to make sure each one links to the correct location. Recall that by clicking a hyperlink you jump to the referenced location. First, test the hyperlink to the merged customer letters.

To test the Merged Customer Letters hyperlink:

1. Position the pointer over the text **Merged Customer Letters** in cell A11. The pointer changes to a pointing hand 🖑, and a ScreenTip showing the address of the linked document appears.

2. Click the **Merged Customer Letters** hyperlink. Word launches and the Merged Customer Letters document opens on your screen. See Figure 6-37. Notice that the Web toolbar also appears on your screen. Figure 6-38 describes the function of each button on the Web toolbar in navigating between documents that contain hyperlinks.

Figure 6-37 ◀
Merged
Customer
Letters
document
opened from
hyperlink

Web toolbar (location
on your screen
may differ)

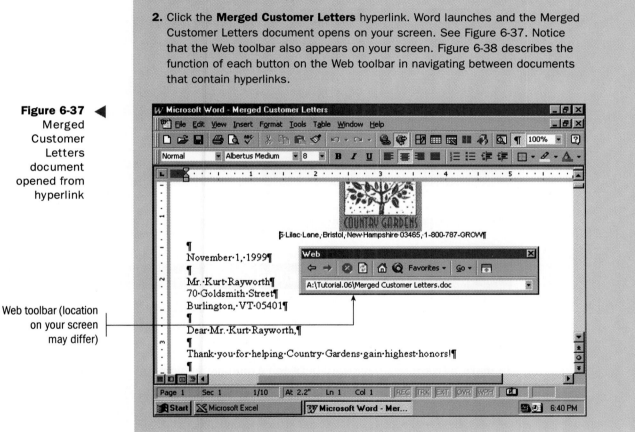

Figure 6-38 ◄
Function of
buttons on
Web toolbar

Icon	Button Name	Description
⇐	Back	Displays the previous hyperlink document
⇒	Forward	Displays the next hyperlink document
⊗	Stop Current Jump	Terminates a jump
▣	Refresh Current Page	Updates the information on a page
⌂	Start Page	Displays the home page of the current site
◎	Search the Web	Uses the Internet Explorer to search the Web
Favorites	Favorites	Adds sites to a Favorites folder for easy reference
Go	Go	Displays a list of all commands on the toolbar
▣	Show Only Web toolbar	Hides other toolbars
N/A	Address	Shows a history of documents and sites visited

Navigating Between the Hyperlink Documents

After reviewing the letter, you are ready to return to Excel. Instead of using the program button on the taskbar, use the navigational buttons on the Web toolbar to move forward and backward between the hyperlink documents.

To move forward and backward between hyperlink documents:

1. Click the **Back** button ⇐ on the Web toolbar to return to the title sheet for the New Products workbook. Notice that the hyperlink reference has changed color, indicating that you have used the hyperlink at least once to jump to the linked document.

2. Click the **Customer List** hyperlink. The Customers workbook opens.

3. Click the **Back** button ⇐ on the Web toolbar to return to the New Products workbook.

 TROUBLE? If the Web toolbar does not appear, click View on the menu bar, click Toolbars, and then click Web. Repeat Step 3.

4. Click the **Forward** button ⇒ on the Web toolbar to jump to the Customers workbook again.

5. Click the **Back** button ⇐ on the Web toolbar to return to the New Products workbook.

6. Save and then close the New Products workbook. Notice that the Customer workbook automatically closed. Remove the Web toolbar.

7. Switch to Word, close the Word document, and then exit Word.

Sue is pleased to have the hyperlinks in place for navigating between these related Country Gardens documents.

Publishing Excel Data on a Web Page

The **World Wide Web** (WWW), commonly called the Web, is a structure of documents connected electronically over **the Internet**, which is a large computer network made up of smaller networks and computers all connected electronically. Each document on the Web is called a **Web document** or **Web page**. These documents store different types of information, including text, graphics, sound, animation, and video. A Web page often includes hypertext links to other Web documents. These hypertext links point to other Web pages and allow you to follow related information by jumping from computer to computer to retrieve the desired information. Each Web page or document has a specific address, called its Uniform Resource Locator, or more commonly, **URL**. The URL indicates where the Web document is stored on the Web.

As a progressive businessperson, Sue recognized early the potential marketing power of the Internet. Understanding this potential, she hired a small firm to develop her company's documents to be placed on the Web. This provides Sue with another means to inform her customers of new Country Gardens products and events, in addition to the customer letter and the in-store flyers.

Now, she plans to develop an additional Web page showing her new products list. Fortunately, Sue can use her existing New Products worksheet to create this Web page. However, she will need to make some modifications first. In order for a document to be usable as a Web document, it needs to be formatted in a particular way.

Converting an Excel Worksheet to HTML Format

When people access the World Wide Web, they use a software program, called a **Web browser**, that enables them to access, view, and navigate all the Web documents on the Web. Web browsers recognize files that are in the HTML format. Therefore, any document that is to be available on the Web needs to be in this HTML format. **HTML**, short for HyperText Markup Language, is the language in which your data needs to be formatted in order to be accessible on the Web. In order to display your Excel data on the Web you need to convert it to HTML Format. Excel workbook data can easily be converted to HTML format. Only then can the workbook be used as a Web document.

Sue has asked you to convert the new products table in the New Products worksheet to HTML format. Excel provides a Wizard that walks you through the process of converting an Excel range or chart to HTML format.

To open the New Products workbook and start the Internet Assistant Wizard:

1. Open the New Products workbook and make sure the New Products sheet is activated. Press **Ctrl + Home** to return to the top of the worksheet.

2. Select the range **A11:H21**. This is the range containing the new products table that you want to convert to HTML format.

3. Click **File** on the menu bar, and then click **Save as HTML** to open the Internet Assistant Wizard - Step 1 of 4 dialog box. See Figure 6-39.

   TROUBLE? If the Office Assistant opens, click "No, don't provide help now" to close it.

   TROUBLE? If the Save as HTML command does not appear on the File menu, click Tools on the menu bar, then click Add-Ins to display the Add-Ins dialog box. Click the Internet Assistant Wizard check box, and then click OK to install the Internet Assistant. Repeat Step 3. (If you don't see the Internet Assistant Wizard in the Add-Ins dialog box, check with your instructor or technical support person.)

Figure 6-39 ◄
Internet
Assistant
Wizard - Step
1 of 4

selected data range
identifies area you
want converted to
HTML format

click to add another
range or chart

click to change
order of objects
on Web page

click to remove range
or chart from the list

In the first dialog box, you specify the range(s) and charts to put on the Web page. The range you selected, A11:H21, is automatically inserted into the Ranges and charts to convert list box. To add another range or chart, click the Add button. You have no more ranges or charts to add.

4. Click the **Next** button to display the Internet Assistant Wizard - Step 2 of 4 dialog box. See Figure 6-40.

Figure 6-40 ◄
Internet
Assistant
Wizard - Step
2 of 4

this option creates
a complete new
HTML Web page

In the Internet Assistant Wizard – Step 2 of 4 dialog box, you specify whether you want to create a complete new Web page or insert the range into an existing Web page. Sue wants to insert the new products table as a separate Web page, which is the default option.

To create a complete Web page:

1. Make sure the Create an independent, ready-to-view HTML document option button is selected, and then click the **Next** button to display the Internet Assistant Wizard - Step 3 of 4 dialog box. See Figure 6-41.

Figure 6-41
Internet
Assistant
Wizard - Step
3 of 4

insert horizontal lines
on Web page

your text here
will differ

specify title for
title bar

specify words you
want to appear on
Web page above data

In Step 3 of the Internet Assistant Wizard, you lay out your Web page. You specify the title you want displayed in the title bar of the Web browser. You also enter any information you want to appear above or below your worksheet data. In the Header section, you type the text you want to appear above the data in the worksheet at the top of the Web document. You can also enter text in the Description below header box. These lines of text appear below the header. You can also insert horizontal lines, the date the file was last updated, and your Internet e-mail address. Now enter the information for Sue's Web page.

2. Highlight the default Web page title in the Title textbox, and then type **Country Gardens Web Page**.

   TROUBLE? If you pressed the Enter key and accidentally advanced to the Internet Assistant Wizard – Step 4 of 4 dialog box, click the Back button to return to Internet Assistant – Step 3 of 4.

3. Press the **Tab** key to move to the **Header** text box, and then type **New Product List** to place this text above the new products table on your Web page.

4. Click the **Insert a horizontal line after the converted data** check box to place a line below the new products table to serve as a separator from the other information on your Web page.

   Now enter the date the page was updated, the name of the person creating the Web page, and an e-mail address to contact.

5. Type **10/1/99** in the Last Update on text box.

6. Type **Sue Dickinson** in the By text box.

7. Type **sd@cg.com** in the Email text box. The completed dialog box appears in Figure 6-42.

Figure 6-42 ◀
Internet
Assistant
Wizard - Step 3
of 4 completed

8. Click the **Next** button to display the Internet Assistant Wizard - Step 4 of 4 dialog box. See Figure 6-43.

Figure 6-43 ◀
Internet
Assistant
Wizard - Step 4
of 4 completed

accept default ———

change to
CGPRICE.htm ——|

In the final step of the Internet Assistant Wizard, you specify the location and name of the HTML file you are creating.

9. Make sure that the Save the result as an HTML file option button is selected so your work is saved as an HTML file.

   Change the default filename MyHTML.htm to CGPRICE.htm.

10. In the File path text box, select just the filename, **MyHTML.htm**, and replace it with **CGPRICE.htm**. See Figure 6-44.

Figure 6-44 ◀
Internet
Assistant
Wizard - Step 4
of 4 after
filename
change

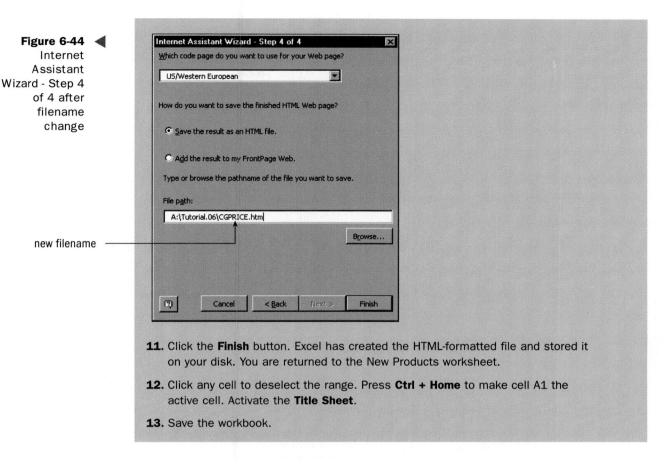

new filename ———

11. Click the **Finish** button. Excel has created the HTML-formatted file and stored it on your disk. You are returned to the New Products worksheet.

12. Click any cell to deselect the range. Press **Ctrl + Home** to make cell A1 the active cell. Activate the **Title Sheet**.

13. Save the workbook.

Viewing an HTML File Using a Web Browser

You have completed your Web page and it is now saved on your Student Disk as CGPRICE.htm. The file extension .htm indicates that it is in HTML format, and therefore readable using a Web browser. Before the document is made accessible on the World Wide Web, Sue wants to view her Web page to confirm that her layout appears as she wants it to. To see how it will appear to people viewing it from the Web using a Web browser, you can open the HTML file on your Student Disk using your own Web browser.

To view the CGPrice HTML file:

1. Click **View** on the menu bar, point to **Toolbars**, and then click **Web**. Excel displays the Web toolbar.

2. Click the **Go** button 🔲 on the Web toolbar, and then click **Open**. Excel displays the Open Internet Address dialog box, in which you can specify the URL of the Internet site or the name of the HTML file you want to view.

3. Click the **Browse** button. Excel displays the Browse dialog box. If necessary, use the Look In text box to display the contents of the Tutorial.06 folder on your Student Disk, click **CGPRICE**, and then click the **Open** button. Excel returns to the Open Internet Address dialog box and displays the address for the HTML file.

4. Click the **OK** button. Excel opens the Internet Explorer (or the Web browser installed on your computer) and displays the CGPrice HTML file. See Figure 6-45.

Figure 6-45 ◀
Viewing New
Product List
Web page from
a Web browser

the appearance of
your Web page may
differ depending on
the Web browser
you are using

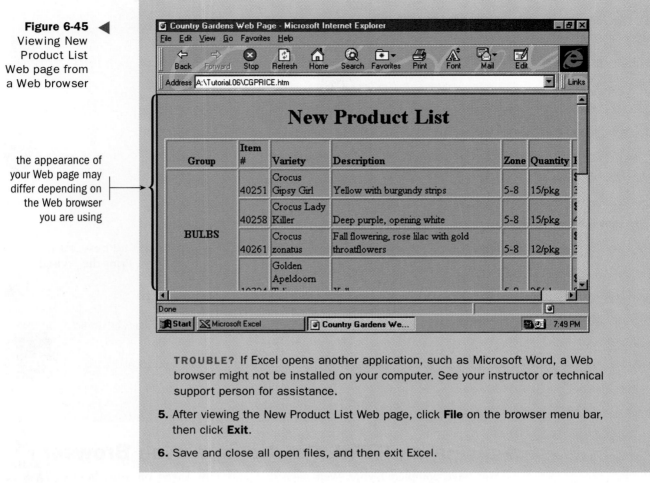

TROUBLE? If Excel opens another application, such as Microsoft Word, a Web browser might not be installed on your computer. See your instructor or technical support person for assistance.

5. After viewing the New Product List Web page, click **File** on the browser menu bar, then click **Exit**.

6. Save and close all open files, and then exit Excel.

Sue is very pleased with the New Product List Web page. It is ready to be added to the series of Web documents Country Gardens currently has available on the World Wide Web.

Quick Check

1. _____ is the language used to present documents on the World Wide Web.

2. You can jump to a document by clicking a _____.

3. A hyperlink can be a _____, _____, or _____.

4. The _____ button on the Standard toolbar is used to insert a hyperlink.

5. You use the _____ and the _____ buttons on the _____ toolbar to move forward and backward between hyperlink documents.

6. A software program called a _____ _____ enables you to access Web documents.

7. To convert Excel data to HTML format, you issue the _____ command.

8. The file extension _____ indicates that the file is in HTML format.

Sue is very pleased to have informed her customers of the new products using a variety of methods—distributing flyers, mailing customized letters, and creating a Web document to be viewed on the World Wide Web.

Tutorial Assignments

Sue is ready to send the merged customer letter to the Massachusetts Country Gardens customers. She also wants to add the NEGHA pie chart to a Web page to be viewable online. Finally, she needs to inform her advisory board, a group of local business professionals, about the company's new products and the NEGHA recognition. Help Sue with these tasks.

Do the following:

1. Start Word and open the document CustLtr2 in the TAssign folder for Tutorial.06 and save it as Customer Letter 2.
2. Use the Merge Mail Helper to modify the selection criteria so only the Massachusetts customers in the city of Andover are selected. Rearrange the letter with the modified criteria. Close the Form Letters 1 document without saving it. (Note: The document Customer Letter 2 is still open.)
3. Print the letter for Ronald Kooienga.
4. Return to the customer list in Excel and change the street address of Ron Kooienga (Customer Number 133) to 20 Freedom Trail. Print the revised letter. Save Customer Letter 2 and exit Word.
5. Open the workbook NEGHA in the TAssign folder for Tutorial.06. This workbook contains a pie chart comparing sales of the top growers in New England. Sue wants to add this chart as a new page on her Web site. Use the Internet Assistant Wizard to create a Web page named NEGHA.htm. The title bar should have the title "Country Gardens," and the Header should be "Top Growers in New England." Add any other information you think is appropriate to Step 3 of the Internet Assistant Wizard. Open your Web browser and view the Web document. Print the Web page from your browser.
6. Open the workbook NewProd2 and save it as New Products 2. Use this workbook to answer questions 7 through 11.
7. Activate the New Products worksheet. Use WordArt to create your own graphic. The text of the graphic is "New Products & Prices." Place the graphic above the new products list. Experiment with some of the features on the WordArt and Drawing toolbar. Save the workbook. Print the worksheet with the graphic.
8. Activate the Title sheet and add a hyperlink to the NEGHA workbook in cell A14. Instead of using a word or phrase as the hyperlink, use the file address of the NEGHA workbook in the TAssign folder for Tutorial.06 as the hyperlink.

9. In cell A15, create a hyperlink to the GardenNet home page on the WWW. Its URL is http://trine.com/GardenNet/. The hyperlink text should be "GardenNet."
10. In cells A17:A18, create a WordArt object with the text "Store Sales." Use the WordArt graphic as a hyperlink to the MonSales worksheet.
11. Save the New Products 2 workbook. Print the Title Sheet worksheet. Close the workbook.
12. Sue has written a letter to her advisory board telling them of the Country Gardens new products and their sales. Open the letter AdvLetr in the TAssign folder for Tutorial.06 and save it as Advisory Board Letter. Open the workbook MonSales in the TAssign folder for Tutorial.06 and save it as MonSales2. Link the MonSales2 worksheet to the Word document Advisory Board Letter. Print the letter.
13. Add the sales for Massachusetts (Figure 6-46) to the worksheet and print the advisory board letter again. Save and close both the letter and the workbook.

Figure 6-46 ◀

Item #	Variety	MA
40251	Crocus Gipsy Girl	600
40258	Crocus Lady Killer	550
40261	Crocus Zonatus	400
10324	Golden Apeldoorn Tulips	200
72211	Astilbe Assort.	300
72621	Hybrid Daylily Assort.	100
74311	Garden Phlox Assort.	650
82480	Exactum Persian Violet	1000
87345	Purple Verbena	500
87730	Salvia Cherry Blossom	450

14. Open the letter AdvLetr in the TAssign folder for Tutorial.06 and save it as Advisory Board Letter2. Open the workbook MonSales in the TAssign folder for Tutorial.06 and embed it in the Advisory Board Letter2. Add the sales for Massachusetts (Figure 6-46) to the worksheet in the Word document. Save and print the letter. Close Word.

EXPLORE
15. Use Windows Explorer to compare the file size of the two Word documents: Advisory Board Letter and Advisory Board Letter2 in the TAssign folder for Tutorial.06. What is the file size in bytes of each file? Explain the difference in file sizes.

EXPLORE
16. Sue is beginning to prepare a PowerPoint presentation for the Growers Association meeting. Create a new PowerPoint presentation. Create a first slide that has the title "Country Gardens" and a subtitle "The Past 15 Years." Include a second slide that shows Country Gardens as the top grower in New England. Embed the Pie Chart from the NEGHA workbook in the TAssign folder for Tutorial.06 into slide 2. Resize the chart as necessary. In the presentation, explode the Country Gardens slice. Print the two slides on one page. Save the presentation as "Growers" in the TAssign folder for Tutorial.06 and exit PowerPoint.

17. Close all open files.

Case Problems

1. Reporting Sales for Toy World Store manager Fred Galt must report to the regional manager each week. He faxes a memo each week to the regional sales office indicating his recommendations regarding any special sales or promotions he feels will be needed, based on the summary sales information he includes in the report. Fred maintains a worksheet that summarizes sales in units and dollars for each day of the week. This sales summary is included in his weekly report, and on the company's Web page.

Do the following:

1. If necessary, start Excel and make sure your Student Disk is in the appropriate drive. Open ToyStore.xls in the Case folder for Tutorial.06. This is Fred's partially completed worksheet. Save it as Toystore Sales.

2. Complete the worksheet by computing total sales in dollars for each day (including the formula for Saturday) by multiplying the number of units sold of each product by the price per unit (the price table is in the upper-right corner of the worksheet). Also, compute total sales for each product and the total sales for the store. (*Hint*: Check number for Monday through Friday: Total store sales = $86,993.90.)

3. Save the worksheet.

4. Start Word and open the document ToyLtr and save it as Toy Memo.

5. Link the worksheet range A1:F15 to the memo. Print the memo.

6. Saturday evening, Fred faxes the memo to the regional manager, indicating that sales are on target for the week, and no special promotions are necessary at this time. Update store sales for Saturday using the following data: 22,6,18,14. Save the workbook.

7. Print the memo.

8. Save the memo and exit Word.

9. Create a Web page named ToySales.htm which includes the range A7:F15. You decide what information should be entered on Step 3 of the Internet Assistant Wizard. Open your Web browser and view the Web document. Print the page from your Web browser.

10. Use WordArt to replace the title "Store Analysis" with the title "Toy World Sales." Print the worksheet excluding the Product Price Table.

11. Save and close the workbook.

2. Quarterly Sales at Happy Morning Farms Casandra Owens is product manager for a line of breakfast cereals at Happy Morning Farms. Casandra is waiting for one figure so that she can complete her Sales Report—Summarized by State for next week's Operations Management Team (OMT) meeting. As she is working on the report, she receives an urgent call from one of her sales representatives indicating that he needs Casandra in Denver immediately to deal with a customer problem that requires management attention. Casandra realizes that she will not be able to make the next OMT meeting, so she plans to complete her report on the road. She will get the last figure she needs, finish the report, and then fax it to John Styles, who will represent her at the meeting. Before she leaves the office, Casandra decides to embed her data in a memo.

1. If necessary, start Excel and make sure your Student Disk is in the appropriate drive. Open the workbook StSales in the Case folder for Tutorial.06.

2. Open the Word document StMemo in the Case folder for Tutorial.06 and save it as State Sales Memo.

3. Embed the StSales worksheet in the Word document, State Sales Memo, which can be found in the Case folder for Tutorial.06.

4. Save the Word document with the embedded worksheet.

5. Print the memo with the embedded worksheet.

6. After arriving in Denver Casandra gets a call with the missing sales figure—sales in Idaho this quarter were $21. Update the Word document by entering the Idaho sales number in the embedded worksheet.

7. Save the Word document and print the memo again. Close the Word document.

8. Print the source worksheet, StSales. Comment on the sales data in the source worksheet versus the sales data in the Word document.

9. Now repeat the process using a different approach. Open the workbook StSales in the Case folder for Tutorial.06 and save it as State Sales.

10. Open the Word document StMemo1 in the Case folder for Tutorial.06 and save the document as State Sales Memo1.

11. Link cell D49 in the State Sales workbook to the end of the first sentence in the State Sales Memo1 Word document. (Hint: For the best placement of the linked object, use the Unformatted text option instead of Microsoft Excel Worksheet object when you link the object.) Save the document. Print the letter.

12. Update the State Sales workbook by entering the Idaho sales number ($21).

13. Save the Word document. Print the State Sales Memo1.

14. At the bottom of the State Sales Memo1 document, add the line "Details for Sales are in the State Sales workbook." Create a hyperlink in the Word document to the State Sales workbook. The hyperlink text should be "State Sales workbook." Save the Word document. Test the hyperlink.

15. Save and close any open documents.

3. Horizons State Alumni Office Charlene Goodwin, director of alumni affairs, has been planning a marketing "blitz" in which she will use three methods to reach Horizons' alumni. For campus visitors she will develop a flyer inviting friends of HSU to visit the campus store to view its new line of Horizons affinity products. For World Wide Web users, she plans to create a Web page highlighting these products. For alumni, she plans a letter announcing the affinity products that alums can order using a mail-order form. Help her get these jobs completed.

Do the following:

1. If necessary, start Excel and make sure your Student Disk is in the appropriate drive. Open the workbook AlumProd in the Case folder for Tutorial.06, and save it as Alumni Products. This is the product list.

2. Open the Word document Alumltr in the Case folder for Tutorial.06 and save it as Alumni Letter. Link the product list from the Alumni Products workbook beginning at the line [insert price list here]. Remember to remove the note [insert price list here]. Print the letter with the linked object.

3. You notice an error in the product list—the price of item 3 should be $75. Return to Excel and correct the error in the worksheet. Print the letter. Save and close the Word document.

4. Create a logo for Horizons State using WordArt. Insert it at the top of the product list in the Alumni Products workbook. Save the workbook and print the price list with your graphic.

5. Create a Web page for the product list in the Alumni Products workbook (do not include the WordArt graphic in the range) using the Internet Assistant Wizard. You decide the titles, headers, ruled lines, and so on you want to include on the page. Name the page HorzPrc.htm. View the page using your Web browser. Print the Web page using your Web browser.

6. Create a title sheet with appropriate information to describe the workbook. Print the title sheet.

7. In the title sheet, insert a hyperlink to the Word document Alumni Letter.

8. In the title sheet, insert a hyperlink to your institution's Web page.

9. Save and close any open files.

4. Inwood Design Group of Japan Spurred by the Japanese passion for the sport, golf enjoys unprecedented popularity in Japan. Inwood Design Group plans to build a world-class golf course, and one of the four sites under consideration is Chiba Prefecture, Japan. Other possible sites are Kauai, Hawaii; Edmonton, Canada; and Scottsdale, Arizona. You and Mike Nagochi are members of the site selection team for Inwood Design Group. The team is responsible for collecting information on the sites, evaluating that information, and recommending the best site for the new golf course.

Your team identified five factors likely to determine the success of a golf course: climate, competition, market size, topography, and transportation. The team has collected information on these factors for all the four potential golf course sites.

Mike created a worksheet that the team can use to evaluate the four sites. He brought the completed worksheet to the group's meeting so that the team could analyze the information and recommend a site to management.

Prepare a memo to the site selection committee with your team's findings. Do the following:

1. If necessary, start Excel and make sure your Student Disk is in the appropriate drive. Open the workbook Inwood in the Case folder for Tutorial.06. Save the workbook as Inwood 1. Review the worksheet.

2. Open Word and write a brief memo to the site selection committee. State your recommendation for a site selection and reason(s). Support your narrative by referencing the Weighted Score section of the Inwood worksheet. Paste the Weighted Score section of the worksheet into your memo.

3. Save the Word document as Inwood Memo in the Case folder for Tutorial.06.

4. Print the memo. Close Word.

5. Explain why pasting rather than linking or embedding is appropriate in this situation.

6. In the Inwood 1 workbook, activate the Title Sheet and insert a hyperlink to the Inwood Memo. Test the hyperlink.

7. Use your Web browser to access one of the following sites: www.yahoo.com, or www.altavista.com. Use the information at these Web sites to locate an interesting golf-related Web site. In the Inwood 1 workbook, below the hyperlink to the Inwood Memo, insert a hyperlink to this site.

8. Replace the Inwood Design Group title in the Title Sheet with a WordArt image with the same text.

9. Save the Inwood 1 workbook, print the title sheet, then close and exit the workbook.

Developing an Excel Application

Employee 401(k) Planning at CableScan

OBJECTIVES

In this tutorial you will:

- Arrange worksheet in sections

- Assign data validation rules to a cell

- Assign and use range names

- Use IF and FV functions in formulas

- Create a series using AutoFill

- Protect worksheets

- Delete unnecessary sheets from a workbook

- Plan and record Excel macros

- Run a macro using menu commands

- Run a macro using a shortcut key

- View Visual Basic for Applications code

- Run a macro using a button object

CableScan

CableScan intends to implement a 401(k) plan this year, and Mary Kincaid, benefits administrator, will travel to the company's three sites to present the plan and its features to all of the employees. A 401(k) plan is a retirement savings program that allows employees to deduct funds from their monthly pay, before taxes, provided that they invest them directly into various options within the 401(k) plan.

To introduce the 401(k) plan, Mary will hold formal meetings at each company location. At the meetings, she will give employees an audio-visual presentation that includes an overview of the plan, the administrative procedures, and the investment options. Because there are currently no other retirement plans available to the employees, other than personal savings, the company wants to be sure that there is high participation in the 401(k) plan. Management has set a goal of 80 percent of all eligible employees to participate in the plan. To help ensure this high rate of participation, the company will match, dollar for dollar, whatever the employee contributes, up to four percent of the employee's salary. Additionally, employees can contribute up to a total of 20 percent of their salaries.

Mary has asked you to work with individual employees after each of the formal presentations by answering any questions they may have. She also wants to provide an Excel workbook that can be used by employees to determine the appropriate amount they can contribute to the plan, and see the effects different amounts will have on their retirement savings over the next five to 30 years. Employees can use this workbook to conduct their own what-if analyses on their retirement plans.

SESSION

7.1

In this tutorial you will develop a more complex workbook than you have in any previous tutorial. You'll build it in three sessions. In this session you will start the process by dividing your worksheet into separate sections for input and calculations. You'll use the Excel data validation feature to specify the type of data that a cell can store. You'll assign names to cells and use these names instead of cell addresses to build the formulas in your worksheet. Finally, you'll use the IF function to build formulas where the value you store in a cell depends on the result of a condition.

Planning the 401(k) Workbook Application

You have been asked to develop a simple investment model that will allow each CableScan employee to see the effect (dollar accumulation) of investing a percent of his or her current salary each year at an annual return on investment over a 30-year period. You can use Excel to create a workbook that the employees can use to make these calculations and plan their retirement funding.

You realize that many of the employees at CableScan are familiar with Excel, and will have no trouble using a 401(k) planning workbook. However, there are others who will require assistance in using the workbook, and you will be working with those employees one-on-one after Mary presents the plan. Because the CableScan employees using the workbook will be of varying skill levels with Excel and computers in general, you want the workbook to be as easy to use as possible. It needs to produce valuable information clearly, while being nearly foolproof to use.

Figures 7-1 and 7-2 show the planning analysis sheet and the sketch that Mary has created to assist you in completing the workbook. You can see from the planning analysis sheet that the formulas to be used in the workbook are somewhat complex. Fortunately, Excel provides a few means of simplifying complex formulas. Mary also wants you to build the worksheet so that employees enter only valid data in the correct cells in the worksheet. Note in the sketch in Figure 7-2 that the worksheet will be divided into manageable sections—sections where the employee provides (inputs) information, and sections containing information produced from calculating the input to produce output. Also note that the workbook allows the employee to view and analyze the information numerically and graphically, by including a line chart.

Figure 7-1 ◀
Planning
analysis sheet

Planning Analysis Sheet

<u>My Goal</u>
To develop a simple investment planning worksheet

<u>What information do I need?</u>
Name of employee
Current salary
Percent of salary invested—enter a percent of salary. NOTE: The maximum percent an employee can contribute is 20 percent.
Annual rate of return—enter as a percent

<u>What calculations do I need to perform?</u>
Employee contribution—monthly = current salary * percent of salary invested/12
Employer contribution—monthly = monthly employee contribution
NOTE: Remember that for every dollar employee contributes, employer invests a dollar, up to 4% of employee's salary; employer invests nothing above 4% of employee's salary
Total monthly contribution = monthly employee contribution + monthly employer contribution
Value of investment at 5, 10, 15, 20, 25, and 30 years. NOTE: use
=FV(monthly rate of return, number of periods, total monthly contribution) to compute future value of investment

<u>What output do I want to see?</u>
Table showing future value of investment at 5, 10, 15, 20, 25, and 30 years
Line chart displaying future value of investment

Figure 7-2 ◄
Sketch of
worksheet plan

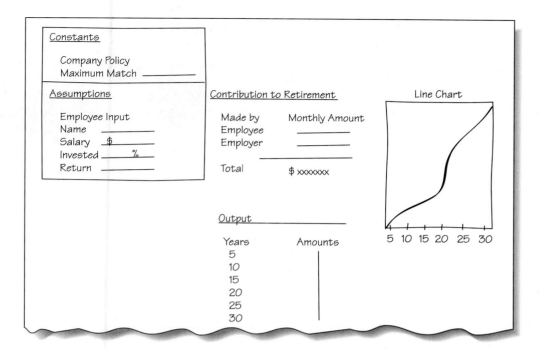

Use these planning documents to build the worksheet for Mary. She has already started to create the workbook.

Open the 401k file and examine the work Mary has done so far.

To open the 401k workbook and save the workbook as 401kPlan:

1. Start Excel. Make sure your Student Disk is in the appropriate disk drive, open the workbook **401k** in the Tutorial.07 folder on your Student Disk, and immediately save it as **401kPlan**.

2. Click the **401kPlan** sheet tab. In the 401kPlan worksheet, the labels and column headings have already been entered. See Figure 7-3.

Figure 7-3 ◄
Initial
401kPlan
worksheet

input section →

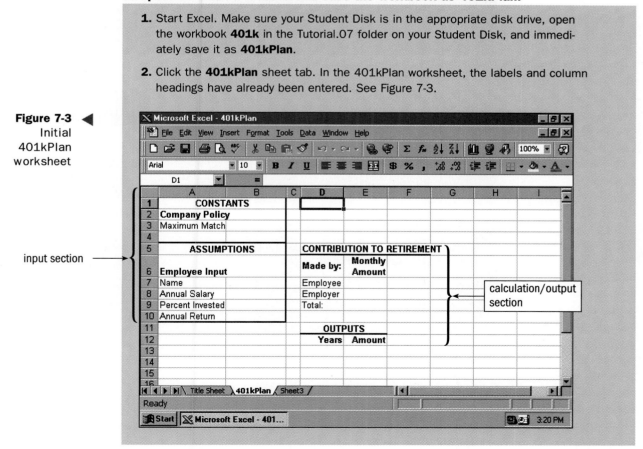

Arranging a Worksheet in Sections

Since many people will be using the worksheet, and will want to change assumptions such as current salary, percent of salary invested, and annual return on investment, Mary has divided her worksheet into two sections: input and calculation/output. The **input section** contains the data values used in formulas. Sometimes the input section is said to contain the worksheet's **initial conditions and assumptions** because the results of the worksheet are based on the values in the input section. A second section, the **calculation/output section**, performs the calculations and displays the results of the model. The formulas in this section do not contain constants; instead they reference cells in the input section. For example, the formula to calculate the monthly employee contribution to the 401(k) plan (cell E7) will reference cells B8 and B9 in the input section, which contain values for the employee's salary and the percent of salary the employee invests in the 401(k) plan, rather than constants, such as 30000 and .05.

Dividing the worksheet into sections has the following benefits:

- The user knows exactly where to enter and change values—in the input area. Changes to the worksheet are made only to values in the input area.

- The user clearly sees what factors affect the results of the worksheet.

- The user doesn't have to change specific values in formulas to reflect new assumptions.

Entering Initial Values

Now that you have examined the current status of the workbook, it's time for you to continue creating the 401(k) application. Since the labels and headings have already been entered, you'll begin by entering and formatting the values shown in Figure 7-4.

Figure 7-4 ◄
Initial
assumptions

Cell	Value	Formatting
B3	.04	Percent style
B7	Mike Tobey	
B8	30000	Currency style, no decimal place
B9	.05	Percent style
B10	.08	Percent style

To enter and format the input values:

1. Click cell **B3**, type **.04**, and press the **Enter** key. Return to cell B3 and click the **Percent style** button 🔲 on the Formatting toolbar.

2. Click cell **B7** and enter the remaining values and formatting shown in Figure 7-4. When you're finished entering the data, your input section of the worksheet should look like Figure 7-5.

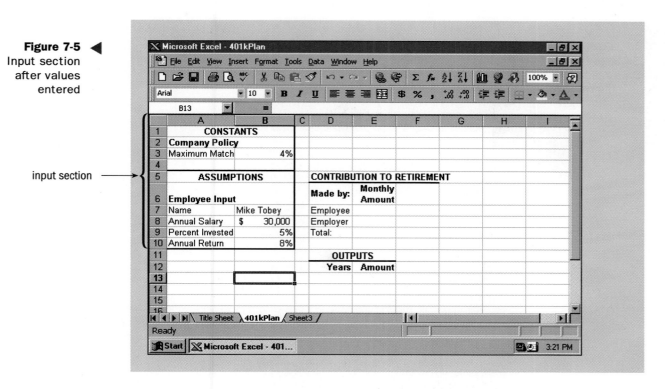

Figure 7-5 ◀
Input section
after values
entered

input section →

Mary is concerned that an employee may accidentally enter invalid data into the worksheet, which will result in output that is not correct. For example, employees are not allowed to invest more than 20 percent of their salary in the 401(k) plan. If an employee entered a value greater than 20 percent of his or her salary, the value of future investments would be inaccurate, because the plan does not allow for this level of investment.

You can use the Excel data validation feature to prevent a user from entering an invalid value. This will allow you to minimize errors introduced by the workbook user.

Validating Data Entry

One way to make sure the correct data is entered in a cell or range is to use the Excel data validation feature to restrict the information being entered in the worksheet. For instance, you can specify the type of data (whole numbers, dates, time, or text) allowed in a cell, as well as the range of acceptable values (for example, numbers between 1 and 100). If you wish, you can display an input message that appears when a user enters data in a given cell, reminding the user of valid entries for this cell. You can also display an error message when the user enters an invalid entry. Since the maximum percentage of salary an employee can invest is 20, Mary asks you to establish a validation rule so that a user cannot exceed this limit.

Specifying Data Type and Acceptable Values

The first step in using the data validation feature is to specify the type of data as well as the acceptable values allowed in a cell or range of cells. You need to specify that in cell B9 only decimal values less than or equal to .2 (or 20 percent) are permitted.

To specify a data type and acceptable values:

1. Click cell **B9**, the cell where you want to apply data validation.

2. Click **Data** on the menu bar, and then click **Validation** to display the Data Validation dialog box. See Figure 7-6. This dialog box allows you to specify the parameters for the validation, the message that appears as the user inputs a value, and an error alert message that appears if the user enters an invalid value.

Figure 7-6 ◀
Settings tab of
Data Validation
dialog box

3. Make sure the Settings tab is selected, click the **Allow** list arrow, and then click **Decimal** from the list of allowable data types. Notice the number of text boxes in the dialog box changed to reflect the selection you made in the Allow list box.

   Next, specify the range of values you will allow.

4. Click the **Data** list arrow, and then click **less than or equal to**. Notice that when you select this data operator, additional text boxes appear in the dialog box, allowing you to further specify the criteria for validation.

5. In the Maximum text box, type **.2**. The data validation rule of a value of less than or equal to 20 percent is now specified.

   TROUBLE? If you accidentally pressed the Enter key or clicked the OK button and the Data Validation dialog box closed, you can reopen the dialog box by clicking Data on the menu bar, and then clicking Validation.

Next, establish a prompt that will appear when users select that cell, indicating the type of data they can enter into the cell.

Specifying an Input Message

Now create an input prompt that informs the user what kind of data is allowed in the selected cell. The message will appear as a ScreenTip beside the cell when the user selects it. Although the input message is optional, Mary asks you to include the input message "Percent of salary invested by employee cannot exceed 20%," as an aid to the user during data entry.

To enter a data validation input message:

1. In the Data Validation dialog box, click the **Input Message** tab. See Figure 7-7.

Figure 7-7 ◀
Input Message
tab of Data
Validation
dialog box

2. Make sure the Show input message when cell is selected check box is checked. This will ensure that the message will appear when the user selects the cell.

3. Click the **Title** text box, and then type **Valid Data**. This title will be at the top of the input message when it appears.

4. Click the **Input message** text box, and then type **Percent of salary invested by employee cannot exceed 20%**. This message will be displayed as a ScreenTip beside the cell being validated whenever the user selects that cell.

The input message that you have entered will help minimize the chances for employees to enter an invalid percent of salary value. However, if users still enter a value above 20 percent, then you want them to be prompted to reenter a correct percentage.

Specifying an Error Alert Style and Message

You can also use the Data Validation dialog box to establish an error alert message, which is a message that appears if an invalid entry is typed in the cell. This message should inform the user of the error, and identify a means to correct the error and enter a valid value.

Now create an appropriate error alert message for this cell.

To enter the error alert message:

1. In the Data Validation dialog box, click the **Error Alert** tab. See Figure 7-8.

Figure 7-8 ◀
Error Alert
tab of Data
Validation
dialog box

2. Make sure the Show error alert after invalid data is entered check box is checked. Now select the message style: Stop, Warning, or Information. Figure 7-9 describes the function of each style.

Figure 7-9 ◀
Error
message
alert styles

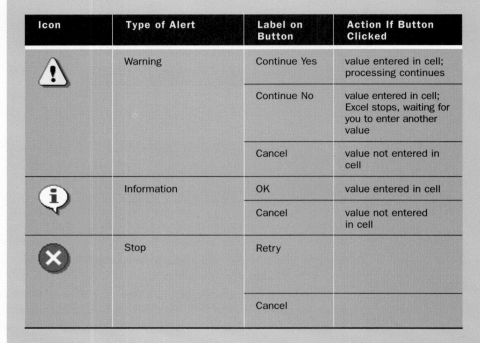

Icon	Type of Alert	Label on Button	Action If Button Clicked
⚠	Warning	Continue Yes	value entered in cell; processing continues
		Continue No	value entered in cell; Excel stops, waiting for you to enter another value
		Cancel	value not entered in cell
ⓘ	Information	OK	value entered in cell
		Cancel	value not entered in cell
✖	Stop	Retry	
		Cancel	

You decide to use the Stop style, since you don't want to continue data entry until the percent invested is 20 percent or less.

3. If necessary, click the **Style** list arrow, and then click **Stop**.

Now specify the error alert message.

4. In the Title text box, type **Invalid Data**.

5. In the Error message text box, type **You entered a value above 20%. A valid percent is 20% or less.**

6. Click the **OK** button to close the Data Validation dialog box.

The data validation rule is completely specified. Now test the validation rule to make sure it is working correctly when invalid data is entered in the cell.

To test data validation:

1. If necessary, click cell **B9**. The input message for Valid Data is displayed. See Figure 7-10.

Figure 7-10 ◀
Display of input
message

input message
displayed when
cell B9 selected

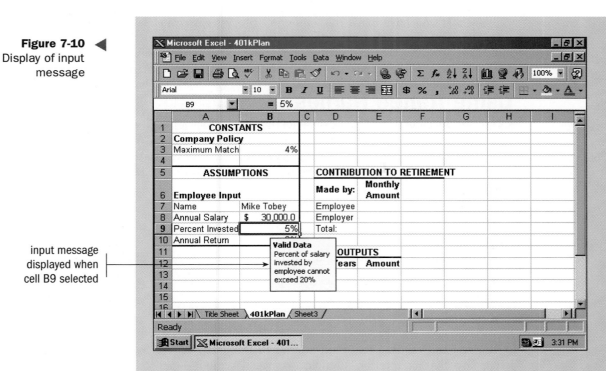

Now attempt to enter an invalid value.

2. Type **.25** and press the **Enter** key. The error alert message for Invalid Data is displayed. See Figure 7-11. Your choices are to click Retry to correct the value, or
click Cancel to start all over. You decide to correct the value.

Figure 7-11 ◀
Display of error
alert message

Stop alert indicator

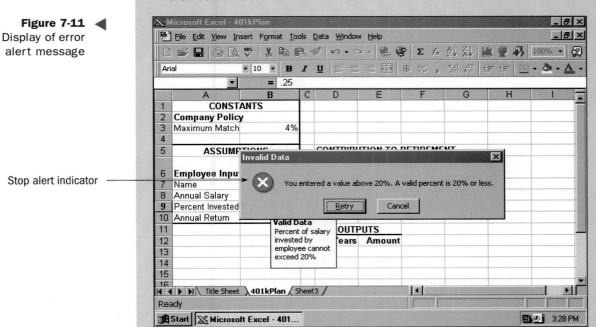

3. Click the **Retry** button. Cell B9 is highlighted and Excel waits for you to enter a
corrected value.

4. Type **.05** and press the **Enter** key. Excel recognizes this entry as valid and moves
the cell pointer to the next cell, cell B10.

Now that you have made the data entry process easier and less error-prone for users, enter the formulas needed to perform the calculations in the workbook. Some of the formulas are complex. To avoid overwhelming users, you want to simplify the formulas a bit. This will also allow users to clearly see how the inputs are calculated to produce the output.

Using Range Names

So far in Excel you have always referred to cells by their addresses. Excel provides a valuable feature that allows you to assign a name to a cell or a range of cells so you don't have to remember the cell address. A **range name** is a descriptive name you assign to a cell or range of cells that can then be used to reference the cell or range of cells in formulas, print ranges, etc.

The ability to name a cell or range allows

- easier formula construction and entry

- improved documentation and clarification of the meaning of formulas

- navigation of large worksheets simply by using the Go To command to move the pointer to a named range

- specification of a print range

Range names must begin with a letter or the underscore character (_). After the first letter, any character, letter, number, or special symbol—except hyphens and spaces—is acceptable. You can assign names of up to 255 characters, although short, meaningful names of 5-15 characters are more practical.

REFERENCE window	**DEFINING A CELL OR RANGE NAME**
	- Select the cell or range of cells you want to name.
	- Click Insert, point to Name, and then click Define to display the Define Name dialog box.
	- Type the range name in the Names in workbook text box.
	- Click Add to add the name to the Names in workbook list.
	- Click the OK button to return to the worksheet.

Defining a Range Name

You decide to assign range names to several cells in the input area. This will make it easier for you when you create the formulas to be used to calculate the output. Use the range name MaxMatch in cell B3, Salary in cell B8, Invested in cell B9, and Return in cell B10.

To define a range name:

1. Click cell **B8**, the cell you want to assign a range name.

2. Click **Insert** on the menu bar, point to **Name**, and then click **Define** to display the Define Name dialog box. See Figure 7-12 Notice that Excel has already placed the name Annual_Salary in the Names in workbook text box using the text label in the cell to the left of the selected cell. You can keep that name or change it by typing a new name in the text box. In this case, shorten the name to Salary.

Figure 7-12 ◄
Define Name
dialog box

name suggested
by Excel

address name
is assigned to

click here to remove
a selected
range name

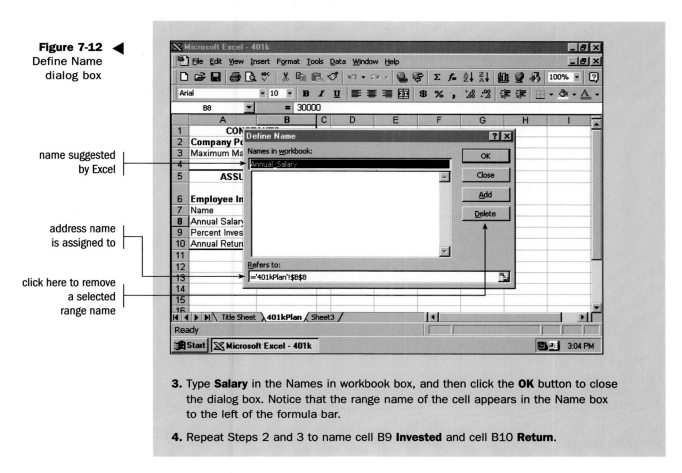

3. Type **Salary** in the Names in workbook box, and then click the **OK** button to close the dialog box. Notice that the range name of the cell appears in the Name box to the left of the formula bar.

4. Repeat Steps 2 and 3 to name cell B9 **Invested** and cell B10 **Return**.

As you have noticed, the range name of the selected cell appears in the Name box to the left of the formula bar. This Name box allows you to work with named ranges more easily.

Using the Name Box to Define a Range Name

You can also use the Name box as another means of assigning names to cells. You can use this Name box to define a range, or to select and move to an already defined range. Assign the name MaxMatch to cell B3 using the Name box.

To assign a range name using the Name box:

1. Click cell **B3**, the cell you want to name.

2. Click the **Name** box to the left of the formula bar. See Figure 7-13.

Figure 7-13 ◄
Using the Name
box to assign a
range name

Name box

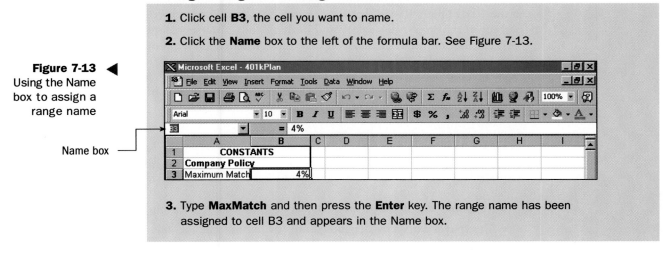

3. Type **MaxMatch** and then press the **Enter** key. The range name has been assigned to cell B3 and appears in the Name box.

Now that you have assigned names to the input cells, you can use them as you create the formulas for the 401(k) investment model. First, calculate the amount the employee plans to invest each month.

Using a Range Name in a Formula

You can use the name of a cell or range in a formula instead of cell addresses as you enter your formulas into the worksheet. Rather than using the formula =B8*B9/12 to compute the amount the employee plans to invest each month, you can enter the formula using the range names =*Salary*Invested*/12. Now enter the formula to compute the monthly employee contribution.

To enter a formula using a range name:

1. Click cell **E7**, the cell where you calculate the monthly amount the employee contributes to the retirement plan.

2. Type = **Salary*Invested/12** and press the **Enter** key. Excel performs the calculations and displays the value 125.

3. Click cell **E7** and examine the formula in the formula bar. Notice that the range names appear in the formula instead of the cell addresses. See Figure 7-14.

Figure 7-14 ◄
Range names
appear in
formula bar

formula bar displays
range names

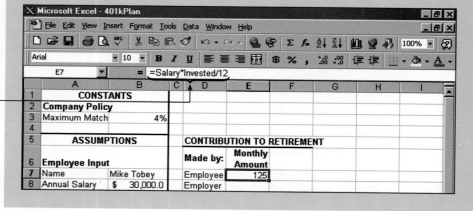

Next you need to enter a formula to calculate the amount of money the employer will contribute to the employee's 401(k) investment. The formula to calculate the employer's contribution is not as straightforward as the one for the employee's contribution. The amount the employer contributes depends on the percent of salary the employee invests in the 401(k) plan. Recall that the company policy is to match dollar for dollar up to four percent of the employee's salary and nothing above four percent of the employee's salary. This calculation requires that you determine whether the employee is contributing more than four percent. If the employee is investing more than four percent of his or her salary, then the employer will only match four percent of the salary. On the other hand, if the employee is investing four percent or less, the employer will contribute an amount equal to the employee contribution.

Inserting the IF Function

There are many situations where the value you store in a cell depends on certain conditions. For example:

- An employee's gross pay may depend on whether that employee worked overtime.

- A taxpayer's tax rate depends on his or her taxable income.

- A customer's charge depends on whether the size of the order entitles that customer to a discount.

In Excel, the IF function allows you to evaluate a specified condition, performing one action if the condition is true and another action if the condition is false. The IF function has the following format:

IF(*logical_test, value_if_true, value_if_false*)

where

- A *logical_test* evaluates a logical expression (condition) as either True or False.

- A *value_if_true* is the value returned if the *logical_test* is True.

- A *value_if_false* is the value returned if the *logical_test* is False.

An example may help illustrate how the IF function works. Suppose you need to determine whether an employee earns overtime pay, that is, whether he or she worked more than 40 hours in a week. Figure 7-15 illustrates the logic of this function.

Figure 7-15 ◀
Flow chart of
the IF function

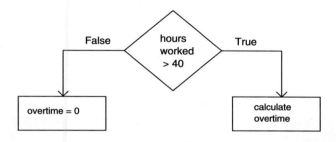

Using the IF function syntax

In this example, the condition is the comparison between the hours an employee works and 40 hours. The *value_if_true* is returned if an employee works more than 40 hours; then the condition is true and overtime pay is calculated. The *value_if_false* is returned if an employee works 40 hours or less; then the condition is false and overtime pay is 0.

The most common condition, a simple condition, is a comparison between two expressions. An **expression** may be a cell or range, a number, a label, a formula, or another function that represents a single value. For example, B5, B6*B7, and "West" are expressions. In addition to expressions, a condition contains a comparison operator. A **comparison operator** indicates a mathematical comparison, such as less than or greater than. Figure 7-16 shows the comparison operators allowed in Excel.

Figure 7-16 ◀
Comparison
operators

Type of Comparison	Comparison Operator Symbol
Less than	<
Greater than	>
Less than or equal to	<=
Greater than or equal to	>=
Equal to	=
Not equal to	<>

A comparison operator is combined with an expression to form a condition. For example, say the hours worked value is stored in D10; then the condition "the number of hours worked is greater than 40" would be expressed in Excel as IF(D10>40...). Figure 7-17 illustrates several examples of conditional situations and how they can be expressed in Excel.

Figure 7-17 ◀
Examples of
conditional
situations

Conditional Situation	Excel Formula
If salesperson's sales are > 5000 THEN return the value 0.1 (10% bonus) ELSE return the value 0.05 (5% bonus)	=IF(B24>5000,0.1,0.05) Note: cell B24 stores salesperson's sales
IF company's region code equals 3 THEN return the label East ELSE return the label Other	=IF(N7=3,"East","Other") Note: cell N7 stores code for region
IF person's age is less than 65 THEN amount x under 65 rate ELSE amount x 65 or over rate	=IF(A21<65,B21*C21,B21*D21) Note: cell A21 stores person's age; cell B21 stores amount; cell C21 stores under 65 rate; and cell D21 stores 65 or over rate

Mary developed a flowchart to establish the logic behind the formula needed to calculate the employer's matching contribution to the 401(k) plan. See Figure 7-18.

Figure 7-18 ◀
Flow chart of
employer's
monthly
matching
contribution

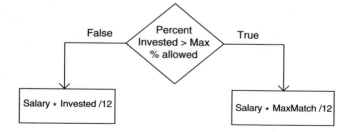

Now enter the IF function needed to calculate the employer's monthly matching contribution to the 401(k) plan.

To enter the IF function:

1. Click cell **E8** to select the cell where you want to enter the IF function.

2. Click the **Paste Function** button ![fx] on the Standard toolbar to display the Paste Function dialog box. Click **Logical** in the Function category list box, click **IF** in the Function name list box, and then click the **OK** button to open the IF function dialog box.

   TROUBLE? If the Office Assistant opens and offers help on this feature, click the No button.

   Now enter the condition.

3. In the Logical_test text box, type **Invested>MaxMatch**.

4. Click the **Value_if_true** text box, and then type **Salary*MaxMatch/12**, the value to be returned if the condition is true.

5. Click the **Value_if_false** text box, and then type **Salary*Invested/12**, the value to be returned if the condition is false. See Figure 7-19.

Figure 7-19 ◀
IF function dialog box after arguments entered

formula developed by Excel based on your entries in the IF function dialog box

6. Click the **OK** button. Excel places the IF function in the worksheet. Since the condition, in this case, is True, the value 100 appears in cell E8. Notice that the formula =IF(Invested>MaxMatch,Salary*MaxMatch/12,Salary*Invested/12) appears in the formula bar.

Now compute the total amount invested each month, which is the sum of the employee and employer contributions.

To calculate the total contribution:

1. Click cell **E9**, click the **AutoSum** button ![Σ], and press the **Enter** key. The total amount invested is 225.

   Now name cell E9 TotContribution.

2. Return to cell **E9**, click the **Name** box, type **TotContribution**, and press the **Enter** key.

   TROUBLE? If the label TotContribution appears in cell E9, click the Undo button ![undo] on the Standard toolbar, and then click the Name box, type TotContribution, and press the Enter key.

3. Format the range **E7:E9** using the Currency style and zero decimal places.

4. Click any cell to deselect the range.

5. Save the workbook.

Quick Check

1. When you select a named cell or range, the name appears in the _____.

2. Which of the following are invalid range names?
   a. Annual_Total
   b. 3rdQtr
   c. Qtr3
   d. Annual total

3. During data validation, the error alert message is displayed _____.

4. Rather than enter constants in formulas, you should reference values from a separate section of your worksheet referred to as the _____.

5. When you restrict the information being placed in a particular cell, you are applying _____.

6. During data validation, the input message is displayed when you _____.

7. When the value you store in a cell depends on certain conditions, you should consider using a(n) _____ in your formula.

8. The symbol <= is an example of a _____.

You have completed the input section of the 401kPlan worksheet. By applying data validation rules, defining range names, and using range names and IF functions to create formulas, you have made the worksheet easier for you to develop and the numerous CableScan employees to use. In Session 7.2 you will complete the worksheet's calculation/output section.

SESSION

7.2

In this session you will finish the 401(k) planning workbook by entering the remaining formulas using the Excel AutoFill feature and FV function, creating a line chart, and protecting worksheet cells.

Computing the Retirement Fund

The last set of calculations will determine the dollars accumulated over time, or the total retirement fund, often called the "retirement nest egg." In the first column, range D13:D18, the values 5, 10, 15, 20, 25, 30—representing the years left until retirement—need to be entered. Although you can type these numbers, there is an easier approach you can use when the values represent a series.

Creating a Series Using AutoFill

When working in Excel you sometimes need to enter a series of data. You enter one or two initial values in a series of numbers, dates, or text, and using the **AutoFill** feature, Excel completes the series for you. Figure 7-20 shows several series that AutoFill recognizes and automatically completes. You can quickly enter the series of data with the assistance of the fill handle. Enter the series 5, 10, 15, 20, 25, and 30 to represent the number of years left until retirement.

Figure 7-20 ◀
Examples
of series
completed
using AutoFill

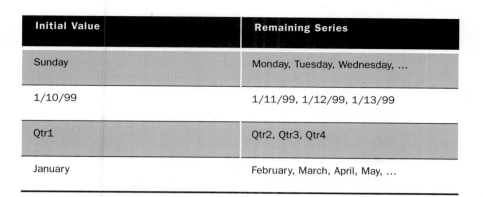

Initial Value	Remaining Series
Sunday	Monday, Tuesday, Wednesday, …
1/10/99	1/11/99, 1/12/99, 1/13/99
Qtr1	Qtr2, Qtr3, Qtr4
January	February, March, April, May, …

To generate a series using AutoFill:

1. If you took a break after the last session, make sure Excel is running, the 401kPlan workbook is open, and the 401kPlan sheet is active.

2. Scroll the worksheet so row 5 is the first visible row in the worksheet window.

3. In cell D13, enter **5**. In cell D14, enter **10**.

4. Select the range **D13:D14**.

5. Click and drag the fill handle in cell D14 through cells D15:D18. Notice that a ScreenTip displays each number in the series as you drag the mouse pointer. Release the mouse button. Excel has created the series, using the interval between the two selected values.

6. Click any cell to deselect the range. See Figure 7-21.

Figure 7-21 ◀
Series created
using AutoFill

series ⟶

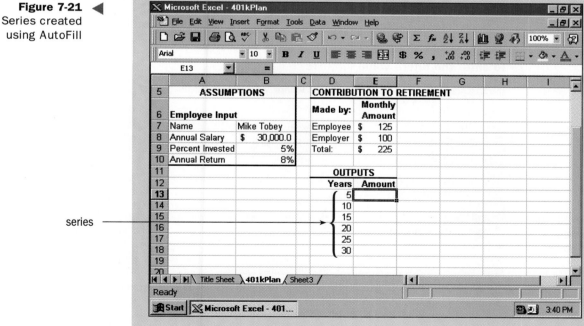

Inserting the FV Function

Now enter the formula to calculate the future value of the investment, the retirement nest egg. The future value of an investment is its value at some future date based on a series of cash flows of equal amounts made over a number of periods earning a constant interest rate. You will use the financial function FV to compute the future value of the investment. The FV function has the following format:

$$FV(\textit{rate, nper, pmt})$$

where

- *rate* is the interest rate per period.
- *nper* is the number of periods in which payments will be made.
- *pmt* is the payments made each period. It cannot change over the life of the investment.

This is one of several financial functions available in Excel. Figure 7-22 lists some of the other Excel financial functions.

Figure 7-22 ◀
Selected
financial
functions

Function Name	Description
PV	Computes the present value of a series of equal payments
PMT	Computes the periodic payment required to amortize a loan over a specified number of periods
RATE	Computes the rate of return of an investment that generates a series of equal periodic payments
DDB	Computes an asset's depreciation using the double-declining balance method
IRR	Computes an internal rate of return for a series of periodic cash flows

Now enter the future value formula, using the Paste Function button on the Standard toolbar.

To enter the future value formula:

1. Click cell **E13** to select the cell where you want to enter the FV function.

2. Click the **Paste Function** button [fx] on the Standard toolbar to display the Paste Function dialog box. Click **Financial** in the Function category list box, click **FV** in the Function name list box, and then click the **OK** button to open the FV function dialog box. See Figure 7-23.

   TROUBLE? If the Office Assistant opens offering help on this feature, click the No button.

Figure 7-23 ◀
FV function
dialog box

name of function ⟶

arguments ⟶

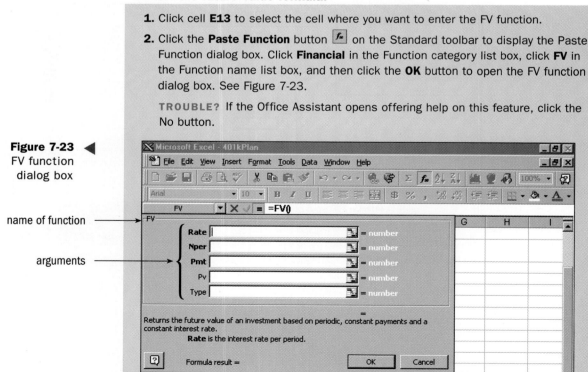

Now enter the arguments for this function. First, calculate the monthly return on the investment by dividing the annual return by 12.

3. In the Rate text box, type **Return/12**. Notice that the monthly return of .006666667 appears to the right of the Rate text box.

Next, calculate the number of monthly payments during the life of the investment.

4. In the Nper (number of periods) text box, type **D13*12**. Notice that 60, the number of months in five years, appears to the right of the Nper text box.

Now, enter the total amount invested each month.

5. In the Pmt text box, type **TotContribution** and press the **Enter** key. The value ($16,532.29) appears as a red negative value. See Figure 7-24. This value, ($16,532.29), means that if an investment of $225 is made each month for 60 months and earns interest at a rate of 0.67% per month, you will have accumulated $16,532.29 in 5 years. By default, Excel shows this value as a negative number. You think the employees will be confused if they see the value of their investment as a negative number, so edit the formula and place a minus sign in front of the function name in order to display the future value as a positive number.

TROUBLE? If the width of column E is too narrow, increase the column width to display the value.

Figure 7-24 ◀
Future value
computation for
five years

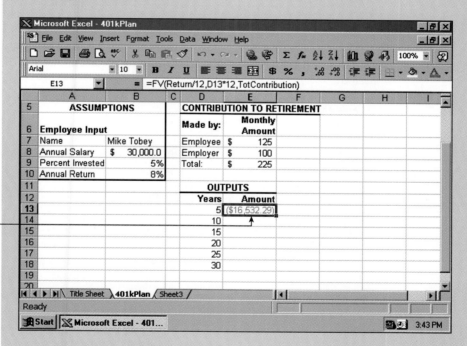

future value appears
as negative number

6. Double-click cell **E13**. Position the insertion point to the right of the equal sign (=) and type -, and then press the **Enter** key. The value appears as a positive number.

7. Copy the formula in cell E13 to cells **E14:E18**.

8. Format the range using the Currency style with zero decimal places.

9. Click any cell to deselect the range. See Figure 7-25.

Figure 7-25 ◀
Future value
computations
over 30-year
period in
five-year
increments

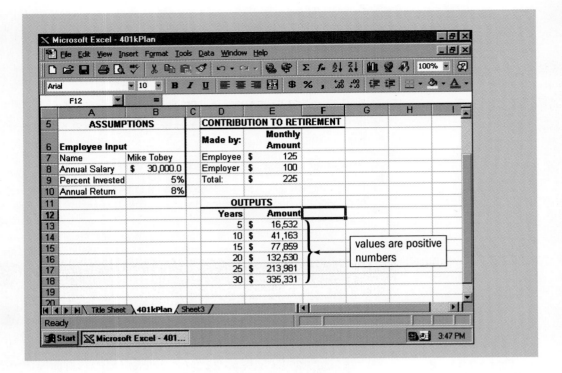

The output table showing the dollars accumulated over 30 years is complete. Now display this information as a line chart showing the accumulation of dollars over the 30-year period.

To create the line chart:

1. Select the range **D13:E18**.

2. Click the **Chart Wizard** button 📊 on the Standard toolbar to display the Chart Wizard - Step 1 of 4 - Chart Type dialog box.

3. Click the **Line** chart type. Seven line chart subtypes are displayed. Click the **Line** chart subtype (the first subtype).

4. Click the **Next** button to display the Chart Wizard - Step 2 of 4 - Chart Source Data dialog box. On the Data tab, make sure the Data range box displays ='401kPlan'!$D$13:$D$18. Click the **Series** tab. With Series1 selected in the Series section, click the **Remove** button. Click the **Category (X) axis labels** box, click the **Collapse dialog box** button, and select the range **D13:D18**. Click the **Collapse (Expand) dialog box** button to return to the Chart Wizard. See Figure 7-26.

Figure 7-26 ◀
Source Data
dialog box after
modifications

Series1 removed ——

entered as
category axis

5. Click the **Next** button to display the Chart Wizard - Step 3 of 4 - Chart Options dialog box.

   Next, add a title to the chart.

6. If necessary, click the **Titles** tab, click the **Chart title** text box, and type **Retirement Nest Egg** for the chart title. Click the **Category (X) axis** title box, and then type **Years in future**. Click the **Value (Y) axis** title box, and then type **Dollars**.

   Since there is only one data series, remove the legend, as it is not needed.

7. Click the **Legend** tab and then click the **Show Legend** check box to remove the check and deselect that option.

8. Click the **Next** button to display the Chart Wizard - Step 4 of 4 - Chart Location dialog box. Embed the chart in the 401kPlan worksheet (the default option).

9. Click the **Finish** button to complete the chart and display it in the 401kPlan worksheet. See Figure 7-27.

Figure 7-27 ◄
Completed
line chart

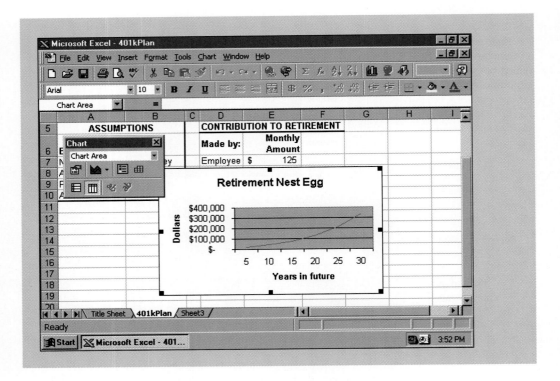

You need to move and resize the chart to improve its appearance.

To change the size and position of the chart:

1. Scroll the worksheet until row 5 appears as the first visible row and column D as the first visible column in the worksheet window.

2. Move and resize the chart object so it appears in the range F6:L18. See Figure 7-28.

Figure 7-28 ◄
Line chart after
being moved
and resized

floating Chart toolbar
may appear in a
different location
on your screen ⟶

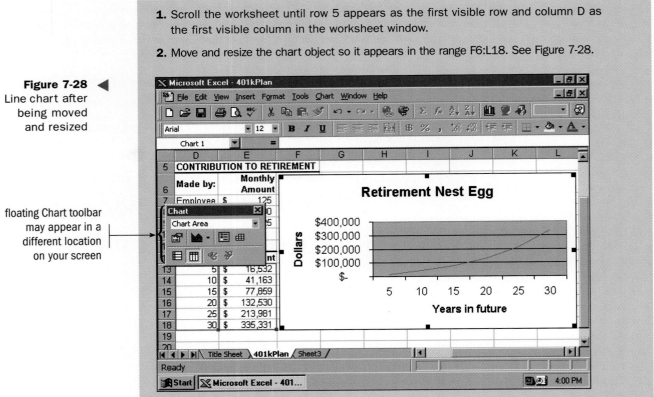

Now enhance the chart's appearance.

To improve the appearance of the chart:

1. Double-click the **Series 2** (Line object) to display the Format Data Series dialog box. On the Patterns tab, click the **Weight** list arrow, select the thickest line weight, and then click the **OK** button.

2. Click the **Value-Axis** object, and then click the **Format Axis** button 🖼 on the Chart toolbar to display the Format Axis dialog box. Click the **Font** tab, click **8** in the Size list box, and then click the **OK** button.

3. Click the **Category-Axis** object, and then click the **Format Axis** button 🖼 on the Chart toolbar to display the Format Axis dialog box. If necessary, click the **Font** tab, click **8** in the Size list box, then click the **OK** button. See Figure 7-29.

Figure 7-29 ◄
Final version
of line chart

thicker line

8-point font size

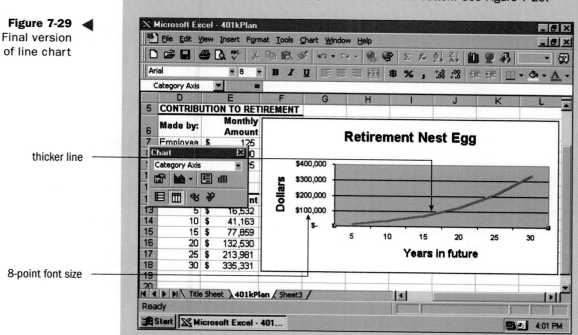

4. Click anywhere outside the chart area to deselect the chart.

5. Save the workbook.

Now that all the components of the worksheet are complete, you still need to make a few enhancements to make the worksheet less susceptible to user error. Mary realizes that others will use the worksheet to explore what-if alternatives, and she worries about a user accidentally deleting the formatting or formulas in the calculation/output section of the worksheet. To preserve your work, Mary asks you to protect all the cells in the worksheet except the cells in the input section.

Protecting Cells in a Worksheet

When you **protect** a worksheet, data in protected cells cannot be changed. Once you have protected worksheet cells, the data in these cells can be viewed, but not edited or modified. Once you protect a worksheet, you cannot enter data, insert or delete rows, or change cell formats or column widths. Only the values in unprotected cells can be changed.

Unlocking Individual Cells

Most of the time you will not want to lock every cell in a worksheet. For example, in a worksheet that you share with others, you might want to protect the formulas and formatting, but leave particular cells unprotected so that necessary data may be entered. When you want to protect some but not all worksheet cells, you implement protection by following a two-step process. By default all cells in a worksheet have the locked property turned on, which means the cell is capable of being protected. First you need to identify the cells you want unprotected and turn off the "lock" associated with each of these cells. Once you have "unlocked" the selected cells, you activate the protection command to "turn on" protection for the remaining cells. Figure 7-30 illustrates this process.

Figure 7-30 ◄
Process of protecting worksheet cells

Default Status

By default, every cell in the worksheet has a locked property turned on, which means each cell has the capability of being protected, but at this step no cell is protected. You can enter data in any cell.

Step I

The worksheet after some cells have their locks removed (locked property turned off). At this step no cell is protected. You can enter data in any cell.

Step II

The worksheet after the Protect Sheet command has been activated. The cells in the bottom two rows are protected—no data may be entered in these cells. You can still enter data in the first row.

REFERENCE window

PROTECTING CELLS

- Select the cells you want to remain unprotected.
- Click Format, and then click Cells to display the Format Cells dialog box.
- In the Format Cells dialog box, click the Protection tab.
- Remove the check from the Locked check box, and then click the OK button.
- Click Tools, point to Protection, and then click Protect Sheet to display the Protect Sheet dialog box.
- If desired, enter a password in the Protect Sheet dialog box, and then reenter the password in the Confirm Password dialog box.

You start by unlocking the range of cells where the user can enter data, which in this case would be the input area of the 401kPlan worksheet. Then activate the protection for the rest of the worksheet, which will protect the data and formulas you do not want the employees to change.

To unlock the cells for data entry:

1. Click cell **A5** to make it the active cell, so you can view the input section.

2. Select the range **B7:B10**, the cells the user can change and therefore do not require protection.

3. Click **Format** on the menu bar, and then click **Cells** to display the Format Cells dialog box.

4. Click the **Protection** tab. By default, the Locked check box contains a check. See Figure 7-31.

Figure 7-31 ◀
Protection tab
of Format Cells
dialog box

check means cell
is capable
of being locked

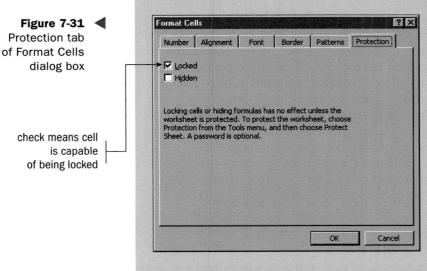

5. Click the **Locked** check box to remove the check.

6. Click the **OK** button. Nothing visible happens to the worksheet to show that cells are unlocked.

Since Excel does not provide any on-screen indication of the protection status of individual cells, you decide to change the background color of the unlocked cells to distinguish them from the protected cells. This will be a nice visual cue for the employees using the worksheet, indicating which cells they should use to input their investment information.

To change the fill color of unprotected cells:

1. If necessary, select cells **B7:10**.

2. Click the **Fill color** button list arrow [icon] on the Formatting toolbar to display the Color palette.

3. Click **Yellow** in the fourth row, third column of the Color palette.

4. Click any cell to view the yellow color applied to the unprotected cells.

Protecting the Worksheet

Now that you have unlocked the cells for data entry, you will turn on protection for the entire worksheet to protect every cell that you didn't unlock.

When you protect the worksheet, Excel lets you enter a password that must be used to unprotect the worksheet. If you specify a password, you must make sure to remember it so you can unprotect the worksheet in the future. Unless you are working on confidential material, it's probably easier not to use a password at all.

To turn protection on:

1. Click **Tools** on the menu bar, point to **Protection**, and then click **Protect Sheet** to display the Protect Sheet dialog box. See Figure 7-32. The Password text box lets you enter a password of your choice. The Contents check box locks the cells in the sheet. The Objects check box prevents changes to charts or graphical objects, and the Scenarios check box locks any scenario you've created.

Figure 7-32 ◀
Options for protecting a worksheet

if you want a password, enter it here

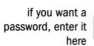

2. Click the **OK** button. If you had entered a password, a Confirm Password dialog box would appear and you would be asked to retype the same password to make sure you remember it and that you entered it correctly the first time.

Testing Cell Protection

After protection is enabled, you cannot change a locked cell. Before you distribute the workbook to the employees to use, you decide to test the worksheet to assure yourself that protection has been implemented successfully.

To test worksheet protection:

1. Click cell **E13**, and then try typing **40000**. A message indicating that this cell is locked and cannot be changed is displayed. See Figure 7-33.

Figure 7-33 ◀
Message displayed when you attempt to change a protected cell

2. Click the **OK** button to continue.

   Now enter a value in a cell that is unlocked.

3. Click cell **B8**, type **40000**, and press the **Enter** key. Notice that the calculation and outputs changed.

Now that you are done creating the workbook, and have customized it so it is user-friendly and appropriate for use by all CableScan employees, you give it to Mary to review. She is very pleased with the finished workbook. Her only suggestion is to further simplify the workbook by removing any unnecessary sheets. She thinks this will eliminate any possibility of people trying to enter data in the wrong area of the workbook.

Deleting Unnecessary Worksheets

If you want to remove an empty worksheet or a worksheet you no longer need, you can delete it. You decide to delete Sheet3 since it is not used in the 401(k) application.

To delete a worksheet:

1. Click the **Sheet3** tab to activate the Sheet3 worksheet.

2. Click **Edit**, and then click **Delete Sheet**. Excel displays a message letting you know that the selected sheet will be permanently deleted.

3. Click the **OK** button. Notice that Excel has deleted Sheet3 from the workbook.

4. Save the workbook.

Quick Check

1 You can use the Excel _____ feature to complete a series of numbers, dates, or text values.

2 Why were the unprotected cells filled with color?

3 Protecting a worksheet is a two-step process. You _____ and then you _____.

4 How does cell protection differ from data validation?

5 What happens when you try to enter a value in a protected cell?

6 The FV function stands for _____. This function is found in the _____ category.

You have now completed the worksheet. In this next section you will create two macros that will simplify some of the tasks a user performs when using this workbook.

SESSION

7.3

In this session you will learn what macros are, and how they can be used to automate tasks in a workbook for the user. You will also plan and create two macros using the Excel macro recorder.

Automating Tasks Using Macros

Typically macros are used to automate repetitive tasks. A **macro** is a series of commands and functions that you can initiate whenever you want to perform a particular task. That is, you create them to automatically perform a series of Excel operations, such as menu selections, dialog box selections, range selections, or keystrokes. They carry out repetitive tasks more quickly than you can yourself, making your work more productive while helping you make fewer errors. For example, you can create macros to automate the following tasks:

■ Move through a large worksheet quickly.

- Add a date and time stamp to a cell in the current worksheet.

- Extract data from an Excel list and create a chart.

- Print several reports from a worksheet, each with different print specifications.

- Apply a common set of formats to any sheet in a workbook.

Macros simplify the use of workbooks for both experienced and novice users. In reviewing the 401kPlan workbook with Mary, you realize that macros would be useful to include in this workbook. You know that all users will need to clear the input section to enter data as it changes. You also know that people will most likely want to have a hard copy of some or all of the worksheet. Therefore, printing is another task that would be good to simplify.

Creating Macros

You can create a macro in two ways: you can use the macro recorder to record your keystrokes and mouse actions as you perform them (recording the selection of ranges, menu commands, dialog box options, etc.), or you can write your own macros by entering a series of commands in the **Visual Basic for Applications (VBA)** programming language, which tells Excel how to do a particular task.

The easiest way to create a macro in Excel is to use the macro recorder. When you record a macro, Excel automatically translates your keystrokes and mouse actions into Visual Basic instructions (code) that you can play back, or run, whenever you want to repeat those particular keystrokes and tasks. Excel records your actions, and then translates them into a series of instructions in the Visual Basic for Applications (VBA) programming language. When you run the macro, the instructions are read and executed in sequence, thereby duplicating the actions you performed when you recorded the macro.

In this section, you will create two macros using the macro recorder. The first will be a ClearInputs macro that will automate the task of clearing values from the input section of the workbook, so the user can enter new data. The second macro you will create will be a Print macro, which will simplify the printing process.

Planning Macros

As with most complex projects, you need to plan your macro. Decide what you want to accomplish and the best way to go about doing it. Once you know the purpose of the macro, you should carry out the keystrokes or mouse actions before you actually record them. Going through each step before recording a macro might seem like extra work, but it reduces the chances of error when you actually create the macro.

Mary realizes that many different employees will use the worksheet and will enter different sets of input assumptions. She wants you to create a macro that will automatically clear the values in the input section and place the cell pointer in cell B7—ready for the user to enter a new set of data.

She sits down at her computer and goes through the steps to include in the macro before you actually record them. This way you will be familiar with the steps to include in the macro, and the chances for errors in the macro are fewer. Figure 7-34 lists the steps Mary plans to include in the macro.

Figure 7-34 ◀
Planning the
ClearInputs
macro

Action	Result
Select the range B7:B10	Highlights the range you want to clear of data
Press the Delete key	Clears the contents of the selected range
Click cell B7	Makes cell B7 the active cell

Excel

Recording the ClearInputs Macro

After planning the macro, you are ready to record it. There are several actions you need to take before actually recording the macro. First, you want to decide on an appropriate name for the macro. For example, the first macro Mary asked you to create is for clearing the input section of any values, so a good name for this macro would be ClearInputs. A macro name can be up to 255 characters long; it must begin with a letter, and it can contain only letters, numbers, and the underscore character. No spaces or other punctuation marks are permitted. For multiple-word macros such as Clear Inputs you can use initial caps (ClearInputs) or the underscore (Clear_Inputs).

When you record a macro, every keystroke and mouse click is stored by Excel. Therefore, your second task before you can record the macro is to specify where you want the macro stored. The macro is stored in the form of a Visual Basic for Applications program, and its storage location plays a part in how you will be able to access and use the macro once it is created. There are three possible locations you can choose to store the macro. By default, Excel assumes you want to store the recorded macro as part of the current workbook. In this case, Excel stores the recorded macro in a hidden module that is part of the workbook. Macros stored in a workbook are available only when the workbook is open. If a workbook is closed, the macros stored within the workbook can't be used. Use this storage option to store macros that you plan to use only when using this workbook. If you use some macros on a regular basis, you may want to make them available at all times. In that case, you would choose to store the macros in the Personal Macro workbook. With this option, Excel stores the macro in a special workbook file named Personal Macro. When you start Excel, this workbook is opened and hidden automatically, making the macros in it available to any open workbook.

You can also store the macro in a new workbook file. In this case, Excel opens another workbook to store the recorded macro. To use macros stored in another workbook, you need to open the workbook with the macros as well as the workbook containing the application.

In addition to considering where you want to store your macro, before you record a macro you also need to make sure your worksheet is set up exactly as you want it to exist at the time you play back the recorded macro. This may involve opening a specific workbook, activating a specific sheet in which you want the macro to run, and moving to the location where you want to start recording. Otherwise the macro may not work as planned, and you may have to record it again.

REFERENCE window

RECORDING A MACRO

- Click Tools, point to Macro, and then click Record New Macro to display the Record Macro dialog box.
- In the Macro name text box, type a name for the macro.
- If you want to run the macro by pressing a keyboard shortcut key, enter a letter in the Shortcut key text box.
- In the Store macro in list box, click the location where you want to store the macro.
- In the Description text box, type a description of the macro.
- Click the OK button. The macro recorder starts recording.
- Perform the tasks you want the macro to automate.
- Click the Stop Recording button on the Stop Recording toolbar, or click Tools, point to Macro, and then click Stop Recording to stop the recording process.

When you record a macro, you name and describe it. You can also set up a shortcut key to run the macro, and specify the workbook in which to store the macro.

To record a macro to delete a range of cells:

1. If you took a break after the last session, make sure Excel is running, the 401kPlan workbook is open, and the 401kPlan sheet is active. If necessary, press **Ctrl + Home** to make cell A1 the active cell.

   Now start the macro recorder.

2. Click **Tools** on the menu bar, point to **Macro**, and then click **Record New Macro** to display the Record Macro dialog box. See Figure 7-35.

Figure 7-35 ◀
Record Macro
dialog box

enter new name here

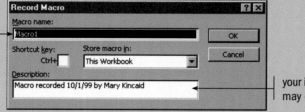

your information here
may differ

Excel proposes a default name for the macro. This default macro name consists of the word "Macro" and a number corresponding to the number of macros you have recorded in the workbook in the current work session. You should change the macro name to a name more descriptive of what the macro will do. Name the macro ClearInputs.

3. Type **ClearInputs** in the Macro name text box.

   Now specify the location of your macro. You want the macro to be accessible only to this workbook, and when this workbook is open. Therefore, you want to store the macro as part of this workbook.

4. Make sure the option This Workbook is selected in the Store macro in list box.

   Notice that Excel provides a brief description indicating the date the macro is being recorded and by whom. You can add additional comments to explain the purpose of the macro.

5. Click anywhere within the **Description** text box. If the insertion point is not at the end of the default description, move it there. Press the **Enter** key to start a new line. Type **Clear the values from the input section.** See Figure 7-36.

Figure 7-36 ◀
Completed
Record Macro
dialog box

Record Macro	? X
Macro name:	
ClearInputs	OK
Shortcut key: Store macro in:	Cancel
Ctrl+ This Workbook	
Description:	
Macro recorded 10/1/99 by Mary Kincaid	
Clear the values from the input section.	

6. Click the **OK** button to start recording the macro. See Figure 7-37. Excel returns to the worksheet and the message "Recording" appears in the status bar at the bottom of the screen. You are now in Record mode and all keystrokes and mouse clicks will be recorded until you stop the macro recorder.

Figure 7-37
Stop Recording
toolbar

click here to stop
recording of macro

Relative Reference
button

status bar indicates
macro is being
recorded

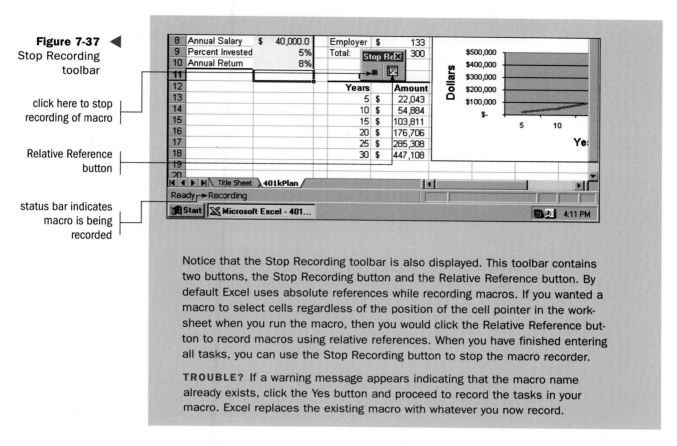

Notice that the Stop Recording toolbar is also displayed. This toolbar contains two buttons, the Stop Recording button and the Relative Reference button. By default Excel uses absolute references while recording macros. If you wanted a macro to select cells regardless of the position of the cell pointer in the worksheet when you run the macro, then you would click the Relative Reference button to record macros using relative references. When you have finished entering all tasks, you can use the Stop Recording button to stop the macro recorder.

TROUBLE? If a warning message appears indicating that the macro name already exists, click the Yes button and proceed to record the tasks in your macro. Excel replaces the existing macro with whatever you now record.

Now perform the tasks you want recorded.

To perform the steps to be recorded:

1. Select the range **B7:B10**.

2. Press the **Delete** key. The input section is now cleared.

3. Click cell **B7** to make it the active cell.

   You have completed the actions that you want recorded. Next, you will stop the macro recorder.

4. Click the **Stop Recording** button ◻ on the Stop Recording toolbar. Notice that the message "Recording" is no longer displayed in the status bar.

   TROUBLE? If you forget to turn off the macro recorder, it continues to record all of your actions. If this happens to you, you may need to delete the macro and record it again. To delete the macro, click Tools on the menu bar, point to Macro, and then click Macros in the Macros dialog box, select ClearInputs in the Macro Name list, and then click the Delete button. Click the Yes button to verify you want to delete the macro.

You have completed recording your first macro. Now test the macro by running it.

Running the ClearInputs Macro from the Tools Menu

After recording a macro, you can play it back, or run it, at any time. When you run a macro, you are telling Excel to execute the previously recorded instructions contained within the macro. It is a good idea to run the macro directly after you create it, as a test to ensure that it works correctly. If it doesn't work correctly, you can:

- re-record the macro using the same macro name as before

- delete the recorded macro and then record the macro again

- edit the incorrect macro by opening the Visual Basic Editor

REFERENCE window

RUNNING A MACRO

- Click Tools, point to Macro, and then click Macros to display the Macro dialog box.
- In the Macro Name list box, click the name of the macro you want to run.
- Click the Run button.

The first time you run the macro, you are testing it to determine whether it works as expected. Run the macro you just created to see if it automatically clears the values from the input section. To do this, you need to first enter values in the section to be cleared.

To run a macro using the Macro command on the Tools menu:

1. Enter a new set of input values in cells B7:B10. Enter **Mary Higgins**, **45000**, **.02**, **.06**.

2. Scroll to the calculation/output section to see the results of the new set of input assumptions.

3. Press **Ctrl + Home** to move to cell A1.

   Now save the workbook before running the macro for the first time in case anything goes wrong while running it.

4. Click the **Save** button 🖫 on the Standard toolbar to save the workbook. Use the ClearInputs macro to erase the input values.

5. Click **Tools** on the menu bar, point to **Macro**, and then click **Macros** to display the Macro dialog box. See Figure 7-38. A list of all macros found in all open workbooks appears in the Macro Name list box.

Figure 7-38 ◀
Macro dialog box

click here to run selected macro

click here to delete selected macro

Excel

Select the name of the macro you want to run.

6. If necessary, click **ClearInputs** to display ClearInputs in the Macro Name text box, and then click the **Run** button. Excel executes the ClearInputs macro and clears the values in cells B7:B10. See Figure 7-39.

Figure 7-39 ◄
Worksheet after
macro run

input values cleared ——

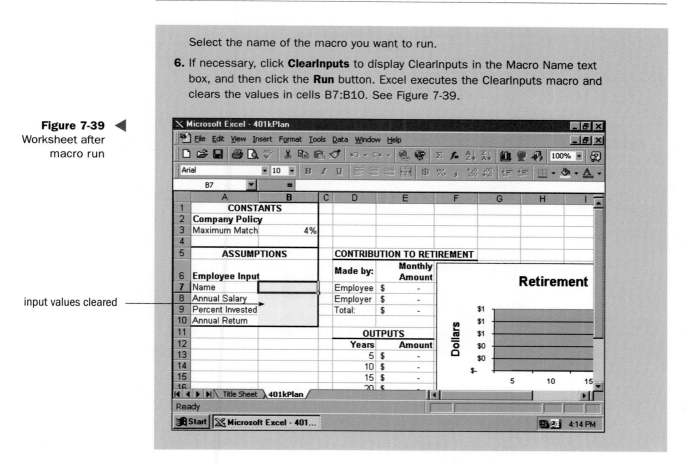

The macro ran successfully. Now that you know the macro works, you want to make it easy for users to run. There are several ways to do this.

Creating a Macro Shortcut Key

You can use the Macro command on the Tools menu to run macros that you execute infrequently, but this approach is inconvenient if you need to run the macro often. There are several ways to make it easier to run a macro. You can:

■ assign the macro to a shortcut key that enables you to run the macro by using a combination of the Ctrl key and a letter key

■ assign the macro to a command that appears on one of the Excel menus

■ assign the macro to a button on a toolbar

■ assign the macro to a drawing object

A quick way to run a macro is to assign it to a shortcut key, a key you press along with the Ctrl key to run the macro. The shortcut key is a single uppercase or lowercase letter. If you use this option, you can run the macro by holding down the Ctrl key and pressing the shortcut key. Normally you assign a shortcut key when you first record a macro; however, if you didn't create a shortcut key at the time you recorded the macro you can still assign one to the macro.

Mary asks you to create a shortcut key to execute the ClearInputs macro. She wants users to type Ctrl + c to execute the macro.

To assign a shortcut key to the macro:

1. Click **Tools** on the menu bar, point to **Macro**, and then click **Macros** to display the Macro dialog box.

2. If necessary, click **ClearInputs**, and then click the **Options** button to open the Macro Options dialog box. See Figure 7-40.

Figure 7-40 ◀
Macro Options
dialog box

enter shortcut
key here

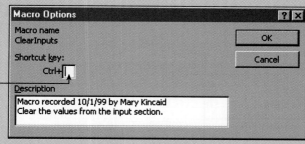

Assign a keyboard shortcut to the macro.

3. Make sure the insertion point is in the Shortcut key text box, type **c**, and then click the **OK** button to return to the Macro dialog box. Click the **Cancel** button to return to the worksheet. The shortcut key is now assigned to the ClearInputs macro.

Now test the shortcut key to see if the macro runs when Ctrl + c is pressed.

To test the shortcut key:

1. Enter a new set of input values. In cells B7:B10, enter **FJ Miles, 50000, .06, .10**.

2. Press **Ctrl + c** to run the macro. The input values are erased and B7 is the active cell.

   Note that shortcut keys are case-sensitive, so if a user types Ctrl + Shift C, the shortcut will not run the ClearInputs macro.

The shortcut key successfully ran the macro. Now let's take a look at the code behind the ClearInputs macro.

Viewing the ClearInputs Macro Code

As you may have realized, you can successfully record and run a macro without looking at or understanding the instructions underlying it. For simple macros this approach is fine. There will be times, however, when you may welcome the greater flexibility that comes from understanding the commands underlying the recorded macro.

As Excel records your actions, it translates them into a series of instructions in the Visual Basic for Applications programming language. Figure 7-41 represents the Visual Basic code generated while your ClearInputs macro was recorded.

Figure 7-41 ◄
VBA code for
ClearInputs
macro

start of macro ——
comments ——
body macro ——
end of macro ——

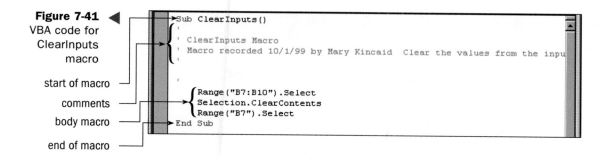

```
Sub ClearInputs()
'
' ClearInputs Macro
' Macro recorded 10/1/99 by Mary Kincaid  Clear the values from the inpu
'
'
    Range("B7:B10").Select
    Selection.ClearContents
    Range("B7").Select
End Sub
```

Visual Basic for Applications Code

The Visual Basic for Applications code shown in Figure 7-41 has the following components: **Sub/End Sub** are keywords that mark the beginning and end of a macro. The keyword Sub in the statement

    Sub ClearInputs()

signals the start of the macro. It is followed by the macro name ClearInputs and then by left and right parentheses. The keywords End Sub signal the end of the macro. **Comments** are statements that explain or document what is happening in the macro. Any line of the code that is preceded by an apostrophe is a comment and is ignored by Excel when the macro is run. In Figure 7-41, Excel includes as comments the macro name, the date recorded, and the description you entered in the Record Macro dialog box.

The **body of the macro** is the series of statements between Sub and End Sub representing the VBA translation of the actions you performed while recording the macro. In Figure 7-41 the statement

    Range("B7:B10").Select

is the VBA equivalent of selecting the range B7:B10.

The next statement

    Selection.ClearContents

is the VBA equivalent of pressing the Delete key to clear the contents of the selected range.

The last statement

    Range("B7").Select

is the VBA equivalent of clicking B7 to make it the active cell.

Now that you have viewed the code behind the macro, you're ready to create your next macro, a macro to print a portion of the 401kPlan worksheet.

Recording the Print401k Macro

Because your worksheets may be large, containing input sections, data, tables, reports, charts, etc., you may want to use a macro to help you simplify the steps for printing different parts of a worksheet. Also, the addition of one or more print macros will make the printing process much easier for other users.

After an employee has made changes to certain input values and viewed the revised table and chart, Mary wants the employee to be able to print a hard copy of the worksheet for his or her records. Some employees may only want to print the table and chart from the 401k worksheet. Instead of the user having to establish print settings to get the output of just the table and chart, for example, you could create a macro to print just these sections of the worksheet. Because you would be printing only part of the worksheet, you would need to specify the print area for the portion of the worksheet you are printing. Mary also wants the user's output to automatically have informative headers and footers. Before printing, the user should also be able to view the output in the Print Preview window. Figure 7-42 shows the planning for this macro. Using this planning sheet, record the macro for Mary. Mary suggests that you name the macro Print401k and that it be stored just in this workbook. Now, set up the worksheet just the way you want it before you begin the macro recorder.

Figure 7-42 ◀
Planning the
Print401k
macro

Action	Result
Click File, click Page Setup	Opens the Page Setup dialog box
Click the Sheet tab, click Print area, type D5:L18	Defines print area
Click Margins, click Horizontally check box	Horizontally centers output
Click Header/Footer tab, click Custom Header, click the Tab Name button, click OK	Defines custom header
Click Custom Footer, click Date, click OK	Defines custom footer
Click Print Preview	Displays output in Print Preview window
Click Close	Closes Print Preview window
Click cell A5	Makes cell A5 the active cell

To record the Print401k macro:

1. Enter a new set of input values. Enter **Tammy Beach**, **25000**, **.1**, **.12** in the appropriate cells in range B7:B10. Click cell **A1**.

   Now start the macro recorder.

2. Click **Tools** on the menu bar, point to **Macro**, and then click **Record New Macro** to display the Record Macro dialog box.

   Excel proposes Macro2 as the name for the macro, because this is the second macro you have recorded during this work session. Change the name of the macro to Print401k.

3. Type **Print401k** in the Macro name text box.

   Now add a shortcut key.

4. Click the **Shortcut key** text box, and then type **p**.

   Add an additional comment to explain the purpose of the macro.

5. Place the insertion point at the end of the default description. Press the **Enter** key and type **Print preview output table and chart**.

6. Click the **OK** button to start the macro recorder.

7. Click **File** on the menu bar, and then click **Page Setup** to display the Page Setup dialog box.

   By default, Excel prints the entire worksheet. To print only a part of the worksheet, you must specify the part you want.

8. Click the **Sheet** tab of the Page Setup dialog box, click the **Print area** text box, and then type **D5:L18**.

   Now specify the print settings so the output is centered horizontally.

9. Click the **Margins** tab, and then check the **Horizontally** check box to select it.

10. Click the **Header/Footer** tab, and then click the **Custom Header** button. In the center section, click the **Tab Name** button, and then click the **OK** button.

11. Click the **Custom Footer** button, click the **Date** button 🗓 in the Right section, and then click the **OK** button.

Review the output in the Print Preview window.

12. Click the **Print Preview** button on the right side of the dialog box to preview the output. See Figure 7-43.

Figure 7-43 ◀
Print Preview
as result of
running macro

13. Click the **Close** button to close the Print Preview window and return to the 401kPlan sheet. Note that you cannot stop the macro until you leave the Print Preview window.

14. Click cell **A5** to make it the active cell.

You have completed the tasks for the macro; now turn off the macro recorder.

15. Click the **Stop Recording** button ■ on the Stop Recording toolbar to stop recording the macro.

Now test the Print401k macro using the shortcut key.

To test the macro using the shortcut key:

1. Save the workbook.

2. Press **Ctrl + p** to run the macro. Excel displays the output table and chart in the Print Preview window.

3. If you want a hard copy, click the **Print** button on the Print Preview toolbar, and then click the **OK** button in the Print dialog box; otherwise click the **Close** button.

The shortcut key successfully ran the print macro. However, Mary thinks it may be easier for a user to run the print macro by clicking a button placed on the worksheet. Mary asks you to create this button.

Assigning the Print401k Macro to a Button on the Worksheet

Another way to run a macro is to assign it to a command button object. You place the command button object on a worksheet, assign the macro to the button, and then run the macro by clicking the button. This approach makes the macro easier to use. It will speed up your own work, as well as make the macro easier for others to run.

REFERENCE window

ASSIGNING A MACRO TO A BUTTON OBJECT ON A WORKSHEET

- Click the Button button on the Forms toolbar.
- Position the mouse pointer where you want the button, and then click and drag the mouse pointer until the button is the size and shape you want.
- Release the mouse button. The button appears on the worksheet with a label and the Assign Macro dialog box opens.
- Select the name of the macro that you want to assign to the button from the Macro Name list box.
- Click the OK button.

Since the workbook is still protected, you need to turn protection off in order to make any changes to the worksheet (except in unlocked cells), such as placing a button on the worksheet.

To turn protection off:

1. Click **Tools** on the menu bar, point to **Protection**, and then click **Unprotect Sheet**. The worksheet is unprotected. If you had password-protected the worksheet, the Unprotect Sheet dialog box would open so that you could enter the password.

Now place a command button object on the worksheet.

To place a button object on the worksheet and assign a macro to the button:

1. Click cell **D2**.

   Next, display the Forms toolbar, which contains the tools you need to place the button object.

2. Click **View** on the menu bar, point to **Toolbars**, and then click **Forms** to display the Forms toolbar. If necessary, drag the Forms toolbar out of the way. See Figure 7-44.

Figure 7-44 ◀
Forms toolbar
displayed in
worksheet
window

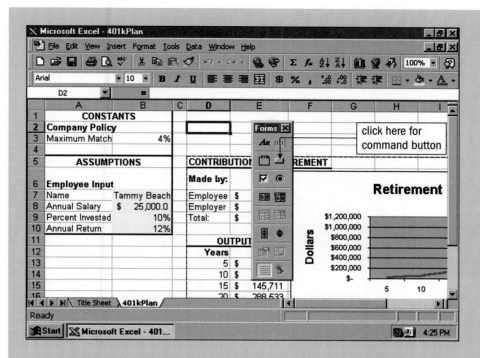

Now place a command button on the worksheet.

3. Click the **Button** button ▭ on the Forms toolbar. Now position the mouse pointer in the worksheet where you want the button to appear.

4. Position the mouse pointer in the upper-left corner of cell D2. Click and drag the mouse pointer until the box covers the range D2:E3. When you release the mouse button, the Assign Macro dialog box opens. See Figure 7-45. Here you select the macro that will be run when this button is clicked by the user. This is referred to as assigning a macro to a button object.

Figure 7-45 ◀
Assign Macro
dialog box

select this macro ─────▶

5. Click **Print401k** in the Macro Name list box, and then click the **OK** button. The macro is assigned to the command button object. The button object appears on the worksheet. It is selected (sizing handles appear around the button), and the default name Button 2 appears as a label on the button.

TROUBLE? If the button is too small, too large, or in the wrong location, you can resize or move it just as you move or resize any object. If the button is not selected, press the Ctrl key while moving the mouse pointer on top of the button, and then click the mouse. Selection handles appear around the button, indicating that you can move or resize it.

TROUBLE? If the Forms toolbar is in the way, click and drag it to move it out of the way, or click the Forms toolbar Close button to remove it from the screen.

Now change the name on the button to one that indicates the function of the macro assigned to it.

6. Highlight the label on the command button and type **Print 401k Report**. See Figure 7-46.

Figure 7-46 ◀
Command
button to run
Print401k
macro

command button
with new label

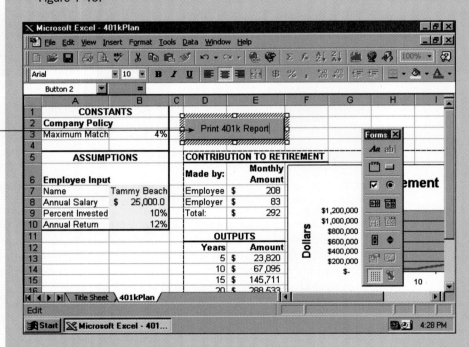

7. Click anywhere in the worksheet to deselect the button.

8. If you haven't already removed the Forms toolbar, click its **Close** button to remove it now.

Now test the command button to make sure it runs the macro.

To test the Print401k macro using the command button:

1. Type **.08** in cell B10 and press the **Enter** key.

2. Click the **Print 401k Report** button. Excel displays the output and chart in the Print Preview window.

3. If you want a hard copy, click the **Print** button on the Standard toolbar and then click the **OK** button in the Print dialog box; otherwise click the **Close** button.

Your Print401k macro worked successfully using the button object.

4. Save the workbook, and then close it and exit Excel.

Quick Check

1. A _____ automates repetitive tasks.

2. You can create a macro by _____ or _____.

3. A recorded macro stores instructions in the _____ programming language.

4. Name three ways to run a macro.

5. Macros are stored in a _____, _____, or _____.

6. To stop recording a macro, you _____.

7. What is the purpose of a shortcut key?

8. "Print Chart" is a valid macro name. (True/False)

You have created a workbook for the CableScan employees that will allow them to easily and efficiently plan and establish 401(k) plans.

Tutorial Assignments

After the formal presentation at the first of CableScan's three sites, you have received feedback from the employees on how to improve the usability of the 401kPlan workbook. Do the following:

1. If necessary, start Excel and make sure your Student Disk is in the appropriate disk drive. Open the workbook 401kPln2 in the TAssign folder for Tutorial.07 and save it as 401kPlan3. Since this workbook contains macros, Excel displays a message informing you of this. Click the Enable Macros button to continue.

2. Remove cell protection from the worksheet.

3. Specify a data validation rule for the Salary value, cell B8. You want to allow integer values between 5000 and 150000.

4. Test the data validation. Enter a salary of 200000. What happens?

5. Modify the data validation you just assigned in cell B8 to include an input message. The message should state "Valid salary values are between 5000 and 150000" and have the title Valid Data.

6. Modify the data validation you assigned in cell B8 to include an error alert message. The error message should have the title Invalid Data, and the message should state "You entered a value less than $5000 or greater than $150,000." Use the Warning style in defining the error alert.

7. Test the data validation again. Enter a value of 200,000. What happens?

8. Change the error alert style to Information. Enter 200000 as the current salary. What happens?

9. Assign the name Contributions to the range E7:E8. Replace the formula in cell E9 with the formula =Sum(Contributions). What value is displayed in E9?

10. The FV function in cell E13 assumes that payments are made at the end of the month. A more realistic assumption is that payments are made at the beginning of the month. Use the Paste Function button on the Standard toolbar to modify the FV function in cell E13 by placing a 1 in the Type argument. Copy the modified formula to the other cells in the output table. Use the Print 401k Report button to print the worksheet.

11. Modify the IF function in cell E8 so the condition is expressed Invested <=MaxMatch instead of MaxMatch > Invested. Modify the other arguments of the IF function so you get the same results as in the tutorial. What formula did you enter in cell B9?

12. Plan and create a macro to print preview the entire worksheet except the range A1:B4. Include the label "CableScan 401k Plan" as a custom header in the center setting and change the page orientation to Landscape. Name the macro PrintWorksheet. Assign a shortcut key to the macro. Place a button on the worksheet next to the Print 401k Report button. Label the button Print Worksheet. Test your macro twice, using the Print Worksheet button and the shortcut key. (*Note*: By default, the macro button does not print.)

13. Delete Sheet3 from the workbook, and then save and close the workbook.

14. a. Open a new workbook and use AutoFill to create the series Q197,Q297,Q397,Q497,Q198,Q298,...,Q199,...,Q499. Print the series.
    b. What values must be entered in the worksheet in order for Excel to recognize the pattern and create this series?
    c. What value does Excel display after Q499?
    d. Save the workbook as AutoFill Exercise in the TAssign folder for Tutorial.07 on your Student Disk.

15. Open a new workbook and create two macros that are identical, except that in the first case you'll record the macro using absolute references and in the second, you'll record the macro using relative references. Both macros enter a company's name and address into three worksheet cells. Figure 7-47 describes the steps required for each macro.

Figure 7-47 ◀

<u>**Name of Macro:**</u> NameAddress1 Shortcut key: x Description: using absolute references
Click cell A1
Type Adobe Development Corporation
In cell A2, type 101 Terra Way
In cell A3, type Tucson, AZ

<u>**Name of Macro:**</u> NameAddress2 Shortcut key: y Description: using relative references
Click Relative Reference button
Click cell A1
Type Adobe Development Corporation
In cell A2, type 101 Terra Way
In cell A3, type Tucson, AZ
Click Relative Reference button

Do the following:
   a. Record the NameAddress1 macro as described in Figure 7-47.
   b. Before you record the second macro, clear the contents of cells A1:A3, and then make A3 the active cell.
   c. Record the Name Address2 macro described in Figure 7-47.
   d. Activate Sheet2.
   e. Click cell D5 and run the NameAddress1 macro using the shortcut key.
   f. Click cell D12 and run the NameAddress2 macro using the shortcut key.
   g. Activate Sheet3.
   h. Click cell D5 and run the NameAddress1 macro.
   i. Click cell D12 and run the NameAddress2 macro.
   j. Save the workbook as Relative vs. Absolute in the TAssign folder for Tutorial.07. Close the workbook.

Comment on the differences between the two macros.

Case Problems

1. Travel Expense Worksheet for Tax Purposes Jack Conners, an accountant for a manufacturing company, has been preparing tax returns on weekends and evenings for several years to earn extra income. Although Jack uses a commercial tax package to prepare tax returns for his friends and clients, he has discovered that the package doesn't provide any assistance in determining the portion of a business trip that is tax deductible. Jack has asked you to develop a worksheet to determine deductible travel expenses that he can use with a client who travels on business.

The IRS rules state that a taxpayer can deduct travel expenses incurred while pursuing a business purpose. Those travel expenses include transportation, lodging, incidentals, and 50% of meals. Incidentals are items such as local transportation, telephone calls, laundry, and similar small items that are necessary while traveling. Sometimes a trip may involve both business and personal activities. If fewer than 50% of the travel days are devoted to business, the IRS rule states that none of the transportation expenses are deductible; otherwise the transportation expenses are fully deductible. The costs for lodging, meals, and incidentals are deductible to the extent that they are related specifically to business activities. Only 50% of meals associated with business travel, such as taking a client to lunch, are deductible.

Figure 7-48 incorporates the information you need to complete the travel expense worksheet.

Figure 7-48 ◀

```
Inputs
  Name of taxpayer
  Dates of travel
  Destination
  Purpose
  Number of travel days: business
  Number of travel days: personal
  Transportation (total cost)
  Lodging (cost per day)
  Meals (cost per day)
  Incidentals (cost per day)


Calculations
  Transportation = IF Number of travel days: business is greater than Number of travel days: personal THEN
                      Transportation = Transportation (total cost)
                  ELSE
                      Transportation = 0
                  END IF
  Lodging = Number of travel days (business) x  Lodging (cost per day)
  Meals = Number of travel days  (business) x Meals (cost per day) x 50%
  Incidentals = Number of travel days (business) x Incidentals (cost per day)
  Total deductible travel expense = Transportation + Lodging + Meals + Incidentals
```

Do the following:

1. If necessary, start Excel and make sure your Student Disk is in the appropriate disk drive.

2. Prepare a travel expense worksheet based on the information in Figure 7-48. Name the sheet Travel.

3. Divide the worksheet into two sections: input and calculation/output. As you develop the input section, assign range names to each cell.

4. The IRS guideline limits the deduction for meals to $75 per day, unless the taxpayer has receipts to justify a higher expense. Set up a data validation rule in the input section to comply with this guideline. You should include an input message and determine appropriate text for the message. Also, include an error alert message using the Warning style. You determine the text of the error alert message. Test the data validation.

5. Use the range names to build the formulas in the calculation section of your worksheet.

6. Improve the appearance of the worksheet, so you have a professional-looking report you can output.

7. Print the worksheet using Taxpayer 1 data from Figure 7-49.

Figure 7-49 ◀

Input Field	Taxpayer 1	Taxpayer 2
Name of taxpayer	Ken Turner	Ellen Wymer
Dates of travel	Jan 5 - Jan 12	April 21 - April 28
Destination	Austin, TX	San Antonio, TX
Purpose	Sales call	Consulting
Number of travel days (business)	5	3
Number of travel days (personal)	3	5
Transportation (total cost)	350	375
Lodging (cost per day)	125	110
Meals (cost per day)	50	60
Incidentals (cost per day)	20	15

8. Save the worksheet as Travel Expense in the Case folder for Tutorial.07 on your Student Disk.

9. Print the formulas for the worksheet. Include row and column headers. Output the formulas on one page.

10. Create macros to clear the input section and print the worksheet. Assign each macro to a button. Use Taxpayer 2 data from Figure 7-49 to test your macros.

11. Apply cell protection to all cells in the worksheet except cells in the input section. Test the cell protection. Assign a color to identify the range that is unprotected.

12. Delete any unused worksheets in the workbook, then save and close the workbook.

2. Sales Agreement Application for Desert Dreams Desert Dreams, a self-contained community, is being developed in New Mexico by Adobe Sun Corporation as an environment that appeals to people of all ages. Desert Dreams offers lifestyle features such as an 18-hole golf course, clubhouse, state-of-the-art fitness center, swimming and tennis center, hiking and bike paths, and open space with beautiful desert views. In addition, the floorplans for the houses in the development are said to be the best in the area as well as winners of numerous architectural awards.

Interest in the community has been abundant. To assist the sales associates, you have been asked to develop a Sales Agreement worksheet to use with potential home buyers as they finalize the sale of a home.

The worksheet should summarize the total purchase price, which consists of the cost of the lot, the base price of the home, and the cost of extras (options). In addition, the worksheet should lay out the payment schedule for two alternative financing schedules: a cash plan and a mortgage payment plan. Figure 7-50 shows the information you need to include in your worksheet.

Figure 7-50 ◀

Input
  Name of buyer
  Lot cost
  Base price of home
  Options

Calculations
  Purchase price = lot cost + base price of home + options

  Financing Plan - Mortgage
    Deposit at signing sales agreement $5000
    Down payment at start of construction   (15% x total purchase price) less deposit
    Final payment at closing   total purchase price less (down payment and deposit)
    Total cash paid out   sum of 3 payments
  Financing Plan - Cash
    Deposit at signing sales agreement $10000
    Down Payment at start of construction   (30% x total purchase price) less deposit
    Payment at start of framing   (35% x total purchase price) less deposit
    Final payment at closing   total purchase price less (sum of 3 payments) less cash
                                              Discount
    Cash discount   2.5% of base price
    Total cash paid out   sum of 4 payments
    Total purchase price   total cash paid out plus cash discount

Do the following:

1. If necessary, start Excel and make sure your Student Disk is in the appropriate disk drive.

2. Design the worksheet with the two users in mind. Make it useful to sales associates as they enter data but also attractive and easy to follow for home buyers, who will receive a copy of the sales agreement. Consider dividing the worksheet into input and calculation/output sections. In your calculation/output section include a payment schedule for both the mortgage and cash financing plans. Use the information in Figure 7-50 as you build your worksheet. Name the sheet Sales Agreement.

3. Apply the following data validation rules:

   ■ base price of home does not exceed $300,000

   ■ lot prices are between $20,000 and $100,000

   For each rule you should include an appropriate input and error alert message.

4. Create and use range names as you build formulas and in any other way you see fit. (*Hint*: Values in the input section and selected calculations are the most useful choices for range names.)

5. Format an attractive sales agreement worksheet, using features you have learned throughout the tutorials.

6. Save your workbook as Sales Agreement in the Case folder for Tutorial.07 on your Student Disk.

7. Enter the data in Figure 7-51, and then print the worksheet.

Figure 7-51 ◀

Name of buyer	Helen Chomas
Lot cost	25,000
Base price	150,000
Options	12500

8. Develop macros to:
   a. Clear input values from your input section. Name this macro ClearInputs and assign it to a button.
   b. Print the portion of the worksheet that includes inputs and costs of both financing plans. Name this macro PrintData, and assign it to a button.

9. Helen Chomas has just selected some additional options which increased the options cost to $15000. Make this change to the input section of your worksheet and use your PrintData macro to print a new output of the financing plans.

10. Create a title sheet. Print the title sheet.

11. Use the Index tab in the Help dialog box to learn how to "paste" range names and their associated addresses into your worksheet. Create a section in your title sheet to include all range name information in your worksheet. Print the modified title sheet.

12. Protect all cells in your worksheet except the cells where a user enters input values.

13. Save your worksheet, and then print the worksheet formulas. Remember to include row and column headers in your output.

14. Modify the Financing Plan - Mortgage to include a line for the monthly mortgage payment. Assume 8% annual interest, 25 years, and amount borrowed (use final payment at closing). Use the Office Assistant to learn about the PMT function. Use your print macro to output the Sales Agreement worksheet.

15. Save and close the workbook.

3. Customer Billing for Apex Auto Rental Apex Auto Rental is the only car rental company in a midwest city. The company has been in business for two years. John Prescott, president and founder of Apex, has asked you to help him computerize the bills he gives to his customers.

Apex rents two types of cars: compact and luxury. The current rental rates are shown in Figure 7-52.

Figure 7-52 ◀

Type	Charge/Day	Charge/Mile
Compact	$38	$0.22
Luxury	$50	$0.32

1. If necessary, start Excel and make sure your Student Disk is in the appropriate disk drive.

2. Develop a worksheet that calculates and prints customer bills. Divide your workbook into the following sheets:

   ■ A title sheet that includes a title, your name, date developed, filename, and purpose.

   ■ A worksheet for the customer bill. Name the worksheet Customer Bill. The customer bill should include the information shown in Figure 7-53. Divide your worksheet into input, calculation, and output sections. Use the layout in Figure 7-54 to design your output section. As you create your input and calculation sections, assign range names to these cells.

Figure 7-53 ◄

Assumptions
  Rental rate information (Figure 7-52)

Rental Inputs
  Customer name
  Type of car (compact or luxury)
  Number of days rented
  Number of miles driven

Calculations
  Charge per day (depends on type of car rented, which is entered in input section. Get charge from rental rate information)
  Charge per mile (depends on type of car rented, which is entered in input section. Get charge from rental rate information)
  Amount due = (days driven x charge/day) + (miles driven x charge/mile)

Figure 7-54 ◄

Apex Car Rental
Customer Bill

Customer Name: xxxxxxxxxxxxxxxx

Type of Car: xxxxxxxxxxx

Days Driven: x   **Charge/Day:** xx

Miles Driven: xxxx   **Charge/Mile:** xx

Amount Due: $ x,xxx.xx

3. Apply the data validation rules from Figure 7-55 to the input section. You decide on appropriate input and error alert messages.

Figure 7-55 ◄

Field	Rule
Number of days	< 30
Number of miles	< 5000
Type of car	List (use values from rental rate information)

4. Use the range names as you build the formulas for the customer bill.

5. Improve the appearance of your worksheet.

6. Save your worksheet as Apex Rental.

7. Enter the Customer 1 data from Figure 7-56 into the input section of your worksheet. Print the entire worksheet.

Figure 7-56 ◀

Input Field	Customer 1	Customer 2
Customer name	Masirsa Elders	Henry Fuller
Type of car	Compact	Luxury
Days driven	2	7
Miles driven	150	1200

8. Create macros to

- clear the rental input section. Name this macro ClearInputs. Assign the macro to a button.

- print only the customer bill. Name this macro PrintBill and assign it to a button.

Use the Customer 2 data from Figure 7-56 to test your macros.

9. Print the formulas (include row and column headers).

10. Apply cell protection to the worksheet cells, while permitting the user to enter data in the input section. Use color or shading to identify the unprotected area.

4. Managing Tours for Executive Travel Services Executive Travel Services (ETS) of San Diego is a travel agency that specializes in selling packaged tours to business executives from Fortune 500 companies. ETS was started in 1982 by Tom Williams, a retired executive from a Fortune 500 company. As an executive, Tom often wished he could socialize with other top executives in an informal setting for several days so he founded ETS. ETS books tours that last from one to three weeks. The tours are designed to let executives enjoy a variety of activities while becoming acquainted with other executives.

In the last several months, the number of tour requests has nearly doubled. ETS accidentally overbooked several of its more popular tours. Tom decided to develop an Excel list that could be used to provide information necessary to avoid future overbooking problems. One of his first steps was to develop the data definition shown in Figure 7-57.

Figure 7-57 ◀

Field Name	Description
Tour	Tour name
Month	Month tour is scheduled to start
Type	Type of tour: Golf, Photo, or Relax
Sold	Number of seats sold for tour
Open	Number of seats still open for sale
Price	Price of tour

The Excel list was created to track the Tours information. Tom would like you to make several changes to improve the operation of the tour management. Do the following:

1. If necessary, start Excel and make sure your Student Disk is in the appropriate disk drive. Open the ETS1.XLS workbook in the Case folder for Tutorial.07 and save it as Executive Tours. Review the Tours list. What is missing from the list?

2. Complete the information in the Title Sheet worksheet. Activate the Tours Data sheet and add the appropriate field names in the order in which they are listed in the data definition. Center and bold each field name.

3. Replace the report title and subtitle with a WordArt graphic.

4. Tom wants to know how much revenue the tours are producing. Add a Revenue field to the Excel list and place it immediately to the right of the Price field (column G). Revenue for a tour is calculated as the number of seats sold for a tour multiplied by the price charged for the tour. Add the column heading Revenue in cell G7. Use the Format Painter button to copy the formats in cell F7 to G7. Use a natural language formula to build a formula to compute revenue for each tour.

5. Insert a formula in cell G5 to sum the revenue for all tours. Assign the range name TotalRevenue to this cell (G5). Use color, shading, or some other enhancement to draw attention to the total revenue cell. In cell F5 enter the label Revenue.

6. Use the Pivot Table feature to produce a report that summarizes tour revenues by month and type of tour. Enhance the appearance of the report. Place the pivot table on a separate page. Name the sheet RevenueSummary. Print it.

7. Use the Zoom box on the Standard toolbar to change the magnification so you can see all the columns in the list without scrolling.

8. Insert a new sheet into the workbook and in it, prepare a professional-looking income statement for ETS based on the model in Figure 7-58. Name the sheet IncomeStmt. As you enter the input assumption section in this sheet, assign range names to each cell in this section.

Figure 7-58 ◀

Revenue:

    Total revenue = sum of revenue from all tours (use the formula =*TotalRevenue* to link to total
        revenue in the Tours Data sheet)

Expenses:

Commissions = Commission rate × Total revenue

Administration = Administrative rate × Total revenue

Reservation System = Reservation system rate × Total revenue

Supplies = 6000 + Supplies rate × Total revenue

Rent = 12000

Miscellaneous = 5000

Total expenses = sum of all expenses

Net Income = Total revenue - Total expenses

Input Assumptions:

Commission rate   25%

Reservation system rate 35%

Administrative rate   5%

Supplies rate   3.6%

9. Use the ranges as you enter the formulas to build the income statement.

10. Save the worksheet. Print the formulas for the income statement (include row and column headings in the output).

Questions 11-13 involve the creation of macros.

11. Create three macros to sort the Tours list. The macros should sort by:

   - Tour

   - Type field as the first sort key and Tour field as the second sort key

   - Revenue (descending order)

   Assign each macro to a button that when clicked performs the desired sort. Place the buttons in a convenient location on the Tours Data sheet. Test the macro.

12. Create a macro that will print the Tours list. Assign the macro to a button. Label the button. Place the button in a convenient location on the Tours Data sheet. Test the macro.

13. Create a macro to print the income statement and input assumptions. Assign the macro to a button. Label the button. Place the button in a convenient location on the IncomeStmt sheet. Test the macro.

14. Based on the income statement and the Goal Seek feature, determine how high the commission rate must be raised for ETS to break even (net income zero). Print the input assumptions and income statement on a single sheet.

15. Apply cell protection to all cells in the IncomeStmt sheet except the cells in the input section and save the workbook.

Answers to Quick Check Questions

SESSION 5.1

1 Record
2 Field
3 List
4 Sort by major and within major by last name
5 New button
6 Assuming you have the fields FirstName and LastName as part of the employee list, you would click the Criteria button in the Data Form dialog box. In the FirstName field text box type "Jin"; in the LastName field text box type "Shinu". Click the Find Next button to display the record in the data form.
7 Primary; alternative answer might be sort field or sort key
8 Descending

SESSION 5.2

1 In order to have Excel calculate subtotals correctly, you must first sort the data because the subtotals are inserted whenever the value in the specified field changes.
2 Page Break Preview view
3 Natural language
4 AutoFilter, Data
5 Use the AutoFilter feature. Click the Major field filter arrow and then click Marketing. For the GPA field, click Custom from the list of filtering options. Enter the comparison operator > and the constant 3.0 to form the condition GPA greater than 3.0.
6 Outline
7 Conditional formatting

SESSION 5.3

1 Sums the field
2 Refresh
3 Rows, columns, or pages
4 a. AutoFilter
   b. Pivot table

SESSION 6.1

1 Paste Special
2 Object linking and embedding
3 Linked
4 WordArt
5 Has no effect
6 The Excel menus and toolbar replace the menus and toolbar in the Word window. The embedded object now has column and row headings and the sheet tabs appear. Excel becomes the active program.
7 Embed
8 Link

SESSION 6.2

1 Main, merge fields
2 Merge field
3 Linking
4 Position the insertion point where you want the merge field; click the Insert Merge Field button, and then click the name of field you want to insert.
5 Click the View Merged Data button on the Mail Merge toolbar

SESSION 6.3

1 HyperText Markup language, Web
2 Hyperlink
3 file address, text, graphic image
4 Insert Hyperlink
5 Forward, Back, Web
6 Web browser
7 Save As HTML
8 .htm

SESSION 7.1

1 Name box
2 b and d
3 If you enter a value that violates the validation rule
4 Input section
5 Data validation
6 When you enter a cell
7 IF function
8 Comparison operator

SESSION 7.2

1 AutoFill
2 To help users identify them
3 Remove the Locked property from cells you want to be able to enter data nto, activate the Protect Sheet command
4 Cell protection prevents you from entering any data in a protected cell. Assuming a cell is unprotected, data validation allows you to specify what values users are allowed to enter in the cell.
5 A message box appears informing you that the cell is protected
6 Future Value; Financial

SESSION 7.3

1 Macro
2 recording, or entering Visual Basic code
3 Visual Basic for Applications or VBA
4 Shortcut key (Ctrl + letter), command button object, Run button from Macro dialog box
5 Current workbook, another workbook, Personal Macro workbook
6 Click the Stop Recording Macro button
7 To quickly execute the macro
8 False. Macro names cannot contain embedded blanks. Use an underscore.

Microsoft Excel 97 Introductory **Index**

If you are using this text as part of our Custom Edition Program you will find entries in the Index and Task Reference that do not apply to your custom tutorials.

Microsoft Excel 97 **Task Reference**

TASK	PAGE #	RECOMMENDED METHOD
AutoComplete, use	E 1.15	To accept Excel's AutoComplete suggestion, press Enter. Otherwise, continue typing a new label.
AutoFill, create series	E 7.20	Enter the first or first two values in a series. Select this range. Click and drag the fill handle over cells you want the series to fill.
AutoFilter	E 5.16	Click any cell in list. Click Data, point to Filter, then click AutoFilter. Click list arrow in column that contains the data you want to filter, then select the value you want to filter on.
AutoFilter, custom	E 5.19	Click any cell in list. Click Data, point to Filter, then click AutoFilter. Click list arrow in column that contains the data you want to filter. Click Custom, then enter the criteria in Custom AutoFilter dialog box.
AutoFormat, use	E 2.29	Select the cells to format, click Format, then click AutoFormat. Select desired format from Table Format list, then click OK.
AutoSum button, use	E 2.9	Click the cell where you want the sum to appear. Click **Σ**. Make sure the range address in the formula is the same as the range you want to sum.
Border, apply	E 3.20	See Reference Window: Adding a Border.
Cancel action		Press Esc, or click ⮌.
Cell contents, clear	E 1.28	Select the cells you want to clear, then press Delete.
Cell contents, copy using Copy command	E 2.15	Select the cell or range you want to copy, then click 🗐.
Cell contents, copy using fill handle	E 2.11	Click cell(s) with data or label to copy, then click and drag the fill handle to outline the cell(s) to which the data is to be copied.
Cell reference types, edit	E 2.14	Double-click cell containing formula to be edited. Move insertion point to part of cell reference to be changed, then press F4 until reference is correct, and then press Enter.
Chart title, add or edit	E 4.15 E 4.19	Select the chart. Click Chart, and then click Chart Options. In the Titles tab, click one of the title text boxes, then type the desired title.
Chart, activate	E 4.11	Click anywhere within the chart border. Same as selecting.
Chart, add data labels	E 4.16	Select the chart, then select a single data marker for the series. Click Chart, click Chart Options, then click Data Labels. Select the type of data label you want, then click OK.
Chart, adjust size	E 4.11	Select the chart and drag selection handles.
Chart, apply a pattern to a data marker	E 4.18	See Reference Window: Selecting a Pattern for a Data Marker.

If you are using this text as part of our Custom Edition Program you will find entries in the Index and Task Reference that do not apply to your custom tutorials.

Microsoft Excel 97 **Task Reference**

TASK	PAGE #	RECOMMENDED METHOD
Chart, apply a texture	E 4.28	Click Format Chart Area on Chart toolbar, click Patterns tab, click the Fill Effects button, and then click the Texture tab. Select the desired texture.
Chart, create	E 4.6	Select data to be charted. Click [icon], then complete the steps in the Chart Wizard dialog boxes.
Chart, use picture	E 4.31	Create column or bar chart. Select all columns/bars to be filled with picture, then click Insert, point to Picture, then click From File. Select picture from Insert Picture dialog box, then click OK.
Chart, delete data series	E 4.13	Select the chart, select the data series, then press Delete.
Chart, explode pie slice	E 4.25	Select the pie chart, then click the slice to explode. Drag the selected slice away from center of pie.
Chart, format labels	E 4.27	Select chart labels, then use Formatting toolbar to change font type, size, and style.
Chart, move	E 4.11	Select the chart and drag it to a new location.
Chart, rotate a 3-D chart	E 4.26	Select a 3-D chart. Click Chart, then click 3-D View. Type the values you want in the Rotation and Elevation boxes.
Chart, select	E 4.11	Click anywhere within the chart border. Same as activating.
Chart, update	E 4.12	Enter new values in worksheet. Chart link to data is automatically updated.
Chart Wizard, start	E 4.6	Click [icon].
Clipboard contents, paste into a range	E 2.15	Click [icon].
Colors, apply to a range of cells	E 3.23	See Reference Window: Applying Patterns and Color.
Column width, change	E 2.24	See Reference Window: Changing Column Width
Conditional formatting	E 5.21	Select the cells you want to format. Click Format, then click Conditional Formatting. Specify the condition(s) in the Conditional Formatting dialog box. Click the Format button and select the formatting to apply if condition is true.
Copy formula, use copy-and-paste method	E 2.15	Select the cell with the formula to be copied, click [icon], click the cell you want the formula copied to, then click [icon].
Data form, add record	E 5.11	Click any cell in list, click Data, then click Form. Click New button, type values for new record, then click Close.

Microsoft Excel 97 **Task Reference**

TASK	PAGE #	RECOMMENDED METHOD
Data form, search	E 5.13	Click any cell in list, click Data, then click Form. Click Criteria button, enter criteria, then click Find Next.
Data form, delete record	E 5.14	Click any cell in list, click Data, then click Form. Click Criteria button, enter criteria, then click Find Next. After finding record to delete, click Delete button.
Data, validation	E 7.6	Select the cell for data validation. Click Data, then click Validation. Use the tabs in the Data Validation dialog box to specify validation parameters (Settings tab), the input message (Input Message tab), and the error alert message (Error Alert tab).
Embed, object	E 6.15	In Excel, select object and click Copy button. Switch to another program and open document. Select location where document will appear and click Edit, click Paste Special. Click the Paste option button, click Microsoft Excel worksheet Object, then click OK.
Excel, exit	E 1.32	Click File, then click Exit, or click Excel Close button.
Excel, start	E 1.5	Click the Start button, then point to Programs, if necessary click Microsoft Office, and then click Microsoft Excel.
Font, select	E 3.17	Select the cell or range you want to format. Click Format, click Cells, and then click the Font tab. Select the desired Font from the Font list box.
Font, select size	E 3.17	Select the cell or range you want to format. Click Format, click Cells, and then click the Font tab. Click the Font Size list arrow, then click the desired font size.
Footer, add	E 2.34	In the Print Preview window, click Setup, then click the Header/Footer tab in the Page Setup dialog box. Click the Footer list arrow to choose a preset footer, or click Custom Footer and edit the existing footer in the Footer dialog box.
Format, bold	E 3.16	Select the cell or range you want to format, then click **B**, which toggles on and off.
Format, center text across columns	E 3.15	Select the cell or range with text to center. Click Format, click Cells, then click the Alignment tab. Click the Horizontal Text alignment arrow and select Center Across Selection.
Format, comma	E 3.10	Select the cell or range of cells you want to format, then click [,] .
Format, copy	E 3.9	Select the cell or range of cells with the format you want to copy. Click [brush], then select the cell or the range of cells you want to format.

Microsoft Excel 97 **Task Reference**

TASK	PAGE #	RECOMMENDED METHOD
Format, currency	E 3.6	Select the cell or range of cells you want to format. Click Format, then click Cells. Click the Number tab, click Currency in the Category box, then click the desired options.
Format, italic	E 3.17	Select the cell or range you want to format, then click **I** which toggles on and off.
Format, indent text	E 3.15	Select the cell or range you want to indent. Click .
Format, center in cell	E 3.13	Select the cell or range you want to format. Click , which toggles on and off.
Format, font	E 3.16	Select the cell or range you want to format. Click the Font arrow and select the desired font.
Format, percent	E 3.11	Select the cell or range of cells you want to format, then click %.
Format, wrap text	E 3.13	Select the cell or cells you want to format. Click Format, click Cells, then click the Alignment tab. Click Wrap Text check box.
Formula, enter	E 1.17	Click the cell where you want the result to appear. Type = and then type the rest of the formula. For formulas that include cell references, type the cell reference or select each cell using the mouse or arrow keys. When the formula is complete, press Enter.
Formulas, display	E 2.37	Click Tools, then click Options. Click the View tab, then click the Formulas check box.
Freeze rows and columns	E 5.6	Select the cell below and right of row or column you want to freeze. Click Window, then click Freeze Panes.
Function, enter	E 2.21	Type = to begin the function. Type the name of the function in either uppercase or lowercase letters, followed by an opening parenthesis (. Type the range of cells you want to calculate using the function, separating the first and last cells in the range with a colon, as in B9:B15, or drag the pointer to outline the cells you want to calculate. See also Paste Function button, activate.
Gridlines, add or remove	E 3.31	Click Tools, click Options, then click View. Click Gridlines check box.
Header, add	E 2.34	In the Print Preview window, click Setup, then click the Header/Footer tab in the Page Setup dialog box. Click the Header list arrow to select a preset header, or click the Custom Header button to edit the existing header in the Header dialog box.
Help, activate	E 1.26	See Reference Window: Using the Office Assistant, and Figure 1-23.

Microsoft Excel 97 **Task Reference**

TASK	PAGE #	RECOMMENDED METHOD
Hyperlinks, insert	E 6.33	Select text or graphic to serve as hyperlink, then click Insert Hyperlink button. Click the Browse button, select the file you want to link to, and then click OK.
Labels, enter	E 1.15	Select cell, then type text you want in cell.
Link, objects	E 6.10	In Excel, select object and click Copy button. Switch to another program and open document. Select location where document will appear and click Edit, and then click Paste Special. Click the Paste Link option button, click Microsoft Excel Worksheet Object, then click OK.
Link, update	E 6.13	In Excel, edit data. Switch to other program to view changes in destination document.
Macro, assign shortcut key	E 7.34	Click Tools, point to Macro, click Macros. Select name of macro, click Options, enter shortcut key letter in Shortcut key text box, click OK.
Macro, assign to button	E 7.39	See Reference Window: Assigning a Macro to a Button Object in a Worksheet.
Macro, recording	E 7.36	Click Tools, point to Macro, then click Record New Macro. In Record New Macro dialog box, enter a descriptive name in the Macro Name box, select location where you want to store macro, assign a shortcut key, then click OK. Perform the tasks in the macro. Click ■.
Macro, run from Tools menu	E 7.33	Click Tools, then click Macro. Select the name of macro you want to run, then click Run button.
Macro, run using shortcut key	E 7.34	Press Ctrl + shortcut key.
Natural language formula	E 5.23	Use column headers and row labels in place of cell references to build formulas.
Non-adjacent ranges, select	E 4.22	Click the first cell or range of cells to select, then press and hold the Ctrl key as you select the other cell or range of cells to be selected. Release the Ctrl key when all non-adjacent ranges are highlighted.
Numbers, enter	E 1.16	Select the cell, then type the number.
Page Break, insert	E 5.28	Click row selector button where you want to start new page. Click Insert, then click Page Break.
Page Break, remove	E 5.28	Click row where you want new page to start. Click Insert, then click Remove Page Break.

Microsoft Excel 97 **Task Reference**

TASK	PAGE #	RECOMMENDED METHOD
Paste Function button, activate	E 2.19	See Reference Window: Using the Paste Function button.
Paste, graphic object	E 6.8	Select cell where you want to place object. Click Insert, point to Picture, then click From File. Select object, then click Insert.
Patterns, apply to a range of cells	E 3.23	See Reference Window: Applying Patterns and Color.
PivotTable, create	E 5.30	Select any cell in list. Click Data, then click PivotTable Report. Identify source, location, layout of data, and placement of pivot table.
Print Preview window, open	E 2.30	Click [icon].
Printout, center	E 2.32	In the Print Preview dialog box, click the Setup button. Then click the Margins tab, then click the Horizontally and/or Vertically check boxes.
Printout, landscape orientation	E 3.33	In the Print Preview window, click the Setup button. Then click the Page tab in the Page Setup dialog box, then click the Landscape option button in the Orientation box.
Protection, cells	E 7.24	Select cells you want to remain unprotected. Click Format, click the Protection tab and remove check from Locked check box. Click Tools, point to Protection, then click Protect Sheet. Click OK.
Range, highlight	E 1.18 E 1.28	Position pointer on the first cell of the range. Press and hold the mouse button and drag the mouse through the cells you want, then release the mouse button.
Range, move	E 2.27	Select the cell or range of cells you want to move. Place the mouse pointer over any edge of the selected range until the pointer changes to an arrow. Click and drag the outline of the range to the new worksheet location.
Range name, defining	E 7.12	Select the cell or range you want to name. Click Insert, point to Name, then click Define. Type the name in Name in Workbook box, then click Close.
Range, nonadjacent	E 4.22	See Non-adjacent ranges, select.
Range, select	E 1.18 E 1.28	See Range, highlight.
Row or column, delete	E 2.25	Click the heading(s) of the row(s) or column(s) you want to delete, click Edit, then click Delete.

Microsoft Excel 97 **Task Reference**

TASK	PAGE #	RECOMMENDED METHOD
Row or column, insert	E 2.25	Click any cell in the row/column above which you want to insert the new row/column. Click Insert and then click Rows/Columns. Above the selected range, Excel inserts one row/column for every row/column in the highlighted range.
Sheet tab, rename	E 2.16	Double-click the sheet tab then type the new sheet name.
Sheet, activate	E 1.11	Click the sheet tab for the desired sheet.
Shortcut menu, activate	E 3.24	Select the cells or objects to which you want to apply the command, click the right mouse button, then select the command you want.
Spell check	E 2.23	Click cell A1, then click ⬚.
Sort, single sort field	E 5.7	Select any cell in column you want to sort by. Click ⬚ or ⬚ on Standard toolbar.
Sort, more than one sort field	E 5.9	Select any cell in list. Click Data, then click Sort. Specify sort fields and sort order, then click OK.
Subtotals, insert	E 5.25	Sort the list on column you want to subtotal. Select any cell in list, then click Data, then click Subtotals. Specify the criteria for subtotals, click OK.
Text box, add	E 3.27	Click ⬚ on the Drawing toolbar. Position pointer where text box is to appear, then click and drag to outline desired size and shape. Type comment in text box.
Toolbar, add or remove	E 3.25	Click any toolbar with right mouse button. Click the name of the toolbar you want to use/remove from the shortcut menu.
Undo button, activate	E 2.26	Click ⬚.
Web page, converting worksheet	E 6.37	Select range you want to convert, click File, then click Save As HTML. Specify the information using the Internet Assistant Wizard.
WordArt, embedding	E 6.7	Click ⬚, then click ⬚. Select WordArt style, enter the text, specify font, then click OK.

Microsoft Excel 97 **Task Reference**

TASK	PAGE #	RECOMMENDED METHOD
Workbook, open	E 1.11	Click [icon] (or click File, then click Open). Make sure the Look in box displays the name of the folder containing the workbook you want to open. Click the name of the workbook you want to open, then click Open.
Workbook, save with a new name	E 1.21	Click File then click Save As. Change the workbook name as necessary. Specify the folder in which to save workbook in the Save in box. Click Save.
Workbook, save	E 1.21	Click [icon].
Worksheet, close	E 1.31	Click File, then click Close, or click the worksheet Close button.
Worksheet, delete	E 7.28	Click sheet tab of sheet you want to delete. Click Edit, click Delete Sheet, then click OK.
Worksheet, print	E 1.29	Click [icon] to print without adjusting any print options. Use the Print command on the File menu to adjust options.